Stephen Crisp

Scripture Truths Demonstrated, in Thirty-Two Sermons

Stephen Crisp

Scripture Truths Demonstrated, in Thirty-Two Sermons

ISBN/EAN: 9783337114305

Printed in Europe, USA, Canada, Australia, Japan

Cover: Foto ©Lupo / pixelio.de

More available books at **www.hansebooks.com**

SCRIPTURE TRUTHS
DEMONSTRATED,

IN THIRTY-TWO

SERMONS,

OR

DECLARATIONS

OF

STEPHEN CRISP,

Late of COLCHESTER, in ESSEX, deceased.

CAREFULLY TAKEN IN

Characters or Short-Hand,

AS THEY WERE DELIVERED BY HIM AT THE PUBLIC

MEETING-HOUSES

OF THE PEOPLE CALLED

QUAKER

In and about LONDON.

FAITHFULLY TRANSCRIBED AND PUBLISHED, TOGETHER WITH

PRAYERS AFTER SERMONS

PHILADELPHIA:
PRINTED AND SOLD BY JOSEPH JAMES, IN CHESNUT-STREET,
BETWEEN FRONT AND SECOND-STREETS.
M.DCC.LXXXVII.

TO THE
READER.

THO' the Writer of these Sermons doth out of Modesty decline to print his Name, yet he does assure the Reader, that he has not in the least altered or imposed upon the Preacher's Sense, either in the taking or transcribing of them: And he does further declare, that he neither is, nor ever was, one of the People called Quakers, *but always of another Persuasion: Yet being willing, according to the Apostle's Rule, to try all Things, he has sometimes been present at their Meetings; and having the Art of Short-Writing, he has taken many of their Sermons and Prayers from the Mouths of divers of their Preachers; and among others, those of* Stephen Crisp, *deceased; which, upon Perusal, appeared to him, as well as to emi-*
...rsons of another Sect, to contain so
...spel Truths, delivered with such Plain-
...al and Demonstration, and generally
...le to the known Doctrines of Christi-
...that it is hoped the publishing of them
...e useful to the World: And, that the
... and Intent of them may be the more
...y comprehended, there is a Title given
...very Sermon, agreeable to the Subject-
...ter chiefly treated of therein.

LONDON, March, 1694.

SERMON I.

The GREAT MEDIATOR *of the* EVERLASTING COVENANT.

Preached at GRACE-CHURCH-STREET, APRIL 25, 1688.

My Friends,

HOW should we all admire the workings of the Holy Ghost! You may know from your own experience, that all the operations of the Holy Spirit, from the beginning, have been in order to the cleansing, and purifying, and preparing you for the kingdom of God. This experience is given to a little remnant, to know that the manner of his working, that the end, aim and design, of all the operations of his power, is for our good, and in order to our eternal happiness.

Now, this is a great engagement upon the minds of the people of God, diligently to wait upon him, that they may be opened more and more into the mystery of life and salvation, that hath been hid from ages and generations, and is now revealed by his spirit.

And they that are thus exercised with the measure of grace given unto them, they do grow and encrease in holiness and righteousness, by the working thereof; and they encrease in knowledge in the great things of the law, and the mysteries of the kingdom of grace: By the eye which God hath opened, they discern, that the working of his power in all ages, has been for the extirpating, rooting out and destroying of that root of iniquity, that hath brought forth such a crop of sin and wickedness, which was not of his planting, nor of his creating.

For, from the beginning of the creation of God, unto this day, God hath had a singular love and favour to the sons and daughters of men, as being (as, I may say) the master-piece, or greatest piece of the creation, most nearly related to himself, created in his own image, in righteousness

ousness and holiness; and in that they now are not so, but marred, and spoiled from bearing the heavenly image, is not the Lord's doing, but hath been wrought by the enemy both to God and man; yet the Lord continuing his love unto the work of his hands, hath from age to age revealed and made known his power, for the restoring and bringing back again lost man, fallen man, sinful man, to be reconciled unto him; that he may, as was intended, enjoy and possess the love and favour of his Maker; but there was no possibility found for his reconciliation with the holy God, but by making him holy: For as the making him unholy, seperated him from his Maker; so the making of him holy again, would unite him again unto his Maker: So that there must be a way and means for the reducing of him to his primitive state, before he could enjoy and obtain his primitive enjoyments; that is, the love and favour of God: And there hath been a general universal sense, upon the sons and daughters of men, of this alienation, and estrangedness from God; and they have put themselves upon divers ways and methods to obtain reconciliation, and to try if they could restore themselves; and they have found out ways, and tried and proved the inventions and imaginations of their own minds, in their fallen wisdom, what they might do to please God, and be reconciled to him.

We are sinners, and we will sacrifice, we will bring a sacrifice for our sins; and when men have brought a sacrifice, it hath not been accepted, because there hath not been a Mediator known, that might mediate for them with the Lord; so that all the sacrifices they have offered, have never been accepted with him, in order to an atonement and reconciliation. Now only those that have relation to the Mediator by faith in him, doth he intercede for, that he might present them again to God; and this hath been the difference between sacrificer and sacrifice, from the days of *Cain* and *Abel*, unto this day. Some have had relation to the Mediator in all their services and sacrifices, and some have had relation only to the thing offered, and the service performed; but they have not in all ages sped alike: They whose service and worship was performed to God, with a relation to the Mediator, they

have

have found acceptance; and they whose worship and service was performed only with a relation to the thing offered or done, that was but their own act, that was but their will-worship, and that was always turned back again upon them; *for there is no name given under Heaven, by which any can be saved, but only the name of Jesus Christ;* that is the Mediator of the new covenant, for the old one was broken: And when *Aaron* was set up to be an high-priest to God, he was appointed to offer sacrifices for the sins of the people, and he that committed a sin, was appointed by the law to bring an he-goat of the flock unto the door of the tabernacle, and to deliver it to the priest, and he was to make an offering for the sin committed after such and such a manner, and it was to be an atonement with God for him: So here was seemingly, a reconciliation by a sacrifice; and some saw no farther than the bringing of a goat, and a ram, and the performance of the priest's office, and they counted all was well: And others saw farther, long before the apostle spake or wrote it, *it was not the blood of bulls or goats, nor the blood of a ram, that could purge away sin from their consciences.* And after the apostle had opened the mystery of Divinity, who had a divine and spiritual skill, in unfolding the restoration of mankind, he declared plainly, that *when the offering was made by* Aaron *for sinners, even then there remained still a conscience of sin; for it was not possible that the blood of bulls and goats, should take away sin:* So that their outward performances, and their outward services, they did but point out the Mediator; they had a pointing finger, as it were, to the real, true and everlasting Mediator, Christ Jesus; who is made a Mediator betwixt God and man; that by and through him, man might be again reconciled to God.

So that now in these gospel-days, wherein God is opening the mysteries of life and salvation, to the intent and purpose, that the sons and daughters of men might be restored again into their primitive enjoyment of the favour of God; now in these days, it is the duty of all Christians, and of all that are seeking the welfare of their immortal souls, to have their eyes and hearts unto Jesus, as unto one that is able to reconcile them unto God; to him it is committed, to him wisdom and power is committed, and to him authority is

committed,

committed, that he should be an everlasting high-priest; and that all the services, and all the worship and religious performances that people offer up to God, should be in his name, that so by him they might be recommended to God: For none will find acceptance with the Father, unless in all their performances they have an eye unto him.

So that it comes plainly to pass, according to that short and confident assertion of the author to the *Hebrews*, *that without faith, it is impossible to please God*: But it is possible to offer sacrifices without faith, and possible for people to perform religious services without faith, as woful experience hath taught us in our days, that many have been exercised in a kind of religious service, that never in their lives had faith enough to believe the things that they pray for, and they are without faith. When people pray to God to send his Holy Spirit into their hearts, that they may keep his commandments to their lives end, and have not faith to believe it, and when they pray, *Thy will be done on earth, as it is in Heaven*, it is a religious performance; but if it be not done in faith, it is but an encreasing in sin, and an addition to sin. Where is the man that is exercised in praying to God, that believeth that ever such a thing is like to come to pass? Go where you will in this or the other nation, and enquire of people about their faith; they believe there is no possibility of extirpating and rooting out of sin, while they live upon the earth; therefore all their prayers for it are vain, and their faith a vain faith: And it is high time in such a day as this, when men are faithless and unbelieving, to preach up the object of faith, the Lord Jesus Christ. People are of divers faiths, and of divers beliefs; but we have found by experience, that they do them no good, they do not bring a thing to pass, that of necessity must be brought to pass, before they can be reconciled to God; their faith doth not cleanse the heart, nor extend so far as to believe that ever they shall be cleansed; in all the worship and religion that they perform, they come not to this faith, that they shall be made clean: All that is done is but in sin and uncleanness; they cannot bring a clean sacrifice out of an unclean vessel: And our Lord Jesus Christ saith concerning this subject, *an evil tree cannot bring forth good fruit*; but there must be good fruit brought forth; how muſt we do it? *Make the tree good, and the fruit will be good.* When mens vain janglings about religion and religious fancies come to an end, then all this religion will appear to be in vain, and will not anſwer the end for which it is performed, till men believe that it will make the tree good, and cleanſe the heart, and transform men by renewing the ſpirit of their minds. So that religion muſt begin within; and it is not our changing of forms of worſhip, from one form to another, and taking up this and the other opinion, that doth change our hearts. Sad experience doth teach us, that men may carry over their old luſts into a new religion; we can carry over our old inclinations into our new opinions: For though the form of worſhip be changed, the heart remaining unchanged, and the luſts unmortified, *their religion is in vain,* let them be of what perſuaſion they will.

Now the remedy of this great calamity, that hath overſpread all ſorts of people; for there is no ſort of people, but there are thoſe among them that are under this great calamity, of holding the profeſſion of godlineſs with an ungodly mind, and the profeſſion of truth with a falſe and treacherous ſpirit.

And for the remedying of this, there is but one way that all men be brought off from having their eye unto their performances, and to the doctrines and tenets that they hold, and do, as the apoſtle faith, *fix their eye upon Chriſt, and look upon Jeſus.* This is the firſt thing that muſt begin our religion; for Chriſt muſt be the *Alpha* of our religion, as well as the *Omega* of it. If I begin not there, let me begin where I will, I begin wrong; let me begin at the moſt ſerious and ſound doctrine, and at the moſt apoſtolical religion; if Chriſt and his apoſtles were here upon the earth; if I walked among them; if I believed all they ſaid and did, I ſhould begin wrong, if I did not fix mine eye upon Jeſus Chriſt, that is the taker away of ſin, and is the ſanctifier of the ſoul by his Spirit. There muſt be the beginning, and there muſt be the concluſion; he is the author, and the finiſher of all true faith. There are authors of other faiths: Men have their different faiths, and creeds, and articles, and they have expoſed and impoſed them too; but this is the worſt of it, none of
' them

them are right; let them be exposed and imposed with ever so much force and violence, none of these will cleanse the heart; but that faith which is delivered over by Christ Jesus, that hath the quality of cleansing and purifying; that is the faith when all is done, that will do the work; that is it that will save and sanctify, and do the business that all the world is about. Every one would have a reconciler with God, and sin rooted out, and be as God would have them be; this is the public profession of Christendom; at least they would find out something by which it might be done: Altho' many are willing enough to continue in sin and drunkenness, whoredom, lying and hypocrisy; these are a sort of *fools, that make a mock of sin,* and that swim in the stream of pleasure; and what care they, so long as they make a profession of christianity?

But I am speaking of a people that are struggling under their corruptions; that would mortify sin, and serve God in holiness and righteousness, and do God's *will on earth as it is done in Heaven*; and do it not in form, but would have power to do it; and they have tried several ways to do it, and it is not done; and many have been at this work till grey hairs are upon their heads, and it is not done. Now God hath given Christ to make reconciliation; now how can we, that have the love of God extended to us, but extend our good-will to our friends, and signify to them, that all the travel and pains they are at, and all the prayers they make, will do nothing till they have their faith fixed upon Jesus, that is able to save and deliver them, *and save to the uttermost all that come to God by him.*

But here some will object and say, it is true what you say, but is it needful to preach such doctrines to us? for we all believe in Christ, that is, the only Mediator and Saviour. We know that Christ Jesus is the only Mediator, and that unless he commends us to God, we cannot be accepted of him. This is our general doctrine, therefore what need it be urged and pressed upon us, that are come into the faith already.

Let me search into the matter; it is of greater importance than to search into a bargain of worldly things. Men would fain have others open and discover to them wherein
they

they may be cheated, to prevent their being imposed on in a worldly bargain. I hope then they will hearken to know how, and wherein they may be deceived by themselves, and deceived by others in matters of eternal concernment. There are no Protestants, but they reject any Mediator but Jesus Christ, and believe that no Mediator can reconcile them to God, but Christ alone, and they say he is the object of their faith. I would ask them this question, whether they believe in Christ at a distance, or as present, really present with them? If their faith be historical and at a distance, that they believe in Christ, as one born of the Virgin *Mary*, and was crucified and dead before they were born, and arose again, and ascended into Heaven, and is set at the right hand of God, if the reason of my belief be, that I have heard of this relation of Christ, or whether the reason be, because by his Spirit, he hath visited me in this age; the one is, I believe, because good men have told me so; but the other is, I believe, because, by this Spirit he hath promised to send, to lead me into all truth, he hath visited me. Now let me examine whether I am aware of such a spiritual visitation, by this quickening Spirit, which is the Lord from Heaven, and not only the Lord in Heaven. Whether I am aware of such a quickening power and virtue, which I have received upon my spirit, that he is not only at the right hand of God on high in Heaven, but is now come to knock at the door of my heart, and hath raised in me a life, as opposite to sin, as his was. Let me consider if I be aware of a secret touch of his quickening virtue upon my soul, whereby he hath begotten me into a life opposite to sin; so that if sin remains, it remains as a burthen, and oppression upon me, so that I am a sufferer; for as much as I am quickened, and made sensible of a better life, of a godly life, I would fain be at it, and live in it, but iniquity, lust and corruption lie in the way. He that hath quickened me so far, as to bring me to a sense of the burthen of sin, my faith tells me, he will take the burthen off, else my faith will do me no good, if corruption still prevail upon me, if my faith tells me this, it will tell the wickedest man in the world as much; but if my faith tells me I am a sinner, and my sins consist of this and the other evil thing I do, and am inclined to do, it tells me me again, that he that hath quickened me, and brought me to a sen'e of sin, he can take the burthen off from me.

Here now is a true faith, that begins in conviction, and ends in true conversion; this is the word of faith, delivered to the saints, and which we are to preach. They said of old, that the word of faith, they had to preach, was that which was nigh in their mouth, that they might receive it, and do it. I have something nigh that reproves me for sin; if I be obedient to it, then faith gives me victory over that which is sinful, for which the world reproveth me; and as I see faith gives me victory over any corruption, which I have been struggling under, I am encouraged to fix my faith upon him that hath thus quickened me: So that this is the difference between faith in Christ at a distance, and faith that quickeneth me by God's Spirit; that Spirit that hath been so much slighted in our days, by the highest notionists in our age; they supposed it to be a meer fiction; some have mocked and derided, and others have been discouraged to speak of the Spirit of Christ, and his operation upon the soul; some have declared both in the press and pulpit, that they have had no experience of the touches of God's Spirit upon their souls. But our experience hath brought us to another degree of knowledge. We know, and you may know if you please, and that before you sleep, that there is a way opened, God has made way for his Spirit to reach the spirits of men, to signify immediately to their spirits without means, herein thou doest wrong, and herein thou mayest have life, and seek after it. Now the Spirit that thus worketh, is the Spirit of Christ, the Spirit that proceeds from the Father and the Son, that voice in men that tells them they might believe and be saved. When he comes, saith Christ, *he will lead you into all truth.* How shall the world know this is he? *He shall convince them of sin.* If there be any convincement that ariseth in man of this and the other sin, it must be from the way the Holy Spirit hath upon their spirits; he hath a way to speak to men, and every one that is a lover of his own soul, is bound to hearken to that voice.

In the latter days, saith the Lord, *when I shall raise a prophet in the midst of you, whosoever will not hear that prophet, shall be cut off.* All commentators agree on this text,
that

that that prophet was no other than Chrift Je'us; it was not *John* the *Baptift*, nor *Paul*, nor *Peter*; but Chrift that was promifed to be raifed. There was fuch an abfolute command went along with that prophecy, *that all fhould hear him*, and it had a threatening at the end of it, *that all that will not hear him, fhall be cut off*. Are they not whoremongers, and drunkards, and liars, that will not hear this prophet? They will not hear him, becaufe they love their fins. What becomes of them? They are cut off from the enjoyment of the love and favour of God, and when they draw nigh to God in prayer, and other religious exercifes, it is with them, as it was with *Cain, fin lies at the door*. When they come into a ftorm at fea, or are arrefted with ficknefs, and death looks them in the face, they would have peace, but there is diftrefs, and trouble in the room of it. What is the matter? Waft thou not baptifed in the Chriftian faith? Did not the minifter tell thee, *that thou art a child of God, and an inheritor of the kingdom of Heaven?* Alas! my fin lies at my door; O! that I had time to live a better life! What ails thy life, man? My life hath been a life of deceit, luft, and vanity, corruption and hypocrify. Did not thy teacher teach thee, that a believer hath no guilt upon him, but that all his fins are pardoned from the day he became a believer? This doctrine will not hold in a ftorm, tho' it will do in fair weather; when men are fwimming in their pleafures, it will ferve them; but when they come to deal with their Maker, no faith will ferve them, but that which *purifies the heart*, and that which makes a change *from the earthly image to the heavenly*.

It were better for you and I, and every one of us, to take thefe things into confideration, while we have health and ftrength, and while fome fand (as I may fo fpeak) is in our glaffes, to confider what is my faith? What is the object of it? Have I a dependency upon my duties, and alms, and good deeds? They will fail me. But if my dependency be upon Chrift as a Saviour, and a Sanctifier, and my fanctification is carried on gradually, *he that hath begun a good work in me will perfect it*. And if the reafon of my going to meetings, and going into my clofet, and bowing myfelf before the Lord, is to keep clofe to him that carries on the work of sanctification, *he will work all my work in me and for me.* I cannot expect to live in the world, but I shall meet with temptations; the Devil will tempt me, but my Saviour will be nigh me, as nigh to me as the Devil can be; if I will keep close to him, he will keep close to me. *My Father,* saith *Christ, is greater than I, and none is able to pluck you out of your Father's hands.* I must expect to be tempted; *for the adversary the Devil goes about like a roaring lion, seeking whom he may devour.* Alas! saith one, though I have made some progress in the work of sanctification, yet for all that, he may one day betray me. Am I grown strong enough to resist his temptations? and wise enough to foresee all his gins and traps, which he lays to ensnare me? But I know who can see them, and defeat them. I have my faith fixed upon one that can bind the strong man, and cast him out. The life that I now live, is not in my own parts, and by my own understanding and sense: *But the life that I now live, in the flesh, I live by the faith of the Son of God:* This is that faith that gives me victory. The apostle had a battle for it; *I have fought the good fight; and henceforth is laid up for me a crown of righteousness, and not for me only, but for all them that love the appearing of our Lord Jesus Christ;* and that come to have familiarity with Christ, with his Spirit and truth, with his grace and word, in their hearts: Though these are several expressions, they all signify one immortal seed of life, by which men are united to God: It is a leaven there, to leaven them into the Divine Nature.

Whenever such a one is tempted, he resists not the tempter in his own power, but he waits to feel the arisings of that life, and power, and virtue that was in Christ Jesus, and is in him still: He waits for that power, that in the name of Christ he may say, *get thee behind me Satan.* Being fortified by Christ's name, and armed with his power, what is it that a Christian cannot do? What valiant, noble and wonderful things have they done, that have been shielded with this faith? See the eleventh chapter of the epistle to the *Hebrews.* All the repetitions of that chapter, from one end to the other; in all of them the apostle ascribes all the valiantness and courageousness of those noble acts, to the power of faith. They looked to Jesus, before ever the

Virgin

the EVERLASTING COVENANT.

Virgin Mary brought him forth out of her body. The prophets did earnestly seek to know those things, which the Spirit of Christ that was in them, did signify unto them, that there was to be this great Prophet, before ever the *Virgin Mary* was born : So that Christ was always the object of a true believer's faith. Though under the law, they had an high-priest, and he was placed at the altar, and they had offerings burnt upon it, yet they had an eye unto Christ, they had an undervaluing of all that their sacrifices could do for them. *If thou wouldest have had burnt offerings,* saith *David, I would have given them ; I would not have withheld them from thine altar ; thou shouldest have had enough of them.* He was bold to say, in respect of acceptance and reconciliation, *burnt offerings and sacrifices thou wouldest not ; a body hast thou prepared me ; for it is written in the volume of the book, I come to do thy will, O God.* He had an eye unto Jesus that was to come, upon whom help was laid : There was a Redeemer, that should come from *Zion,* and a law-giver from *Jerusalem.* They had an eye beyond sacrifices, unto Christ. In all ages the people of God have had the answer of their souls, which is reconciliation, and the favour of God: They that had this answer, never had it but by Christ. No man can be accepted with God, can ever have the desire of his soul answered in peace and reconciliation with God, until his faith be placed on Christ Jesus : Neither can any man have faith in Christ at a distance, and thereby be reconciled unto God, but must know his Spirit. I must have an experimental knowledge of his power and wisdom, and this I cannot have without his Spirit : Let me believe ever so othordoxly, except I have the Spirit of Christ, it will do me no good, it will be no advantage to me.

This is the word, that was in my heart as a well-wisher to the souls of all men : As God hath done good to my soul, so I cannot but wish well to the souls of others; that as he hath found out a way for my redemption and salvation, so likewise I wish the same for others that are bond-men and bond-women, and under the power of their corruption. God's work hath been to destroy the bondage and the oppression, and to destroy the tyrant that reigns over the souls of people ; God having made them for his glory, and the Devil has stolen them away : That they do not that which
pleaseth

pleaseth God: But God's good pleasure is, that all *may be saved, and come to the knowledge of the truth: And God so loved the world, that he gave his only begotten Son, that whosoever believeth in him, should not perish, but have everlasting life:* And he is called, *the Lamb of God, which takes away the sins of the world.* He can take away sin; if my sin do not obstruct my faith and confidence in him, he will take it away; and if he takes that away, then he makes the tree good. Nothing hinders us from the enjoyment of God, but sin; and if Christ will take it away by the blood of his cross, no matter for all the scorn, contempt, hardship, reproach and persecution of this world; no matter, for he hath not deceived us, but told us before hand, if we will be followers of him, and be led by him, we must expect these things; sufferings, reproaches, persecutions, disdain and envy. These things come not uncertainly upon us; the world loves its own, and cannot love them that are not of it; but they that are not of the world, may be brought to the terms of God, and they may not be any longer in the world. Christ prayeth not that his disciples may be taken out of the world, but kept from the evil: So that Christ is a Mediator, and a propitiation for all men; and he is working by his Spirit for the redemption of all men, *that to as many as believe in him, to them he gives power to become the Sons of God.*

The sum of all this is, that we have an opportunity put into our hands; we cannot deny it; you must all upon search, confess, that the grace of God doth often work in your hearts against any corruption, against any evil: Let not this price be put into your hands in vain, as into the hands of fools. If I knew that this and that was a sin, I would leave it; let us be of that mind, and we shall soon know it; and then say, if I knew such a thing to be a sin, and could get a thousand pounds by it, I would not do it. Why should'st thou love sin for profit or pleasure? I am sure it is an ill bargain when it is done. Whatsoever I am convinced is a sin, I will not do it.

Resolve upon this, and then the grace of God will be at work; we shall soon see that we must leave off sinning. There is such a thing I must leave; God hath set up a judgment in my mind against it; though it bring profit and pleasure, away it must go. Here is a step, a following step, to follow Christ. He that will deny himself, will follow Christ: My Redeemer shews me this to be an evil, I will not do it, but follow him, and imitate him. Here the soul is led step by step, even by Christ, the Captain of our Salvation, till it is gradually cleansed from sin, and reconciled unto God; and this can be done by no other means; for prayers and alms will not do it; all that can be done by us will not do it; none can do it but Christ alone, that God hath laid help upon, that you may all wait for the Divine operation of his grace in your hearts. That is it which we labour and travel for, as knowing that God hath wrought wonderfully by it, for the redemption of all those that love him more than they love their pleasures, more than they love their sins. It must be concluded, that following of him, and leaving father and mother, husband and wife, children, brethren, and sisters; all these things as they stand in competition with him, and the obedience of his Spirit, must be looked upon as nothing to him: Then above all things, I must not displease him: *He can speak peace, and none can take it away; and if he take it away, none can give it.* If we follow Christ, when this is done, then all is done according to the will of God; then the blessing descends upon the whole creation; then every man will speak truth to his neighbour, and every man will govern his family with discretion; so God is glorified, and his name comes to be exalted; who is worthy to be beloved, adored, and exalted above all blessings and praises. To him be glory, who is God over all, blessed forever and ever. *Amen.*

His Prayer *after* Sermon.

MOST *glorious God of life and power, and of everlasting kindness; a God of long-suffering and patience, else we had not been here at this day.*

Lord, we are monuments of thy mercy! thou hast spared us long, and hast called unto us in a day when we turned away our ear from thee: Thou hast stretched forth thy hand all the day long, and thou hast gathered a little remnant of the lost sheep of the house of Israel to partake of thy pastures of life; and now all our souls have been greatly refreshed and comforted

forted, since we came to understand and comprehend with the rest of thy saints, the height, and length, and breadth, and depth of thy love, which in the Son of thy love, thou hast revealed to us.

And, blessed Father of Life! our souls do breathe and cry unto thee, on the behalf of strangers, which are aliens from the commonwealth of Israel, that are yet breathing and enquiring after thee, asking the way to Zion.

O Lord! remember them and hear their cry, and let their sighing and complaining enter into thine ears; that all they, in whom thou hast begun to kindle holy desires after thee, may have them grow into a flame, to burn up all enmity to thee; that so they may be purified by thy judgments, and receive of thy heavenly grace. This is the way which thou hast used with thy children; thou hast commanded them to worship thee in thy dwelling-place; thou hast taken them into thy house, and fed them with thy finest wheat, refreshed them with thy loving kindness, and filled them with thy Holy Spirit.

Dearest God of Love! this is the design and purpose of our meeting together, that we may enjoy the presence, and feel the operation of thy word, and have communion with thee, and thy Son Jesus Christ, through thy Holy Spirit; the way into rest and life is with thee. Thou canst open, and none can shut. Lord! open the hearts of this people, to receive of thy goodness, and receive of thy blessings; that so every one may be sensible, that thou art at least knocking at the door of their hearts, that thou mightest have an entrance, and bow the hearts and wills of all, to receive what thou givest and hast to offer; to receive the word of life, by which thou art quickening them, and kindling holy desires after thyself, that every one may recive the truth in the love of it: That so blessed God of Life! thy glorious work of redemption may be carried on, and we may all feel it carried on in our souls.

Hear thy poor people that are crying unto thee, the God of Gods in Zion! that are sensible of their weakness and feebleness, and how unable they are to overcome the enemies of their souls: Arise in thy power, O Lord! and these enemies shall be scattered; let the souls of thy people be raised from the dust, and delivered from their sin, that they may rejoice and praise thy name for their deliverance.

Righteous

Righteous God of life! our eyes are unto thee, to set forth thy g'ory, for thou haft made bare thine arm for the falvation of the poor and needy fouls, and thou haft been ftretching forth the cords of thy love to gather them that were fcattered; and haft been bringing home to thee, thofe that were hurried away in a dark and cloudy day.

Thou haft made us fenfible of thy operations; and haft conftrained thy fervants to labour in the word and doctrine, for the gathering of fuch home; that fo they and we may enter into thy holy covenant, and may found forth thy praifes to the ages and generations to come: That fo, Holy God of Life and Love! thou that haft faved us with a marvellous falvation, mayeft receive for all thy mercies, and bleffings to thy children, praifes, glory, honor, and thankfgiving; for thou alone art worthy, who art God over all, bleffed forever. Amen.

SERMON II.

HEART PREPARATION *for receiving the* GOSPEL.

Preached at DEVONSHIRE-HOUSE, FEB. 12, 1687.

IT is in my heart at this time, to defire that every one's heart were prepared to be made a partaker of the bleffings of the gofpel; for there is a certain preparation that every one muft witnefs in themfelves, before they are capable of receiving divine bleffings; for in all ages of the world, the bleffings of the Lord have been manifold, and his arm hath been always ftretched out in all ages, to the fons and daughters of men, that are fenfible of the love he hath unto them; and where thefe tenders of the love of God have met with prepared hearts, they have received it to their eternal welfare: But this hath been the lamentation that hath been taken up upon the greateft part of mankind, that they have not been prepared to receive the love of God; their hearts and minds have been fo filled with the love of vifible things, and carnal objects, that they have not been truly fenfible of the riches of the grace, mercy, and love of God unto them.

Now,

Now, it was said of old by the prophet, *that the preparation of the heart is of the Lord;* and there is something that belongs to us on our part, that we may attain this preparation, that we may be brought into this spiritual frame of mind; and that is, by returning to the Lord, for people to think upon his name, and have regard to his appearance: And although this is not the work of nature, for by nature the minds of people are abroad, and they are crying out as the Psalmist speaks, *who will shew us any good?* Yet to help that defect, the Lord hath been pleased to send forth his grace and his truth, and to call unto the sons and daughters of men, that they might seek after him, that they might *seek the Lord while he is to be found;* and they that hearken to his voice, they will readily confess, that there is nothing doth so well satisfy an immortal soul, as to be gathered into fellowship with its Maker; and that one time or other, it is the desire of all men and women, that they might attain peace with the Lord; and they know there is no peace to the wicked; they know wickedness will remain until it is abolished and destroyed; and they know it is not in their power to destroy it; and therefore of necessity there must be a waiting upon the Lord, who is *Almighty*, that he may reveal his power in our weakness.

And they that are thus prepared in their minds, meet religiously together, with expectation from God; that he, according to his promise, will appear, and reveal his arm, and do in them, and for them, that which they cannot do for themselves; this is a fit occasion for people to meet together, and to have their expectation from God, and say, Lord, thou knowest my weakness, and thou knowest the enemies I have to deal withal; thou knowest I am not able to overcome them: Therefore we are now met together, in the presence of the Lord, to wait to receive at his hands, that power, that life, that virtue, by which we may be made more than conquerors. Such a religious meeting thus gathered together, hath a promise; *I will be in the midst of them,* saith the Lord; and therefore, having a promise, we may reasonably expect that we shall be made partakers of the living virtue and power, by which we may do that, which of ourselves we cannot do.

And

And, friends, it is my soul's desire, that you were all thus qualified, that every one had an evidence in himself of this right preparedness; for where the eye is abroad upon any visible thing, that it seeks satisfaction in any thing below the Lord himself, it will wear away and wax old. All those objects that people fix their mind upon, they will wax old; but they whose desires, and the breathings of whose souls are, that they may grow into acquaintance with their Maker, this will never wax old. When peoples minds are fixed, as the people of the Lord of old were, when they made a comparison between the state of their minds, and the minds of others, and signified it in these words, *they are saying; they are crying* (that is, they that are of the world) *who will shew us any good?* But for our parts, our cry is, *Lord lift up the light of thy countenance upon us, and we will be more glad of that, than they can be with all the increase of corn, and wine, and oil.*

Now they that feel in themselves that the reason of their meeting together is to enjoy the light of God's countenance, and to partake of the blessings of God, they have their expectation from God, their minds are retired into God; knowing right well, that if the tongues of men and angels are moved to declare the heavenly and divine mysteries of the kingdom of God, they cannot be edified or benefited by them without the divine help and assistance of God's Spirit; for there is a *seal* upon them, and none can open that *seal*, but the *Lyon* of the tribe of *Judah*; he only is found worthy to unseal the mystery, and unseal the divine blessings that are with the Lord: So that people must come to that retiredness of spirit, to that resignation of soul, to be as a little child waiting upon the Lord, crying out unto the Lord, that he will prepare them, *that he will make them hungry, and then feed them, that he will raise a thirst in them, and then satisfy them with those divine springs of life, which through the Lord Jesus Christ are opened to every one that believeth.* So far as your minds are stayed and settled in waiting for the Lord, so far you will feel in yourselves an openness and readiness, that if the Lord speaks, you are ready to hear him, ready to submit to his word, ready to obey him; there will be such an openness in the mind, not to the words of any man, but unto the word of God

God, to receive that; for where the words of men are received, though never so excellent, they convert not the soul, *but the word of the Lord is pure, converting the soul*. And this word is that which is able to quicken those that are dead in sins and trespasses, and bring them to be made partakers of life. For it is not an increase of knowledge that will do the turn, but it is the increase of life and virtue, the increase of godliness, and submitting our wills unto him that made us: It is this that will do our turn, this will bring peace to the soul, and bring us into the favour of God, through our Lord Jesus Christ. Now, that you may all feel that which prepares the heart for this resignation, and quietness, and subjection, you must wait upon the Lord, that you may be made partakers of the blessings of his everlasting gospel, and of his divine presence: This is that which is most profitable, most advantageous: And then the Lord will *open to you the windows of Heaven, and rain down these blessings upon you*, whereby you will be comforted and refreshed, far beyond all the works that we can do; for it is an *inward work* that must be done upon the soul, to convert people that have been alienated and estranged from God, and bring them to a reconciled state, through the Lord Jesus Christ, whereby they may partake of the divine virtues, which sanctify and justify the soul in the sight of God.

His PRAYER *after* SERMON.

M O S T *g'orious and powerful Father! thy arm of power is made bare in this our day, to bring salvation to the poor.*

O Lord! thou hast lifted up the light of thy countenance upon a people that have waited for thy glory and thy salvation; a little remnant whom the good of this world could not satisfy; but O Lord! in an acceptable time, thou hast brought thy salvation near; and the light and brightness of the everlasting gospel, thou hast commanded to shine into the hearts and souls of the mourners and bowed-down ones, who are seeking the living God, not among the outward forms and ways of men.

But, O blessed Father of Life! thou hast now brought us to the day of thy power, and bowed our wills, and made us a willing people therein to serve thee, and to do thy will on earth, as it is

done

His PRAYER after SERMON.

done in Heaven; and for that end, O Lord, thou hast put it into the hearts of thy people to wait upon thee, in whom all our fresh springs are, that from thee we may receive the renewing of power from day to day.

In all the hours of our temptations and trials, our eyes, O Lord, have been to thee and to thy power; and we acknowledge, to the glory of thy power and goodness, that thou hast been a God nigh at hand, when we have been seeking thee, and trustings in thee, so that we are a people sensible of thy power and presence with us; for that eye which thou keepest open to thy children it brings thy glory to our view, and shews it breaking forth over the nations; and we have great joy and satisfaction in beholding the progress of thy mighty power in our day, how thou hast broken down and confounded, and art still breaking down and confounding, all the dark imaginations and devices of the sons and daughters of men, that have conspired to hinder the breaking forth of the glory of thy Son, Christ Jesus.

O powerful God of Life! arise more and more in the greatness of thy power and love, and make known thy counsel, and thy will among the inhabitants of the earth; and bow their minds, O Lord! and their wills, that none may dare to withstand thy appearance, lest they be found fighters against God, and destroyers of themselves.

O powerful Father! for this end, make bare thine arm unto the rulers and governors of these nations, that they may know thy counsels, and bow to thy heavenly will, and may promote thy law of righteousness in their own hearts, and the hearts of others; that by thy power, a blessed reformation may be wrought, and a stop put to iniquity; that it may not run down in a mighty stream, as it hath done in time past; but that truth and righteousness, and sound judgment may be known in the earth: That they that hunger and thirst after righteousness, may have their souls desires satisfied; and so praise and thanksgivings shall arise from their souls to thee.

O powerful Father of Life! preserve and keep thy children, whom thou hast gathered, and purged, and purified, and to whom thou hast made known the way of life, and made them a willing people in the day of thy power, to do thy will, and to wait for the coming of that kingdom that thou hast promised to establish under Christ Jesus, the King of Kings and Lord of Lords; and

that

that it may grow, and increase, and be spread abroad upon the earth, and let every one desire to be the subject thereof.

Powerful Father of Life! the arm of thy power and invisible strength hath been revealed, that nothing hath been able to resist or stand against and prevail, by which thou art planting Zion and building Jerusalem, and establishing it: By the same power, let thy work be carried on, and let many be brought in to be subject to Christ, for the good of their immortal souls: As thou hast multiplied thy blessings upon us, so from day to day thou hast made us sensible of thy love unto us, owning us to be thy children and peculiar people, by thy presence in the midst of us, whenever we meet in thy name to wait upon thee, that so, Living Father, all thine, both here and every where, may be encouraged to attend upon thee, and to be faithful to thy power; that waiting for the opening of thy counsels, and the enlightening their understandings, they may be able to comprehend, with all saints, the height, and depth, and length, and breadth of thy love in Christ Jesus; that in the sense of the freeness and greatness thereof, all thy children here and every where, that in an everlasting covenant of grace thou hast gathered to thyself, may have communion with thee and thy Son and Spirit; and may return thee the honor, glory, and praise of all thy love, and mercy, and grace; for thou alone art worthy, who art God over all, blessed forever and ever. Amen.

SERMON III.

The FIRST and GREAT COMMANDMENT.

Preached at DEVONSHIRE-HOUSE, May 27, 1688.

WHEN God gave forth his *Law* on *Mount Sinai*, which *Israel* was to hear and obey, the first and great commandment was, *thou shalt have no other Gods before me.* Here is the sum and substance of all *true religion* that ever was upon earth to this day. All the commandments, all the precepts, prophecies, and all the dealings of God with his people, from that day to this, have all been contained in this short precept, *thou shalt have no other Gods*
but

The FIRST *and* GREAT COMMANDMENT.

but me. And as long as Ifrael stood in obedience to this command, their blessings were multiplied upon them, their good things were increased from day to day; the Lord was with them, as long as they were willing to be his people; he appeared as their *God,* and as their defender wrought their deliverances, *fought all their battles* for them, gave them dominion and strength, courage and wisdom; ministered out of his *treasury* all good things unto them; for the great care of God Almighty was with all his people, he had regard to them, and visited them at all times, to keep them from idolatry; *I am,* saith he, *a jealous God,* take notice of me to be so; I am jealous of my name; if thou wilt be mine, *thou shalt have no other Gods but me.*

And all the precepts about offerings and sacrifices, and making atonement for sinners, and the divers services and worship, the various offices in the temple and *sanctuary,* they were all outward means appointed of God, to keep this outward church in an inward conformity to the command of God. This command was written in tables of stone, and these tables were laid up in the *ark of God,* and all this appertained to the *first covenant,* and typed and figured out the dispensation of the *new and everlasting covenant* that God would make with his people, not like unto the old: How not like it? Not like it in the outward shadows, the types and shadows of things, but he would bring forth the substance of all those *shadows* and *types,* and would alter the form and outward appearance of things; *for as God is unchangeable,* so is his *law* unchangeable.

Moses saith, the first and great commandment is, *Thou shalt have no other Gods but me.* This was put into the stone tables. Christ Jesus saith, the first and great commandment is, *Thou shalt love the Lord thy God with all thy soul, and with all thy mind,* Matt. xxii, 27. This is put into the *tables of the heart.* So here is a difference between the first commandment by *Moses,* and the first commandment by *Christ*; they both acknowledge the first and great command to be the subjecting of the creature to him that made him, as his God, that he may only serve him, and that he may love him with his whole heart: The *Jew* could prove this by his *stone tables,* and *Christ* proves this by the fleshly tables of the heart, for
there

there he is bound to love the Lord with his whole heart, and to serve him only; *him only shalt thou serve*.

Now, here the Jews law is brought over to the Christians, in the greatest point of religion that ever was preached; shuts out all idolatry, all superstition, all variety of religions; all is shut out by this commandment, and the Christian that hath the law written in his heart, according to the new covenant, he can go as readily to it and read it, as ever the Jew could go to his *stone table*, and read the law there; you cannot deny, that if there be a thing written and engraven in my heart, I can go as readily to it as I can go to any book or table, tho' I have the keeping of it: But the Jews had not the keeping of it, for generally it was laid up in the *ark of God*.

Now, friends, that which lies upon my mind to speak to you at this time, and that out of the great love that I have to all your precious and immortal souls, as God hath had *love to mine*, is, that you would all consider and weigh in the fear of the Lord, whose presence is among us, which of you, and how many of you are come to the obedience of this commandment: I do not doubt but the most of you can say them *all*, but a happy people are you if you can do *one*: I dare pronounce that soul a blessed soul, that can perform this one commandment, that can or dare stand before his *Maker, and say, O Lord! I love thee with all my heart, with all my soul, and with all my might*; my love is withdrawn from all other things in comparison of thee; there is nothing in this whole world hath a place in my mind, but as it is in subjection to the love of thee.

Here is the first and great commandment, the unchangeable law, the *law* that was good in *Moses'* days, and good in *Christ's* days, and it holds good in our days; and indeed it is such a definitive law, that the breakers of it can neither be good *Jews*, nor good *Christians*. There is an absolute necessity lies upon us, of abstracting and drawing away our minds and souls from all other gods, from all images and other dependencies and trusts that people are naturally liable to trust to, and to have their whole confidence set upon the Lord; but alas! with grief of heart I speak it, there are but very few that as yet have known the right giving forth of the *law*, and there are fewer that are subject to it. This law was not

The FIRST and GREAT COMMANDMENT.

given forth at first without thunder and lightening, and a terrible noise, and the mountain smoking (he that hath an ear to hear, let him hear) infomuch as *Moses* himself said, he feared greatly, and he quaked exceedingly, because of the thunder of the Almighty, and the mountain that smoked and burnt with fire, so that *Israel* could not draw nigh.

Now I say, there are but a few that have come to the knowledge of the giving forth of this law, that have certainly known those thunders, and that terrible work that the Lord of the whole earth makes, when he comes to set up his law; for a great many that have come nigh to it, and might have heard and received the words of the law of God, they have gone backward, they have done like unto the Jews of old, though they had suffered much, and gone through much, and had seen the wonders of the Lord; how he had led them and delivered them; yet when it came to this, that they must hear the voice of God, they said we cannot bear it; we cannot endure it: We have devised for ourselves an easier way; for the voice of thunder and dreadful noises, put them into terror and quaking, and trembling, and great dread came upon them; but we have found an easier way, say they; what is that? Go thou, said they to *Moses*, *and hear thou what the Lord saith, and come thou and tell us*, thou shalt be a Mediator between us; let God speak unto thee, and do thou speak the same to us, and we will hear thee.

Thus the Jews that were not come beyond the law of God written in *tables of stone*, they would not come to receive it in their hearts, as the *Christian* must; so *Moses* received the law from the *mouth of God*, and he was faithful as a servant in the house of God, and he ministered forth the law of God, his precepts, statutes and judgments, and testimonies; and he made them a book of laws for all of them to walk by, from the highest to the lowest; how they should act in criminal matters, and to do justice between man and man, and what they should do in the worship of God, and what they should do towards the priest, whose lips should preserve knowledge for them; and so he brought up a form of religion; but his work was according to the precepts of God; and he brought them into the form of national religion, and government, and national laws. And so *Moses* and the priest ruled over them; and the prieſt offered ſacrifice for them, and made atonement for them, and *Moſes* enquired of the Lord, and asked council for them, and taught and inſtructed them ; and what became of all this at laſt ? When this was done, the prieſt made atonement for ſin, but he could not pluck away the guilt of one ſin ; *there remained the conſcience of ſin* after he had made his offering ; and *Moſes* taught them the counſels of God, and the commands of God, but he could not bind their hearts to the obedience of them; for he declared openly againſt them, that they were *a rebellious and ſtiff-necked people*, notwithſtanding they had a law without them. Indeed, time would fail me to run through the manifold miſcarriages of the church of the *Jews*, in reſpect of their idolatry, in reſpect of their contempt and rebellion, both to God and his ſervant *Moſes*, who was to teach and to guide them : I ſay, the time would fail me to mention the manifold miſcarriages that happened among this people, that had a law and religion without them, and a teacher without them.

Now in the fulneſs of time it pleaſed God in ſending his Son, Chriſt Jeſus, to raiſe up a prophet like unto *Moſes*, in reſpect of faithfulneſs, though higher in reſpect of dignity ; for *Moſes* was faithful in all his houſe as a ſervant, but this man was faithful as a ſon in his own houſe, in the houſe that he was heir of, that houſe wherein he was as King, even a prieſt, a prophet, and a ruler in. When the Lord ſignified by the ſpirit of prophecy, the coming of the *Juſt One*, he ſignified to the people that his miniſtry ſhould not be as that of *Aaron* ; the people ſhould not have their religion without them, and their laws and precepts without them, and their prieſts without them, and their worſhip and church without them ; but that they ſhould have it all within them. *I will write my law in their hearts, I will put it into their inward parts, then they ſhall be my people, and I will be their God, and they ſhall not forſake me.* Your fathers brake my old covenant, but I will make a new covenant in the latter days, a new covenant, not like that your fathers broke ; they brake the law without them, *but I will write my law in their hearts ;* this prophet that is like to *Moſes, he ſhall teach my people, he ſhall be a leader to them, and guide them in the way they are to go, and ſhall be a captain for them,*

them, to lead them to *salvation*; and it *shall come to pass, in the day that I do this, if there be any that will not hear him, he shall be cut off from among the people*. That is, the judgment that comes upon the contemners of the gospel, upon them that will not hear Christ Jesus, they shall be cut off from the people; from what people? From the people of God; they shall have no part of the privileges that are enjoyed thro' Christ; they shall be cut off from the benefits that others reap by their faith in Christ.

So that now we are to expect the operation and working of a ministry, that leads a people to an inward religion, a heart religion, where the heart is fixed entirely upon the true and living God, as the object of their dependence and trust; and they have no other. This is a strange word to flesh and blood; what, no other dependence than on the invisible God? Flesh and blood, and sensuality, can never come to this; this is a religion that hath been hid from ages and generations, and will be hid to all ages that ever shall be in the world, where sensuality prevails. What, will you have me to have my whole dependence for the comfort of my life here, and of the life that is to come, the other life, to have my dependence upon an invisible God, that invisible power that made me, and created the world? How is it possible for me to sequester myself, and draw myself off from all visible objects? I must trust to this, and trust to that: Flesh and blood can never attain to this, with all the wit and reason it hath; it can never separate itself from idols; they are little children; they are children of another birth, born of another seed, that keep themselves from idols.

Friends, idolatry is a great deal more common, I find, than most are aware of. Am I commanded to *love the Lord with all my heart, and soul, and mind, and might?* What is left when the whole is taken away? If God hath my whole heart, what have I to bestow upon the world? What love, what affection, what eagerness, what fervency can I bestow upon the world, or any object in the world, when my whole heart, and soul, and mind, is gone before, is gone toward the Lord?

This is the first and great commandment; and the second

cond is like unto it, that is, *thou shalt love thy neighbour as thyself*. Here it is that the law and the prophets, faith, creeds, prayer, religion and worship, all that ever was in the world, all are comprehended in this, *thou shalt love the Lord thy God with all thy heart, soul and strength, and thy neighbour as thyself*. So what need is there for us to be disputing about religion; about this tenet, and the other tenet; this text, and the other text? For my part, I should only desire you to understand this text, and I should not doubt your going to Heaven. Here is the sum; here is all at once; here is the quintessence of all religion, of all types, shadows, figures, ceremonies and priest-hood, and all that ever was or could be named and practised in the world; all brought to this, *the heart given up to God;* our love set upon him.

What, is this sufficient, will some say? This will make you a good moral man; but what is this to the Christian religion? You may be led into error, and become a heretic for all this.

How can this be, that I should not be of a sound faith, but led into error and heresy for all this? When people let in error, and heresy, and unsoundness of faith, where do they let it in? Do they not let in the principles of error and heresy into their hearts? I believe this, and that, and the other error, that it comes into the heart, and hath a seat in the heart; but how can we let it into the heart, *when the heart is given up to God?* Cannot I keep out error and heresy, if I give up my heart and soul to him? Cannot I trust him with all?

This kind of talk of error and heresy hath come among men that have had the keeping of their own souls: They have taken their own souls into their own hands, and have ordered their religion themselves, or have had somebody to order it for them; and a great many of them have met together to make creeds, and catechisms, and confessions, and orthodox doctrines, that might certainly be professed and subscribed. So afterwards some have come and found fault with them; then they must have a council to try them; then these go off and are laid aside, and others are given in the room of them; so that these men have

have set up for themselves. These would not be under the government and prescription of God, as children under the government of a father; but they will set up religions themselves, and say to the rest of the world, if you own any thing contrary to our principles, you are a heretic; and being a heretic, you are to be rooted out and cut off. Do not you read in the scripture, that *whoever hears not the Prophet that was to come into the world, should be cut off?* What, will not you hear Christ speak in the church? Will not you hear Christ speak? The church cannot speak without a head; if you will not hear the church, you must be cut off. Then they have fallen to hanging, and burning, and killing, and destroying people, and nations not a few: And this comes from their making faiths, and creeds, and ordering religion themselves: All their barbarous and inhuman cruelties, martyring and dungeoning people, comes from their making faiths themselves; and of all things nothing is more desperately wicked, and they did not know it. *The heart is deceitful above all things, and desperately wicked, who can know it?* Men know not how proud and arrogant they themselves are, and yet they would be ordering the hearts, and minds, and consciences of others; and out of this hath sprung all superstition and idolatry, because men would not give up their hearts to God; *thou shalt have no other Gods but me.* This commandment is great in itself; strict in the terms; *thou shalt love the Lord thy God with all thy heart, and thy neighbour as thyself.* Their neighbours could not see with their eyes; therefore they would be hanging, and burning, and destroying one another.

But, blessed be God, who is now bringing forth true Christianity upon its old basis and foundation, whereon it was placed at first, for Christianity hath been justled off from its first foundation; for instead of loving God with all their hearts, and loving their neighbours as themselves, they hated them: Now this is the day, O friends! the weight of it is great; this I say is the day wherein God is bringing Christianity upon its old foundation.

I would not have you think that I am here judging our fore-fathers, that are fallen asleep, that, therefore, they are gone

gone to Hell, because they saw not this day, and lived not to see that benefit of it that we enjoy; I am far from it: This was the thing that they believed and prayed to God for; they did not see this day outwardly, but they saw it by faith. When I was a child, I remember the people of God, when they met three or four together, they would rejoice in the hopes of what they foresaw; they gave thanks to God for the blessed days that he would bring forth, though they could not tell when; they did say, and believe, that God would scatter the fogs, and mists, and bring forth a happy day, wherein his people should have the gift of his Spirit: When they saw the impositions and persecutions of those times, when they that did not conform, and comply, were cast into prisons, dungeons and gaols; well, it will not always be thus, say they, there is a day coming, wherein the Lord will set his people free from all the yokes of oppression, and from the oppressor.

Indeed, my soul did rejoice in hearing the prophetical sayings of those good men, and I thought I might live to see that day. Blessed be God that hath preserved my life to this day, and to this hour, to enjoy what they prayed for: They prayed to God to scatter the mists and fogs, that they might no longer cloud and darken men's minds, and hinder them from enjoying God's teaching. Blessed be God, that we are now in the enjoyment of the prayers of the faithful, that left the world before we were in it. Now the day is come that they prayed for, and enquired after.

How strangely doth the man talk, will some say, concerning the Christian religion; the Christian religion is all *England* over; go to any meeting in *London*, except one, and they will tell you they are Christians; I would to God they were; that is the worst I wish them all. But what should we talk of the Christian religion without the Christian life? except we find that amongst them, what signifies the name and profession of it? And the Christian doctrine is wanting in many places too. There is many in this city, urging this very command, of loving God with all their hearts, and their neighbours as themselves, as fervently as I can do, or any body else; and yet they will tell you in the next breath, that no man in *London*, nor in the world, can do this; no man can possibly love God with all his heart; never a man can be found that can

perform

perform such an act, as to love his neighbour as himself: Not every neighbour, it may be, but some one choice affociate he may pick out, that he can love, and bear with his infirmities and affronts, and *love* him as himself; *love* thy neighbour, that is every body, that there may be a good-will for all people throughout the whole race of mankind, *peace on earth, good-will towards men*: This is the fruit of the gospel. Christian words will not make the Christian religion, there must be a Christian life; but where shall we find that, or seek it?

I know not, I have nothing to do to judge any body, but there is one that judgeth who it is that liveth the Christian life, and who doth not? Who is this? what one is this? *The* HEAD *of the Christian church*: Why, is he here? Yes, the head of the Christian church is here, and he speaks and gives sentence; if you have an ear you may hear him, and if you will turn your mind inward, for he is an *inward minister*, every one of you, if you will turn your minds inward, he will tell you whether you live a Christian life, and what *life* it is you *live*: If there be a drunkard here, let him ask whether his life be a Christian life; will a man go away ignorant from this place, and have no answer? If there be a drunkard here, let him ask inwardly in his own bosom, Lord is my life a Christian *life*? I dare affirm, on God's behalf, he will have an answer, no, thy life is not a Christian *life*, but a shameful, beastly life, a brutish one.

Who told you that the *Head* of Christians, Christ Jesus, is present? Christ Jesus, is he present? How came he here? He is ascended up into Heaven such a day, say they, how came he here? Let him be ascended up into Heaven, yet he is not so ascended into Heaven as not to be here also; how should he fulfil his promise, if he be circumscribed in Heaven or earth? How should he make good his promise, if when *two or three are met together in his name, he is not in the midst of them*? Here now are many more than two or three met together in the name of Christ, and that hope for acceptance with God, through the *Mediator*, Christ Jesus; if you think that here are two or three met together in the name of Christ, it follows that Christ is in the midst of them.

I know not what you may enjoy, some may possibly say, I do not find any such presence of Christ; I hear of the presence of Christ in the sacrament, and I have heard talk of the presence of Christ at a meeting, but I have been at many a meeting, and I never found such a presence of Christ.

Can you read the scriptures? Yes, I can read the scriptures as well as you but that cannot give me a sense of it; I do read the scriptures and believe them; but what signifies my reading the scriptures concerning the presence of Christ, if I have not a sense of it? I have been at many a meeting, but never had the sense of such a Divine Presence as you talk of, nor it may be at the sacrament neither: What is the reason thou hast no sense of it? If thou wilt take my counsel, and turn thy mind inward, and enquire whether the thing I speak of be true, whether there be such a voice as I speak of, that will tell thee what thy state is: If thou wilt be true to thyself, thou mayest know the Divine Presence, and thou mayest hear Christ speak.

The soul hath eyes, and ears, as well as the body. What eyes doth the apostle mean when he saith, *the God of this world hath blinded the eyes of them that believe not, lest the light of the glorious gospel of Christ, who is the image of God, should shine unto them*? If the soul hath eyes, and ears, as well as the body, it can hear, and see as the body; as the bodily eye can see visible things, so the eye of the soul can see things that are invisible, and heavenly; you can hear my voice outwardly, and you may hear the voice of Christ inwardly. I have known some that have been so afraid to hear ill of themselves, that they would not enquire; some have been so guilty in their own consciences, that they have been afraid of hearing ill, and would not enquire about themselves: So it is inwardly; some have been so conscious that their life and conversation is naught, that their life is a sinful life, that they dare not put it to the question: It would certainly have been told them, thy life is not a Christian life; thou must mend thy life, before ever thou comest to have peace with God: If this should be thy portion and mine, that upon search we should find our condition bad, what harm is it?

I would put one question to thee, be serious in considering of it: We are all children of wrath by nature, none of us differ about that, and that *unless we be born again, we cannot enter into the kingdom of God*. The question is, whether I am am one of those or not? Suppose upon enquiry it be discovered to me that I am not, that is bad enough; this is hard, but not so hard as it is true; this is the thing which I would have you consider: Am not I in a better case to know that I am in a natural state, than to go on and perish to eternity? As long as there is life, there is hope; as long as a man is upon the earth, and taking care for his soul, and enquiring about the state of his immortal soul, if his soul is not in a good condition, is it not better for him to know it, and to seek for a cure? For there is no greater infirmity and infelicity can be upon man, than to have some occult and hidden disease, that he cannot be made sensible of; for this wastes and spoils him, and he cannot be persuaded to look out for a remedy: So it is inwardly; if a man be ignorant of his condition, and go on to his dying day, and hour, and does not seek after a remedy, this man perisheth without all peradventure. When you are in this enquiry, be content to be controlled, be willing to have the truth spoken, though it be against yourselves. I might instance in divers things that I have spoken of: If a man be satisfied that his life is not a Christian life, I say, if the swearer or liar, if the proud person, or the effeminate, as soon as they come to be satisfied that their life is not a Christian life that they now live, what can this man expect? What counsel should we give him, and what counsel should he take? I will go on in the way that I am in: What, after thou knowest thy life is not a Christian life? God forbid: Wilt thou go on and perpetrate sin upon sin, and heap up wrath against the day of wrath; I am a sinner, my life is unchristian, I make account to live in sin, and die in sin; is this good policy? Consider another text which our Lord spake, *if ye die in your sins, whither I go, ye cannot come.*

O friends, lay these things to your hearts; what have I to do but to tell you that the love I have in my soul for you all, makes me desire in my heart that you might be saved? *This is the will of God, that you might all be saved, and come to the knowledge of the truth: Blessed are they that know the truth; the truth as it is in Jesus.* Truth in the inward parts, hath a speaking voice; and if thou hearken to it, it will tell thee that thy state is naught. Canst thou believe the truth when he tells thee so, that thy state is naught, and that thou art like to go to eternal destruction, unless there be repentance and regeneration to prevent it? Canst thou believe this doctrine, when it founds in thy own heart? If thou canst not believe it, unbelief will be thy ruin. *The spirit of truth is come to convince the world of sin, because they believe not in Christ*: He tells them their condition, and they will not believe him. The Spirit of Christ convinceth men of sin, and they believe him not. The spirit of truth convinceth thee of thy sin, but thou believest him not. If thou lovest thy pleasure, and thy profit, and thine honour, then thou lovest not God with all thine heart; and then thou art not a Christian, but out of covenant with God. Art thou sensible that thy condition is bad, were it not best to get it mended? After we are convinced of our own sinful state, is it not our best course to seek to have it mended? Who shall mend it? faith one; I have done all I can to mend my life, and I cannot mend it.

I have concluded so in my younger years; I have fasted, and prayed, and spent time in hearing, reading, and meditation, and did all in my own power, and all to mend my state, but I could not mend it; and as I grew up in years, sin and corruption more prevailed, and there was no help; and I came so far as to believe there was no help, and that if God did not help me, I was undone to all eternity. I many times wished that I had never been born: I went to ministers and meetings, and to all sorts of separate people, and to all manner of ordinances, and to all manner of means, to mend this bad heart of mine, to see if I could get a power that would give me victory over my corruptions; but my arm was never so long as to reach thereunto; it was far out of my power and reach.

Many have sought to get this power of reforming their hearts and lives; to attain it by their own hands, by their own endeavours, but they could never do it; they could never better their condition, nor bring forth fruit worthy of amendment of life. I wish that every one was come to that pass, that they knew not which way to turn them; that they were come at last to their wits end: They will

will come to it sooner or later; the sooner the better. I have done all I can; I can do no more; I am at my wits end, and I know not what to think, concerning my eternal state; I know not what to judge of it; I strive against my lusts and corruptions, but for all that they prevail against me: Temptations come before me, but I cannot conquer them. O I am glad when people come to that pass, that they know not what to do, but despair of their own arms, of their own strength, and their own wit, and despair of all other help in the world; I am glad of that.

I am not preaching up despair of God's grace and mercy; but let me tell you, when men despair of their own doings, and of all outward means, and helps, then they are fit objects for the mercy of God; and not till then: *When the Lord looked, and saw that there was none to save and deliver, then his own arm brought salvation.* God will not save till then; God will not reveal his power, till men have done with their own power; they will never trust God, while they think they can do something for themselves. All the forms of religion of the several people of this nation, will do them little good without the power. What is the meaning of that principle, to have such masses, and prayers, and performances? What is the meaning of it? Let us search to the bottom. They say we are sinners; when we pray to God for his blessing, and for salvation by Christ, there is this at the bottom, they think these duties and performances will be very helpful to their state; helpful towards the knowledge of it: To speak plain English, these are their Gods. If I speak of prophane and wicked people, I would say their lusts are their Gods: But when I speak of righteous people, that are meer formalists, then I say their duties, as they call them, are their Gods. When they have done all, they can do nothing for them, and then they have no Gods at all; then they are *godless*: And if God doth not help them, then they are undone to all eternity.

When poor creatures are cast out, as it were, into the open field, to the loathing of their persons, not salted at all, nor swaddled at all, but lying in the guilt of their blood: *When*

I

I passed by thee, faith the Lord, *and saw thee polluted in thy own blood, I said unto thee, when thou wast in thy blood, yea, when thou wast in thy blood, I said unto thee, live. When I passed by thee, and looked upon thee, behold, thy time was a time of love, and I spread my skirt over thee, and covered thy nakedness; yea, I sware unto thee, and entered into covenant with thee*, faith the Lord God, *and thou becamest mine.* What, was it a time of love, when I was such an object in mine own eyes, that I thought I was the most miserable creature in the world; one that could not make a good prayer, nor dispute for religion, nor perform any duty; a poor creature cast out into the open field, to the loathing of my person; lost all that I gained; my name was from among the living; my days were passed over in sorrow, and I said there is nothing but darkness, and death, and misery for me: I used all means, and tried all things, saving only a living trust in God alone, and that flesh and blood cannot do. Flesh and blood cannot know him, therefore flesh and blood cannot trust in him. Alas! said I, I cannot trust in the Lord, I cannot cast my soul and all my concerns, my fame and reputation in the world, I cannot cast all upon the care of the Almighty; I cannot know him, nor trust in him; how can I do it? nobody can do it. *They that know my name*, faith the Lord, *they will put their trust in me*: Never a truer word was spoken; but how they should know God, and trust in him, I know not.

When thou comest once to this pass, to be at thy wits end, and not know which way to turn thee, nor to whom to run for help, or to ask counsel for thy soul's welfare, when thou art come to the end of all, and without hope, then God reveals himself by his Son Jesus Christ; Christ the Son of God, is known by our coming to him; but none can come unto Christ, *except the Father which hath sent him, draw him: When thou hast done with thy Gods, and thrown away thy idols to the bats and moles*, then thou wilt find the Lord; and thou wilt cry out, O! that God would have mercy upon me, and lift up the light of his countenance upon me; I am a poor, miserable creature. There are many that make such a whining and complaining, that they take a pride in their very complaints,

plaints, their hypocrify is fo great. I have known fome that have prided themfelves in wording their condition, and expreffing their miferable cafe before the Lord; but fuppofe thou canft not fpeak at all, but feeleft thyfelf miferable, thou canft not exprefs thy condition; at fuch a time as this, God was drawing thy foul to Chrift Jefus, the Mediator of it: I have heard of a Mediator, and that there is *Balm* in *Gilead* for me; that there is a phyfician there; that there is one phyfician, even Jefus Chrift, the Mediator of the new covenant; thou haft finned againft him, and grieved him, yet he ftands with open arms for thee, ready to receive thee and embrace thee; where ftands he? He ftands at the door and knocks; it is a fmall matter, one would think, to let him in: *Rev.* iii, 20. *Behold, I ftand at the door and knock; and if any man hear my voice, and open the door, I will come in to him, and fup with him, and he with me.* Here is good news for an hungry foul, if any fuch be here; Chrift the Mediator, ftands at the door and knocks, he will come in and fup with thee, if thou open to him; then we fhall meet with the Lord's fupper: *This is the Lord, I will wait for him;* he will bring his bread with him, the bread of life, and the wine of his kingdom, and the Lord's fupper will be celebrated without cavilling and jangling.

Now, becaufe we will not pervert the fcripture, I would have you that underftand books, read what *commentators* of this and former ages fay upon this text; whether they do not deliver in their opinions, that this knocking at the door, is Chrift calling the foul by his grace; and this door is the door of the heart, and Chrift's calling the foul by his grace and Spirit, to let him in by faith: This is their judgment and fenfe, and their fenfe is mine; and I believe the genuine fenfe of this text, that Chrift would have people think he is near to them, and would have them open their hearts, and receive him by faith, to be a Saviour to them.

No; that, faith flefh and blood, I cannot bear, I cannot confent to have him for my Saviour, I will not let him in, for he is like *Micaiah* to *Ahab*, *he never fpake good concerning me*: For if I have him for my Saviour, I muft part with my lufts and pleafures; if there be any other Saviour, I will try, and not meddle with him; he will fpoil all our mirth and good society; he will tell me that every idle word that I shall speak, I must give an account thereof in the day of judgment: What, do you think that I can like such a Saviour? That I can live with such a one as will call me to an account for every word I speak; and that if I speak one idle word, judgment will come upon me? No, I will try one and another, rather than accept of him on such terms; I am one that am joined to such a church, and enjoy such and such ordinances, and such helps: I am in covenant with God, and under the seals of that covenant; I am baptized, and do partake of the Lord's supper, which is another seal of the covenant; I hope it will go well with me. I will go something farther: Another saith, he must have a Mediator; I will go to the *Virgin Mary*, and offer something to her, and pray to her: Saith another, I will go to Saint *James*, and Saint *John*, and other Saints to intercede with God for me. They must have some Mediator: This is the twisting and twining of the sons and daughters of men, to keep out Christ, the great Mediator, who came into the world for this purpose, to destroy the works of the Devil. Alas! I have nothing left but my bare life and living in this world; I have nothing left me but some *little desire I had to please God*, and that he will never judge and condemn me for; but my false dealing, and buying and selling with deceit, he will judge this, and condemn me; and my discoursing of things without me; all my carnal friendship of the world, and my vain fashions, all this is corrupt and defiled; these he came on purpose to destroy; he came to destroy both the Devil and his works. What, can a man live in the world, and never join with the Devil? never sin at all? never do any thing that the Devil would have him to do? There is no perfection in this world; no living without sin here; then I am sure there is no unity with Christ here; and if there be no unity with Christ, then there is none with God the Father. What will become of thee now? What will all the pleaders for that opinion say now? There is something stands between God and me, and I shall never have peace; and what is that? It is sin; I would have my sin taken away, else I had better never been born. Canst thou remove sin out of thy heart? I have tried, but I cannot do it; I have heard of Christ the

Mediator

Mediator of the new covenant, he faith, he came into the world, and that for this purpofe he was manifefted, that he might deftroy the works of the Devil. Now fin in my heart is the Devil's work, I will fee if he will deftroy that for me; I will truft and rely upon him, and fee if his great power can deftroy it in me.

Here people come rightly to believe in him that God hath fent, and truft in him, and he will take them in; and, like a Chirurgeon, he will rip their hearts, and let out their corruptions, though there hath been ever fo much rottennefs; and he will heal them, and purify them, and pardon them, though they have been ever fo wicked, if they come to him; when thy fins are fet in order before thee, then thou crieft out, *O wretched man that I am! who shall deliver me from this body of death?* Is it God that hath thought on me, and waited to be gracious, hath born my fins long? how wonderful is his patience towards me! All thefe things working in the foul, tends to beget a love of God, and fervent defires after being cleanfed and purified from fin, and earneft prayer to the Lord, to make the holy fire to kindle that would burn it up: The more the foul trufteth in Chrift, the more doth this heavenly fire burn up our lufts, and then a man feels a great change in his mind: The things, faith he, that I delighted in, are now grievous to me; I hope I fhall never be found in thofe things again; my mind is now taken off them; who took it off? Didft thou not ftrive before to take it off? I did, but I could not do it. There are many, I believe, in this affembly, before the Lord, that are my witneffes in this matter, that when they came to Chrift the Mediator, he changed their minds, and he untied the Devil's fetters; they were tied to their fins and lufts, but he hath unloofed them; they are afhamed of thofe things that they formerly took pleafure in. *What fruit* (faith the apoftle) *had you in thofe things, whereof you are now afhamed?* So I fay, what pleafure have you in fporting, and gaming, and drinking, and company-keeping? What pleafure have you to think on your wanton difcourfes? What pleafure in pride and vanity? What pleafure in wrath and bitternefs of mind? And what pleafure in malice and envy? What pleafure have you in thefe things whereof you are now afhamed? So far as you are convinced, you are ashamed to think of them; I am ashamed to think that the Devil at such a time, by such a temptation, should prevail over me.

I would to God you were all come to this, to be ashamed, that you might remember your past evil ways and actions, with sorrow and shame: There is a secret joy in this. Sure it is better to be ashamed, than to continue in impudence. God hath wrought this change at last; and who shall have the glory of it? God shall have the glory of it; for his own works will praise him. What men do, many times they do for their own praise; but when they are at their wits end, and know not what to do, they cast themselves upon their Maker, to see if he will have mercy upon them; if not, they must perish: Then for what he doth, he gets the glory and the praise of it.

There are some here, that are bound to praise God while they have a day to live, for what he hath done for them. They could never have loved God with all their hearts; but they would have continued strangers to God, and the Devil would have led them captive at his will. They would not have loved God with all their hearts, had not God first *shed abroad his love upon their hearts*, and constrained them to love him: It is he that hath first loved them, and *wrought in them, both to will and to do, of his own good pleasure*. Whatsoever we are, we are by the grace of God; this grace is magnified in them that believe and obey the gospel.

My friends, we know there is so much peace and pleasure in the ways of God; so much soul-satisfaction in walking with God, and loving of him with all our hearts, I should be glad if every one of you were of the same mind, and had experience of it. We labour diligently for this purpose; and we would set before you these two things:

First, how we may come to know our miserable state by nature.

And what a blessed and happy state they are in, that have been converted and changed; that have been translated out of the kingdom of darkness, into the kingdom of God's dear Son. Consider

Confider your ftate by nature is evil; we hope that many of you believe the reports of the gofpel, concerning the goodnefs of the Lord, his great love in fending his Son into the world, to feek and to fave you that were loft, and that you believe in him. And we are perfuaded, that by the foolifhnefs of preaching God will fave fome of you, that you may be his redeemed ones, and truft to no other Saviour: *For there is not any other name under Heaven, but the name of Jefus, by which we can be faved.* He only can take away the fins of the world; his fpirit fearcheth the heart, and trieth the reins, which he promifed to fend into the world when he was about leaving of it. Now I dare proclaim that Holy Spirit to be the Spirit of the God of Heaven, that now fees what refolution thou art of, and what thou art now propofing to do; whether to go on in fin, or to return to God. This I can fpeak without blafphemy, it is God's Spirit that fearcheth the heart, and knoweth thy thoughts and purpofes, and convinceth thee of thy fin: God hath fent his Son Chrift Jefus into the world to enlighten you, that by his light you may fee him; and that by his grace you might receive him; and that by his grace you might be faved.

To him I commit you all, and thefe words that we have fpoken in the evidence and demonftration of the fpirit, according as he hath wrought in us.

I muft tell you we were never called of God to ftudy *Sermons* for you, nor to preach things that are made ready to our hands; but as the *Lord our God* hath wrought in us, and as God hath been pleafed to make known his mind to us, and by his Spirit given us utterance, fo we fpeak, and fo we preach. You that are come to believe and receive the things of the Spirit, you will judge what I fay. *I fpeak unto you that are fpiritual; judge ye what I fay,* faith the apoftle. So when I fpeak of divine and heavenly things, you that are fpiritual, judge what I fay? And as you come to judge and determine in yourfelves that thefe things are true, you will feel the power of them in your own fpirits, and we fhall all be of the fame mind; and as we have *one God,* we fhall ferve him in fincerity, and worfhip him with reverence. Then his name shall be exalted in the midst of us, and we shall edify one another in *love*, and we shall instruct one another, and call upon one another; *come, let us go to the house of the God of* Jacob, *he will teach us, and preserve us* in his way, and do us good, and keep us from all evil.

Turn your minds inward, and consider that God is a God at hand, ready to help you; and he requires no more of you than of other people in former times, to love the Lord with all your hearts, and to abstract and withdraw your mind from all other things that do come in competition with him; and be sure to have no trust or dependence but upon him; then see what God will do for you: No tongue can express, nor pen write; *neither hath it entered into the heart of man to conceive, the things that God hath prepared for those that love him.* That wisdom and knowledge, that joy and peace, and consolation, that passeth all understanding, he will reveal and communicate by his spirit to them that love him, and trust in him, and rely upon him, and receive teaching from him; he will feed them *with food in due season; he will bring the former and the latter rain, and they shall be as trees planted by the rivers of water, and bring forth fruit in due season; and their leaf shall not fade or wither.*

This hath been London's wonder, and England's wonder, how it comes to pass, that such a people's leaf hath not withered, nor faded, as many have done: Our root was by a river; if we had stood in ourselves; if our dependence and support had been upon doctrines, tenets, and commandments of men, then our leaf would have been upon the ground as well as others; but because we have been upon our root, *Christ Jesus,* that is always green, both in summer and winter, therefore our leaf hath not withered; to the praise of God, and to the honour of his name, be it spoken: He hath preserved us, for we have no power of ourselves, no more than others; but we trust in God, and have received power from God, to stand as witnesses for him; we have trusted in the Lord, and he hath stood by us, and delivered us, when we were compassed about with dangers and distresses; if we continue to trust in him still, he will bring us through all

our

our trials and troubles, and he will be with us, and *never leave us nor forsake us*; if we take him for our God, we shall never need any other.

We read that *Senacherib*, king of *Assyria*, sent *Rabshekah* to *Jerusalem* to *Hezekiah*, with a great army, saying, *what confidence is this wherein thou trustest? And he spake also to the people, and cried with a loud voice, hear you the word of the great king of* Assyria; *let not* Hezekiah *deceive you, for he shall not be able to deliver you; neither let* Hezekiah *make you trust in the Lord, saying, the Lord will deliver us.* Hezekiah went and prayed to the Lord, *saying, O Lord of hosts, God of* Israel, *that dwellest between the Cherubims, thou art the God, the God alone of all the kingdoms of the earth; thou hast made Heaven and earth; incline thine ear, O Lord, and hear; open thine eyes, O Lord, and see and hear all the words of* Senacherib, *which he hath sent to reproach the living God*, &c. And we read, that after he had presented his supplication before the Lord, *the angel of the Lord went forth and smote in the camp of the* Assyrians, *one hundred four score and five thousand; and when they arose early in the morning, behold, they were all dead corps.*

Thus you see what came of it at last; and thus it hath been in our day; they that trust in the Lord, he will deliver them, and they shall never be ashamed nor confounded; but as for all other Gods, they that trust in them, shall be confounded and covered with shame, and they and their Gods will perish together.

And now, my friends, I beseech you all to have respect to this great duty of putting your whole trust in the *Lord*, who is the living *God*, and he will be always present with you, and work in you both to will and to do of his good pleasure; he will support and preserve you in all your trials and sufferings, that you may be vessels of honor, to bear his name in the earth, and so sound forth his praise to the following generations.

His Prayer *after* Sermon.

MOST *glorious, infinite, Powerful Father! who hast created us, and given us life and breath, and lengthened out our time to this day, and hast long waited to be gracious to us, and art still waiting upon the sons and daughters of men, holding forth*

forth the hand of thy love, and offering thy grace and tendering salvation unto them, and hast brought a day of visitation upon the inhabitants of this city and nation.

Glory, praise and thanksgiving be to thee, O Lord! that by thy power, thou hast inclined the hearts and consciences of the sons and daughters of men, to submit to thee, and bow their necks to the blessed and easy yoke of thy Son Jesus Christ, that they may do thy will on earth, as it is done in Heaven. They that are travelling, and distressed, and afflicted in their souls because of their bondage, do thou arise, living Father, and reveal, and discover thy power to them; shew them the exceeding greatness of thy power, that they may trust therein, and be safe; make bare thine arm for their salvation. Those that are slumbering in their profession, let them be awakened; and bring to thine heavenly kingdom, those that have passed through thy refining fire, and whom thou hast cleansed and sanctified.

Powerful Father of Life! carry on thy work among thy people every where: Gather them that are scattered, and bring back to thyself, those that are wandering and out of the way, and seeking the living among the dead. Lord, teach them and let them hear a voice behind them, and guide them to the holy mountain; that they may be brought to the path of life, and to the place which thou hast provided for thy little flock to meet and feed together, offering unanimously the sacrifices of praise and thanksgiving, which thou hast ordained and appointed in thine house.

Blessed and powerful Father! all thy little ones be pleased to surround with thine Almighty Power; and wherever they are, let them feel thy preserving hand, delivering them from the evil of the world: We pray not that thou shouldest take them out of the world, but to preserve them from the defilements and pollutions of it: That holy people may serve thee the holy God, and bear thy holy name upon their hearts; that so it may be exalted and magnified above all, and humble thanksgivings and praises may be given unto thee, through Jesus Christ, for all thy love thou hast manifested, and for thy abounding mercies, and renewed favours which we have received at thy hands.

To thee, living Father, through Jesus Christ, thy well-beloved Son, in whom thou art well pleased, be all honour, praise and dominion rendered by us, and all thy people, from henceforth, and forever. Amen.

SERMON

SERMON IV.

The STANDARD of TRUTH.

Preached at GRACE-CHURCH-STREET, *May* 29, 1692.

THERE is a universal standard of truth, that God hath set up over all the sons and daughters of men; he hath given the knowledge of it in, and through Jesus Christ; he hath dealt it out to them, that they may be capable of joining and adhering to the truth, and to be delivered from eternal condemnation. This *standard and measuring-rule* is revealed and manifested in every man and woman, by the light that shines in their hearts, by which they are able to discern, and to give a sound and true judgment, (if they are but willing) upon all *their own ways*. A man or woman may know in every word they speak, in every action they do, whether they speak, and do, according to the truth, or whether they are justified by the truth, in what they speak and do.

I tell you, my friends, this is no small mercy, that mankind hath obtained at the hand of his Maker, that he is brought into a capacity of not acting blind-fold, but that he may see his way, and his own inclinations, and pass judgment upon them, whether they are good or evil? Whether they will stand justified in the sight of his Maker, or whether they will be condemned.

I confess, the veil of ignorance, that is come over the sons and daughters of men, through sin, transgression and rebellion, is very great. And I may say, as the apostle said, *sometime you were darkness*: And what can darkness see? what can darkness discover? The Lord our God, that made us, hath not left us in that state of darkness, blindness and ignorance; but through the riches of his mercy and goodness, hath found out a way, to *command that light should shine out of darkness,* into people's hearts, for all that the Devil did to darken man, to alienate and estrange him from his Maker.

The same Almighty Power, that said in the creation, *let there be light, and it was so;* he hath shined into our hearts;
and

and the way by which he hath done so, is through the Mediator, through Jesus Christ the Redeemer, *in whom the fulness of the God-Head dwells.* He hath received power from his Father, not only to be a light and salvation, but to impart and communicate of that divine light unto them, even *unto every one that cometh into the world;* that so by means thereof, they may be delivered from their darkness, and ignorance of the mind of God, that they were liable to in the fall, and might be restored, through the Mediator, to a capacity of judging of their own actions, and of their own words, and ways, and inclinations.

This is the *standard* which God hath pitched in every one of our bosoms, for the trial of ourselves, either for our justification, or condemnation, of every word and action.

Now, to make every one sensible of the greatness of this blessing, consider, it is not only given to augment and encrease knowledge, but it is given on purpose to allure and persuade men into a liking of truth, into a love of truth: The apostle esteemed it a wonderful mercy that came by Christ; *he hath sent him to bless us, in turning every one of us from the evil of his ways:* So that here is a capacity that the sons and daughters of men have, through the Mediator, of being turned from the evil of their ways and doings, to that which is well-pleasing to God.

The next work, after God hath wrought thus mercifully for the sons and daughters of men, is, that they would be good to themselves, and merciful to themselves, and take pity of themselves, by a due improvement of the grace, and mercy, and kindness of God, that he hath bestowed freely upon them; and in bringing all their deeds to that standard, all their words and actions to that rule; that so whatsoever they may be, or how many soever, if they do not answer that standard and rule, they may deny, withstand and resist them, that so they may keep out of condemnation: For the apostle declares it plainly without scruple, *there is no condemnation to them that are in Christ Jesus:* If he had said to them that profess Christ Jesus, there had been a large latitude, especially for those nations; but the words are limited, and you will find them so; that is, *to them that are in Christ Jesus;* and (as if he should say) that you may know rightly what I mean; I mean, *such as as walk not after the flesh, but after the spirit*. They that are in Chrift, walk after his Spirit; for, *they that walk not after the Spirit of Chrift, are none of his*; but they that are his, walk after the fpirit, the fpirit of truth, and there is no condemnation to them.

It is not only the fcriptures that ratify and confirm this doctrine, but you yourfelves are all living witneffes of the truth of this, that fo far as you do act and fpeak in obedience to the principle of truth, that God hath planted in you, you feel no condemnation upon you: Such a thing I did at fuch a time, and I had no condemnation: Why fo? becaufe I did it in obedience, and fubjection to that meafure of grace that God fet up in me; and fuch a thing I did, for which I was condemned: Why fo? becaufe I did it according to the inclinations of my own corrupt mind, and in contradiction to the truth that opened in me.

My friends, I would have you in point of the doctrine of chriftianity, to be the better for what you read and hear: It is poffible for me to preach the truth, and you may believe what I fay, and you may read the Holy Scriptures, and have the belief of what you read; but if you come to a fenfible feeling of the fulfilling of things you hear, you will give a greater feal to the truth of the doctrine, than by all you have read and heard; and you will *grow wife to falvation*, by trying and experiencing the effect of every thing you underftand; and not like the carnal men of this world, that have not faith, that mind only their worldly profits and pleafures, fuch are *earthly, fenfual and devilifh*; but I would judge of actions and words, according to truth, and according to the effect I find in me. I did fuch a thing, and I had peace in the doing of it; I feel no reproach, no condemnation upon me. Here is a way for people to grow up in the life of chriftianity; to keep to the ftandard of truth; for whether men will or no, they muft do it at laft, and may now, if they pleafe, make a trial of their words and actions.

As for the moft part of you, you are got paft *Pilate*: *Pilate* could make that enquiry; *what is truth?* faith he: And I confefs, it is not long ago, it is within the memory

mory of man, that a more serious and better sort of people were so confounded with the darkness and ignorance of those times, that they were ready to cry out, what is truth ? and where is truth ? Their eyes were so blinded, and things were so jumbled and confused by the disputations that men raised, that made things so dark people could not see their way : But *God who hath commanded the light to shine out of darkness*, hath brought a *glorious day;* hath dissipated, and scattered, and driven away a great deal of that fog and mist, that did overspread men's minds. As many as have sincerely sought the truth in the inward parts, they have found a divine principle of truth, that hath a self-evidencing quality in itself, to convince the minds and consciences of the sons and daughters of men, that it is the truth : And to this the Lord hath brought most of you, to be sensible of something that is truth in itself. There are many things that are true in the words of them ; many true expressions ; but there is truth in itself, the essential truth of God, which, as it is in God, is everlasting and eternal, and will stand over all error, and falshood, and deceit : The truth, as it is in Christ Jesus, is a standard and rule for men to act by ; he hath given it to the sons and daughters of men ; and as it appears in them, it is either a Judge to condemn them, or a Saviour to save them from their sins, and to justify them.

Now, that which concerns us, is to find out the measure of truth, or manifestation, or principle of truth, which it hath pleased God to reveal in ourselves : And whosoever will turn their minds a little while inward, into the serious search and consideration, how the Lord hath dealt with them, they will find they are not quite destitute of truth. One that makes it his practice to lye, cheat and cozen, is not utterly destitute of truth; for there is a principle of truth in him, that doth check and reprove him for his theft, lying and falshood, and he lives under condemnation himself. He cannot draw near to the God of truth upon any occasion, but his lying and falshood stand in his way. Now, if so be, that this liar be made sensible of a principle of truth in him, and do but bring his words and actions to the truth, so much of it as he
knows

knows will make him leave lying and deceiving, and to practife truth to efcape condemnation; if he will but leave lying and falfhood, and live in the truth, and fpeak the truth to his neighbour, he will find another ftate, condition and frame in his foul, than there was before: He is now more at peace, and hath a clear and ferene way, to come to God by prayer, and for pouring out his fupplication, which he had not before; for he had barred up his own way by his fin, which lay continually at his door; *if thou deft not well, fin lies at thy door,* faith God to *Cain*: So, when you do evil, you cannot but know it; when you are drunk, or fwear or tell a lie, and deceive your neighbour, and carry on the defign of finful profit, thou knoweft it, whether men know it or no, and God that made thee knoweth it; and there thy fin lies at the door, and blocks and bars thee out, that thou canft not offer thy prayers to God with that clearnefs, as if thou hadft fpoken the truth: So that it highly concerns every one of us, to be waiting upon God, for the difcovery of his truth to us; and then we muft embrace, adhere and join to the truth, as our chiefeft good.

But fome will fay, this adhering and joining to the truth, is a hard leffon: It is pretty eafy to find out a principle of truth, that ftandeth againft, and oppofeth all manner of evil: Very few, now a-days, will deny a fettled principle of truth in all men, that judgeth falfhood, and condemneth deceit, and witneffeth againft it in others, and in themfelves: But this fame joining, and adhering to it, that cannot be done, without a crofs to a carnal mind.

Now, if the crofs of Chrift be not taken up, there is no good Chriftianity among us; where this is neglected, it fpots and ftains the profeffion of Chriftianity, becaufe it is fo directly oppofite to the doctrine of Chrift; *he that will be my difciple, muft;* it is not, he may if he will; but, *he muft take up the crofs of Chrift, and follow* HIM. There were a fort of people, that were never like to be made Chriftians, that would be exempt from taking up a daily crofs; therefore he preffeth it upon them to deny themfelves, and take up his crofs and follow him. No man is like to live a Chriftian life, without taking up a daily crofs.

This I cannot do, fays one; I know how to carry myfelf among

among Christians with serioufness, sobriety and watchfulness, without shaming any profession; but I cannot deny myself, I cannot contradict my own will: This is that which keeps a man from leading a Christian life, when he cannot deny himself, and take up his daily cross.

Now, it is come to this now a-days, when a light is broken forth, and men have a principle of truth in their own hearts, it comes to this; faith one, I ought to be *holy in all manner of conversation*, and to be watchful over my words, and have my conversation honest and just without deceit: See what a deal I know, yet I can never live this life, for all I know it so well; I cannot take up a daily cross, which is so much against the contrary inclinations working in me; then the question I put to myself is, shall I take up a cross or no?

Here it comes to the point with every man or woman, after they come to the knowledge of this *standard* of truth: If the world would but come to this rule and standard, there would be no more cheating nor cozening, no more fraud, deceit nor dissimulation, nor war and bloodshed; but if men would, in every thing they do, answer the principle of truth in themselves, they would put the question to themselves, shall I take up my daily cross, or no? Shall I deny myself those pleasures that my conscience doth condemn; and those ungodly gains that I seek after by falshood, by lying, prevaricating and departing from the truth? Shall I do this, that I may be rich and great in the world, or shall I not?

You know what I say, many of you, and have put this question to yourselves, and some have made a good answer to it: I will take up my daily cross, by the grace of God; this standard of truth shall be the rule of my words and actions, to my dying-day.

They that have learned this lesson, and obtained peace with God, through our Lord Jesus Christ, that have not only made a resolution, but performed it in act and deed, by the power of Christ's cross, they are purified, and sanctified, and washed from their old conversations, and *have their conversation in Heaven*; that is, live after a heavenly manner, live a godly life here upon earth, when they have come to this resolution, and also the practice of it.

I would desire, and it is my labour, that you that hear me
this

this day, who are aware of what I am speaking, *viz.* The STANDARD *of* TRUTH, the principle of Truth, that unerring Guide, which is placed in the conscience of every man, and justifieth, or condemneth, his actions and words. You who are come to be aware of this, that you may all come to this godly resolution in yourselves, I would have this dispute carried on in every one's bosom. When the question is stated, I would have you really answer it; shall I guide my actions and words according to this unerring rule, or no? I cannot tell what to say, say some, there is danger in it: What danger can there be to answer that which a man knows to be truth? I will tell you what danger: The world is perverse, and most men live out of truth, and the Devil is a cunning adversary, and he would have none live in it: *He abode not in the truth;* and he would not have us live in it, nor regulate our words and actions by the truth in our own souls: What if most men in the world pervert the truth? What if so few walk in the *narrow way,* and so few come to life eternal; is that an argument that I must not come there? Should it not stir me up to greater diligence, that by any means I may be of the number of that few that shall obtain salvation, and not go with a great company in the way that leads to destruction? If we improve our times, and seasons, and opportunities, and mercies, and blessings, that are vouchsafed to us, we at last may obtain life eternal.

But some may say, I must sit down in despair, for I cannot come thither of myself, though I do what I can to *work out my own salvation.* There is a decree against me; what, tho' I should pray ever so much, and spend my nights in grief and sorrow? If I be decreed to eternal damnation, there is no help for me, no hope that I should escape. And if I be decreed to salvation, though I take my liberty to sin, and be loose and wanton, as others, it cannot hinder me from attaining salvation at last.

For this reason, many have laid aside the spiritual warfare against corruption, and their spiritual travel, that they will do nothing in order to their everlasting happiness; therefore they think they had as good take their pleasure: But, my friends, the case is not now so with us; let every soul among us praise the Lord for his mercy, in expelling that thick

thick cloud of darkness, which is vanished and gone: This I know, and I hope you do all believe, that God doth every where, and in every nation, call sinners to repentance, and that *he delighteth not in the death of him that dieth, but rather that they would turn and live*; and in order thereunto, he hath given his Son, Jesus Christ, to be a Saviour and a Mediator; and *he hath sent forth the Spirit of his Son into our hearts*, to give direction to us in our way: Now our duty is, to make improvement of those visitations of mercy, that God hath bestowed upon us, in order to our salvation, and not live in *rioting and drunkenness, chambering and wantonness, strife and envying*, and following the fashions of the world: But we must *work out our own salvation with fear and trembling*.

But some will say, is not this done already? Is it not already wrought by our Saviour and Mediator? *Christ hath tasted death for every man*, and laid down a price for the soul of every man.

But yet there must be a change wrought in us; there must be a translation of our souls, from one state to another. This is called in the scripture, regeneration, and being born again; this is called a being baptized into Christ, and described also by other expressions: But the matter is, to change thy life; for there is a sinful source of wickedness, that is stirred up by the motions of the powers of darkness, and our own concupiscence; but God is always ready to bring us under the government of his Holy Spirit, that will lead us into all truth; and this cannot be done without a Cross. But the question lies here, shall I take up this Cross or no? If I do, it will *crucify me to the world*. Let me see; how much do I love the world? A great deal: But do I love the world better than my own soul? *What will it profit me, to gain the whole world, and lose my own soul? Or what shall I give in exchange for my soul?* I cannot get to Heaven without denying myself; let me take care of my immortal soul: I am a poor creature; I will serve the Lord my Maker, and make it my business to glorify and please him. He can snatch me away by death when he pleaseth; therefore will I labour, that my thoughts, words, actions and conversation,

tion, may anfwer to that rule that he hath fet before me, as a ftandard of truth, to fquare and regulate my actions by. I will not live any longer in vanity, as many do; I do not know but my breath may be ftopt to-day, before to-morrow; therefore *to-day, while it is called to-day, I will hear* God's voice, *and not harden my heart*, but receive that counfel, that is offered to me, for the benefit of my foul. I am bought with a price, I am none of my own; I will live to him that died for me: I have more reafon to live to Chrift, and ferve him, that fhed his precious blood for the redemption of my foul, and to be fubject to him, than to be fubject to Chrift's enemy, to the prince of the power of the air, who rules in the children of difobedience. I will take up a refolution to ferve God, but I can do nothing of myfelf; but *the grace of God which brings falvation, will teach me to deny ungodlinefs, and worldly lufts, and to live righteoufly, foberly and godly, in this prefent world.* Take heed of being deceived and beguiled, for there is no way will bring you to Heaven, but a holy and undefiled way.

Therefore, come and take this ftandard of truth in your hands, to guide you in your way, that you may neither turn to the right hand, nor to the left: This will fhew you the way you fhould walk in, and be like the cloud and pillar of fire to the *Ifraelites*, in their journey to *Canaan*, which was a type of Heaven; the cloud they could fee by day, and the pillar of fire by night; fo this ftandard of truth will direct you in your travel to the heavenly *Canaan*. Let this be the rule and meafure of your thoughts, words and actions.

If a workman, that is a builder, hath a rule to work by; if he goes on, and never examines his work by his rule, but makes his eye his rule; if he doth not bring his rule to his work every little while, to fee whether his work be right; if he worketh on, and never minds his rule, what fad work will he make. But a prudent skilful workman will fay, I will not truft mine eye too much, but I will look to my rule, my rule will not fail me; if there be bad work, it will difcover it to me, that I may mend it before I go any further. Thus a difcreet workman

workman will often bring his rule to his work, and ufe his line and plummet, that he may make it workman-like. He will fay, if I let my rule alone, and not make ufe of it, but work as I pleafe, and truft to mine eye, no wonder if I make bad work, and what I build fall down again, and tumble about mine ears.

You to whom God hath given the ftandard of truth, as a rule and meafure to govern your thoughts, words and actions by, let every thing be tried with it, before you die, and leave this world: If you do fo, and make this your daily practice, then ask yourfelves, and you will be able to tell yourfelves, and tell me, and fay, I have now obtained more hopes of God's favour, and a greater fenfe of his love and goodnefs to me, than ever I had before. The apoftle doth exhort us, to *walk circumfpectly, not as fools, but as wife, redeeming the time.* We have fpent a great deal of time in vain, let us now be wife, and improve our time, for our eternal advantage; let us walk circumfpectly, that is, look round about us, confider our ways, and try all our thoughts, words and actions, by the ftandard of truth. *To-day* (my friends) *while it is called to-day*, hear the voice of God, and *harden not your hearts*, and receive that heavenly counfel, that is tendered to you, that you may be *partakers of the inheritance, among the saints in light.*

His PRAYER after SERMON.

BLESSED *and eternal Father! thou haft brought forth thy glorious name, and revealed thy power and thy mighty arm; and thou haft caufed a remnant to bow and worfhip at thy appearance: Thou art wonderful; thy majefty is great; they that do behold thee, will, with reverence, worfhip before thee. Thy power is gone forth, and hath reached the hearts of thy people; thou haft humbled them, and fubjected them to thy Divine, Almighty Power, that they might appear in the earth, to the praife and glory of thy great name.*

And, O Lord, as thou haft begun a great work in the earth, fo thou haft committed this work to thy fervants and children, that bear thy name among the fons of men, that they should fhew

forth

His PRAYER after SERMON.

forth thy righteousness, among the inhabitants of the earth; and our souls have said many a time, who is sufficient for these things? All our fitness and sufficiency, our meetness and preparation is from thee: Do thou reveal thy power, and make bare thy Almighty arm. We have found thy presence from day to day, and thou hast upheld them that know thy love.

O glorious God of Life! herein we have encouragement to go on in the work which thou hast called us to; hereby we are enabled to worship before thee, and to offer up living praises unto thy great name, for that refreshment and consolation, which thou hast ministered unto thy people.

And, O Living Father! we have never waited on thee in vain; whensoever we have met together in thy name, we have found thy Divine Presence, and the opening of the treasures of thy love, of thy wisdom, and of thy favour to thy children: So that from day to day, and even at this day, thou rememberest thy people, and thou givest them fresh occasion to draw nigh to thee, and receive their daily nourishment and strength, from the operation of thy power.

O living God of Life! gather up the hearts of thy people more and more, and draw them into a nearness to thyself, that their understandings may be more and more opened to discern thy will, and subject themselves to thy wisdom, that every thought that is exalted against thy divine power, and living voice, in their own consciences, may be brought down; that so all the nations of the earth may bow before thee; that so thy truth may reign, and thy power may be exalted, and the righteousness which thou hast revealed, may shine forth more and more, in the brightness and glory of it, and enlighten those that are afar off, that they may be brought to seek after God.

And, Living God of Life! let those that are bowed down under the weight of sin, be supported and raised up; and those that are weary and heavy laden, let them have rest to their souls.

Powerful God of Life! keep thy people in a fresh and living sense of thy love, and of thy heavenly virtue, by which thou nourishest thy children, and satisfiest them from day to day; not only when they are met together, but when they are separated from one another. Let thy people be preserved from the evil of the world, while they are in it, and let thy wisdom

and

and power give them victory over it, that thou mayest have the g'ory of all thy mercies and bleffings, vouchfafed to them. For thou alone art worthy, who art God over all, bleffed forever, and ever. Amen.

SERMON V.

The GREAT DUTY of REMEMBERING our CREATOR.

Preached at DEVONSHIRE-HOUSE, April 6, 1692.

THERE is only one living and true God, Creator of Heaven and earth, whom we are obliged to ferve and worfhip : I have fo much charity as to believe, there are none among us, but will own and acknowledge this : And my foul wifheth, that this obligation did always reft upon every one's mind, that they might remember their Creator, that hath given us all life and breath, and continued all our bleffings to us ; that fo every one might apply their hearts unto that univerfal duty, that we are all convinced of.

And they that are thus employed and exercifed, they are confidering how, and after what manner, they may quit and difcharge their duty, and perform the obligation that lies upon them, fo that it may be accepted at the hands of God ; I fpeak now of thofe that are confiderate, not of thofe that go on in a form of religion, and matter not, nor regard whether they are accepted of God or no ; but all that are confcientious towards God, they are defirous to ferve God, and worfhip him, fo as they may be acceptable to him, fo to perform duties that they may receive their reward, and that encouragement that God in all ages hath difcovered, and made manifeft to be in his purpofe towards them that truly ferve him.

When people come to this confideration, how they may ferve God aright, and worfhip him acceptably, the Lord is nigh unto them, to inftruct them, to teach them, and guide them in that way that is everlafting : And, bleffed be his holy name !

name! a great many in our days, have met with this divine teaching and inftruction; and are taught in this age, as in former ages, to underftand the worfhip of God that he requires; that is, in fpirit and truth; and do find, that the Father doth feek fuch worfhippers, and where he finds them, rewards them, and they have an anfwer of peace in their bofoms, and they are encouraged to go on in the worfhip and fervice of God, to the end of their days.

And it is a great mercy and benefit; a great bleffing that God hath beftowed upon a remnant, to open their underftandings, to let them fee and know the way of being near to God, that fo they may know whom they worfhip; for you have read, there have been worfhippers, that do worfhip they know not what: As our Saviour faid to the woman of *Samaria, you worfhip you know not what; we know what we worfhip*: So all that are taught of God, do know which is the firft leffon of Chriftianity, as the apoftle faith; *he that cometh to God, muft firft know and believe, that he is*; that is, people muft firft be fenfible, that *there is a God, and that he is a rewarder of them that diligently feek him*, before they can rightly worfhip him.

Now, for want of this knowledge, the world is fcattered, and people are divided into a great many forts of worfhips, and fafhions, and ways of religions, for want of the knowledge of the true worfhip, of the true and living God; fo that though men are univerfally convinced, that there is a God, and that a worfhip is due to him from every one of us; yet people are confounded, fcattered, and divided about the performance of their great duty; and in the day that the Lord hath vifited his people, he hath come to anfwer this doubt, and queftion for them; it hath been the great queftion of the world, and is ftill of many thoufands; I know we fhould worfhip God, but I know not the way and manner wherein to find acceptance: The Lord hath anfwered that queftion in abundance; *they that have ears to hear, let them hear what the Spirit faith*; there is a fhort anfwer to it in all.

Let people profefs what religion they will, there is no acceptance with God, but through Chrift: So that if people come to be of this, and that, and the other profeffion, and change

change their religion ever so often, and go from one religion to another, if they come not to Christ, they come not to him in whom they may find acceptance; in him God is pleased with every one; but out of him he is pleased with no one. The great mystery of religion lies in Christ; people must come to God, by faith in him; *for without faith, it is impossible to please God.* Let people perform ever so much service and duties, all must pass through the hand of the Mediator, before ever their performance will reach unto God, or before peace and comfort will reach to any man's soul. Therefore, it is the wisest way for every one, that would have acceptance with God, to come to him, in the name of the great Mediator. People would be glad to have acceptance with God, and not to have their services turned back upon them, as *Cain's* was: Now, every one that will have acceptance with God, must come this way; there is but one way, it is not the way that men have invented; some by their works and merits, some by their made-faiths, and made-beliefs, and by divers articles and principles, holding this principle, and the other principle; but our Lord and Creator, he hath found out one way, in his infinite wisdom, and unspeakable mercy to mankind, that was forever lost, and could never return to God, by all his sacrifices, offerings and performances; he was never able to return into unity with his Maker, if God had not found out a way; and the way that God hath found out, is by his beloved Son Christ Jesus: *God spared not:* He spared not what? He spared not his only begotten Son: Why, what did he do with him? *He gave him for the life of the world;* in him that God gave, there is life. *It pleased the Lord that his Son should have life in him, as the Father had life in himself;* for Christ was *with the Father before the world began; in him was life, and the life was the light of men;* John i. 4. It was no created life; that life that is in his Son, is not a created life, but is an eternal life, and it was given for the life of the world, and the life is the light of men: *This is the true light, which lighteth every man that cometh into the world.* So that here is the dignity of that life which God hath bestowed upon us; we are endued with that life, which was with the Father through Jesus Christ, before the world was. Let us consider the dignity of that light, that we are lighted with. The

The question is, whether we should obey this light, or no: It is the question of every one; I am enlightened, faith a man, shall I obey it, or no? If I obey, I must take up a cross, and part with my beloved lust and corruption. No doubt of that; we must persuade people to do that, before we can bring them to Heaven and happiness, and fellowship with God; it must not be by that way they lost it, but by the contrary way, by which God will bring men to happiness again. They lost it by transgression, and sinning against God; by this way and means men came out of the presence and favour of God; but what way shall they obtain it again? Shall it be by committing iniquity, and breaking God's law? No; here is the way that God hath found out, to bring poor man back again to himself, by the sufferings and obedience of his Son, Jesus Christ: *He hath given to him all power in Heaven and Earth*, that all should be subject to him; here is a dignity which Christ hath obtained.

It comes to the question with us, whether we are enlightened? now we know we are enlightened; God hath bestowed something upon us, that wars and fights against sin and iniquity. How came we by it? Is it any faculty in nature? No; nature is corrupted and defiled, because *the carnal mind is enmity against God; for it is not subject to the law of God, neither indeed can be;* yet there is something in me that answers the pure law of God, which makes me to hate things that are reprovable; that is, light: How came I by it? It is not natural; for then it would run parallel with the natural inclination that is in my soul, to lead me further and further from God. These are set in opposition one against another, the flesh and the spirit; *the flesh lusteth against the spirit, and the spirit against the flesh.* Here is part of an inward war, that you may all be sensible of. Now, these two warriors, the flesh and the spirit, make war one against another, and one of them is overcome. It is true, there is such a principle in me, that strives against sin and corruption: How came you by it? If you believe the scriptures, I say, it is the life of the Son of God, *that lighteth every man that cometh into the world*. Now, many that
have

have rejected and despised the light; I believe they did not think, at the same time, to mock and make a scorn of the life of Jesus, tho' it was really so: But if people come to a true esteem and value of that light that God hath planted in the soul, they will give more reverence and respect to it. It is this that brings those that preach Christ, to preach him in those terms, and under those denominations, that he is nigh them.

We do not doubt of Christ's being born of a Virgin, in the land of *Canaan*, and that he wrought miracles, and preached many godly sermons, and that he was crucified, dead and buried, and rose again from the dead, for these things are certainly true: But we would have him our Saviour in this age, we would have a nearer knowledge of him, and a sense and feeling of the virtue of that power, by which he saved them that lived in former ages: He is not a Christ and a Saviour of one age only, but of all ages to this day; from *Adam*, to the last man that shall live upon the earth. That age and generation that knoweth not Christ, will not be saved by him, if there be any age wherein he is not known: *There is no other name under Heaven by which you can be saved.* If you ask where is this Saviour? *Say not in thy heart, who shall ascend into Heaven? that is, to bring down Christ from above; or, who shall descend into the deep, that is to bring up Christ again from the dead? The word is nigh thee, even in thy mouth, and in thy heart; that is the word of faith, which we preach.* He is nigh thy soul, he is the Lord of life, and a quickening Spirit, if I know that quickening Spirit, after this I know the Lord Christ; when he comes to work in me by his power, changing my heart, and translating me from death to life, then I know the true Christ: God hath manifested, in all ages, that it is the duty of people to come to the knowledge of the Son of God; for *he hath sent forth his Spirit to teach us, and to lead us into all truth.*

For when Christ was with his disciples, he told them that he would pray the Father, and he should *send the Spirit, the comforter;* and when he came, he would be known by his divine and inward teachings and operations, guiding and *leading them into all truth;* that was his work to them: But what shall other folks do? He will be made known to others too : When he comes, *he shall convince the world of sin* : So that his work to his disciples was, to *lead them into all truth* ; and his work to the world is, to *convince the world of sin* : Who will deny, but that there is a Spirit in our age, as well as in other ages, that will convince men of sin? Is this the Spirit of God, that convinceth the world of sin, or is it the spirit of the *QUAKERS only* ? When people come to consider really and truly, how they may serve God aright, they will find there is no serving God aright, unless they come to Christ the Mediator, that in and by him they may put up supplications to God; and through him, they may expect at the hand of God, peace and comfort; and there is no other way, nor ever will be.

The Jews, they had another way, they had an outward way of serving God ; this stood in divers offerings, sacrifices, washings and observations ; this was a way of worship of God's own institution to that people ; but what came of it ? When the apostle came to grasp it, he said, *the comers thereunto, were not made perfect* : What were the transgressors of it then ? They that would sin on, and continue in sin, and not bring a goat, or a ram, or other oblation ; they that did observe it, and came up to the point of the law, they did bring their offering when they were convinced of their sin : If a man sinned, he was to bring an he-goat, and to bring it to the door of the tabernacle ; but when he sinned, the conscience of sin, the guilt of sin remained upon him. For *it was impossible*, saith the apostle, *that the blood of bulls and goats should take away the sin : For if the blood of bulls and goats, and the ashes of a heifer sprinkling the unclean, sanctifieth, to the purifying of the flesh, how much more shall the blood of Christ (who, through the eternal Spirit, offered himself without spot to God) purge your consciences from dead works, to serve the living God.*

When there is no hope of atonement and reconciliation with God, by all those offerings under the law, he tells you of *one offering of the Son of God himself, through the eternal Spirit, by which he became a propitiation* ; for this will do ; if I believe that Christ offered an holy offering to the Father for my sins, I believe he offered his body, and that through the eternal Spirit, that he might be a propitiation for sin, and

take

take away sin, and have power over sin and death, and conquer death and darkness: The apostle drives the matter further; you must come to the inward work of this outward offering, this eternal offering, that was in due time offered to God; you must come to know the operations of it, by the *sprinkling of the heart from an evil conscience* : So that there was to be an applicatory faith for the offering of that. The way to a Saviour was not made by man, no more than the way of salvation by Christ was found out by man; no more than the application of the benefit is effected by man.

When it pleaseth God to call a people by his grace, he calleth them by his Son; not by this and the other form: *No man cometh to me*, saith Christ, *except the Father, which hath sent me, draw him*. The first thing that a man or woman comes to be aware of, is the secret sense and feeling of the Lord's Divine Power upon the heart, to seek Christ Jesus; as soon as they feel this, and embrace it, this is a token of the love of God. I hope all this congregation will acknowledge, that they have sometimes felt his drawings, and that they have not embraced and closed with them so well as they ought.

When people are aware of these drawings inwardly to holiness and righteousness, and are sensible that they should, with care and attention, close with them, for the good of their poor souls; and that it concerns them to be happy in the other world that is to come, and therefore resolve to be led by these drawings of the Spirit of God, these are not weeds that grow in the fields naturally; these are Sparks of Divine Fire, kindled in the hearts of men by God himself: No man comes unto God, till God comes to him, and touches him, and gives him sense and motion: These are the motions and stirrings of God's Holy Power, in the hearts of many that are wicked and abominable; yet the Lord doth not despise the work of his own hand, but reacheth to such.

When the Lord meets with those that despise not, but highly prize this wonderful grace, and close with it, and are glad of it, such a one saith, I feared that the Lord had forgotten me, and had passed by me, and had done with me; but I see he visits me again, and he hath visited fited my foul this day, inclining me to walk more anfwerably to his love; he hath doubled his power upon me, and hath kindled a holy fire in my heart, and caufed me to feek after him; he hath touched my heart, and I will pour out my foul in fupplication; feeing he hath touched me, he will take hold of me by his power, and he will keep me from being any more drawn away: I will live in the fenfe of his power and mercy, that keeps me night and day, that I may encreafe in it, and grow in grace. When the Lord meets with fuch a one, he will draw him into the way that he hath appointed: *None can come unto me,* faith Chrift, *except the Father, which hath fent me, draw him.* If I am drawn, into what form fhall I go now? and what ordinance fhall I take up now? This is all under feet; this is none of my work; I will come to Chrift the Mediator, and he will take the government and rule of me: It is not my beft way to ftudy a form, and an outfide religion; I will wait upon that power that hath thus touched my heart, that he may by degrees bring me to the obedience of Chrift.

But fome are ready to fay, who, and what is this Chrift Jefus that you are fpeaking of; that immediate Chrift Jefus that is extant and prefent, that I am to have to be the object of my faith; that I may believe in him, and come to an acquaintance with him, that I may partake of the life of Jefus Chrift, and have it communicated to my foul?

We have not a thought, or a word to fpeak, that may derogate from the wonderful grace of Chrift, who died in his perfon on earth for the falvation of our fouls: Yet we muft know, that the Lord Jefus Chrift may be fpiritually prefent with us, and take the government of us, and we are to be fubject to him: How fhall this be? I am fpeaking of one that hath felt the Father's drawings, when he draws them to his Son, and draws them to fomething that is holy and pure: This God the Father hath begotten: We read in fcripture, *that God hath begotten Chrift, who is the only begotten of the Father.* It is ftrange, you will fay, to fpeak of begetting Chrift again, God begets Chrift again, that is, fpiritually; he being the firft born in many brethren, in every true believer, and there is a travel of foul that Chrift may be formed

in

in him. See what travel of foul the apoſtle *Paul* falls into the ſecond time, for the *Galatians*. They were a brave people, they worſhiped God in Spirit, and believed in Chriſt Jeſus, and afterwards they came to be ſeduced by falſe prophets, and falſe teachers, that ſet them about their works, and told them they could not be juſtified and ſaved without their own works: Theſe falſe teachers that came among them, were as bad as Popiſh prieſts and friars. It is not your obedience to Chriſt, and the Spirit, that will ſave you, you muſt be doing: So theſe poor people were deluded and bewitched; and to give you the apoſtle's own words, they were infatuated, and *drawn away from the ſimplicity of the goſpel,* and they thought by the works of the law to obtain ſalvation: The apoſtle writes a letter to them, and tells them that he *travelled in birth again, till Chriſt was formed in them.* If this was not ſcripture, it would look like a ſtrange work; there muſt be a forming of Chriſt, a birth there muſt be, and a begetting: Who muſt beget in this and that moment, but the ſame that begat from the beginning? the ſame is the Father, he begets Chriſt in all that believe and obey the goſpel. He is begetting ſomething in me that is holy, though I be unholy; the Father, by the operation of his divine hand, begets ſomething in me that is holy. This I find, though I am not ſo good as I ſhould be; I have that given me, that will tell me, that the more I adhere and join myſelf in my deſires and affections to this good principle, the more I ſhall partake of the quality of it; this good principle, though it be like *a little grain of muſtard-ſeed,* I cannot tell what to compare it to for littleneſs, in compariſon of the great lump and maſs of ſin, corruption and filthineſs, that wars againſt it; yet this will overſpread all that is bad, and make me *holy,* as that is *holy; pure* as that is *pure,* and to have a love for him, from whom it came, even to Chriſt and God; it will gather the affections from corruptible things, and place them upon things above.

This faith tells people that it is *the ſubſtance of things hoped for, and the evidence of things not ſeen;* ſuch a one lives by faith, ſuch a one that comes to be joined to that, that is begotten of the father, he *lives by the faith of the Son of God,* and can do nothing of himſelf, but through Chriſt that

ſtrengthens

strengthens him; he says unto God, I perceive I can do nothing without thee; I cannot pray unto thee, nor serve thee; of myself I can do nothing acceptably, but through Christ the Mediator; such a one becomes like a little child, and he must be led; and who must lead him, but the Spirit of Christ?

You cannot preach, says one to him, unless you be moved by the Spirit: You cannot pray until you be moved by the Spirit: How should I? No, without him I can do nothing, I cannot preach, nor pray, nor do any thing acceptable to God the Father, but by Christ; and he hath revealed him in me.

This is no new doctrine, we see the new and living way; it was an old way to old Christians, and a new way to the new; and so a thousand years hence, if the world lasts so long, men will see that they cannot do any thing pleasing to God, but as they are gathered into Christ; they will see their own righteousness, works and doings, will avail them nothing at all. This is all laid at the feet of Jesus, whom God hath exalted to be a Prince and a Saviour, to be Lord and King.

Now, my friends, we are engaged in this age, abundantly engaged, to offer thanks to God, through Jesus Christ, that he hath provided and opened a way for the sending forth the Spirit of his Son: And that God hath gathered a people, and hath made known to them the way of life, that they might walk in it; but there is no walking in it, but through a daily cross, and self-denial. It is not likely that a man should be brought back to God the same way that he went out from God; and the prophets and apostles do allude to this turning to God; *when thou turnest aside to the right hand or to the left, thou shalt hear a voice behind thee, saying, this is the way, walk in it.* There is a voice, that calls to people in our days, to look behind them, for they are out of the way. This prophecy is fulfilled in our day; we cannot turn away from the good ways of God, but we may hear a voice behind us, saying, thou art sinning against God, and breaking the holy law of God. Now, if people return, it must be by the cross: I will not return to God, saith one; I have pleasure, profit, and honour, and whatsoever my heart can desire, in this evil way that I am walking in; if I return, I shall have nothing but shame and reproach; I shall be undone and ruined, and

I shall lose the favour and friendship of my friends and relations; I cannot return to God, but through a daily cross, and self-denial: What then? It is likelier to be the right way, by this bearing the cross. Christ tells us, *if any will come after me, let him deny himself, and take up his cross and follow me.* This voice of Christ calls me to repent and turn from sin, and giveth me a strong argument, that it is true; that it is the same way that will bring me back to God, by the Mediator. It brings its own evidence with it; we need no argument to prove that it is a right way; it is a right way, because it is the *narrow way*; it is the right gate, because it is the *strait gate.* Every body can walk in the broad way with ease, without any cross.

When people are come thus far, that they are convinced of their duty, when they are called to amend their lives and conversations, to forsake their lives and turn to the Lord, this is the great question, have I power to do this? This question hath stumbled a great many, when they have some beginning thoughts of turning to the Lord; and at last they have settled themselves in a belief that they cannot do it; it is true, and nothing truer, that men, convinced of their sins, have not power to leave their sins of themselves; this is true, but not all the truth; to men that God convinceth of sin, he gives them power to be made willing to forsake their sins. He hath given power to all that *are in Christ Jesus, to believe and become the sons of God; then they have denied ungodliness and worldly lusts,* if they be the sons of God, and *live righteously, soberly and godly, in the world.*

But what shall they do that are sensible they have not power to forsake their sin, till God is pleased to give them power? Such have nothing to do but to wait upon the Lord, for the giving of this power; and there is a duty incumbent on them then to answer this power. The apostle, upon this subject, tells us what people are to do for their own conversion. He ascribes the power of conversion to Christ Jesus: The prophets and apostles, they tell us, there is something for man to do, that is, if he hath not power, he is to be willing to receive it. The apostle hath a notable

table expression to this purpose; he puts them in mind, how they used to do by the devil, when they were the devil's servants; they did obey his commands, and yielded their members servants to unrighteousness: How did they yield? They did it heartily, with pleasure and delight. Thus you did when you did not know the power of God; but now you are come to the knowledge of the power of God, *yield not your members as instruments of unrighteousness unto sin, but yield yourselves unto God, as those that are alive from the dead, and your members as instruments of righteousness unto God*: Rom. vi. 13. Let your minds, and wills, and affections, be joined to that power which God visited you with; in love to God, give up your members as servants unto righteousness.

Here is something for man to do in the day of God's visitation; *thy people shall be willing in the day of thy power*; when they come to that, and experience that, this shews that they are the people of God: But they that are not a willing people, are none of God's people, God's people are so; and I pray God make you all so, to be a people willing to be God's people, when he gives you power, and it will not be long before he gives you power to forsake your sins, to forsake this, and the other foolish, proud and vain action and fashion; he hath made Christ Jesus to be Lord and King, and he shall reign over death; he hath made all things by Christ, and he is become the Saviour of all men, but especially of them that believe; so that I would have a special salvation, and thou wouldest have it too: Christ hath made a way, and opened a door for us to be saved, *that we might have an abundant entrance into his everlasting kingdom*: But I would have a special salvation, that would invest me with the love of God in my heart, before I die; it is to be had through Christ, therefore to him will I come, to him must every one come, and every knee bow to his name, and every one must wait for his appearing in the Spirit. When Christ appears, truth stirs. Now, if a holy, divine life is in thee, it is he; if a principle of truth stir in thee, it is he: The same Jesus, only in a smaller manifestation: He that is faithful in a little, he will make him ruler over much: This is he that God hath ordained to be the Captain of our Salvation;

vation; this is that which we preach in his name, and testify and declare to all people, that there is no other salvation, no deliverance from death and hell, but by and through him; *in him there is a reconciliation, and that peace which passeth all understanding,* and power over all those things which have captivated us, and made us disobey our great Lord and Maker: Let us wait for the coming of Christ; *he is our King, our Lord and Law-giver, and he will save us:* This was the cry of his people of old, for the glorious and great salvation he hath given, and the work he hath wrought. Let the prayers and supplications of all people, that desire salvation, be put up more and more, that he will visit the earth, and give power from above, and *bring us into that new and living way, which he hath consecrated for us, through the veil, that is to say, his flesh;* to whom be glory, for ever and ever. *Amen.*

His Prayer after Sermon.

MOST *blessed and glorious Father, and Fountain of Life, and of all living Blessings! whose glorious day dawneth; by thy power thou hast brought the children of men out of darkness, that they might walk in the light thereof: Great joy, and strong consolation, hast thou brought unto thine Israel, unto the people that thou hast gathered by thy arm of power; thou hast made them, O Lord, to take great delight in thy ways; for thou hast caused the light of thy countenance to be lifted up upon us, and thy holy and divine presence hath gone along with us, from time to time, through all those states and conditions, and through all those trials and exercises that we have met with, and that thou hast led us through.*

The right hand of thy power, O Lord! hath been with us, and therefore we have not failed; and thy heavenly blessings have been rained down upon us, that have made thy heritage to grow and become fruitful, to the honor of thy great name, and the eternal consolation of our souls.

And, therefore, O heavenly Father! in the consideration and feeling of the great things thou hast wrought for us, and for the continuance of thy love to us, our souls are always engaged

His PRAYER after SERMON.

engaged to offer high praises, and humble thanksgivings to thy great name; and the supplications of our souls, whom thou hast quickened and brought to life, are daily poured forth upon thine altar, that as thou hast hitherto helped us, thy holy and divine presence and power may still accompany us to the end of our days; and that in all the exercises, and trials, which thou art pleased we should meet withal, we may find thy presence with us, that thy eternal, heavenly power may surround us, that so we may be more than conquerors, through Christ, that hath loved us.

And O powerful God of Life! our souls rejoice, and our hearts are made glad to behold the progress of thy power in our day, how thou hast brought down the mighty from their seats, and hast exalted those that are of low degree; how thou hast laid the mountains low, and exalted the inhabitants of the vallies.

O blessed Father of Life and Power! praises, praises wait for thee in Zion; and dear Father! by the operation of thy wonderful power, preserve and keep thy children, whom thou hast gathered into a living sense of thy presence, that they may bow before thee, and be exercised in a daily, holy, divine worship unto thee; that so, powerful God of Life! thou mayest daily pour down thy blessings upon us, and delight to manifest thyself to be our God; and let us live as becomes a people that are gathered unto thee.

O Lord God Eternal! carry on thy great work in the earth, and make known thy power more and more; there are many breathing-ones, and many that cry to thee daily. Living Father! it is the operation of thy Spirit that hath raised these breathings, and kindled these desires in them, and it is thou alone who art able to answer them; therefore, living God and Father, they are committed to thee; the mourners, the bowed-down, and those that are laden with sin and iniquity, and that groan under the pressure and burden of it, let their burdens be taken off, and the yoke of Christ, that easy yoke, be put on, and let none of thy commandments be grievous to them, that they may be made meet to enter into thy kingdom; let them be brought through the labour and travel of regeneration, and let none be exalted into the airy vision and sight of things, but by thy living power, be rising to eternal life in their souls.

And

And Lord, we pray thee, fit and prepare all thy people for the work and service which thou hast been pleased to call them to, that so thy name may be exalted over all, and thy truth spread more and more; and let all error and darkness be expelled, and let the power and influence of thy name be great in the earth, that all thy scattered people may be brought home, to reside in thy house, that there may be unity and concord amongst them, and they may all with one heart and mind, return, and ascribe praises and honour, and glory to thy holy name, for all thy blessings, mercies and living refreshments, that we have received at thy hands, for thou alone art worthy, and God over all, blessed forever and ever. Amen.

SERMON VI.

The DIVINE MONITOR; or, LIGHT from HEAVEN.

Preached at GRACE-CHURCH-STREET, *June 19, 1692.*

IT is a great privilege to the sons and daughters of men, that it has pleased God Almighty to open a way, how they may come to the true knowledge of himself. And O that there was a heart in every one of us, that could rightly prize this privilege as we ought to do! for in the knowledge of the true God consists our true happiness; and without this, the mind of no man or woman can be good. There is nothing seasons the mind and soul of man, and prepares and fits it for an everlasting well-being, but the divine knowledge of the living God that made him. And there is a propensity in the soul of man, even since the fall, to return again to God, and to have that acquaintance and communion with the Lord that man had before he fell: And they that have regard to that inward spark of divine love, that they find in their own souls towards God, they will experience that the Lord is merciful and gracious, and propitious to that which is of himself

For

For tho' the foul is loft, and man is loft through tranfgreffion, and a great alienation has happened between him and his Maker, yet the mercy of the Lord endureth forever; and his kindnefs and favour to loft man is fuch, that he ftretcheth out his hand all the day long, and prefents and offers to the children of men a friendfhip and acquaintance, and a communion again with him. And tho' by fin and tranfgreffion, there is a rebellious nature grown up in the fons and daughters of men, yet the foul of man is not wholly fo; there is fomething that ftrives and labours in a contrary way, and perfuades the foul to turn again unto the Lord, and to wait for the knowledge of God; and whofoever hearkens with care and diligence, to that divine Monitor, that is daily drawing and perfuading people to feek after God, they come to underftand, that the Lord is not fo angry with mankind, but his love, and mercy, and good will, reaches towards all the fons and daughters of men; and the bar that hinders their communion with God, and peace with God, it is not in the Lord, but it is in themfelves; and therefore the remedy muft be wrought in themfelves.

This is evident to every eye, that there is fomething gotten into mankind, which the Holy God cannot own, and can never have fellowfhip with; that is, another contrary fpirit hath wrought upon the fouls of people, and hath feduced and drawn them out to that which is unholy and contrary to God, and the terms of God's covenant to mankind, which is, that he fhould forfake that which the contrary fpirit hath wrought. *Let the wicked forfake his ways, and the unrighteous man his thoughts.* Why fhould he forfake his ways? Becaufe the Lord never led him into thofe ways. He that made him, never led him into them; but the devil, the enemy of mankind, feduced him into thofe ways; therefore the Creator cries out to him, *let the wicked forfake his ways, and the unrighteous man his thoughts;* I cannot have union with him, as long as he walks in his evil ways; I cannot dwell in his mind, fo long as evil thoughts are in it: So may the Lord complain of the works which the devil hath wrought, that man is carried away from God, by his evil thoughts, and the works of the devil. Why

The DIVINE MONITOR ; or,

Why doth not God deftroy thofe works, when he is Almighty, and able to do it? Very true, God is fo; but he hath offered to mankind, through the fon of his love, a way and means, how man may come to be purged, and cleanfed from the evil that the devil hath wrought in him, and how he may come to be reconciled to God: God hath not chofen the way of coercion and force, and to work altogether by irrefiftible power, that man fhall go to Heaven whether he will or no: There was no force ufed for his going to hell and darknefs, but it was the choice of his will: The devil could not have forced him, and led him away out of covenant with God, he could not compel him to break the holy command of God; but the devil tempted him, and he yielded to the temptation, and now man is driven out of the prefence of God; yet God hath found out a way for the fons and daughters of men, to turn again to him: What by force and coercion, and irrefiftable power? No, but the fcripture faith, He hath offered life and falvation to all men: *He hath freely given the Son of his love, out of his own bofom, who making himfelf an offering for fin, hath prefented a way and means for men's returning again to God.*

How doth God prefent Chrift to us? He prefents him to the view of every one's mind, to the underftanding of every foul; he offers and prefents him for falvation to the ends of the earth. There is a damnation come in by man's being fubject to Satan, but falvation comes in by his being fubject to Chrift; as damnation came in by his being defiled, fo falvation came in by his being cleanfed: As the devil is the defiler, fo Chrift is the cleanfer, and man is the object upon which both do work; and they that have been defiled and corrupted (as we all have) by the unclean Spirit, can any of us give a reafon they fhould not be cleanfed by the holy Spirit? We have loft our right to Heaven by fin and tranfgreffion, in the firft *Adam*; and can any give a reafon, why we fhould not be reftored, and redeemed, by Jefus Chrift, the fecond *Adam*? No reafon can be given of our redemption, but that God is free in his love, and Chrift in his offering: *He hath offered himfelf a facrifice for fin: Every prieft hath fomething to offer; this man, the man Chrift*

Christ Jesus, offered himself, through the eternal Spirit, a sacrifice for sin; and now the sacrifice is offered, and a door is opened, and a new and living way consecrated through the veil, that is to say, his flesh.

Now, who can be wise enough to find out a reason, why all men enter not in at this door? For all men enter in at the other door, which the devil and Adam opened, to run from God; all could run in at that door. What is the reason, that all go not in at that door which Christ hath opened, and God hath revealed, and which cost Christ so dear to work our way back again, for mankind to return to God? If we go about to enquire into the reason, we shall find it very little, for there is all the reason in the world we should serve God, and seek our own happiness; there is all the reason in the world we should part with sin and iniquity, and with the devil's work, which he wrought, if we knew but how: Now this, I say, is a great privilege, that God hath afforded to the sons and daughters of men, that they may know; for here the terms of the gospel and of salvation, are brought into a narrow compass, to a short sum, there need no catalogue of them; they that will be ruled by the wicked one, must have their part with him; and they that will be ruled and governed by the Holy One, shall have their part with him, *that where he is, there they may be also.*

Is this in the power of man's will? No, there lies the mischief in the will of man; for you cannot but know by experience, if a man may have his own will, he will always run headlong to destruction, and run in the way of wickedness: And if ever he comes to turn out of that way, into the way of righteousness, he must do it in a way that is a cross to his own will. Some have said, because we have spoken of the free grace of God, in a way that is universal, of his kindness to mankind, through Jesus Christ, they have said, that we hold free-will, that men might be saved if they would; but alas, we have tried it, and we have an universal knowledge, that is able to convince us, and all the world, that it is far enough from our own will. Man is far enough from being able to save himself, from being saved by his own will: He can run on to damnation, there is a current goes with his affections, and with his corrupt defires, they go with the current and ftream ; as long as a man goes on in fin, he fwims down the ftream.

Now many, after they have long gone on in fin, and their evil ways, they think of returning to God ; for they think there is a better way, a furer and fafer way for their fouls, than to go on in wickednefs: So there is ; if there be fo, faith the fincere foul, O that I might walk in it: Why doft thou not? I am convinced that I fee a more excellent way than my way is, a better walking and converfation than my life is; but alas! it is too hard for me to walk in it: Why? what is the matter, what makes it hard ? becaufe of my own will ; I cannot walk in it and have my will, I cannot walk in it, and enjoy my affections and defires, and my intereft in the world: This is no wonder that thou telleft me; now thou art convinced of a better way, and wouldeft walk in it, and thou canft not walk in it, but thou muft take up a daily crofs ; we might all of us tell that, and read it before ; I pray God you may come to read it within, what a crofs it is you are to take up, and what way it is you are required to walk in; that is the way of God, the way that leads to Heaven, it is a narrow way; but the way that the devil would have you to walk in, is a broad way, there is no rub in it.

O would you but once come to experience how hard it is to walk in that *way that leads to life*, you would find that you cannot do it without felf-denial: It comes to this point ; I have read of it before, but now I find it fo. Such a man, or fuch a woman, will ferioufly apply themfelves to live blamelefs, harmlefs, and inoffenfive towards God and men ; they will fet a bridle, and a watch before their mouths, that they may not fpeak a vain word ; they will take care of the frame and temper of their minds, that they fin not in their thoughts, that they fin not with their lips, nor with their hands. This is not as I was wont to do ; I was ufed to have my liberty ; now I find myfelf yoked, I dare not fin againft God : Now I find, by experience, what I heard before, that no man can follow Chrift, without denying himfelf, and taking up a daily crofs.

I

I would have you experienced in this work; wicked men think it a pleafant life, to follow the devil's work, and to walk in the *broad way*; but the way of felf-denial is uneafy, there is much ftrife and oppofition in that way; If I have a mind to fpeak a vain word, I am limited; if I have a defire to wrong my neighbour, and cheat and defraud him, I am limited, I am not to do it, that belongs to the broad way: If a man will feek after the Lord, and walk in the way of holinefs and righteoufnefs, the end whereof is peace, he will find it is a narrow way, wherein he cannot enjoy his own will; fuch a one muft be a *David*, who faid, *I behaved myfelf as a weaned child*; that is, as one that is afraid to be beaten.

But thou wilt be ready to fay, I am a man, and not a child; I am come now to be a man, a man of parts; I have feen much, and read much, and would you have me become a child? How great a man was *David*: If you fpeak of a man, he was a man of dignity and honour, a man of valour and experience; yet when he fpeaks with refpect to the frame of his mind before the Lord, he faith, he behaved himfelf *as a weaned child*, as one that feared to be beaten, feared to commit an offence; he feared the rod of his God upon him; he feared fomething of judgment upon his confcience. *David* was an old teftament man, but he had regard to that which never waxeth old, which is the fame in all times, new and old, *Alpha* and *Omega*. Chrift Jefus was his leader, before he was born of the *Virgin Mary*; his word was a light to his feet, and a lanthorn to his paths: *David* had acquaintance with God, who did lift up the light of his countenance upon him.

And when Chrift himfelf came to preach upon earth, he faith himfelf, *every one that comes into the kingdom of God, muft become as a little child.* He muft become as a little child in fimplicity and fubjection; he muft be under government; he muft become as a little child, or he muft in no wife enter the kingdom of Heaven; they muft not think to enter into Chrift's kingdom becaufe they are men; men of parts, men of courage, men of underftanding, learned doctors, mafters of liberal arts and fciences:

Thefe

These may help to make them men, but they must be children; all their wits, and parts, and manhood, courage and valour, will do them no good; for little children, babes and fucklings, may underſtand more than they of Divine Myſteries, and have greater communion and intercourſe between God and their ſouls than they; ſo that all who enter into Chriſt's kingdom, muſt become like little children.

So that here is a way provided by Jeſus Chriſt, for man to come again into the favour of God, which is by Chriſt alone, not by any thing that a man can do; Chriſt muſt be their leader and their counſellor, he alone can give them the true knowledge of God. *No man can know the Father but the Son, and he to whom the Son reveals him.* Men can never attain to the ſaving knowledge of God by ſtudy, and by diſputation and reading books, and commentators, and obſervators of matters of religion. Time would fail me to ſpeak of the multitude of books that have been written about the knowledge of God. You muſt come to Chriſt for divine knowledge; theology, the knowledge of God, and divine and heavenly things, are from Chriſt: He ſhall have this divine knowledge, be he ever ſo ſimple, that comes unto Chriſt for it; he cannot have it any other way, for God hath ordained this way: Saith God, he ſhall have it of my Son, who is the Reconciler, the Mediator between God and man, he ſhall be beholden to Chriſt for all. All men's own works and labours will not juſtify and ſave them, for God hath committed the whole work of ſalvation to Chriſt. One would think it ſhould be no great matter for men to lay aſide their own works and duties, and ſubmit to Chriſt; but I tell you it is very hard, and I found it hard myſelf.

Men think by reading and learning, and hearing this and the other man's notions and opinions, they may be edified and profited, and come to the true knowledge of God; but while they are waiting upon God, in the way he hath appointed, they may receive knowledge from Chriſt, and be more certain and infallible in what they do know, than by conſulting all the wiſe men and learned doctors in the world. For no man knows all at once; and no man

knows

knows all things neither: It is not a thing neceſſary that man ſhould know all things in relation to God; for as he is in himſelf, he is incomprehenſible: *For no man knows the Father but the Son, and he to whom the Son ſhall reveal him;* yet that which he knows of God, he may know it is certain and infallible.

Suppoſe a man know nothing of God, but that he is the *ſearcher of the heart, and trier of the reins.* There are many that have tried this, and ſay they know it, that yet doubt whether there be a God or no. But when God comes within them, and convinces them of ſin, and ſearches them, and brings judgment upon them for what they have done, then they know infallibly, that God is *the ſearcher of hearts.* This is not a man's work, this is the work of God; if I find God doth approach my ſpirit, I know it is God's work; I have now got ſome knowledge of God, how came I by it? Who gave it me? No one but he that hath all knowledge; he that was with the Father from the beginning, and was glorified with the Father before the world began, he gave me this knowledge; and how did he give it thee? By his Spirit; *for he hath ſent forth the Spirit of his Son into my heart;* and that Spirit of Chriſt ſearches the hearts, and tries the reins. He tells me this is evil that thou haſt done, this is that which God that made thee hath againſt thee; this thou muſt forſake, and this thou muſt repent of; here I have an infallibility of what I know, but I cannot get rid of my evil.

Now, if I can believe in the power by which my heart is ſearched, and truſt in him that hath begun to deal with me, then his work is not only to reveal his light to convince me, but to put forth his power to convert me; ſo that by the power of that truth by which my heart is ſearched, I come to be converted, and turned from my ſin, and break off from it; and when I am broken off from it, I am ſure, and have a certainty that it is ſo, that I am broken off from ſuch a ſin, and that my heart is turned againſt it; I am ſure that now I hate it, and deteſt it, and that God hath turned my inclinations another way: I am ſure this is God's work, I can witneſs this infallibly, that ſomething is now done in
order

order to my redemption: But there is something yet remaining to be done: What then? I will go step by step; by following my guide, I shall be sure to be making some progress every day, to that state to which the Spirit of Christ will lead me: These persons come to a certainty of knowledge by their own experience.

Some will say, take heed of being deluded and deceived by the *Quakers*; so say I too: Take heed of being deluded by any body; if any go about to persuade thee, to believe that which thou knowest to be a lye, I am sure they are about to delude thee; I would have every one to have an evidence in themselves of what they believe.

Doth a man believe that such a one is a drunkard, because the scriptures declare judgment against the drunkards? the scripture saith, *wo to the drunkards of* Ephraim: There are judgments denounced against the drunkards in the old testament; consider the scripture doth not tell such and such by name, that they are drunkards; but the Spirit of God, by a work and operation upon a man's conscience, singles him out, and charges him with the guilt of drunkenness.

There is a great condemnation pronounced against whoremongers in scripture, but it doth not tell us who they are by name; but their consciences tell them so, and gives infallible judgment against them, and say, *thou art the man, thou art a person that God doth judge and condemn; whoremongers and adulterers, God will judge*; but that doth not concern thee, and affect thee, except thou be one; I may read this an hundred times in the scripture, and not have a reflection in my own conscience, except I be guilty: But when God meets with a guilty person, and judgeth and condemneth him, there will be an infallibility in what such a one knows. If a whoremonger is reflected upon by his own conscience, if his conscience tell him he is the man, if all the world should flatter him, and say he is not guilty, he would certainly know that they tell him a lye.

So that here is no dependence upon any man's judgment, but upon an invisible judge in a man's own heart: Who shall delude and deceive this man, that hath this experimental knowledge? those persons will not deceive a man, that would turn him from the evil of his ways; thefe do not go about to deceive him, that will tell him he muſt hearken to that principle of truth and holineſs in his own heart; they would deceive him that tell him he is converted when he is not, and leave him there: But when he is really converted and turned from fin to God, fome will tell him he is deluded and deceived; I pray God every one of us may be fo deceived: Saith the apoſtle, *we are deceivers, yet true:* All that are truly converted, though men cry out they are deceivers, though they are deceivers, yet true; they are come to the favour of the knowledge of God, through Chriſt; and fo ſhall certainly *come to be partakers of the inheritance that is undefiled, and that fadeth not away.*

Friends, you know that this hath been the propofition of all the prophets, and apoſtles, from the beginning to this day; the thing that they have propoſed to the fons and daughters of men, hath been to enquire after the knowledge of the true God: It hath been wonderful to confider, what the devil hath done to prefent divers doctrines that he hath found out, and ſtirred up others to invent a company of Gods, that other people have adored and worſhipped. It is hard to find any nation that do not worſhip fome God; it is natural for man to defire to come to fome God, he thinks he muſt come to fome God, and cannot be happy if he come not to GOD: But the devil hath invented many Gods, and fet the people a worſhipping of idols, the work of men's hands, fuch Gods that are fo far from helping their worſhippers, that they cannot help themfelves, they cannot wipe off the duſt from their own faces; and if they fall down, they cannot rife again.

But this is not our cafe, we have but one God preached among us, and but one Lord Jefus Chriſt, the Mediator between God and man: Our condition is happy, in having but one God, in comparifon of theirs that have many Gods.

If the true God, that you worſhip, were but truſted in, you would be the happieſt people in the world: If you do but fearch, you will find that the devil hath in this nation, and in this age, ſtirred up people to worſhip as many Gods, as he did in other nations in ancient times, among the *Sidonians*, and *Amorites*, and others.

But

But you will say, we worship one God, and trust only in one God, and one Christ, and one Holy Ghost, the only living and true God.

Do not tell me what God a man professeth to worship, but what God he trusteth in, that gives it the name: Whatsoever a man trusteth in, that he makes his God, whether it be gold or silver, or the honours and pleasures of this world, if he trusteth in these things, he makes them his God. Let a man but search and try himself, and he will find something hath got a place in his heart, that he cannot part with for Christ's sake. He will be ready to say, I cannot part with my house and land, with my wife and children, and my goods and possessions, because I have a confidence in them, and believe they will do me good, and be a defence for me; I trust that in times of peril those things may do me good. Here is a divine adoration, here is that trust, that confidence, that all true Christians ought to have in the true God, and this is placed in these earthly things. Now, wheresoever the trust and confidence is placed in transitory and earthly perishing things, these men trust in transitory Gods.

Nothing so shews that a man makes the Lord his God, as when he casts all care on him, and puts his whole trust in him, when he makes a profession and acknowledgment of his dominion and greatness, and of all his other perfections, that by his wisdom he can procure for them all that is good, and by his power, keep off from them, and secure them from evil. When I make the Lord my trust and refuge, and trust him for my God, I choose him before all the Gods of the Heathen, and trust in him above all things under Heaven, upon the account of the profundity of his wisdom, and the almightiness of his power: When a man hath this sense upon him, he will walk before the Lord with resignation of mind, and be willing to be at God's disposal, and he will not only give up himself to God, but he will hearken to him, and hear his voice when he speaks to him.

God, who at sundry times, and in divers manners spake in time past, unto the fathers by the prophets, hath in these last days spoken to us by his Son: But, where is his Son, you will say? He is in Heaven; but though he is *the high and*

and lofty one that inhabits eternity, yet he dwells with meek, humble and contrite hearts, that tremble at his word. If I be one of the number of those that tremble at God's word, I have that promise that he will come home to me, and dwell with me. It is well for thee, if the over-ruling power of God hath prevailed upon thee, that thou canst be willing to be at God's disposal, and say, Lord, what wouldest thou have me to do?

Therefore, friends, I would advise you all to love your own souls, that when God desires your hearts, you would give them up to him, that there he might delight to dwell, and have his habitation. Hearken to God's voice, and have regard to his word, which is a more sure word than any man's in the world. *There is a more sure word of prophecy,* saith the apostle, *unto which you will do well to take heed.* This will check you, and reprove you, when you do evil, and shew you wherein you have transgressed; and will encourage you, and be a comfort to you, when you do that which is good. This will *make you wise to salvation, and thoroughly furnish you, and give you understanding for every good work.* This word will tell you, this you must not do, lest you offend God, and wound your conscience, and grieve the Holy Spirit; this word will help you so to speak, as to administer grace to the hearers; such a one as hath regard to this word, hath a chaplain in his own bosom, that will direct and teach him how to steer his course, and order his conversation among men, and how *to serve God acceptably.* This *High Priest's lips will preserve knowledge,* even Jesus Christ the righteous, who speaks to us in his word; we can do nothing but by his direction: If you come to him to lead you into all truth, he will bring you to the Father, and reconcile you to him, that so you may obtain his favour and everlasting life. When one of Christ's disciples said, *shew us the Father, and it sufficeth us,* Jesus saith unto him, *he that hath seen me, hath seen the Father, and how sayest thou then, shew us the Father?* If you subject yourselves to Christ, and to the government of his Spirit, he will bring you to that life and immortality, that *fadeth not away.*

This hath been our labour and travel from time to time,

to preach Chrift among you, and not to preach ourfelves, and gather a church for ourfelves, but to gather a people unto Chrift, who is Lord of Heaven and Earth. We would preach Chrift Jefus the Lord; we would not have you admire men's words and fayings, and charge your memory with them; but we would have you remember the words and fayings of Chrift, who is the great Mediator, to reconcile man again to God, that you may know him by his power, working effectually in your hearts; we labour for nothing elfe, and we want nothing elfe.. *We are ambaffadors for Chrift, as though God did befeech you by us; we pray you, in Chrift's ftead, be ye reconciled to God: That you may fo live, that whether you eat or drink, or whatfoever you do, you may do it all to the glory of God,* your great Creator, that hath given his Son to die for you, and *redeem you from all iniquity, that you might be a peculiar people, zealous of good works.*

Let God have all the honour and glory, for all his mercies and bleffings; let us render unto him hearty praifes, and thankfgiving, for his wonderful love, and acknowledge that it is a great privilege that we may obtain by Jefus Chrift, even to be brought again to have the knowledge of the living God, which we loft by our tranfgreffion.

His PRAYER after SERMON.

GLORIOUS art thou in thy appearance, O Lord! and very wonderful is thy power, and thy ways paft finding out: And in this thy glorious day, thou art opening a way for the fons and daughters of men, to turn to thee.

And, O Lord! thofe whofe eyes thou haft opened, rejoice and are glad, becaufe they have feen the way of thy falvation; and the breathings of their fouls are, that their feet may be kept therein, and that they may make ftrait fteps in their way to thy kingdom.

O Lord! we are fenfible that our ftrength, and our power, and our ability is only in thee; and therefore are the fouls of thy children bowed and fubjected to thee, waiting for the renewing of thy power, that as our temptations are renewed from day to day, thou wouldeft make known thy power in us, that

His PRAYER *after* SERMON.

that we may feel the stretching forth of thy hand to save thy little ones, out of the hands of the destroyer.

And so, powerful God of Life! break forth more and more in thy glory, and make known thy power in expelling the clouds of darkness and ignorance, and bring the minds and understandings of thy people to know thee more and more, till they come to the blessed inheritance, among the saints in light.

Holy and powerful Father! break in upon thy people by thy Almighty Power, and scatter the dark clouds of temptation, and cause the light of life to shine upon them; thou that hast commanded the light to shine out of darkness, do thou shine into the hearts of the sons and daughters of men; open their hearts, that they may receive the truth, and make tender their hard hearts, that they may live to thee that made them, and give a comfortable account to thee of their thoughts, words, and actions, and let them turn to the Lord before it be too late to repent of them.

Powerful God of Life! thy mercy and loving kindness doth abound, to a little remant that do believe in Christ, and do trust in thy name; thou hast been with them in their fiery trials and tribulations, and to this day thou hast been the glory of our assemblies, and the joy of our meetings. We are sensible of thy holy power working in our souls, and of thy renewing thy love upon us: All that desire a full sense thereof, that are seeking and crying after thee for it, O let them be brought to a due sense of thee the living God! O arise for the help and the comfort of the sorrowful, the sighing and the needy soul: Pour forth the treasures of thy love upon them that follow hard after thee, and breathe for deliverance; that so, powerful God of Life! praises may arise to thee for all thy mercies, and abundant blessings, for thy goodness and loving kindness, bestowed upon us from time to time.

Most powerful God of Life and Light! let the eye of thy favour be turned upon this land of our nativity; spare the inhabitants of this city and nation, that they may seek after thee; let them know the weight of thy hand upon them, to bow them down to humility and brokenness of heart; give them repentance for their sins.

Living God of Life! display thy power to all, from the highest to the lowest among us, and advance the kingdom of
our

our Lord Jesus Christ, to whom thou hast given a name above every name; and let his kingdom and glory be exalted over all, and shine in the midst of us.

Blessed Father of Life! give wisdom to our counsellors, that they may counsel for thee; make known thy will, and send help from Heaven to all that stand in need thereof, and that wait upon thee for it; give them thy Holy Spirit, that they may be guided in thy way. Let thy Son Jesus Christ have the steering and governing of all things, and let glory be rendered to thy great and worthy name, and keep us in the love of God and in union with one another; let the stroke of thy power remain upon the hearts of all whom thou hast touched at this time; let them be bowed down always in thy holy worship, and remain in a belief of thy truth, and cease to do evil, and learn to do well, and walk acceptably before thee, that so transgression may be finished, and sin and iniquity may be put an end to; and that truth and righteousness may be set up, and shine among us, and that our souls may rejoice in thee, that we may magnify and praise thy power, and glorify thy name; for thou art worthy of all honour, praise and glory, and humble thanksgiving, for the manifestation of thy love and power. All which we desire to offer thee through Jesus Christ, who art God over all, blessed forever and ever. Amen.

SERMON VII.

The INWARD PREACHER; or, the OFFICE of CONSCIENCE.

Preached at GRACE-CHURCH-STREET, June 21, 1692.

My Friends,

MANY have been sent among you, that from living experience have declared their testimony for the truth, that you might all be brought to wait for the testimony of truth in yourselves. This is that which will

will stand you in stead, to know the testimony of truth in your own hearts to be for you ; therefore you are to wait, especially at such times as these, to hear the voice of truth in your own souls : For whatsoever the preacher preacheth, if the truth in thine own heart doth not speak peace, it is not well with thee. Whatsoever testimonies are born of the truth itself; it is the truth that must bear testimony of thee, that unerring word, that gives to every one an infallible evidence of their peace with God, or against that which hinders them.

You know our labour hath been to persuade all people to hearken to the truth in themselves, and to make it their business, and travel, and endeavour, that they might have unity with the truth in their own hearts, that their consciences may not condemn them.

For such as you, in whom God hath raised his witness, and hath exalted the truth for a judge, you are not ignorant, nor covered over with darkness, as many others are; you do not remain in doubt, but you know the truth, and have an answer of peace in well-doing, and a condemnation in evil-doing; not administered to you only by preachers without, but by the evidence and demonstration of the Spirit of God in your own hearts. This is that standing mystery which God hath raised, which can never be put down again, but as each one may put it down in themselves.

I grant that men may put it down : You have read, and had it plainly witnessed to you, even *killing the just, and crucifying the Lord of Glory; and of spiritual* Sodom, *and* Egypt. These things you have read of, and you that are turned to the light, know the meaning of those sayings, by woful experience; for when ever you have turned aside, from a due subjection to the grace of God, by which we are convinced, then there hath been a piercing, *and crucifying of the Son of God afresh, and vexing and grieving the Holy Spirit, by which you should be sealed to the day of redemption* : Then there hath been anguish and tribulation upon your souls; and if this be minded, it will plant a fear upon your minds, and make you afraid to do the like again; but where this tribulation and anguish is neglected and put off, there a custom of sin takes away the sense of sin. You know many have had more judgment at some time upon them for a vain word, or a vain thought, than afterwards they have come to have for the most abominable wicked action. How came this to pass? Was sin ever the better? Or hath it changed its nature? No; but they are further off from the sense of the evil of it. This is the word of truth, to which you must stand or fall; this is the stone, that whosoever falls upon it, shall be broken and tendered; but if they stay till the weight of truth fall upon them, it will grind them to powder.

They will have a life of liberty, let the truth say what it will: I will have my liberty, and use my tongue as I list, I will be wanton and proud, and envious and malicious, tho' I know these things be naught, and the witness in my conscience testifies that these things are wicked, and contrary to the will of God, yet I will have them: Whosoever comes to this mind, the stone is near falling upon them, and they will be ground to powder; they are like to barren earth, which beareth thorns and briers, and is rejected, *and is nigh unto cursing, whose end is to be burned.*

Therefore, friends, I entreat you to hearken to the word of the Lord, it is a holy word, and an old word; many have professed it: There are many preachers that will cry, hearken to the word of the Lord in such a chapter, and such a verse. My testimony this day is, hearken to the word of the Lord: But where shall we find it, some will say? I tell you, it is written with the finger of God in your own consciences; and it is either for you, or against you. Let your profession among men be what it will, this Minister of the Covenant hath no respect of persons, or regard to profession; he will not excuse this or that man, because he makes a greater profession of his name than others; this rather is his judgment, and his condemnation shall be more swift and sharp upon him that makes a profession of Christ's name. *If judgment begin at the house of God, what will the end of them be that obey not the gospel of God.* Those that take upon them a strict profession, they do greater dishonour to God, than those that cry out there is no reforming; there can be no living

ing without fin: Thefe profefs what they do, and they do as they profefs. But when people come to profefs holinefs and righteoufnefs, and profefs a power alfo by which righteoufnefs is obtained, but live not ftrictly according to their profeffion; thefe are they *that caufe the name of God to be blafphemed among the Heathen*, more than they that fay there can be no living without fin.

Now this witnefs of God hath no refpect to profeffion, but hath refpect to the ftate and frame of the mind of a man or woman, that they ferve God with, whether it be with fincerity and uprightnefs of mind, and with breathing defires, that *they may know the good and acceptable will of God, and what is well-pleafing in his fight*; and that they might perform that which is according to his heavenly will. Where this fincerity is, where this cry of the foul is, the Lord hath regard to it; but where people's religion is only to bear up a profeffion, and hold up an external fellowfhip and communion one with another; when this fincerity is wanting, the Lord abhors their worfhip, it is an abomination to God, and no benefit or advantage to themfelves: It is not for the glory of God, that they make a profeffion, but for fome defign to themfelves, and fo they become abominable.

This was the ftate of *Ifrael* of old, and it is the ftate of a great many now, that think they do great matters, if they conform fo far to the truth, as that outwardly they may not be charged with a lye, and that they are of fuch a fociety. It is well if fome would come fo far as to maintain their fociety with God's people, and their external profeffion; but if they have not regard to the truth in their own confciences, what is their profeffion worth? What will all thy unity with them fignify? If there be a breach between God and thine own foul, who can heal that breach? What will the profeffion fignify and amount to at laft? But, *go ye curfed into everlafting fire, prepared for the devil and his angels*. And all the reafon to be rendered for it, is this; depart from me, *ye are workers of iniquity*: He did not fay in that fentence, ye are lyars, you never prophefied in my name, and I never preached in your ftreets; but allowing what they faid to be truth, that they had made a profeffion, and

held

held communion with other Christians, allowing these things, yet notwithstanding it is, *go ye cursed;* and the reason of the sentence is, *you are workers of iniquity.*

Let the dread of the God of Heaven rest upon you. My friends, it is another thing to make a profession of the Lord God of Heaven and earth, than most are aware of; *let every one that names the name of Christ, depart from iniquity.* What is iniquity? It is all things that men or women do to gratify their own wills contrary to the will of God; that is iniquity: Where had all men liberty? Where had *Adam* and his sons their liberty to fulfil their own wills, and to contradict the will of God? Yet nothing is more common in nations, countries and families, than for people to assume a liberty to perform and fulfil their own wills, and to bring about their own interest, designs and contrivances, though at the same time they are convinced that it is contrary to the will of God. Where this liberty is taken, there iniquity is wrought; that is iniquity that is unjust, that which is committed against him upon whom we have all our dependence every moment for life and breath, for food and raiment, and every thing we enjoy; we have a dependence upon that God that made us, yet vain men and women assume a liberty of gratifying their own wills, and setting up for the flesh.

You may remember that passage of the good apostle, when he saw some libertine professors of Christianity, grow loose and careless; they thought it was well they did acknowledge God in their meetings and worship, but as to the affairs of the world, they had forgotten that God was concerned in those things; the apostle takes notice of such libertine loosness, *go to now, you that say, to-day or to-morrow we will go into such a city, and continue there a year, and buy and sell and get gain; whereas you know not what shall be on the morrow: For what is your life? It is even a vapour, that appeareth for a little while, and then vanisheth away: For that you ought to say, if the Lord will, we shall live and do this or that.* You ought to live in subjection to him that made you, you ought to have regard to God's honour in whatsoever you do: *Whether you eat or drink, or whatsoever you do, do all to the glory of God.* Is not

not this fcripture? Is not this found amongft the apoftle's writings? Do not we hold the name of Chriftians which was given to them at *Antioch?* Yea, we are called Chriftians, and thefe writings of the apoftle are holy writings, and what then is the matter that we take fo little notice of them? That men do not apply thefe wholefome exhortations to the particularities of their converfation, but that they go from country to country, and from one place to another, and do what they pleafe, without having any regard to give their fubjection to the great God: This loofenefs hath brought into the minds of fome, fuch a liberty, that they live without God in the world; when they go fometimes to religious meetings, and when they hear the name of God mentioned, it may be there is a little awe upon their minds, and they have fome regard to that God that gave them breath and being, for the prefent: But if there be not religion, if there be not a tie (religion fignifies a tie, a being bound to God) if men be not bound and tied to God, by that which is made known to them, every one will defire that *which is good in their own eyes.*

Therefore it is neceffary for you, my friends, above all people, you that are come to a meafure of the miniftration of the Spirit, to know and to mind what it doth fpeak. Such a thing I did this morning, and I am reproved for it; fuch a thing I did well, and I am juftified and warranted in the doing of it: Thus it is when a thing is well or ill done. Sometimes fome men act two or three days together, and never bring their actions to the rule; that is, like a man that is building and never minds his rule, fo what he builds up, tumbles down again upon his head. You know there is fomething in you that hath a fpeaking voice, an infallible voice, and gives judgment on your actions, and paffeth a fentence, either of juftification or condemnation upon you. If you would live fo as to anfwer God in what you do, you need not fear anfwering men. I do not fear anfwering men in all I do or fpeak; if I do but anfwer mine own confcience, I fear no man, tho' he be of another perfuafion and judgment oppofite to me; if I keep peace in mine own confcience, I fhall anfwer the principle of truth in my adverfaries confciences, tho' they hate me, and defpife me, and feek occafion againſt me; if my actions anſwer the truth of God in mine own heart, they will anſwer the truth in any man's heart: This makes a man as bold as a lion.

When the people of God obtain a reputation, to be true and juſt, and holy and righteous, all men will expect holineſs and righteouſneſs at their hands. What if I profeſs to be one of theſe people? If I have not the truth in my own heart, tho' I put on this reputation as a cloak to hide my infincerity, the want of that truth takes away my courage. It is truth that hath a power in all men in the world, and it is the power of holineſs and righteouſneſs that makes wicked men afraid; and therefore the apoſtle argues upon that ſubject, the magiſtrate is cloathed with power. What power hath he? The power of juſtice, and the power of the ſword. What ſword hath he? A ſword of juſtice; and he is a *terror to evil-doers, but a praiſe to them that do well.* It is true, if I have done evil, if I meet with a man that is but my equal; if in buying, and felling, and commerce, I have wronged him, and deceived him, tho' he knows not of it, yet I am afraid of him, I am fearful that he will diſcover me and find me out: But if I ſpeak the truth, and do that which is honeſt in the ſight of all men, I ſhall not fear any man: There is no nation under Heaven, but there is a principle of truth to be found among them in the hearts of men. If I act according to the principle of truth in mine own heart, there is the ſame principle of truth in all men. If I walk up to the principle of truth in myſelf, I ſhall likewiſe walk up to the principle of truth in all men's hearts; if mine own heart doth not condemn me, all the world cannot condemn me.

If profeſſors were reſolved to anſwer the principles of truth in their own hearts, and go thorough-ſtitch in their profeſſion, they might live courageouſly: Truth will crown them with victory. But if they do not live according to the rule and ſtandard of truth, they are like ſalt that hath *loſt its favour, which is trodden under the feet of men.* But where all are one in truth, they are gathered into the truth, and they will live according to it, ſo far as they are *the* OFFICE *of* CONSCIENCE.

are convinced of it. If you would give them a world, they will not give away a hair's breadth of the truth which they have profeſſed. When truth thus comes to have dominion, then truth ſhall overſpread the earth, and the *kingdoms of the world ſhall become the kingdoms of the Lord, and of his Chriſt*, and righteouſneſs ſhall rule, and the ſceptre of it be ſwayed over the nations, and they that rebel againſt it, ſhall be broken by it, and they that are found in it, ſhall have dominion, and they ſhall condemn hypocrites and diſſemblers. Now if you would grow up in this dominion, you have an opportunity for it, becauſe the truth is revealed in your own hearts.

They who undertake to walk in the truth, meerly from what they hear the miniſters of truth preach, laying up in their minds a company of doctrines, notions and tenets, they will ſtumble and fall; but they that will hearken to the truth in their own hearts, and regard the voice of it in all their ways and undertakings; theſe have a miniſter at home with them, they have a chaplain in their own houſes; if there be any thing they know not, and if they know not what to do, they ask the miniſter of the ſanctuary; others will ask their miniſters, but your miniſter is at home with you: Where hath God appointed any man to rule over your conſcience? No, God hath appointed Chriſt only to rule and govern your conſcience, to be *the author of faith, and the finiſher of it* too: You that are come to the diſpenſation of the Spirit of Chriſt, keep to the teſtimony in your own hearts; then you have fellowſhip with one another in the truth; and you have cauſe to bleſs God for it, that God hath ſo opened the hearts of one toward another, that the ſuffering of one, is the ſuffering of all; and the conſolation of one, the comfort and rejoicing of all: But alas! who is in this fellowſhip? Only thoſe that are in fellowſhip with the truth, in their own hearts, and really ſo: If a man ſhall break fellowſhip with truth in his own heart, he will make no bones of breaking fellowſhip with his brethren: As ſoon as men break fellowſhip with truth, they are unruly, heavy, troubleſome, and make no matter of ſplitting, and tearing, and rending of fellowſhip with others. How comes it to paſs that thou haſt done this? Thou didſt not the while thou fearedst sinning against the witness of God in thine own heart. But when men have once made light of the great minister of the gospel in their own hearts, it is an easy matter to make light of the rest; if, as Christ saith, *they have done so to the green tree, no wonder that they do so to the dry tree: If they despise me* (faith Christ) *do you think they will love you?*

It is most evident in a great many at this day, they dispute against truth, they have taken a liberty to speak contrary to the truth in their own hearts, and then they cry down the ministers of it: Do you think they do so that keep their first tenderness? When they were convinced, the power of the Lord rested upon them; when the power of the Lord first wrought upon you, and brought you to yea and nay, and to plain simple language and habit, this was with joy and delight for Christ's sake. They that keep up this tenderness and simplicity of mind, there is no scattering, nor rending, or tearing among them, they *keep the unity of the Spirit in the bond of peace*, and they are kept together in one.

Friends, you have an opportunity in your hands, see that you make use of it; you may bear up, and not be deceived by men, or devils, if you keep faithful to the principle of truth in your own hearts. Let what reproach and persecution soever come, here is a standard, a foundation and a rule, for you to be governed by, every hour of the day; search your hearts, and try your consciences by it. As ye do this, and keep to the rule of the new creature, of the regeneration, being changed from a carnal birth to an incorruptible birth. *If you be born of the incorruptible seed*, the devil cannot corrupt you, evil passions cannot corrupt you; if you keep up that foundation that is incorruptible in itself, then nothing will corrupt you, nor your ways and manners: If you will live according to the simplicity of the gospel, you will serve God, and be examples to others in the life of holiness and righteousness; and hereby God shall be glorified. This is that which will shine forth to the whole nation, and give a good report to truth: But if any that profess the truth, be found false to their profession, and be found unholy, and deceive and over-reach their neighbour, they lose by it, and the devil rejoiceth at it.

Thus

the OFFICE *of* CONSCIENCE. 93

Thus we know the life of righteousness is brought forth through the Spirit of truth, and out-shines all, and will reach God's witness in them that are afar off, and bring them near; and happy and blessed are they that are found in this divine work, conforming their lives and conversations according to the new creature, peace be upon them, *and upon the whole Israel of God.* There is a minister that abides with you, that goes home with you, it is his testimony that you must stand or fall by: 'If any one should be a false professor, and be cried up, if he be not sincere, he hath not peace; though he flutter awhile, and make a shew, the worm of guilt gnaws and torments him; such as these have not peace with God, nor fellowship with the church: Though they seem to be alive, yet they are dead; as it was with the churches in *Asia, they had a name to live, yet they were dead;* though they have an empty name, such a one is a living man or woman, they are esteemed friends to the church; but though they are commended and cried up, and have a name to live, yet they are dead; *there is a few names in* Sardis *which have not defiled their garments, they shall walk with me in white,* saith Christ, *for they are worthy. I know thy works, that thou hast a name that thou livest, and art dead.* See what Christ, the bright Morning-Star, could do: He could look into a meeting, and see whether few or many had only a name to live, or were really alive; if they were dead as to sincerity and truth, though they had been among the church, they would help to break it down, but not to build it up.

You that have this divine life still stirring in you, and feel the operation that first quickened you to God, prize this principle of the divine life above all: What is there can rob you of it? Value not the friendship of the world: Alas! what can it amount to? Count it as *dung in comparison of Christ Jesus;* look upon all things with a sound eye: Peace with God is of that concernment, that you cannot be happy here or hereafter, without it; the friendship of the world I can be without, and the customs and fashions of the world I can be without, I can spare these things; but the favour of God I cannot be without, *and growth in grace and the knowledge of our Lord and Saviour Jesus Christ,* and

a

a sincere profession of the gospel; I cannot be without these things.

My friends, though you do not make a shew and flutter in the world, as some others do, yet your glory is within; they that are living members of this divine body, the glory, and beauty and brightness of such, appears in the sight of God. If you grow in *grace*, you will be a comfort to one another; and as the apostle speaks, *you are our epistle written in our hearts, known and read of all men*. The Lord preserve and keep you simple, keep you in all sincerity, in that truth that hath wrought in your own hearts, that you may have acquaintance with your teacher, that he may not be driven into corners; for you may do it, and stop his mouth, and silence him too. If you let your perverse will rule, you may slay the just; but there will come a day of his rising, then down you go. Whatsoever men may get by it at present, when truth riseth, when the Just One that was slain hath a resurrection in them, then most certain down they go. While you have an opportunity in your hands, and an interest in the covenant of life, walk with God according to the counsel and dictates of his Holy Spirit, that you may be brought to a heavenly fellowship, and to partake of the good things that God hath prepared for his children.

My friends, pray prize your seasons, let no day slip, for fear you miss a day at last; wait upon the Lord, and let his fear and a holy awe be always upon your hearts: Then peace will be upon you, and there will be acceptance of all that you do. *Mark the perfect man, and behold the upright, for the end of that man is peace;* when he can reflect upon his past life, and say, I have walked before the Lord with a perfect heart, and done that which is good and well pleasing in his sight, and have not turned aside to the right hand or to the left, but the Standard of Truth hath been the guide of all my *spiritual* and *temporal* actions. If *truth* hath been thy *guide* here, then *truth* shall be thy portion hereafter. If *truth* guide thee in thy way, then thou shalt rejoice with the saints, and receive an inheritance with the people of God, and enjoy that glory and felicity which God hath prepared for them that love him. *His*

His PRAYER after SERMON.

EVERLASTING, glorious, eternal God of Life! whose kingdom ruleth over all; thy kingdom is an everlasting kingdom; a glorious, blessed day hath dawned, wherein thou art making thyself known to the sons and daughters of men; and thou hast opened an eye in a remnant (which the God of this world had blinded) to see the glory of this day. For tho' we have lived without God in the world, yet thou art near to us, and thou hast called us to repentance, and inspired our souls with a desire to thee, and to the remembrance of thy name: Praise and everlasting thanksgivings belong unto thee, who art the author of our salvation; who hast reached out thy hand and laid hold upon us, and sought us out when we sought thee not, and hast made known thy power and love for our redemption and salvation; and thou wilt make it known more and more to every upright, sincere mind.

O powerful Father of Life! how hath thy power and goodness been revealed on our behalf for thine own name's sake? Thou hast stood by us in all our trials and exercises, and we have found thee a God nigh at hand, and thou hast brought a remnant to desire nothing so much as the enjoyment of thy presence; thou hast brought them to be sensible, that without thee they can do nothing; therefore, in all our assemblies and meetings, we desire to be acquainted with thy power, to hear thy word which speaks life to our souls, by which we may live.

And dear and powerful Father! the continuation of thy goodness among us, doth greatly engage the hearts of thy children, to offer up praises and thanksgivings to thee. Thou hast inclined the minds and hearts of thy people to wait upon thee, and hast opened their understandings to receive thy heavenly truth, and those rich and heavenly treasures which thou offerest them, and hast provided a cup of salvation to refresh the poor and needy soul.

O Living God of Life! reach forth thy hand, to support and save those that are breathing after thee, that are sensible of the want of thy presence, and are frequenting the assemblies of thy people, with a hope and desire that they may enjoy a blessing from thee.

Living

Living God of Life! touch their hearts with the finger of thy power, let them know that thou art ready to open the treasure of thy love, and life unto them, through the Lord Jesus Christ, that their souls may be comforted, and they may offer up sacrifices of thanksgiving. And let all thy children every where, render to thy name, through Jesus Christ, blessing, and honour, and praise; who art God over all, blessed forever and ever. Amen.

SERMON VIII.

SAVING FAITH, the GIFT of GOD alone.

Preached at GRACE-CHURCH-STREET, March 8, 1687.

My Friends,

YOU that are made partakers of that precious faith, which hath brought you to an expectation of that redemption and deliverance that comes alone by Christ Jesus, your minds should be continually exercised in that faith which God hath given you, for it is a great gift, a blessed gift that he hath given to us to believe. This never came of ourselves, never was there a true believer in Christ Jesus, but he received his faith of God, it was the gift of God, it was given to him to believe. Other sorts of believers there are in the world, that can communicate their faith one to another; but they are true believers that have their faith communicated to them by the Spirit of Jesus Christ, it is *given to them that believe;* and because it is so excellent and so heavenly a gift, and hath such large privileges belonging to it, it is necessary that every one that receives it, should have a continual exercise in it; that you may know what it is, and what it doth for you, and so come to be experienced Christians. Now all that are partakers of it, they do believe, and know in whom they have believed, and for what they have believed, even for the saving of their souls.

The true faith, that is the gift of God, it is not at all
short

SAVING FAITH, the GIFT of GOD alone.

short of a complete saving of their souls; they that truly believe, their faith stands in one that they know is able to save to the utmost; and so a true believer hath a great comfort in his faith above all other believers in the world; for he knows that his faith reaches to a complete redemption, unto a complete sanctification, unto a complete fitting of him for the kingdom of God.

Now there is no such faith that ever was made by men, there is no such faith that all the wise and learned men upon the face of the earth, have either preached or given forth to be received; for if you come to consider the divers forms of faith that men have ministered, they will fall short of saving their souls, they fall short of redemption, they fall short of fitting and preparing them for the kingdom of God, and so they have not that comfort, that satisfaction, and that inward refreshment that belongs to the others, or that accrues to their souls, that have *the faith of God's elect*.

And herein hath been the privilege of the people of God in all ages, as well as in our age; their faith hath had a farther extent, it hath reached farther in order to the good of their souls, than the faith of all others hath done: What comfort can a serious Christian take in a faith that falls short of righteousness and redemption? Would it not make a man or woman's heart ach, to think I am a believer, but yet I have no faith that reacheth to sanctification, and holy living, and redemption from sin? All my faith leaves me a sinner all my days; to my dying hour there is no mastery to be had, no getting victory over sin, it will prevail over me as long as I live.

This is not that *precious faith* that God's elect have been made partakers of, that works effectually in their souls; this is not that faith that can minister real comfort to the poor soul that is laden with iniquity, and weary of sin; the faith that falls short of sanctification, and redemption from sin, is such a faith as God never gave his people; it came some other way into the world, and it hath captivated most of the sons and daughters of men, and they have expelled the true faith (as much as in them lies) that saving faith that purifies and cleanses men from sin, and gives them victory over the world, and have got another faith in the room of it; and they live in their fins, and in their lufts and concupifcence, and ftill remain in captivity.

But God was pleafed to hear and anfwer the cry of the fouls of a remnant (for which many of us have caufe to magnify the name of our God) when we had travelled from mountain to hill, to feek where true comfort might be found, where one fhould fay to us that we fhould overcome. We know there is no eating of the tree of life until we do overcome; nor entering into God's kingdom till we be cleanfed. Some laid an impoffibility in our way, which made many a one to mourn. What, muft we never be cleanfed? Muft this crooked heart, and perverfe will, always remain? Muft I be a finner and a believer? A finner, and call myfelf a child of God? How can thefe things hang together? Thefe have made many to faint in their minds, and to fay as *David* did in his diftrefs, *one day I fhall perifh by the hand of Saul*. One day this corruption will be my ruin; for all my prayers, and hearing, and other duties and performances, this fin will be my utter ruin at laft.

After many have mourned, and been afflicted, by reafon of the burden that was upon them, it hath pleafed the Lord to vifit a remnant, and to open their hearts to make known the *precious faith*, the *faith of God's elect*, the *faith that was once delivered to the faints*. Is this the faith that is worthy of an earneft contending for, and preaching for, and fuffering for? Who was ever fo mad, as to fuffer for fuch a faith as will leave a man under the power of fatan, and his own lufts? No wonder that fuch have a faith that is not worth contending and fuffering for. Who will expofe themfelves for fuch a faith that will never do them a kindnefs? Now that faith which belongs to a purified foul, to one that is fanctified, that faith delivered to the faints, it is called a *fhield*; when once a Chriftian comes to make ufe of this faith as a fhield, he will find the power of it. A fhield is that which is worn by perfons that are among enemies; it is for the defence and fafeguard of one that is befet with enemies; and a good Chriftian is fo fituated.

There

SAVING FAITH, *the* GIFT *of* GOD *alone.* 99

There is a fort of blind Chriftians, friends to the world, their chriftianity is worldly, and their faith worldly; but all true Chriftians are in the midft of their enemies, inward and outward; and if they had not the fhield of faith to defend them, they would certainly be wounded every day, they would be flain and lofe their lives: The faith that is called a fhield, it is that by which a Chriftian is to be defended and faved from harm defigned againft him every hour; *for the devil goes about like a roaring lion, continually feeking whom he may devour.* The apoftle fpeaks more particularly to believers; *the devil, your adverfary*, he is an adverfary in himfelf, but more efpecially *your adverfary* that are believers; that have believed to the faving of your fouls. You that believe that Chrift is fent of God, endued with power fufficient to break his head, and power to redeem you out of his fervice and bondage, the devil will be your adverfary: Let him be fo, if I have but my fhield. This is that which if a man ufe, he will *quench all the fiery darts of the devil.*

If a man come once to receive the faith, the true faith, faith in the power of God, this faith will remain victorious over temptation; but if thou doft not keep thy faith in a continual exercife, thou doft not deferve the name of a true believer: If a man receive the true faith, and grow carelefs in his chriftian exercife, will not this adverfary, the devil, be about his ears? Will not he fend forth his fiery darts at him; his temptations, and fnares, and gins, to entangle him, tho' he be a believer, if he doth not keep in the continual exercife of his faith? But a true Chriftian, that feels the power of the grace of God, and is in the continual exercife of true faith, he is like a watchman or fentinel, that hath his armour on, and his fhield ready, he knows he is on the borders of his enemies quarters, and he keeps himfelf in perpetual watchfulnefs, in daily expectation of the devil's fiery darts; he keeps his fhield in readinefs; I fee a temptation lies in fuch a thing, but I fee the Lord's power is able to keep me out of it. I fee there is profit or pleafure in the fnare; it is a hook that is baited, but I fee the hook through the bait, bleffed be God; and I have a confidence in his

power

power, and that he is able to keep me from that thing, for all the baits of profit, pleasure, or the friendship of the world.

A believer keeps in the exercise of his faith, and considers that *his salvation is nearer than when he first believed;* the people that believe, are not presently saved, the work of salvation is to be wrought after they believe; *for without faith, it is impossible to please God, nevertheless the foundation of God standeth sure,* it is founded upon the power of God; when a man believeth, the work is begun; tho' some foolish professors tell us, that the work is done when the act is only in the mind; they will tell you what day of the month, and such a day of the year their conversion was wrought; but they know not what they say. A man may possibly know when it was brought about: A man may know about the time when God communicated faith to him; but he must know after he is a believer, then begins the work of salvation, the believer is to be saved from this or the other enemy; he is not presently saved from all, there must be a warfare, *a fighting the good fight of faith,* before these enemies of his salvation are overcome; the devil will not give over because I am a believer, and because Christ promised to *break his head; the seed of the woman shall break the serpent's head.* I am now but putting on my armour; the battle is not fought; I have not yet gone through the peril of the fight; I am now buckling on my armour; when the fight comes, if I have not my shield and my armour ready, I may be slain for all this; some *have made shipwreck of faith,* they have not held it, nor kept the faith, but given it away: But saith the apostle, *I have fought the good fight, I have kept the faith,* I have gotten the victory.

So people, after they are believers, they must wait to have their faith strengthened by renewed manifestations of the same power in which it first stood: They must wait upon the Lord, and he will renew the strength of their faith, zeal and courage; and as temptations are renewed, they have new courage, and new strength and new ability, and all by this divine, spiritual and Christian exercise; they every day come to see the work they believed, that which their faith tended to, see the work in some measure wrought, they

see

see some enemy of their souls brought down and slain, and they see their souls come up to a little more dominion than they had before; they see the devil's power is weakened more than before, and that he hath not so much power as he hath had over them. These things are some encouragement to raise up in a true Christian, living praises to God; seeing, by believing, he hath found thus much encouragement by the working of the word, why should he not wait on the Lord for the accomplishment of this work, that he may believe to the saving of his soul, that he may come to receive the end of his hope and faith, the salvation of his soul? Now, by thus keeping their faith in exercise, they know that their *salvation is nearer now, than when they first believed*. It is not so with every one, for many that have believed, their salvation is farthest off, because of their negligence, professing one thing with their mouths, and doing another thing in their practice; there are some things which they believe and profess, and yet do the contrary; that puts their salvation further off, and draws them secretly into desponding, and into a losing their courage and zeal for God; the custom of sinning hath at last taken away the sense of sinning. It is so with a man when he first transgresseth the rule, he is somewhat tender, and doth it with some regret; but after he is come to a custom of doing it, he is pretty well at ease, and so by degrees he goes on towards the state of being past feeling. At last such sinners come to dying; they were dead once before, and *were quickened through the operation of the Spirit of Christ Jesus*; they were quickened, and if they shall die again, if you die a second time, pray remember it is a second time; you that are careless and ready to die, remember it is the second death that you are going to; and consider that if you *die the second death, you shall have no part of the first resurrection*: Better such had never been born at all, than after they have lived in hope, to lose it again. This is that which was upon my heart to commend unto you, that you may partake of *this precious faith*, that hath a tendency to the saving of the soul, and fitting you for the kingdom of God. Hath God given you to believe? And will you not believe that you shall live without sin?

If

If you come to obtain this precious faith, you will believe that you shall come to live without sinning against God, and have the light of his countenance shining upon you. He that truly believeth, his faith reacheth to this, and he will say to himself, I am saved a little from the liberty of my tongue, and from many sins of an evil practice: God hath redeemed me from my vanity, pride and passion, and other things that were troublesome, the Lord hath redeemed me from them; I see the work is going on, and I am nearer to the kingdom of God than when I first believed; I have gotten victory over many of my spiritual enemies, and I hope the Lord will carry me on, and keep me by his power through faith unto salvation: Hitherto the Lord hath helped me, I have not fought in vain, I have not been beating the air, but God hath given me victory over the tempter inwardly and outwardly, so that he could not prevail, whilst I kept the shield of faith over my head; but when I have been careless, and not exercised my faith as a shield, I have been weak as other men.

You are not called to weakness and feebleness, but to the power of God, that you may be exercised in it, and by it be kept from the evil of the world: There is a possibility of being kept, if you be faithful to him that hath called you, that is, *Christ Jesus, the Captain of our Salvation*, if you follow him step by step, and do not run headlong all at once; when you see a great deal of sin and corruption before you, and seek to master it in your own strength, you will lose the victory: The same word that sheweth us our sin, sheweth us our own inability to overcome it, and that we can do nothing without divine assistance; tho' we lie long struggling under the weight and burden of sin, we cannot of ourselves get victory over it, we cannot bring judgment into victory, God must have the glory of it. If you keep to Jesus, he will carry on the work; you did believe in him, for he did work this faith in you, and he will carry on his own work, and his own work shall praise him. All others that talk of faith, and make an empty profession, they dishonour God; they talk of perfection, and living without sin,

but

but never experience it, and so bring dishonour to God: If you wait to see this work carried on; if you believe and exercise your faith for the overcoming of your sins, and *perfecting holiness in the fear of God*, you will hereby bring glory to God, who alone is worthy of all praise; who is God over all, blessed for ever more. *Amen.*

His PRAYER after SERMON.

MOST *blessed, holy, and unchangeable Lord God! thou hast visited us by thy dear Son and our Saviour Jesus Christ, to gather us to be a people unto thee, who once were not a people, and once not gathered.*

Everlasting Father! thy mercy is great, and thy goodness is great, and to be greatly prized by us all; thou hadst compassion on us to help us when we could not help ourselves; and thou hast laid help upon one that is mighty and able to save to the uttermost all that come unto thee by him.

Blessed God, and Father of our Lord Jesus Christ! we give thee thanks for thy abundant mercy and goodness extended to us. Lord God Eternal! extend thy mercy more and more; and visit the children of men in all nations with the knowledge of thy truth.

Blessed Father of Life! we pray and cry to thee, that thy work may go on, and that it may prosper and encrease, and let the day of thy visitation be extended, and reach forth thy Almighty Arm, that the children of men may be gathered unto thee.

Blessed Father of Life! thou hast shewn mercy to our souls, and we have seen the goings of God in his sanctuary; thou hast, by an out-stretched arm, gathered us to be a people to thyself; thou hast appeared for thy people in all ages, and thou hast saved them out of oppression, and stilled the fury of the enemy. Thou hast cut Rahab, and wounded the dragon, and made way for thy people Israel, that they passed through the Red-Sea as on dry land. Lord, do so for thy people spiritually in our day, and make way for them, and open the door that thy gospel may spread, and run, and be glorified, and have a free course among us; and

that

that thy worship may be set up, and pure incense may be offered up to thee. O Lord! this is the cry of thy servants, and the voice of their supplications to thee, that thy Spirit may be poured out abundantly and operate upon them, that thy word may be profitable and welcome to their souls.

Blessed Father of mercy! thou hast blessed thy children and people with spiritual blessings in Christ Jesus. Thou hast given us thy pleasure this day; and blessed be thy name, thou hast refreshed our souls at this season; let our praises ascend as a sweet smelling favour, and acceptable service to thee: And for all thy mercies and renewed favours and blessings to us, and to all thy people, both here and every where, let thanksgiving and living praises be rendered to thee; for thou alone art worthy of all blessing and praise, who art God over all, blessed forever. Amen.

SERMON IX.

TRUTH'S TESTIMONY
AGAINST THE
POWER of SIN and SATAN.

Preached at GRACE-CHURCH-STREET, June 3, 1688.

My Friends,

GOD hath made you witnesses of the great work of this day; the Lord I say hath given you eyes to see, and ears to hear, and hearts to understand the great work of the day; he hath called you forth, that you may be faithful witnesses every one in your measure of that which he hath brought to pass in your sight, for he hath revealed his power, the eternal power by which the world was made, he hath revealed and manifested that power for the raising up of life, for the subjecting and bringing under death, and the power of it; for a great while a testimony that hath been born in the nation hath been unto death; he that hath the power of death,

that

that is, the devil, he hath had a great many to found out his power, to declare the continuance of it, that death must reign, and darkness must continue, and that the kingdom of the man of sin will never be brought down.

But now in our day, glory to God on high, here is another sound come forth, the Lord *Jehovah* hath uttered his voice, and who can but prophecy! The word of prophecy is given of God, and many are raised up to publish it, and to sound forth the name of the Lord in the extirpation, the ruin and destruction, that is and shall be brought upon the kingdom of iniquity, upon the kingdom of the man of sin, and to prophecy and declare in the name of the Lord, that righteousness shall run down like a stream; this is the gospel, the glad tidings that we receive from God, and minister unto you, that you might believe, and that believing you might come to wait upon the Lord, and behold the accomplishment of it.

For, my friends, herein hath consisted all the labour, travel and exercise, of the servants of the Lord; and for this cause have we suffered many things, and gone through many trials, *because we have stedfastly believed, and therefore have we spoken it*; that the Lord will, by his Almighty power, lay waste, destroy and bring to an end, that power, that the wicked one, the devil, hath had upon the minds and spirits of the sons and daughters of men, and that he will set up and establish, in the very same soul, a law of righteousness, and a law of truth, and will cause the beauty of holiness to shine forth through them, where iniquity hath lodged, where the wicked one hath ruled.

Now you that have believed this testimony, you have received it, as glad tidings unto you, for you are weary of that old service, you are oppressed under the power of that strange prince. There was a kind of spirit and power that had ruled over you, that neither gave you life nor breath, nor had done any good thing, and yet you were subject; and many there were, who through the grace of God, came to see that a state and condition of sin and iniquity was not a happy state; and by a secret kindling of the *spark* of God's love in your souls ere you knew him, there was a cry raised to be delivered, if it be possible. If there

there be any deliverance, O why may not I be delivered? If there be any redemption, why may not I be redeemed! If there be a power that can set me free from the service of this wicked one, why may not I be set free?

Ah, friends! remember the days and nights in which these living cries run through you, then you were poor indeed; then you were humble and broken, and the Lord beheld you in those days, he saw your state and condition, he saw how helpless you were, and did not he arise to help you? Did not a power spring forth in the day of your humility, in the day of tenderness, by which you became able to make war against the lusts of your own hearts, and did not you overcome and prevail in your war? Did not you make a progress by the power and by the grace that first raised desires in you? And as you made this progress and gained ground, as I may say, of your own corruptions, your faith came to be strengthened, and you were confirmed in the belief and in the obedience of the truth; and the more you trusted and relied upon him, the more did he manifest his power in you; he made known his ability and his strength in your weakness, so that you did become *living witnesses*, every one in your measure, that there was such a power; and that that power was able not only to save from a little, or from a few, but was able to save to the uttermost, to save out of all that was polluted and defiled, and to cleanse and purify the conscience from all dead works, and to enable you to serve the living God.

Now the Lord having thus established you, and confirmed you by his power, that you were found in the *faith*, and firm in the believing of the *truth*, my friends, all the labour, and travel and doctrine, and exercise of the preachers of the gospel, to those who were converted and confirmed, became very acceptable. So we preach, and so you believed; here was a unity in our faith, here grew up a fellowship, a communion in the faith, and the Lord became glorified in the assemblies not only of those that preached, but of those that heard, because each one had a place in the body, and each one had a favour of the word of life by which the body was nourished.

Now, my friends, that which lies particularly upon me
to

to leave with you for my testimony (and I pray God that it may be placed in the hearts of all you that have believed) is, that you may all wait upon the Lord, to see all that brought to pass which you have believed: For I take notice by the eye, that God hath opened in me, by which he hath made me to take care of his flock, and sometimes put his word in my mouth, that I may speak a word in due season: I say, by this eye, I take notice of many that have received this precious faith, and thereby have believed the great and high state; their faith reached so far, they knew that power to be able to bring them into a perfect dominion over their lusts, and passions, and corruptions, and over the spirit of the world, over pride, over anger, over all things that are opposite to the divine life; their faith is as sound as we can preach it in respect of the extent of it, but their faith hath not reached thus far in its operation upon their hearts; they have not had the power going on, to accomplish and fulfil that which remains.

Are there not some here and there that are settled in the belief of the truth, but are got into an case from the labour of the truth? But if I be found in the faith, my understanding is opened; I do not only believe this matter, but have inward evidence and demonstration, that I am certain, past all doubt and question of it, that the Lord reveals his power in them that believe, that purifies them, and makes them every whit clean; and here I have a fellowship and communion with them that preach, and them that believe.

But, my friends, all this will not give you communion with God; though there is communion with the church of God, with respect to men, who are come into one faith and doctrine, yet for fellowship with God, it stands in a life beyond all doctrines, and beyond all words and expressions; therefore your business and mine, and every one's, is what we undertook when our faces were first turned to God, that we may be followers of Christ in the regeneration. For many may be firm in point of doctrine, and yet may not follow Christ Jesus: Many hold the truth, but do not hold it in righteousness, but unrighteousness.

Now, my friends, have a care, your religion and your
souls

souls eternal welfare are concerned. This doctrine I leave you in charge in the name of the Lord God: Flatter not yourselves any one of you, because of the soundness of your belief, but look for soundness of heart, and for a right spirit to be created in you, a spirit that can no way endure any thing that the light of Christ hath made manifest to be evil; if it be truth you own, then exercise faith upon it, and whatsoever sin or temptation assaults you, say, I shall overcome in the name of the Lord Jehovah; I shall bring thee under, be what lust, passion, or corruption soever thou wilt, in the name of the Lord, I shall overcome thee, and bring thee under.

Travel on in the faith committed to you, and you will be more than conquerors; you will not only grow into external fellowship with the people of God in the sight of men, but into fellowship with the church of the first-born, whose names are written in Heaven; and your communion will not be in words and doctrines, and principles of faith; but your communion will be with God the Father, and his Son Jesus Christ; and so in all your meetings together, the joy of the Lord will be your strength, and the joy of his great *salvation* your covering, and he will manifest his gracious presence with you; and that power which hath kept you to this day from your childhood, and preserved you in all your battles and conflicts with the world, and strengthened and encouraged you when you went sometimes sorrowing and mourning night and day, and fearing lest you should not overcome your adversaries; that power that hath kept you hitherto, will do greater things for you than you have yet been witnesses of.

Therefore, dear friends, this I would leave with you, there is nothing will keep you and me in that little time that remains to us here to spend on earth, but that which will keep us in the exercise of faith towards God, and his Son Jesus Christ, who is *able to save us to the uttermost*: Let us wait to see the power of God for *sanctification and holiness*; that will reach as far as saving us from our sins.

This hath been the greatest reproach that ever our adversaries have thrown upon us, that there are some amongst us that talk of believing in the power of God, and talk of an ability to overcome their sins, and living a holy life, and living without sin, while they themselves live in it. This is the greatest reproach that ever our adversaries have thrown upon us: Whosoever have been the cause of this reproach, God will require it of them, for the Lord is jealous of his name and glory; and he will have the praise and honour that is due to his great name, for *working in us both to will and to do of his good pleasure*, saith the apostle; tho' I know nothing of myself, yet am I not hereby justified. When you come to that, that you cannot charge yourselves, then the Lord will not charge you; but take heed that therein you place not your justification, hereby you are not justified.

Therefore have an eye to *Jesus, the author and finisher of our faith*. He begins the work of faith, and he will carry it on until he be the finisher of it, and the justifier of it; he is the Mediator of the New Covenant, that alone justifies the children of God. Depend not upon your own holiness and righteousness for justification; keep your eyes to Jesus the author of your faith, who will be also the finisher of it; keep your hearts with all diligence, and walk humbly with God, watching lest your adversary that you have overcome, prevail against you. By going from the power, there is no safety for the flock, but only while they keep in the shepherd's fold; be faithful and keep yourselves in the love of God, and he will be present with you, and keep you to be his witnesses to the end of your days, and will raise up another generation to be witnesses to his power, when he hath taken you to himself.

To that mighty power of God I commit you, for preserving you in humility of mind and soul; and my prayer for you shall be, that you may go on, and make a progress in the good ways of the Lord, until his work be finished in you.

His PRAYER after SERMON.

*H*OLY *and powerful God of Life! who art the Creator of us all; in whom we live, and move, and have*

our

His PRAYER after SERMON.

our being; thou haſt made us all for the purpoſe of thy praiſe and glory, that we might ſerve thee in the land of the living, among the ſons and daughters of men; and not only ſo, but thou haſt given us thy Holy Spirit, as thou didſt to the people of old.

O living God of Life! thou haſt ordained a remnant to give up themſelves to be led by it; thou regardeſt them, and art with them, and they enjoy from time to time thy holy preſence, which makes glad their ſouls; and they have fellowſhip and communion with thee, and thy Son, through thy Spirit, by which they are quickened to offer up pure and living praiſes upon thine altar.

O living God of Love and Life! thou haſt ſhed abroad thy love upon their hearts, by which they are enabled to pray for enemies, that they may come to enjoy ſalvation, and the pleaſures which are at thy right hand, which are infinitely better than all the pleaſures of this vain world.

Holy and powerful Father! have reſpect to all our ſouls, and touch all our hearts with a ſenſe of thy divine love, that we may feel the cords of thy love drawing our ſouls nearer to thyſelf, and aſſuring us that thou haſt a gracious purpoſe to ſave us.

O powerful God of Life! ſhew forth thy power, that our hearts may be touched and quickened thereby, to come to fear thee, and reverence thy name, and be acquainted with thy operation in our own hearts, that they may be humbled and broken before thee, and bow down and worſhip in ſincerity and uprightneſs: That ſo holy God of Life! if it be thy pleaſure, none may depart out of this aſſembly without ſome ſenſe of thy love, and feeling of the powerful drawings of thy grace, and without being raiſed up to purity of heart, and convinced of the evil of every thing that is contrary to thee, and ſerve thee in holineſs and righteouſneſs, and purſue it with all their hearts, and minds, and ſoul, and ſtrength, that thou mayeſt have mercy upon them, and pardon their iniquity, and love them freely, for ſo thou haſt ordained in thy Son Jeſus Chriſt, that we may receive remiſſion of ſins through the belief of thy everlaſting truth.

And holy, powerful, God of Life! that all thy people may partake of holineſs and ſobriety, to the praiſe of thy name, and that they may all come to obtain a victory over
all

all thofe fpiritual enemies that war againſt their fouls, that thy holy work of redemption and regeneration may be carried on, to the praiſe of thy grace, and the exaltation of thy holy name, to whom praiſe, honour, and wiſdom belong, and pure and humble thankſgivings; and unto thee, the living God of Life, we deſire to offer up our praiſes and adorations, for thou alone art worthy; who art God over all, bleſſed forever and ever. Amen.

SERMON X.

BEARING the CROSS of CHRIST, the true MARK of a CHRISTIAN.

Preached at DEVONSHIRE-HOUSE, October 12, 1690.

HE that knoweth the day of the Lord, and the ſtretching forth of his arm, is quickened to feel the power that is in Chriſt Jeſus, the Head of the Church; that ſo he may be enabled, through his power, to bring forth fruit unto God. The eye of the Lord is upon you all, and he expects at the hand of every one, that they bring forth fruit unto God, that according to the aboundings of his mercy towards you, and of his patience and long-ſuffering concerning you, there might at laſt be an anſwer in the ſoul of every one, unto the mercy and goodneſs of God. They that do not know and experience this, that the long-ſuffering and patience of God leadeth unto repentance, they know no part of Chriſtianity; let them make their profeſſion ever ſo high, and proclaim their notions ever ſo loud, they that know not the work of repentance in their hearts, as yet, need to learn the firſt principle of the Chriſtian religion. You know it hath been the cuſtom of people to learn their children principles, and they that have learned their principles, they go for Chriſtians, whether they repent or no; though they go on in ſin and iniquity all their days, yet they go under the reputation of Chriſtians; and it is high time to examine and find out (if you can) a reaſon for this, that a man ſhall be accounted a Chriſtian upon any other terms now in this age, than the Lord Chrift did preach and publifh in the days of his flefh; for he did abfolutely deny that any man could be his difciple, without taking up a daily crofs, and without felf-denial : Now how fhould a man at this day be a Chriftian, or a difciple of Chrift, without taking up a daily crofs, and without felf-denial ?

It may be fome will tell you, that they are baptized into the Chriftian faith, and have been taught, and have made a profeffion of Chriftian principles, and affociated themfelves among thofe that make profeffion of Chrift; but here is not a word of a daily crofs in all this, nor of felf-denial; fo that they would have you to underftand in this, that the terms of Chriftianity are changed, and that men may be Chriftians without the terms of Chrift, or at leaft reputed fo.

And this hath been occafioned by the great apoftacy that hath been brought into the church by a long night of darknefs, and the revealing of Antichrift. Antichrift hath been difcovered and revealed, and hath fet up, in defpite of Chriftianity, a falfe Chriftianity; and there came in the terms of a man's being accepted, and being reputed a Chriftian upon Antichrift's terms: And if you will conform to do thus, and fay fo, you fhall be admitted into the Chriftian Society. Now all thefe terms of Antichrift, have been fuch things as an unregenerate man could conform to and comply with.

And the opening of this door, hath let into the church abundance of hypocrites and evil-doers, who were in too unregenerate a ftate to conform to thofe things that were required; for in the public fociety of Chriftians, it was not faid, you muft be regenerate, and take up a daily crofs, and deny yourfelves, and walk as becometh faints, and fo behave yourfelves that God may be glorified, and the profeffion of Chriftianity honoured by you. Thefe were the terms of old; but there are other terms of being Chriftians, which are of a later date.

Now this apoftacy hath prevailed and fpread over whole nations and countries, not a few, fo that whole kingdoms have become Chriftians upon thefe latter terms, and God is greatly difhonoured among us, and Chrift the Holy One moft horribly prophaned. It is not fo common among

Heathens

the true MARK *of a* CHRISTIAN.

Heathens and infidels, to find people wronging and deceiving one another, and killing and deſtroying one another; and yet it is the practice of many that are called Chriſtians: Theſe are the fruits and effects of thoſe latter times of Chriſtianity. Now ſeeing it is thus, which no mortal man can deny, I have this queſtion to ask, and I deſire that you would ſeriouſly weigh it in your hearts and ſouls, both while you are together, and when you are ſeparate one from another, whether it is not high time for all of us to return again to the firſt terms of Chriſtianity, and to reckon no man a Chriſtian, let him profeſs what he will, ſaving ſuch a one as doth know and witneſs, that the long-ſuffering, and patience, and goodneſs of God, doth lead him to repentance; and ſaving ſuch a one as hath ſo much faith towards God, that for love to God he will deny himſelf, and take up his croſs, and be a follower of Jeſus in that way and life he lived in.

It is high time for all of us to return again to the terms of Chriſtianity, that were ſet up by a higher authority than ever Antichriſt had, and before Antichriſt was revealed; for tho' it is true that Antichriſt hath obtained power on earth, to eſtabliſh his ſort of Chriſtianity, that is, without the croſs, and a ſort of religion whereby they indulge themſelves in whatſoever pleaſeth their carnal hearts, and corrupt minds; yet Antichriſt hath not all power, he is not Almighty; I hope neither Antichriſt, nor the beaſt, nor the dragon, nor the falſe prophet, nor the whore, have all power on earth, though they have a great deal, and by that power they have eſtabliſhed laws, decrees, canons, and innumerable things about religion; and ſome cry, this is the way you muſt walk in; others cry, the way to Heaven lies here, and here you muſt travel if you will come thither: Some cry, this is truth; others ſay, it is error: So that the world is divided; Antichriſt's government in the world is divided; and when *the houſe is divided againſt itſelf*, there is hopes that it will fall at laſt.

But there is one, to whom all power in Heaven and Earth is given and committed; and his Chriſtians are not divided among themſelves, but they are of one heart, and of one mind; and he that hath all power in Heaven and Earth committed to him, can crush and bruise that power that others have. *Herod* had some, and *Pilate* had some; but saith Christ, *your power is limited, this is your hour, and the power of darkness; and thou hadst not had power*, saith Christ to *Pilate, were it not given thee from above;* here is power given to the dragon, to the false prophet, and the beast, to speak great things; but this power of Antichrist is going away; Christ Jesus was sent into the world in his day, to bring people back again to God, and to primitive Christianity and obedience, and to the first terms of society and communion, and to a fellowship in Christ Jesus through the Holy Ghost.

Now if we had set up a way of religion, as other folks have done, which is contained in some canons, articles, doctrines, and such and such commandments of men; and if men will confess these articles, and observe these canons, they shall be of our society; then we should have done like the rest of the fallen Christians; but we have declared from the beginning, that professing our doctrine, and the principles of religion, doth not give any man fellowship and communion with us; but our communion is in the self-denying life, and a daily cross, in opposition to sensual lust, vanity, pride and bitterness of spirit, corruption, enmity and wrath; this hath brought us to a holy fellowship and communion in the Holy Ghost, and to live in unity from one head, which is Jesus Christ; so that there is not this man's church, and the other man's church among the people of God.

Do you read in the primitive times, that *Paul* had his church, and *Peter* his church, and *James* his church, and *Jude* his church? Indeed they had their meetings as we have now, in many cities and countries among the *Jews* and *Gentiles*; but these holy apostles that were the first publishers of the everlasting gospel, after their great Lord and Master, Jesus Christ, they never did appropriate any church to themselves, that was not their business; but our work and business, saith the apostle, is to gather you to Christ, and *present you as a chaste virgin to Christ*; our work is, to *turn you from darkness to light*, that you may

walk

the true MARK *of a* CHRISTIAN. 115

walk in it, and be the children of it; our work is, to build you up as a spiritual house, to be presented to Christ the Mediator.

This is primitive Christianity that hath its foundation in holiness and righteousness, sincerity and truth, not in words, and terms, and articles, and canons, and decrees, and other observances; this is not the foundation of true Christianity, nor will it ever be, the devil's kingdom must be destroyed, it is shaking, for he in whom we believe, hath power from his Father to break the devil's head, Antichrist and the dragon's head. Christ Jesus is signified by divers names, *the second* Adam, *Lord from Heaven, the Way, the Truth, and the Life,* but he is the same Christ; so Antichrist is expressed by several terms and names, but he is the same power of darkness, he hath made the nations drunk, to stagger and destroy, and devour one another.

This hath been done in the fallen state of Christians, and the design which the *Lord Christ* hath in sending his ministers and workmen to labour among you, is to restore men to the first Christianity, and to bring men to God; that religion is not made up of doctrines, articles, canons and decrees of men, but it hath the word of God for its foundation; *he that hath an ear to hear, let him hear:* There is some spirit, and power, and visible work in a true Christian, which the false Christian never had. The false Christians have taken the name and profession of Christ, and their fruits have been dishonourable to him; they might as well make profession of Antichrist and satan, they have a form of godliness, they have some of the word, but they deny the power. What is their religion and outward profession, when they want the internal life, and the motions of the Holy Spirit; if they bring forth the cursed fruits of the flesh, enmity, wrath, lust and corruption, which belong to the fallen nature and unregenerate state?

The apostle takes notice of this deceit and hypocrisy in religion, which was growing up before he died; *men having a form of godliness, and denying the power thereof, from such turn away.* If there be any brethren *that walk disorderly, have no company or fellowship with them,* if you would have the holy name of Jesus free from scandal.

This

This hath been the design of all the faithful ministers of Christ, to keep their holy profession of the name of Christ free from reproach; that the holiness of God's ways might be seen in the holy lives of the professors of them. Till men come to know this, and take up their daily cross, and exercise self-denial, their Christianity is good for nothing; I would not have you trust in it; neither in articles, tenets, or observations; but see how with your lives you answer your profession: Christ was *holy, harmless, undefiled, separate from sinners*. And why should not Christians be so too? How can Christians be followers of Christ, and not separate from sinners? Christ was so. He went one way, and sinners went another; they followed their sins and lusts, but he followed the work his heavenly father sent him about. If thou art a follower of Christ, thou art worthy of the name of a Christian. Do drunkards and swearers follow Christ? Do the wanton and proud follow him? Do the unclean and hypocrites follow him? you know they do not, why do you call them Christians? This is a reproach and shame to the holy name of Jesus, and to true Christianity, that any of these folks should be called Christians, but such as are followers of Christ, who are *holy, harmless and undefiled, and separate from sinners*.

This seems a strange kind of doctrine, yet if it had been preached in the primitive time, there were people that would have received it as apostolical doctrine, that a man should crucify the flesh with the affections and lusts: For saith the apostle, *mortify your members which are on earth; if you, through the spirit, do mortify the deeds of the body, ye shall live; but if ye live after the flesh, ye shall die. And to be carnally minded is death, but to be spiritually minded is life and peace*. This was sound doctrine then.

Now come and tell a man he shall certainly perish and come to damnation for all his profession, if he does not mortify the deeds of the flesh; if he lives in sin and dies in it, he is like to perish: How many have been hauled to gaols and dungeons, only for preaching this doctrine, and when we were first sent to preach, we durst not do otherwise? And God did not send us to preach till he had washed us, and sanctified us, and fitted us for the work of the ministry.

Now

the true MARK *of a* CHRISTIAN.   117

Now when we faw in the holy fcriptures, that God did work upon others by his Spirit, before he fent them to preach the gofpel, was not here fufficient authority given to preach the downfal of fin, and deftruction of it? One would think that fuch a one, thus called and fent of God, had as good authority to preach the everlafting gofpel, as the laws enacted by all the princes of the world could give him; a man fure that hath an authority for preaching the gofpel, would not need to wait for orders and approbation; he would not ftay for an induction. The apoftle Paul took it for a commiffion that was creditable, when he tells you of his miffion, *it was not by man, but by the will of God*, that he was called to preach the gofpel. If we fhould fay we were made preachers, if you ask by whom, not any man in the world can tell you; but we were made preachers many years ago: Not by man, or by the authority of man, but by the will of God. What was your commiffion? to turn men from darknefs (that darknefs we had formerly lived in) *to turn them from darknefs unto light, and from the power of Satan unto God*. The apoftle fums up his commiffion in a few words; the Lord told me *I muft turn men from darknefs to light*. This is our commiffion that we have received from God in this age, to turn men from darknefs.

But fome will fay, that we have not human learning and qualifications for the work of the miniftry: To this I anfwer, if I heard a man fwear or tell a lie, I could tell him that this was not of God, I have learning enough to know, and tell men that, and fay, whoring, drunkennefs, and fwearing, and lying, were works of the flefh, and fruits of the devil's power; I would have you turn from thefe works to the power of God. What is that power of God? I will tell you, it is a manifeftation of grace in your hearts, that will draw you away from the love of all thefe things; the grace of God, is the power of God to falvation to them that believe: *To as many as received Chrift, to them he gave power to become the fons of God; to fuch as believed in his name*. Such Chriftians will fhew forth the power and life of religion in their converfations: So that here is a fufficient authority, no want of authority.

I have been fometimes examined by what authority do
you

you preach? By the higheſt authority in Heaven and earth, by the authority of God that came by Chriſt, the Redeemer. What do you preach? Truth in the inward parts, grace and truth, and againſt all filthineſs of fleſh and ſpirit.

As long as Antichriſt hath a rule, you muſt not preach down ſin without authority; you muſt have power, you muſt be ordained, and have an induction before you undertake to preach the goſpel, and preach down ſin and wickedneſs: The devil hath got ſuch power and rule, that ſome tell us, that no man can live without ſin; if it pleaſe God here and there to raiſe a man and bring him to a holy and righteous life, this man wants a patent, a commiſſion, an induction, an ordinance to preach and cry down ſin in other folks; what commiſſion had the Pſalmiſt when he ſaid, *Come, all ye that fear the Lord, and I will tell you what he hath done for my ſoul*.

Is it not high time for people that have evidences of the love of God ſhed abroad upon their hearts by the Holy Ghoſt, to bear their teſtimony againſt ſin and wickedneſs? Is it not high time for every one's mouth to be open, to teſtify againſt ſuch a horrible miſt of darkneſs that is come over men; to teſtify againſt hypocriſy, uncleanneſs, and unrighteouſneſs?

It was the great deſign of the primitive preachers of the goſpel, to cry down that which ſome miniſters cry up, ſo that Chriſtianity is not like what it was, for then they told them that there was no happineſs but by breaking off *from ſin by repentance*. No poſſibility of ſalvation without confeſſing and forſaking ſin, and truſting in the mercy of God through Chriſt for the pardon of it. Tell them of the mercy of God, and the blood of Chriſt, they will tell you that they cannot be cleanſed from all ſin, they cannot live without ſin. How comes it to paſs that there are miniſters that preach an impoſſibility of living without ſin, when we are aſſured in the holy ſcriptures, that *without holineſs no man ſhall ever ſee the Lord?* And that *there ſhall in no wiſe enter into the kingdom of God, any thing that defileth, neither whatſoever worketh abomination, or maketh a lie?* Rev. xxi. 27. How comes this, that miniſters preach an impoſſibility of living without ſin? Will any of you, ſaith he, be ſo preſumptuous

the true MARK of a CHRISTIAN.

sumptuous as to say a man may live without sin? I will prove it from good authority, both from scripture and the fathers, that no man in the world can do it.

If any set themselves to it in their own strength, the devil will make fools of them; some indeed have gone about it in their own power and will, and have cloistered themselves up in monasteries, and shut themselves up between two walls, that they might be separated from all society, and live without sin; they would do it in their own power, and the devil is stronger than they.

Let me tell you, men of the greatest wisdom, courage and strength, of the most excellent natural parts that any man can have, are not able to grapple with their enemy the devil by their own power; there are seeds of sin, and lust, and concupiscence sown in all their hearts; so far this is right and sound doctrine, that no man can do any thing in his own power and strength. But here is the mistake; a man hath been a long time wrestling with his sins and lusts, to get the victory over them; but by woful experience he finds his weakness and insufficiency; he is sunk in his harness, and so hath given over the battle, saying, I shall never overcome the devil and his temptations, my sins and lusts are too hard for me, I despair of ever overcoming them in my own strength, by all that I can do; that is true enough, but must thou needs perish because thou canst never overcome thy corruptions? If ever I be saved, it must be the free grace of God, that must save me. How canst thou come to lay hold of the free grace of God? I am told I must lay hold on Christ by faith, who is the Mediator between God and man, and is my only Redeemer; there is no salvation in any other: This is very well; now thou art a believer, what dost thou expect, what dost thou hope that Christ will give thee? He will not give me power over my corruptions, so as to live without sin, that is more than I hope for; but I expect that Christ will reveal his power in me, and give me so much strength and power against my lusts and corruptions, that they may not have dominion over me: Now if you tell me that you hope for strength and power from Christ against sin, satan and corruption, do you now tell

me

me that it is still impossible? It was impossible before indeed to live without sin, when thou didst trust in thine own strength; but now, when thou comest to have grace and assistance from the Lord Jesus Christ, the *Son of God, and Saviour of the world*, that giveth thee ability to withstand temptation, and overcome thy corruptions, and the lusts of thy own heart, is it impossible still to live without sin? Then thou mayest say, the devil's slave I am and must be; for there is no other power in Heaven or earth for thee to lay hold of, if thine own power, nor Christ's power neither can do; then thou dost say, that the devil is Almighty. Thus they tell us, when Christ hath revealed his power, it is impossible still.

If I should call this antichristian doctrine, I could make it out. Blessed be God, I do believe that Christ is able to preserve me from the devil's temptations, and all his instruments, if I believe; though I could not do it in mine own power, yet by Christ's power I may be preserved an hour without sin: If so, then a day, and if one day, then a thousand days, if I live so long; Christ hath promised that he will *bruise Satan, and tread him under feet*, and destroy his works, and judge you whether sin be not the devil's work; shall I despond, or despair to have the devil's work destroyed in me?

Here is ground for you all to believe, he that hath faith may lay hold of this power which is offered of God; therefore lay hold of it, else your religion will be good for nothing. This is the enjoyment of a true believer, that he receives power from Christ to deny himself; therefore all their pretended Christianity and professions at the day of judgment, will melt away like snow. These canons, articles, forms, liturgies, these will melt away when the day of the Lord comes to burn upon them; none but they that feel the redeeming virtues of the blood of Christ, that have their souls filled with the love of God; and they that will part with whatsoever they love in the world, for Christ's sake, shall be accepted.

I am not for setting up this and the other sect or opinion; if it be among those of my own profession, if they profess holiness, and bring forth unrighteousness, it is all one; I
shall

shall not value their profession. There are many in this city and nation, that have sheltered themselves under the profession of truth, and talk of perfection, and have brought their lusts and imperfections with them: Here Antichrist is trying another game to bring them under a profession that will serve his turn; the devil will allow men profession, if they will live according to their own hearts lusts, so that they may save his head from the blow that God's power will bring upon it, so that they may dishonor the holy name and religion they make profession of; thus faith the apostle, *I have told you often, and now tell you weeping;* they were Christians, so called, to whom he spake, but *they were enemies to the cross of Christ*, not to the profession of Christ; he did not say they were strangers to the cross of Christ, but enemies to it; they let it fall, they kept the name, word and doctrine up, but they let the cross fall; how much were these Christians worth? sure but a little.

Nay, Antichrist hath been so silly, that because the words are so put upon the cross, no being disciples of Christ without the cross; the words of scripture are so put upon it. Thinks Antichrist, I shall never persuade the people to be at ease, unless I give them a cross; therefore he sets them a making crosses. They must be baptized with the cross; they say we deny not the cross of Christ, we hang it about our necks, we set it up in our meetings and academies, and many princes, and wise men, and learned men, have been so bewitched and drunk with delusions, that they have called this the Christ which they have made with their own hands; they have made Christs, and prayed to them; and all their religion hath been putting together crosses, crucifixes, forms and liturgies, which they have made with their own hands.

Here is Christianity in an empty profession, but where is the soul of it? I would enquire for the life of it, I would see Christianity living in love to God above all, and loving our neighbours as ourselves. When this Christianity comes, there will be no killing one another, nor persecuting one another, nor fulfilling the lusts of the flesh, nor pleading for it neither.

Blessed be God, that our eyes have seen the witnesses raised, raifed, and life from Heaven come into them; and now religion begins to have a life and foul, and fhews itfelf in a little remnant: There is a people raifed by God that feel life in their worfhip, in their families, in their converfations, and in their behaviour towards relations, they do what they do as to God. Many lads and laffes, men-fervants and women-fervants, they do their work and fervice, not barely to pleafe their mafter and miftrefs, but to pleafe God. *The life they live is by the faith of the Son of God*; they live as becomes the members of his body: Hufbands love their wives, not fimply becaufe they are their wives, as the men of the world do, but they do it upon the account of inward religion, and of the divine fellowfhip and communion they have in Chrift Jefus. Hufbands fhould love their wives as Chrift loved his church, and laid down his life for it; fo a man fhould love his wife, and be tender over her, and minifter to her.

The life of Chriftianity hath taught us to behave ourfelves fo as God may have glory, and Chriftianity be reftored to its ancient luftre and beauty that it had in former times.

But fome will fay, do as well as you can, men will never love you; if you have the foul of Chriftianity, you fhall be reviled and fcandalized. Men will make works againft you, and ftrow papers againft you, and fet the magiftrates againft you; live as well as you can, they will follow you and difturb you.

This is more than you know. If a man once comes to feel the life of Chriftianity working in him, and the power of it keeping him from doing evil, and wifhing evil to his enemies, and difpofing his mind to a frame of praying for them, inclining him to pity them; if a man comes to this ftate, he is at peace in himfelf, and enjoys tranquillity of mind; he looks up to the Mediator, Chrift Jefus, and feels an anfwer of peace in his own foul, and is come to reft in himfelf.

Now concerning perfecution, hatred and enmity, between the woman's feed and the ferpentine feed, and how long it will laft. God whom we ferve, did fay to the devil in Paradife, *I will put enmity between thee and the wo-*
man,

the true MARK *of a* CHRISTIAN. 123

man, and between thy seed and her seed; it shall bruise thy head, and thou shalt bruise his heel. So that it is not to be expected, that the seed of the serpent (those that are born of that seed) can love those that are born of the woman's seed. It is possible, that those that are born of the seed of the serpent, should be translated and brought out of that corrupt state; but it is impossible that those *that are born of the flesh, should love those that are born of the spirit,* while they continue in their unregenerate state, but persecute them. It is like a natural instinct, as for water to run downward, and fire to fly upward. Were not all men and women born children of wrath, and naturally enemies in their minds to Christ Jesus? And did he not die and suffer for them all? So that the very nature of the thing is the very reason why Christ died to redeem those that were his enemies to be his friends.

Suppose I, or any other to be a member of Christ, and men do persecute me, and revile me, and hate me, should I not love them, and do good unto them, when I see one infinitely better than either you or I, do it for us? *when we were enemies,* Christ *hath sent his Spirit into our hearts,* that we might become friends of him, and of him that sent him: This is the effect of the righteousness of Christ, and of his innocence, that enemies may become friends; thus have many been brought to a friendship of truth, that were enemies to it; if we could not suffer for the testimony we have received of God, what were it worth? But seeing God hath not only given us to believe, but to suffer for his name, many have been turned by this means from darkness to light, and many more will; the light breaks forth apace, notwithstanding there hath been so much ado to stop it.

It hath been the design of many learned men of this nation, how shall we stop these men's mouths that preach the doctrine of truth in the inward parts, the light within, and Christ within them? I will not repeat the many laws that have been made against them that will not preach lies, but the power of Christ and his truth; now what will you do? You cannot lay hand on them as you used to do; no, but we will reproach them with the tongue, we will render them odious to the government, as persons that wil overturn

turn church and state, and that preach false doctrine; and when all is done, and they have said their worst, people will still believe that sin and wickedness is hateful to God, that God takes no delight in sin, and that the devil will lead us to sin; he that keeps most from sin, keeps most out of the devil's clutches; and he that lives most holy, is most like to God.

These things we will preach, and we will go on in this testimony, that the best way that man can take, is to break off their sin by repentance, and turn to God, their Maker, with their whole hearts, and they will look to their ways, and search, and try and examine their hearts, and if they see evil, to keep out of it; this is such a thing, as there is no withstanding of it, it will go through this nation, and all the nations of the earth.

What if a company of people should combine together, and say, we will not have the sun to shine upon the city of *London*; what course must we take? When the sun is down, we will build a bank or high wall to intercept its light; but notwithstanding all their endeavours, when the sun riseth, it will get over their high banks and wall; so all their designs, and all the contrivances against the light of the gospel, and against Christ the Son of righteousness, and against the Spirit of Christ, the light will ascend and get over the heads of them all, and it will confound them, and break through all opposition.

I exhort you all, my friends, that laying aside all doctrines, and tenets, and contrivances among Christians, to come to this simple *thesis* and *position*; it is no matter what I profess of *religion*, if my life is not answerable to it, if there be not a love to God, and my neighbour, and to mine own soul; there is no life nor power in my profession of religion. I will rest satisfied in the measure of knowledge that God hath given me; I must not do to my neighbour what I would not have my neighbour do to me; I must be upright and sincere towards God; God will not accept of any worship from me, when I am unclean in body and in mind too; we must see that we be purified, for God will not accept of an offering from an unclean heart; *you cannot bring a clean thing out of an unclean,* saith our Lord Jesus Christ,

Chrift, the great preacher of truth and righteoufnefs; I muft *firft make the tree good, before the fruit will be fo*; you and I are thefe trees; till we have fomething good in ourfelves, we cannot bring forth good fruit.

Therefore you muft have refpect to the principle of fanctification in your own hearts, and turn to what you may feel an experience of in yourfelves, fome principle of grace and light in your hearts, that can diftinguifh between good thoughts and evil thoughts. Is this good for me to do? I will go on in it with faith and courage; but if it be evil, I will not touch it, though there be profit and pleafure to allure and draw me to it; I will not touch it, though I might gain the world by it.

Here is Chriftianity with life and foul in it; we have been fcandalized as if we preached up error for juftification: We fay there is no juftification without fanctification; fo you that know the power, live in it; and you that defire to know, turn your minds to the light and grace of God, and you will feel the power that will oppofe fin in its motion, and it will never trouble you in its act and workings. If I would not do ill to my neighbour, and I judge fuch a motion when it is fuggefted, it will never trouble my confcience, becaufe when the devil moved me to it, I rejected it, I would not follow him. It is no fin to be tempted; for our Saviour, that was perfectly holy, and free from all fin, was yet tempted; he had motions in his mind, but he withftood them, and refifted the devil in all his temptations; Chrift was tempted that he might be able to fuccour us when we are tempted; and he will do it for all thofe that wait for him.

Therefore, friends, truft in the name of the Lord, and you fhall feel the ftirrings of that power, that *hath called you out of darknefs into the marvellous light* of the fun of righteoufnefs wherein you live, and which will fhine to his immortal glory and praife, and the everlafting comfort of your immortal fouls.

SERMON

SERMON XI.

The SPIRIT of CHRIST the only true GUIDE.

Preached at GRACE-CHURCH-STREET, *October* 10, 1690.

YOU that are met together in the name of the Lord, and have your expectation from God, and are really waiting to receive a blessing from his bountiful hand; you are they to whom the Lord will communicate the good things of his kingdom, and instruct you in the divine knowledge which the wisdom of this world cannot find out; you shall have your portion in the blessings prepared for you, and laid up in Christ for you, to be handed forth to you from day to day for your support. And hereby you have been preserved and kept alive unto this day. You have received your nourishment, and divine and spiritual refreshment, always in the presence of God; when you have been out of his presence you have met with troubles, and darkness hath gendered upon your minds, and veiled and clouded your understandings, that you have been sometimes in danger to lose your way, until you have returned again unto the *great shepherd and overseer of your souls, by whom you have had access unto God.* You that have had these experiences, O let your hearts and souls be engaged to continue together in one heart and one mind, serving the Lord and waiting upon him for something that may do you good; that may strengthen and confirm you in the blessed truth.

For there are a great many that are convinced, that do yet want establishment: There are a great many that know the truth, yet cannot be brought to abide in it, but are sometimes drawn out of it, and then they meet with trouble in their minds, and *distress and anguish lay hold upon them*, and they do not enjoy that tranquillity and peace, and that inward joy which they believe others do enjoy at the same time; and which they might have enjoyed if they had abode stedfast in the truth. Now what is it that will establish such a one, but their waiting upon God

to

The SPIRIT *of* CHRIST *the only true* GUIDE. 127

to receive power from him to refift the temptations, and the manifold wiles and fnares of their foul's enemy, whereby they are daily in danger to be drawn away from God; drawn out of the way?

You know, friends, how the Lord brought us into this exercife of waiting upon him, by making us fenfible that there was none could help us but him. Teachers we have always had, and men that have fpoken of God, fpoken of his power, and fpoken of his wifdom; but how to dwell in that power, and ftand eftablifhed in it, fo as at all times to refift the power of the wicked one, is what no man can help us to; and upon this account it was, that the Lord's people were fain to cleave clofe to him, and by faith to have their dependence upon him; and cry in their fouls, Lord, unlefs thou eftablifh me, I fhall never be eftablifhed.

The confirming power that ftays and fettles their minds upon the Lord, it comes from him, it is handed to us through the Lord Jefus Chrift, whom we have believed in; they that kept their faith in him have had longings and breathings of foul, that they might receive fome divine bleffings by him, and through him. So that they that meet together in this mind, they find a fettlement in the truth, as it is manifefted and revealed in them, and goes down into the deep where unity is known, where they are of one mind, and the foul is made capable of putting forth ftrong cries to God, and living breathings and prayers to God, that he will teach them how they fhall profit, how they fhall grow, how they fhall ferve him, and honour him in their day; that he will reveal his power in them, to expel any darknefs or veil that hath been gathered upon their minds, that doth hinder them from beholding fo much glory and excellency in the truth, and in the ways of God, as fome they have beheld. And fo thefe are travellers that are travelling with the Lord in faith, to receive a bleffing at his hands. Their minds are not left to this, or that, or the other man, or to meer words or vifible things; but they feel the word of truth anfwering the truth in themfelves; and they receive a comfort and benefit, becaufe they find a bleffing to arife in them. Thefe words reach my

foul

soul; these administer help to me, and I am comforted in them, because I find those works working in me, or wrought in me.

For, alas! my friends, many of you know, that there are some who hear the word, and the declarations in the word are but sounds unto those who have no experience of the work that is signified by the word; many such people do hear the lovely sound, and they are affected many times to hear talk of the work of regeneration, and of the enjoyments of God's people, and how they are borne up in all their trials by an inward and divine power, and how they are always kept alive to God, and preserved in his living presence; but this doth not bear them up in a time of trial; but if a trial or an affliction comes, they sink under it, and they are filled with anguish and perplexity; so that the word barely heard spoken, and not rooted in the mind, doth not minister to the work; the words spoken do not carry that kind of operation upon them as to witness an inward work wrought upon them.

But where there is an effectual work and operation in the soul, it continues in its labour and travel from death to life. And as those heavenly things, those divine operations of God's power are spoken of, there is an *amen* in your souls, saying as far as you have travelled, thus hath God dealt with me, he hath indeed by his power carried some beyond my state and condition, and my faith is hereby strengthened, and my hope is confirmed. He that hath begun a good work so gloriously in my soul, will carry on his own work, and bring me to higher attainments, and further experiences that some of his servants bear witness of.

So that now being exercised, the work goes on, and *the pleasure of the Lord prospereth in Christians*, that when they meet together *in the name of the Lord*, they know for themselves that the Lord is present with them, they know what the word of the Lord is unto them; if they hear the word preached to another state and condition, yet they abide in and keep that which makes manifest to them in their own state: And this suffers not the soul to be carried away with the word, and sight and vision of a higher state than their faith can witness to; and they keep low, and humble

The SPIRIT of CHRIST the only true GUIDE.

ble and tender, and have a care of their own fouls; as the apoſtle when he was come to glorious and high attainments in the work of the Lord, yet he would not *glory of any thing*, but what the grace of God wrought in him: We do not boaſt of things that are not wrought in us.

It is poſſible for the creature to gather in, and comprehend the form of things, that they have not the work of in them; and a great many have done ſo to their great damage, and ſome, it is to be feared, to their utter ruin. They have comprehended high things, and the notions of great attainments; they have heard them declared and ſpoken of thus, and ſo ſome have in their ſpeculations declared to others their conceptions about thoſe things, yet thoſe things were never wrought in them; they could preach of humiliation, when the root of pride was not removed; they could preach of regeneration, and the *old man not put off*, and the *new man created in righteouſneſs not put on*. All this kind of preaching hath been in the world, and is ſtill too much in the world, but it hath not produced and brought forth any profit and advantage to the ſoul, either to preacher or hearer; for it hath not been accompanied with a divine and heavenly bleſſing; but the true miniſtry ordained of God brings forth a work of holineſs and righteouſneſs in the ſoul.

And therefore every one that God hath thus reached, and hath opened your underſtandings, and hath made you capable of comprehending and underſtanding divine things, take heed leſt by the ſubtlety of Satan, and the wiles of your great enemy, you be at any time lifted up, and exalted in your minds, in the notion of the things that you have not attained; not that you ſhould not ſo underſtand the things of God that God openeth to you, as they are many times opened to the creature, before the work of them is in the heart of the creature: And why ſo? why are they opened to me? It is for thy encouragement, that if thou doſt hold on, and be ſtedfaſt in waiting upon the Lord, theſe things God hath in ſtore for thee.

Now the creature waits, and ſaith, though I have not attained ſuch things as I have ſeen, yet the very ſight of them encourageth me to wait upon the Lord, that I may experience

rience the witness of them in myself: There are many that have some taste of great joy, and apprehensions of heavenly things, which they have not attained, but they know what they are waiting upon God for; not that they may have a little joy, which passeth through them, but come to have that joy and tranquillity which will accompany them in all their doings, and their whole conversation. God hath opened many things to you, and you have seen the way of righteousness which he hath cast up for you; and many have taken strait steps to themselves, till they have attained to say, *now my salvation is nearer than when I at first believed.* Let such go on and follow that guide by which they have been directed, and they shall at last attain to a further state, not only to know that their salvation is now nearer than when they at first believed, but that they may come through the Divine Spirit of grace that they followed, and so closely cleaved to, as their blessed guide in their way, to have an entrance administered to them abundantly into the salvation of God, whereby they may sit down, in the kingdom of God, with Abraham, Isaac and Jacob, and have a wall about them, which is the salvation of God.

Here is a great encouragement for sinners, and upright ones, *to follow on to know the Lord*, and then they are sure they shall know him, for they shall behold his glory, and their souls shall be satisfied, for nothing else will satisfy them.

People may have great openings, and great discoveries of things, and may have delight and joy in the opening of things, as it was with the disciples, when Christ our Lord conversed with them in the flesh; he opened many things to them, and they had great joy and comfort in those things which he opened to them, yet there was something wanting to suffice them. *Philip* said unto Christ, *Lord shew us the Father, and it sufficeth us*: *John* xiv. 8. There was something further to be discovered and revealed, so that they could not find their souls to be satisfied and sufficed, till they had it. Christ gave them such an answer as relates to that ministration that we are now under; *he that hath seen the Son, hath seen the Father.* Now they had seen Christ daily, and conversed with him,

and

The SPIRIT *of* CHRIST *the only true* GUIDE. 131
and had eat and drank with him in that flefhly and bodily appearance wherein he converfed with them; but they had not a fight of the Eternal Son of God in a fpiritual manner, as he was the Son of God, and their Saviour; they had not feen him fo. And he that hath feen Chrift in a fpiritual manner, hath feen the Father alfo.

So it is with us in our day. We have, in our profeffion, the teaching of this and that man. We have converfed with Chrift, as it were, to his flefhly appearance. We have read the hiftory of his birth, and of his life and great miracles, and of the great love he had to mankind, by which he laid down his life for them. We have been converfing with Chrift as to his flefhly manifeftation; but confider whether there doth not, till now, remain an empty place in our fouls, fomething that is not fufficed and fatisfied?

What would you have? Have you not fcripture? Read you not there of the birth, life, death, refurrection and afcenfion of Chrift? I would ftill have fomething more, for that will not fuffice me; I would have pardon of fin, and my peace with God, *and the light of his countenance lifted up upon me*, and further manifeftations of Chrift to my foul. We can never fee the glory of God, but in the face of Jefus Chrift. This is the difcovery that Chrift makes to the foul that believeth in him; this is that which gives fatisfaction.

A Chriftian's work is to be converfing with him, and exercifing his mind under the gathering and teaching of him, that can lead him to the Father. None but Chrift can do that, lead them to the Father, and fhew them the Father; and he hath in our day revealed himfelf, and made himfelf manifeft by his fpirit, that fpirit, by which we come to know his holy teaching, reproof and inftruction, daily difcovered in our fouls. The fpirit is our guide; that fpirit we are led by, and are to walk in. Let men go under what form and denomination they will, *they that have not the fpirit of Chrift, are none of his*, until they come to be guided by his fpirit.

People are not led into fin by the fpirit of Chrift; they will tell you thefe are the devil's temptations, and
the

the frailty of our nature, and the corruption of our hearts, by which we are led into sin; it is not the spirit of Christ. It would be a horrid thing for men to say that the spirit of Christ led them into sin; there are few or none so wicked as to say so. The business we are to do in the world is, to obey the will of God: And where the understandings of men are so illuminated, that they are satisfied in their minds, that God hath been pleased to give them a manifestation of the spirit to profit withal; all those that have this spirit of Christ, are directed by it to do the will of God, and to deny their own wills, and the will of others, that would draw them from their duty that they owe to God in their generation.

It is an excellent state and condition for a man to be guided by the spirit, and to be brought under the government of Christ, who is *the way, the truth, and the life.* So that they that come under this government, are directed and pointed out every day to do the will of God. This thou must do, and God will be pleased with thee; and this thou mayest not do, for if thou doest it, the Lord will be angry with thee; it is sin against God. So that we have a heavenly advantage of being taught of God by his spirit, to have the divine and heavenly teaching of the spirit of God revealed in us; if we are at a loss, or make a question, or dispute about a matter, the *spirit will lead us into all truth,* if we give up ourselves to his guidance and teaching.

This hath been our desire and labour many years, not to draw people to observe what we say; for who can direct another man in all things relating to the service of God? If we were ever so certain ourselves, we could not convey certainty and infallibility upon all occasions to another, if we should speak ever so much, and be ever so conversant with them. Therefore our work is, that all people, in all things relating to their souls, might have recourse continually to the infallible teacher and guide, which God, through Jesus Christ, hath made known to them. If people be ruled by this, they cannot but live in unity, and love one another; they will not fall into malice, contention, and hatred one against another. It is impossible for nations to make war, and deſtroy one another, if they would be guided by the unerring ſpirit of Chriſt; for how ſhould it contradict itſelf? For how can any thing agree with the ſtandard of truth, which Chriſt hath ſet up, that acts in contradiction to it? For nothing is truth but what concurs with it; therefore it muſt needs agree with itſelf. If we be directed by the ſpirit, we ſhall call that good which is really good; and that evil which is ſo. If there be thouſands directed by the ſpirit of Chriſt, which leads into all truth, that which is good to one, is ſo to all; and that which is evil to one, is ſo to all. We muſt firſt know what is good, and then receive power to do it. If we come to be inſtructed by the unerring ſpirit, *to know what is the good and acceptable will of God*, we ſhall receive daily power from him to do the will of God; we ſhall all ſpeak the ſame thing, and be of the ſame mind, and live in love and unity. There is no evil wilfully done againſt God, where the ſpirit of Chriſt, the goſpel ſpirit, comes to prevail upon us; it will bring us to a peaceableneſs of ſpirit, to live in love and unity. And the great work we have in the world, will be to do the good and acceptable will of God, both with reſpect to our ſolemn worſhip of God, and our duties towards our neighbours. Then there will be tranquillity, peace and joy, and comfort to all the churches of Chriſt that are under his government. And it is given to the ſons and daughters of men every where, when they come under the yoke of Chriſt, and take up a daily croſs, and live in ſelf-denial; this will bring peace and concord among them.

Many will come to our meetings, and ſpend a little time to hear what we ſay. We exhort them to give up themſelves to the peaceable government of the ſpirit of Chriſt, that *will finiſh tranſgreſſion, and make an end of ſin*, and bring into the ſoul (where ſin reigned) *everlaſting righteouſneſs*. Where there is a great deal of pride, malice and envy, the ſpirit of Chriſt will root it up; and all that evil that the enemy hath planted in men, he will pluck it up, and bring in *everlaſting righteouſneſs*, and plant love in the ſame ſoul, and eſtabliſh and ſettle it. Such a one will have more joy, pleaſure and delight, under

der the government of the fpirit of Chrift in one day, than any one can have that is governed by the evil fpirit in a thoufand days.

You fay *the manifeftation of the Spirit is given to every man to profit withal;* what profit fhall we get? How doth it appear, that the manifeftation of the Spirit is given to profit withal? Becaufe there is that life and grace ftirring in the heart that makes it profitable, and truth doth fo prevail, that it makes us do thofe things that are good and profitable, and to avoid thofe things that are reprovable. If thou wouldeft hearken to the fpirit, that is the reprover, that convinceth of fin, thou muft turn away thy mind from that which will lead into thofe things that are reproveable, otherwife thou wilt be under condemnation in thine own bofom.

When the Spirit of God illuminates men to fee fin, the evil of fin, he will give them power againft it; but when they come to receive power againft it, and ftedfaftnefs in the ways of God, what will be the effect of that? If I become righteous, and live a holy life, and my companions be wicked, they will mock me, and reproach me, what benefit fhall I have by being righteous? I fee evidently I fhall lofe many advantages which I might otherwife reap, and reach with mine own hand. I muft forfake my profits and pleafure, and other delights of this world.

The difciples faid to Chrift, *we have forfaken all, and followed thee;* what fhall we have? People before they would forfake all would have fomething in the room of it. Chrift tells them, *that he that hath forfaken all, father and mother, brother and fifter, and houfe and land, for his name fake, fhall have in this life an hundred fold, and in the world to come, eternal life.* What is the meaning of that, they fhall have in this life an hundred fold? Chrift that is truth itfelf, that cannot lie, hath promifed, that they that forfake all, fhall receive an hundred fold: Now people are ready to grafp at it; they think it is fomething that will anfwer the lofs of what they part withal; what thou receiveft in this promife, muft not be of the fame fort and kind with thofe things thou didft part withal; but when thou haft parted with all for Chrift's fake, and the gofpel,

thou

The SPIRIT *of* CHRIST *the only true* GUIDE.

thou shalt receive that which thou shalt acknowledge is an hundred fold better, and will make thee an hundred fold richer and happier, and it will give thee an hundred fold more than all that thou hast parted with could give thee.

If we part with sin, we part with that which brings bondage and fear of death; having parted with that, then thy fear and bondage is gone, and thou livest then the rest of thy life-time at liberty: But this is not all, thou livest in the enjoyment of the favour of God, thou shalt have the sense of his love, and the comfort of his Holy Spirit, and you shall live in peace and righteousness, and *treasure up to yourselves glory, honour, immortality, and eternal life;* whereas before you did *treasure up only wrath against the day of wrath, and the revelation of the righteous judgment of God;* thou shalt receive an hundred fold, that which is an hundred fold better. Those that part with the things that are reprovable, and do what Christ in his day performed, the good and acceptable will of God, the enjoyments that he hath in Christ, and the comfort, peace and tranquillity he enjoys, is an hundred fold better and more delightful than all the pleasures of sin, and the pleasures and delights of shows, and sights and plays, and comedies, which vain men entertain themselves with in their carnal state. A carnal man cannot understand and discern the things of God, and the pleasures that are to be had in his holy ways; he only looks *at the things that are seen, which are temporal, and not at the things that are not seen, which are eternal.*

But, my friends, those things which are unseen, are not so unseen, but that when a man hath an eye opened within him of the same nature with those things, he can see them: Blessed be God that we have an eye opened to see spiritual things, to see the heavenly treasure, and enjoy it in these earthen vessels.

For all that have an ear to hear, it would be a profitable change to part with all that is evil in the sight of God, and put themselves under the yoke of Christ, and receive a principle of grace which he will communicate to them, that they may do the good and acceptable will of God, and so may enjoy an hundred fold, and have comfort, peace, and joy before they go hence, and are no more seen.

You

You to whom God hath so graciously and mercifully appeared, that have an understanding, and a taste and feeling of those things which are divine and spiritual, *and which pertain to life and godliness;* of all the people in the world, you are an engaged people to serve the Lord; great obligations lie upon you, that you should abide and continue in that which God hath revealed and discovered to you; I mean grace: For you will never grow, till you be under the government of the grace of God, that grace that appeared to you before you came to the knowledge of God and his ways, that hath been with you in your travel from death to life, and from darkness to light. Prize it as a heavenly jewel, as that which contains in itself all those things that your soul stands in need of. If you have any strength to resist temptation, it is from the grace of God that you receive power to withstand temptations; if you have any living openings in your hearts, it comes to you from that grace that is in Christ. When this, and that, and the other prophecy of the prophets of old is opened to you, prophecying and foretelling that state and condition which you are travelling towards, how the Lord will subdue your enemies under you, you are encouraged hereby to go on cheerfully in your way, to that rest which you are travelling to.

There are many of those that believe the truth, who are not come to establishment; and they will find the reason and cause in themselves. Do but ask and enquire how it comes to pass, that such and such are established, and not subject to fear, and horror, and perplexity, as I am? a little thing will turn me over, and shake and unsettle my mind; this hath been the cause, want of keeping close to the grace of God in your conversation in the world. When you, and your children, and servants are governed by the grace of God in all you undertake, then the devil will endeavour to bring you into darkness, and bring discomposure upon your spirits; for the purpose of Christ Jesus, our Saviour, is to settle you; and the purpose of the destroyer is, to discompose and unsettle you, and to marry you to this and the other changing thing; if he can fix your hearts upon this and that object, then there is instability

upon

The SPIRIT of CHRIST the only true GUIDE. 137

upon the foul; take away that thing, and it brings difturbance upon you. If thou haft any object that thy mind is fet upon, thou wilt be much difturbed at the parting with it; but whofe fault is that? The truth manifefted unto thee from the beginning of thy converfion, did engage thee to feparate thyfelf from all vifible, fenfible things, that God might have thy heart and chief love. If he had been thy God, nothing could difquiet thee, when feparated from thee. If ye will have other Gods befides him, you will lofe your Gods; and when they are taken from you, you will be like *Micah*, and fay, *ye have taken away my Gods, and what have I more?* Judg. viii, 24. The reafon of your difcompofure, and anguifh, and forrow, was this; when you had fome other Gods befides the Lord, and your hearts did cleave to fome temporary thing, and the trial came that you had to part with it, you could not bear it.

If you would live a ferene life, a life of tranquillity, fet your minds upon nothing but upon the Lord, let him be the object of your fouls love; live in the light of his countenance, and you may always rejoice: Confider, as for temporals, you hold them of the Lord; God gives you this hufband, that wife, that child, that eftate, God hath entrufted you with it? but not fo, but he that hath it muft part with it, and be bereaved of it when God pleafeth. Now, if you give up your hearts to God, here will be your eftablifhment and fettlement, and you will have an *abundant entrance into the everlafting kingdom of our Lord and Saviour Jefus Chrift*. And would we feek to know and feel wherein the communion of the faints ftands; doth it not ftand in partaking together of the bread of life, which our father giveth us from Heaven? The father fpreads a table for us in the fight of our enemies, and we are fatisfied. They that come to partake of this table of the Lord, find ftrength and refrefhment; fo do I, and alfo my brethren and fifters that fit at the fame table. We are daily confirmed and ftrengthened by what we receive from God, and enjoy there; here is our heavenly fellowfhip and fociety; and where there is this root of love, love cannot be wanting in the branches: There muft be a departing from the bread of

S life,

life, before there can be any jarring and contention among the members of the same body, for we receive life from the same head, *from which all the body, by joints and bands, having nourishment ministered, are knit together, and encreafe with the encreafe of God, and are built upon the foundation of the apostles and prophets, Jesus Christ himself being the chief Corner-Stone, in whom all the building fitly framed together, groweth unto a Holy Temple in the Lord.*

Now that you may be all preserved in Christ, this is the end of our labour, that so every one that hath begun in the spirit, may go on in the spirit, and never look for perfection in the flesh: That you that have begun in humility, tenderness, and brokenness of heart, may in that meet together at times and seasons, and have daily the presence of God among you, and have the bread of life, which will nourish you to life everlasting, and that you may shew forth to the world, the glory, brightness, and excellency of that holy life, which in Christ Jesus is manifested to you.

SERMON XII.

PURE and SPIRITUAL WORSHIP.

Preached at DEVONSHIRE-HOUSE, *November 12, 1690.*

THE worship of God, of the Great God, is pure; he is a holy God, *of purer eyes than to behold iniquity*; and all they who will worship God, whose souls are breathing to have a return of a testimony in his sight, must offer up pure worship, and it must come from that which is pure: For that purpose, the greatness of the love of God is made manifest in Christ Jesus; and there is a diffusing of his grace and virtue in the hearts of the sons and daughters of men, whereby he hath laid a foundation for his own worship; because his worship must be pure. Therefore he hath freely given unto us, through his son, the knowledge of that pure principle of life and grace, from whence, and out of which, all true worship doth spring, and all true honour to God ariseth; and real obedience to his

holy

holy will springs forth out of that which is from himself.

And therefore all that will be worshippers of God aright, must first know and be sensible wherein the ability and capacity stands, that may enable them to do so great and so good a work. Some have conceived it to stand in their own will, and according to the working of their own will, they have framed worships, religions, and observations, thinking thereby to please God: But you know the apostle in a few short words, lays down a positive Christian doctrine, *without faith it is impossible to please God.*

Now this doth declare and signify, that there must be something upon which this faith must work, that must be the object and foundation of it: Faith as it worketh in the creature, worketh upon something; it lays hold on something in which there is a capacity of pleasing God. Now if *we are all by nature children of wrath*, and that no one of himself can please God, then there must be something that is supernatural, that must be the object of that faith by which men alone can please God; and this must be made manifest to the creature for its help, to be its director and supporter in that work that is too mighty for himself, too great a work for a man or woman, too deep, too profound for any man's abilities, power, wisdom, and acquirements, that he can attain to in this world, to worship God aright. To worship God, that is to perform a pure worship to a pure God; *who can bring a clean thing out of an unclean?* Now if we are all obliged to bring a clean worship, a pure worship to a pure and holy God, who hath created us and all things, where shall we have it? Not out of an unclean heart, not out of a defiled mind; there is no bringing it forth from thence, for that is the state and condition that men are fallen into by sin, in which their minds and consciences are defiled, their hearts are polluted, and their affections depraved and set upon wrong objects; and in this state none can serve God aright: That which is pure and holy must be first made known, revealed, discovered, and believed, before people can perform a right worship to God.

And therefore in vain is it, to go and drive people to this and that worship, and force people to this and that service
and

and conformity, upon the account of the worſhip of God. This is vain worſhip; when they have done all, it is not acceptable to God; the poor creature hath no return from the Lord, for God accepts no ſervice or worſhip, but only through his Son. And if ſo bé, men cannot pray and preach in the ſpirit of his ſon, and cannot preſent their complaints and ſupplication to God, but by the aſſiſtance and help of his bleſſed Spirit, there is no reaſon in religion why people ſhould expect a return and anſwer from God of the prayers they make. For it is the general doctrine of *Chriſtendom*, that Chriſt Jeſus is appointed of God for a Mediator between God and man, and all the acceptance we have, or deſire to have, muſt be through him: And therefore if we pray without him, and perform this and the other duty without him, it is contrary to the doctrine of Chriſtianity, to think that ever we ſhould have acceptance in God's ſight.

Therefore there is a neceſſity for every man and woman that deſires to be religious, that hath a religious mind, and is willing to worſhip God, and ſerve God aright, there is a neceſſity that they come to the knowledge of Chriſt, who tells us that he is *the way to the Father*. They that go any other way, go a wrong way; but they that go unto God by Chriſt, they do receive from him power to draw near to God; and through him they receive from God all thoſe bleſſings that their ſouls ſtand in need of.

So here would be an end of all religions the world is full of; of all the ſeveral worſhips that men have made. They have invented and found out ſeveral ways for people to worſhip and ſerve God. This and the other ceremony; this and the other obſervation and method of preaching and praying. If all this be without the aſſiſtance and divine help of the Mediator, through whom alone we can juſtly expect acceptance at God's hands, it is all good for nothing. Therefore the firſt leſſon of a Chriſtian in point of worſhip, is, that he come to the knowledge of Chriſt, by whom, and through whom, he may expect favour with God.

Now ſome people ſay, we are already come to the knowledge of Chriſt; we have read the relation in the goſpel of his conception, birth, life and death, reſurrection

tion and afcenfion. Now where this belief doth give a man this kind of Chriftian knowledge, it doth open a door and way for him into the prefence of God. This is a queftion that ought ferioufly to be confidered; for if we err in this queftion, we err in all: This is like ftumbling at the threfhold, and never coming into the houfe. If we miftake in laying hold of Chrift, we miftake in our worfhip, and in all matters that relate to life and falvation.

For if we muft have another fort of knowledge of Chrift, than we can have from the reports of others; if I muft have Chrift revealed in me before I can have the hope of glory; if I muft have the fpirit of Chrift in me, to help me to put up my requefts and fupplications, before he can prefent them to the Father, then all literal knowledge and faith cannot ftand men in any ftead; this is evident by the teftimony of all the writers of the New Teftament. Chrift and his apoftles did concurrently fignify, that the hope of a Chriftian, the power and ftrength of a Chriftian, all lies in this, that they had known the revelation of Chrift, and the powerful operation of the fpirit working in them; this was that which was well pleafing to God. Many fcriptures might be fpoken of, but you know the fcriptures, and can read them, and fee in them the concurrent teftimony of all holy men to this day, that the knowledge they had of Chrift was a divine knowledge, a fpiritual knowledge; it was a knowing him after the fpirit; it was a revelation of Chrift in them, that feparated and diftinguifhed them from reprobates; even the knowledge of God through Jefus Chrift their Lord. Why fhould not we come to this knowledge as well as they? The Lord is the fame, and his power is the fame, and his *arm is not fhortened*. We may fee as much need of divine affiftance, and divine love, as ever men did; we can perform no duty, either of prayer or preaching, without divine affiftance; not fo much as a figh or groan, that may have acceptance with God, without the help of his Spirit. *The Spirit helpeth our infirmities, for we know not what we fhould pray for as we ought, but the Spirit itfelf maketh interceffion for us with groanings which cannot be uttered:* Rom. viii, 26. If we go about the duty of

prayer

prayer without divine afliftance, we fee what fad work we make of it; if we pray not in the fpirit, and with the underftanding, how can we receive the thing we pray for? But if we *pray in the fpirit, and with the underftanding alfo*, then the *fpirit helps our infirmities*; the fpirit that came from God brings us the things we ftand in need of.

So that a Chriftian hath a foundation for his worfhip and Chriftian performance; what is that foundation? Nothing that is corrupt, if it be, it is good for nothing; for nothing that is corrupted and that defiles, can be acceptable and pleafing to God; we are all polluted and defiled by nature; how can carnal men worfhip a Spiritual God? Carnal men that are in death and darknefs, cannot worfhip that God that is light, and dwells in light, that is inacceffible, that is *of purer eyes than to behold iniquity*. Carnal men want a foundation for their worfhip, and will until they come to that foundation that God hath laid.

Now, that I may fpeak intelligibly what the Lord hath laid upon my heart, I would fay thus: There is an univerfal benefit and privilege diftributed and given freely of God, unto the fons and daughters of men, in their natural ftate, through his Son, Jefus Chrift, in that he hath caufed his light to fhine, and his grace to be extended to every man; *for the grace of God*, which bringeth falvation (for it is not by works) *hath appeared unto all men*, and bringeth light, by which every man may fee how to worfhip God; God hath enlightened every man, and this light comes by Chrift the Mediator; this Mediator is the way that men muft walk in, if they will come back again to God; for men are run out and departed from God; if men will draw near to God, and take fome foot-fteps towads the kingdom of God, from the kingdom of fin and fatan, they muft mind the way, the way muft be their director, they muft not go which way they lift.

This is that which was prophefied of Chrift; faith God, by the prophet *Ifaiah, I will give him for a leader*. I would fain return to God, and go out of the kingdom of fin and fatan, to the kingdom of God: God hath given Chrift to lead me; if
knew

knew what way he would lead me in, I would go that way. As foon as a man takes hold of Chrift, his grace, and fpirit, and life, he will be ready to fay, I am corrupt; my fenfes are corrupt, my mind is depraved, my confcience defiled and polluted; but I have found out fomething that God hath beftowed upon me, that is effential, holy and pure, that did never confent to my corruption, but is a witnefs for God againft it: Here now a Chriftian lays hold on Chrift, the leader; which way will he lead me? If thou layeft hold of this guide, he will lead thee out of evil, he will teach thee to ceafe to do evil, and fpeak evil: This light will lead thee to nothing that will difhonour God, or defile thine own foul: But this is not all, we muft not only ceafe to do evil, but we muft be doing fomething; there muft be a breaking off from pride, *foolifh jefting, evil communication*; but this is not all that he will lead me to; let us learn that leffon, *ceafe to do evil*. This doctrine was preached before Chriftianity was preached, as it is now preached; the prophets of old preached this doctrine to the *Jews* that were under an outward adminiftration, *ceafe to do evil, and learn to do well,* then I will plead with you, and difcourfe with you, faith the Lord: *Come now, let us reafon together, faith the Lord, though your fins be as fcarlet, they fhall be as white as fnow; though they be red like crimfon, they fhall be as wool.*

This is the firft leffon that a true Chriftian learns in his turning to God, in his change and tranflation, *to ceafe from that which is evil*: Here is a ceffation of rebellion, and here is fome hopes of being reconciled to God; a man hath been a rebel againft his Maker, but he hath now received help to refift thofe temptations that prevail over him: But there is no worfhipping yet, there is a forward mind in men to do fomething that is pleafing to God; but there are fome that are not troubled at all for their evil ways, and dread not God's anger, but make a mock at fin, that draw others to it, and make themfelves merry in it: And there is a fort fo far touched with a divine fenfe of God's love to them, that they have alfo a fenfe of his anger and indignation, becaufe of their fin; and they would be fain out of his anger; and who can blame them? When a man feels the

anger

anger of God burning like a fire in his bosom, who can blame that man if he desire peace with God ? If he be under a sense of the displeasure and indignation of the Almighty, he must not haste too soon out of that condition he is brought into; for this is God's purpose, and this is the fruit of all his troubles and afflictions, to take away sin : God hath no other end or design in the affliction that is upon him, than to take away sin; when God hath brought a people into a distressed and dejected state for their sin, the fruit that God expects, is the *taking away of their sin*, and he will hide pride from them, and humble them before him ; if this be the purpose of God, that he intends to purge and purify his people ; then saith the poor creature, if God design to purify me from sin, then I will pray to God to support me, and bear me up under his indignation : That is the cry of the soul that he may not be brought too soon from under the judgment of God, but may be supported and hid in the hollow of God's hand, until the time of remission and refreshing comes, that he may behold the light of God's countenance.

Here is encouragement for every one that is acquainted with this divine principle of grace, that will be led by it, and follow it so far as to be led out of evil ; then they will be fitted to do something in the work of God ; every sigh and groan that thou hast the assistance of the spirit of God to help thee in, is a part of worship : All thy brokenness of heart is part of worship ; hereby thou acknowledgest the great God, that he is able to help thee on in thy way, and to pardon thy iniquity, and blot out thy transgression, and give thee all those heavenly blessings that thy soul doth stand in need of. Then thy soul will bow down to God in acts of holy worship, and say, with a humble confidence and expectation, God will do all those things in me, and for me, that will promote my salvation. It is nothing in religion for people to go from praying and preaching to sinning ; but God must have a holy sacrifice, and that must come out of a pure heart. Now when a man is brought by the help of God, and by the divine assistance of the Mediator, Jesus Christ, to break off from his sin, then he stands fair to become a child of God,

and

and to be a servant of God, and to do something for God in his generation, and to offer to God praise and thanksgiving, and to perform all other duties that God shall lead him into.

But some will say, what, must not we do any thing? I have deeply weighed that question, what a poor man or woman must do, that is come out of bondage. There is a propensity in people to be doing, they would fain do something, they would be doing; they say, what shall I do? If I do something that pleases not God, I had better let it alone; and I can do nothing acceptable to God without divine assistance: Such a one that sees his own impotency and inability, will cast his care upon God, and will say, the Lord is able to lead me and guide me: I am ready to do thy will, O God! Make it clear to me that this is thy will, and that this is that which thou requirest; I am ready to do it, though it be a cross to mine own will: He is ready to go on in God's way, in the way of Christianity; such a one that hath the true knowledge of Christ, if he speaks, the Spirit of Christ speaks in him; if he prays, it is through the assistance of the Spirit of Christ, through whom God alone is appeased and reconciled, and through whom they may receive a blessing from God's hands: But for men to run on in their own wills, and to do a thing because they will do it, they had better sit still; this doing in their own wills, hath filled the world with a sort of Christians that want acceptance with God, which is to be had alone through the Lord Jesus Christ; and the want of the guidance of God's Holy Spirit, is the misery and downfal of Christianity in our days.

Therefore it is our work and business to build upon that foundation which God hath laid; no worship is pleasing to God, but that which ariseth from that spring that is pure and holy: If I cannot find that which will keep me from all pollution and defilement, if I cannot find that, I must stay till I can; to begin a worship and a religion without I know that it is acceptable to God, is but lost labour, and time spent in vain.

Therefore, friends, let every one that desires to be religious, turn their mind inward, wait for the gift of God, which is essentially pure, that never did consent to evil, that never mixed with the corruption of nature, but bears witness to the light, that will guide you and lead you, and conduct you first out of sin; then it will lead you into that worship and religion, and the performance of those things that are pleasing to God. They that are come thus to worship, they do not only know what the Lord requires of them, and when he requires it of them, but they are given up into the hands of God; they pray, preach, exhort, and live according to the will of God.

It is hard for people in a carnal state to believe this; but you that are believers, that are come to know the gift of God in yourselves, and the necessity of being ruled by him, you will believe us, for none else will believe us; let us preach to as many people and nations as we will, none will receive us as true ministers, but those that have the truth in their own hearts; if there be any that despiseth the grace of God in his own heart, he hates that which chides and reproves him; if there be such a man, he will hate me because I am a minister and a witness of the grace of God, and of that truth in the inward parts, which is the ground and foundation that man hath of acceptance with God. A wicked, carnal wretch will say, I hate such a one, I hate the light, that which checks me, and witnesseth against me; thou art such a one as bearest witness against me, therefore I hate thee: It is very true, it cannot be otherwise. Now our desire and labour is, that men may come to the love of the truth in themselves.

You know there are a great many other ministers, whose labour is to persuade people to believe what they say; to lay down a doctrine, and prove it by scripture and reason, and set it home upon their minds by such testimony as the scripture affords, and hereupon they prevail on the minds and judgments of people, to believe what they lay down.

It is easy to lay down a position, and prove it, and convince people that it must be according to scripture; but when a person is convinced of a principle of truth, he is not regenerated thereby, and come to God; therefore, though he cannot deny the doctrine of truth in words, yet he can deny it in works, and doth not rightly come
to

to love it. If people would believe what we say, and observe what argument, we bring to prove a position, they may be convinced of the doctrine of truth, and come to a profession of it, and yet be strangers to it, till they come to love it in themselves: If it were not for this, we would leave preaching, if God had not given a measure and manifestation of the spirit to every man to profit withal. You have it in yourselves, we are but as monitors to you, to put you in mind of it; you have so much business in the world, that you have not had leisure to take notice of it.

A man may have a rich jewel, and be poor notwithstanding, till he come to know the value of it.

A man hath a rich and precious jewel; a pearl bestowed upon him, that would make him rich in faith and love to God, and qualify him for the kingdom of God, and make him an heir of it; but he knows not, nor understands the value of it, and esteems it not; therefore God hath raised up ministers to put you in mind of it, that you may be happy forever, and live in blessedness to all eternity; *whosoever hath an ear to hear, let him hear*; and when they hear what we say, let them take the benefit of it to their own souls. We bring not truth to you, but God hath bestowed it upon you; you will be rich indeed, if you do as a man that bought a field where the precious pearl was, and digged till he found it. Come to the foundation upon which you should build all your hopes of happiness, and depend not upon your own works, or religious performances, for acceptance with God; for there is no acceptance with God, but only through Christ, we are only accepted of God through him. Those that will become Christians indeed, and worship God as he hath ordained and appointed himself to be worshipped, they must come to the principle of light and grace in their own hearts, which they have in, and through Christ, and they will find acceptance with God.

SERMON

SERMON XIII.

The DIVINE LIFE of CHRIST JESUS.

Preached at GRACE-CHURCH-STREET, *March 16, 1691.*

THE bleſſed life of Chriſt is not of this world; and it ought to be your care in all your religious aſſemblies, that you be gathered into the inward, feeling ſenſe, of this divine life; that you may feel your fellowſhip and communion in that life of Chriſt that is not of this world. And may all of you lay hold upon it; for this is the nouriſhment and the heavenly bread, with which *the children of the kingdom are fed and nouriſhed from day to day;* there are many that feed upon words, that are not the children of the kingdom of God; but the begotten of God are come to know the virtue of the divine life, Chriſt Jeſus; their feeding and their nouriſhment is by every word that proceedeth out of the mouth of God, and they grow up to life eternal by that divine and heavenly gift, that God the Father hath beſtowed upon them, through his Son Jeſus Chriſt; and they enjoy the communion of ſaints, through this divine Head of the Church, that communicates of his life and virtue through every member, by which they are ſanctified, and every day more and more prepared for that living and eternal inheritance laid up for the children of God.

And when there are a people that are thus gathered into the life of the Lord Jeſus Chriſt, they are able to draw nigh to God; they feel the power of entrance, becauſe their ſin is removed that did formerly lie at the door; and the way is opened and conſecrated for them to draw nigh and partake of the table of the Lord, by which they grow ſtronger and ſtronger in his might and power, and are thereby enabled to perform the whole will of God, and that divine worſhip and religious ſervice, which God requireth at their hands in their day.

For it is very certain, and we have found it by experience, that the words of our Lord to his diſciples of old

are

are true; *without me* (faith he) *ye can do nothing.* For though people may meet together, and may pretend and set up a form of worship, and of religion in their own wills, yet it all amounts to nothing, with respect to acceptance with the Lord; there is no return in their souls, no addition of life, nor encrease and growth of life; they are not nearer the kingdom than when they first believed, but many times further off; by leaning upon a formality, and not really entering into the work of God, nor travelling out of death into life; for there must be a path, and a travelling in it; the soul must have an exercise thro' the power and life of Jesus, for the overcoming of death, that did separate from God, and a preparing for life, that life that unites us to God again: And when people are in earnest in this travel, they are resigned up to the government, direction and leading of him that is gone before, that hath made a way for us, and will further our progress towards the kingdom of God.

And, therefore, my friends, you know the way, and know how the power hath reached to you, and hath opened your understandings that you may be faithful to that power in your own souls, and may have the use and true improvement of this, and all other such meetings as this, for the gathering of your minds out of all visible and changeable objects, unto that life which God hath revealed, that so in the exercise of it, you may hold your fellowship with God, and with one another; here is the bond of perfection, here is that in which God hath created peace and rest, and joy for his people; so far as every one is partaker of this innocent life, and feels himself changed into it, they are gathered into the church, and they are gathered into fellowship with the head of it, and are comforted in their membership, in their partaking together.

Though I be but a little one, yet I partake of the same virtue which the Lord administered to the greatest saints, while I am a waiting upon him, and of the same divine consolation, and operation, and power that weaneth more and more from the world, and that which is corruptible, and raiseth up in me daily more and more fervent desires after that bread that perisheth not.

Now

The DIVINE LIFE of CHRIST JESUS.

Now herein men and women have an evidence of that Chriftianity in themfelves, the *Spirit of God bearing* record and *witnefs with their Spirits*, which all the loofe profeffors of Chriftianity in the world are ftrangers to, their evidence in themfelves, being againft them; they feek to have evidence without them, and to gather up fome kind of marks and tokens, and fayings, and fentences, from without them, to make them believe that they are in covenant with God, and that they are in a ftate of falvation by Chrift; but he that truly believeth, hath an evidence of his Chriftianity, and of his reconciliation with God; and he hath this evidence in himfelf, a divine, fpiritual teftimony that anfwereth to his own fpirit, that witneffeth to him, that he is one of the children of God.

And my friends, to this you are called, whether you are come to it or no; it is this you are called to with a heavenly call, that you might no longer live in the rudiments of the world, to be feeking and looking here and there, for a ground of peace and of reft; a ground of hope, but may know and feel the fame thing, the fame ground of eternal hope that the faints of old had; what is that? what reafon did they give and render of their hopes of eternal glory? The apoftle tells you plainly the ground or reafon of their hope of being glorified in the world to come, was *Chrift in* them *the hope of glory.* They witneffed that Chrift gave his life for the world. Take the glorious teftimony that the apoftle did bear in one of his epiftles; faith he, *the life was manifefted in me;* it was not covered up or hidden, that people could not find it; God was pleafed to bring it to *light by the gofpel;* when a thing is brought to light, you may fee it. This he affirmed in his day, and the fame is affirmed in our day. The life is manifefted; what life? Not the life of this world, but a life not defiled, not polluted, but the life that is of God, a heavenly life that is holy and pure; that life is manifefted; we have feen it, and we exhort all to lay hold of it, to lay hold of eternal life: Some had a fight of it, that had not laid hold of it; they faw it in a vifion, and they might fay poffibly, oh that I could live fuch a life, that there were no fin in me, in my words, or thoughts, or actions, what a gracious life would
that

that be! They had seen that life, they had tasted of it, but they did not lay hold of it, but let it go by them: Take heed of that, when you have seen it with open eyes. *Bleſſed are your eyes, for they have seen, and your ears, for they have heard,* faith Chriſt to his diſciples: They ſaw that life that was holy, harmleſs and undefiled. Lay hold on this life, eſpecially when you are thus aſſembled together, in a ſolemn manner in the preſence of the Lord, waiting to behold it, and ſee it more and more diſcovered to you, and labour to have that gathering power that will bring you to it, that you may know the ſtrength that comes by it to the ſoul.

There is none of you, but what will meet with temptations in this world, that will draw you into death and darkneſs, to things *that are carnal, and ſenſual, and deviliſh* ſometimes. How ſhall I ſtand if I be not centered in that life that was before the world began, and before the devil was? If I labour to feel the influence of that divine power, that is able to keep me, my faith tells me ſo: I know that power is able to keep me, if I keep in the exerciſe of it. The truſt of a true believer is, that whatſoever temptations and trials they are exerciſed with, they know one already come, *in whom they have truſted, who is both able and willing to deliver them.* So by this means he is kept harmleſs, and innocent, and blameleſs in his life and converſation. Thus you might be kept, if you would regard, and have reſpect to the life that is manifeſted in you.

Whoſoever comes to know, and feel and witneſs in their ſouls the diſcovery and revelation of the life of Jeſus, they know there is in it a certain dominion over that which is contrary to it; and you have many of you had experience of the exerciſe of the power of God in your own hearts, that hath enabled you to reign over thoſe things, that have formerly ruled over you: That you can now ſubdue vain thoughts, and evil deſires, that you can withſtand temptations that come from without, and from within. Now if you could do this, and if ever you have done it, you did it by that power that God diſcovered and revealed in you from Jeſus Chriſt: You had not ſuch hold of this once, before you believed, but by believing, the word of God ſent it unto you; it being fixed by faith in the heart,

that

that faith which is of the operation of God: You could then do that which you could not do before, and forbear that which you was led away by. Thefe experiences which God hath given you, fhould encourage you to hold on in your labour and travel, and engage you *to grow in the grace of God, and in the knowledge of our Lord Jefus Chrift.* Whatfoever is propounded by men in the profeffion of religion, this ought to be our defign and end, in the difcovery that is made to us of the life of Chrift; that we may grow in it, and live in it; (indeed there is great talking of it) but we fhould labour to fhew forth the refurrection of that life in us.

They that come to be baptized for the dead, are baptized into the death of Chrift; the apoftle tells you, *in that he died, he died unto fin.* There are none baptized for the dead, and made partakers of the death of Chrift, but thofe that died unto fin, as he died. Though Chrift had no fin, yet he died unto fin: What ufe did he make of this, that Chrift knew no fin, but yet did take our fin upon him? *He died unto fin, that they which did partake of his death, might be partakers of his refurrection:* He liveth again, and after death rifeth again.

Thofe that partake of this death unto fin, are crucified unto this world, and have taken up Chrift's crofs, and are dead to all the pleafures and delights of this world, which are withered away and come to nothing. What do they live to now? To righteoufnefs, holinefs, chaftity, temperance; thefe are pleafant to them; thefe come to live to righteoufnefs, through the power of him that loved them. This fhews the glory and the power of the grace of God. It is the grace of God that worketh fuch a change in a man or woman. They that delight in fin and wickednefs, in that which is corrupt and ungodly, they have no delight in this, no delight in fobriety, chaftity, holinefs, and purity of mind. In whom hath it wrought fuch a change? In all that are freely given up to it. Where any one is given up to that life, the grace of God hath the praife of it. This is the exaltation and praife of the power of God; fo that others may find by this, that they may by it come to believe, and by beliving, to be faved.

Thus

Thus the gospel hath gone forth, from one to many, and from these to many more, and is encreasing more and more; for grace, mercy and peace, are multiplied, by which the heritage of God, and so every man and woman that partake of this life, are gathered into fellowship.

So that your end in coming to these meetings, is not so much to hear what this, and that, and the other friend saith; but what you have in yourselves to witness to: The divine operations of the power of God in your souls, bringing down something that is to be brought down, and raising up something that is to be raised. Temptation to sin hath more prevalency upon me, than it hath upon this, and that, and the other man. I am not come to their degree, yet it is better with me than it was at my first convincement. If thou dost say this and deceive others, cry to God, and pray earnestly that all may be brought down which is contrary to his grace. If thou sayest and professest this, to strengthen that, which is known, by the light of Christ, to be against the truth of God, if at the same time there is a deceitful heart, how will this appear at the great day of God? The eye of God is upon thy hypocrisy; he that *never slumbers nor sleeps*, he beholds thee, if there be any sin that thou wouldest keep and save alive. If thou makest a profession, and notwithstanding sayest, this sin I will keep, *the Lord pardon me in this thing*; like *Naaman*, the servant of the king of *Assyria*, who said to the prophet, *thy servant henceforth will neither offer burnt offering, nor sacrifice to other Gods, but unto the Lord. In this the Lord pardon thy servant, that when my master goes into the house of* Rimmon *to worship there, and he leaneth on my hand, and I bow myself in the house of* Rimmon; *when I bow myself in the house of* Rimmon, *the Lord pardon thy servant in this thing.* He knew if he bowed not, the king would take notice of the alteration of his gesture, therefore he would bow in the house of *Rimmon*: That sin he would save alive under a profession: That hypocrisy the Lord did abominate.

Be upright in the sight of God, and be faithful to your own souls; if it be so, then every sin will be a burthen, and you will long to be rid of it; if it be so, you know whose hand it is that hath brought you so far; if you be really cordial, and give up yourselves to Jesus, that *work which he hath begun in you, he will finish for you.* He will finish it for you, stand out with him in nothing; give up yourselves to him, and join not with his enemies; take heed of hearkening to them; take heed of every sin that will at last be a burthen and oppression to your souls.

But if you live this heavenly life of Jesus, you will be set at liberty, to have dominion over sin, and to stand without guilt before the throne of God. Friends, let your hearts be deeply affected with the great mercies that God hath bestowed upon you, and for his gift to you of that divine life that *is acceptable in his sight.*

Many things have been done upon the account of religion, and we could never be satisfied whether they were acceptable to God; we could not be satisfied whether we did any thing pleasing to God: We may say of them as the apostle *Paul* did of the *Jewish* sacrifices, *there remains a conscience of sin,* an accusing conscience, that tells us, that guilt is not removed, nor the sin taken away, till the Lord opens this divine mystery to us, that our justification must be by faith in Jesus; that nothing could reconcile us to God but the life of Jesus, and the merit of his death.

This life of Jesus was a holy, blameless, harmless, and innocent life, which *life he gave for the world ;* which *life is the light of men ;* and our souls being turned to this life, we see the glory and the excellency of it, and desires are kindled in our hearts after it. Many have pursued, and laboured, and travelled, that they might come to the enjoyment of it. The very discovery of this life ought to be highly prized, and your souls affected with it; and when you have obtained it, you will say, O! what a blessed condition am I come into! that Christ hath manifested his divine power in me, not only in *reconciling me to God,* but taking away the conscience of sin; by that alone the accuser is cast out, and I may now sing to God, songs of deliverance. Now you taste of the mercies that God hath bestowed upon you; this will affect your souls with a child-

like

The DIVINE LIFE *of* CHRIST JESUS. 155

like submission and subjection to him, that hath begun to save and deliver you, that so you may resign up yourselves to his will, and forsake the world, and the things of it.

Now when these come to such a meeting as this, their minds may be retired, and they may be sensible of the power of truth upon their hearts; but for want of keeping their subjection to the divine power, that hath opened their understandings, when they come into the world again, they are ensnared and entangled, and many times, for want of watchfulness, through a looseness of mind, and unruliness of tongue, they run into anger and passion, and this grieves the Holy Spirit of God. And how should you come to God through the Mediator, when you grieve his Spirit, and quench the motions of it.

These things have been hurtful to many, that in their time might have been pillars in the house of God. Take heed of this, and let the goodness of God dwell upon your minds, that you may feel and experience the inward administrations of it; there are many that are much affected with the outward ministry, and are very desirous to hear the servants of God declare the things that God hath wrought for them, and in them, and the wonderful things that God hath opened to them; yet when you have heard all that man can say about it, if the divine ministry of the word of God doth not make powerful impressions upon you, and sanctify and renew your souls, the outward ministry of the word will do you no good.

Now that you may be established in the truth that you have been taught, this testimony ariseth in me, to desire every one to heed and attend to the manifestation of this life of Jesus in yourselves. Whatsoever God hath bestowed upon me or another, you may perish for all that, and I am not the better for what God hath bestowed upon you, but may perish notwithstanding; but that God hath manifested eternal life to my soul, let that be every ones centre: This will make you holy and blameless, and preserve you in every state, and in the hour of temptation, and in the midst of snares; this will be a bulwark to you; this will be as the walls of Zion, which is the salvation of the Lord. That so you may be preserved sensible of

the

the goodness of the Lord: That grace, mercy, and peace may be multiplied in your bosoms; this will make you dear and affectionate one to another.

Though there may be an external fellowship among those that preach and profess the same doctrine, yet when they come off from that, when once men depart from the power of truth, they grow stubborn and rebellious; but when men come to be gathered into the inward fellowship that stands not in terms and words, but in the revelation of Christ, and in the participation of his virtue and goodness; the more you are united in this, the more you are knit one to another, and become useful and helpful one to another.

The Lord vouchsafe to every one of you a taste of his goodness, and you will prefer it above all that the devil has, and his instruments can present; and if you retire more into this heavenly and divine life of Jesus, you will feel and enjoy more peace and satisfaction, and true consolation in your souls, than I, or any man in the world can tell you of.

SERMON XIV.

The KINGDOM of GOD within.

Preached at GRACE-CHURCH-STREET, July 26, 1691.

YOU have read and heard much concerning the day of the Lord, as a great and notable day; many of you are now living witnesses that the great and notable day of the Lord is coming, in which the accomplishment of great and notable things, the mighty works of God, which have been prophesied of, may be lawfully expected. It is the work of every Christian to wait upon the Lord in the light of this day, and to be acquainted with the works of the Lord, both inwardly and outwardly; for the day of the Lord is a day of power, and that power of God worketh wonderful things; and if we are not kept in the light of that day, the Lord may work great things, and we not know

The KINGDOM of GOD within.

know it; we shall be looked upon as careless and negligent witnesses of the works of the Lord, as those that do not regard them. If you would be faithful witnesses, you must have regard to the works of the Lord, and the operations of his hands. One that is minded to be a faithful witness, he will take notice of what is said and done; you are called to be witnesses of the works of the Lord Jesus Christ, and of his doings; you must stand where you may hear, and see, and understand what the Lord is about to do at this time.

In testimony and witness bearing, the greatest thing we have to expect in this day of the Lord, is, that God will set up the kingdom of his Son Christ Jesus; and unto this all the prophets did bear witness in their time, and now it is our turn to bear witness of it, by sensible and living experiences of the accomplishment of those things that they prophesied of, that the Lord will set up the kingdom of Christ, and bring down and lay waste the kingdom of Antichrist. This our Saviour taught his disciples to pray for, more than sixteen hundred years ago, that the kingdom of God might come; and all the true disciples of Christ ever since have prayed for the coming of this kingdom, and many of them have seen the coming of it, and rejoiced; and others have died in the faith of it, and have been gathered into the kingdom of Heaven.

But, my friends, that which chiefly concerns us at this day, is to behold the kingdom of Christ, the eternal Son of God, within us, to go forward and prosper; and the kingdom of Antichrist suppressed and destroyed, and utterly laid waste; and this is wrought two ways, first, inwardly; second, outwardly.

First, inwardly; there is a great inclination in the minds of people, to look more at the operation of God's power in this great work outwardly, than to look at it inwardly, but unto that there must be a daily cross taken up, and it is my business at this time to tell you in the name of the Lord, that your duty and mine is to turn our minds to the working of the power of God in ourselves, and to see that other kingdom of the man of sin weakened and brought down within us; then there is no fear but he will carry on his work outwardly, and we shall see as much

of

The KINGDOM *of* GOD *within.*

of that work as belongs to our generation; but the great matter and chief government of you and me, is to see the kingdom of God set up within us, which stands in holiness and righteousness: Our business is to walk till we see the righteousness of this kingdom set up within us, in our hearts and souls, and to have a real change made.

We all know, and we must confess, that we have been subject to the man of sin, whatsoever we are now. We have seen the reign and government, the rage and tyranny of the wicked one, that hath led us into rebellion and disobedience to the Lord our Maker. How do we like that government, to be ruled by the devil, and to be led captive, and to be made to do his will, and to rebel against God that gave us our life, and breath, and being? How do we like the government of satan? I hope we do none of us like it. It was so with me; and they that are under the tyrannical government of satan, have many cries and wishes in their souls, that they were freed and delivered from it, and brought under the government and obedience of Christ Jesus; and that they were able to serve God as they ought to do, that they might be translated from the kingdom of sin and satan, into the kingdom of the blessed and dearly beloved Son of God.

This hath been the cry of some ever since they have known the word; and I am persuaded it is the cry of many at this day. I have good news to bring you; not that the day of your redemption draws nigh, but that it is come; the day of redemption is now come, and there are a great many blessing and glorifying the name of God that they are redeemed, and delivered from the bondage of corruption; and have more joy and delight in the service of God, that made them, than ever they had in the service of the God of this world.

But may not some say, how shall this great work be wrought? For it is a great work, and we verily think that nothing but an Almighty Power can effect it. For there are many in this assembly have been trying to no purpose, and done what they could in their own strength, to deliver their own souls from death, and yet they find themselves in bondage still; nay, they have called in the

help

help and affiftance of thofe that they thought to be ftronger than themfelves, and all have failed, and they are yet weak and entangled, and they cannot find themfelves at liberty to ferve the Lord as they ought to do.

I am of this mind, that nothing but the Almighty Power of God can do it; and when you have come to my experience, to know this as I have done, then I hope you will feek after that, and you will fee good reafon for it; and you will then come to this profeffion, if the Lord puts not forth his Almighty Power, I muft then perifh, for there is no other power can deliver me. When you come to know this, what muft you do? Why you muft wait for the revelation of that power that will take you off from all truft and confidence that you have ever had in any thing elfe: A man that hath nothing to truft to but the Almighty Power, and mercy, and goodnefs of God, he puts his whole truft and confidence therein, or elfe he knows he muft perifh.

When a man or woman comes to this pafs, that they have nothing to rely upon but the Lord, then they will meet together to wait upon the Lord: And this was the firft ground or motive of our fetting up meetings; and I would to God that this was the ufe that every one would make of them that come to them, then they would be juftly and properly ufed, according to the end of the inftitution of them at firft; we fhould ufe them as poor defolate helplefs people that are broken off from all their own confidence and truft, and have nothing to rely upon but the mercy and goodnefs of God; and if he pleafeth to reveal his power among us, we know that he is able to fave us. And when we have met with the revelation of God's power, and we have met together in fimplicity of mind, the Lord was pleafed to communicate his Spirit to us, and open a door for us, and difcover and reveal to us that it was the day of his power: And when we came to examine ourfelves whether we were willing in this day of God's power (for the prophet gives us a note of diftinction between the people of God, and other people; *thy people fhall be willing in the day of thy power;* which is as much as to fay, when God difcovers and

reveals

reveals his power to them, such a people are willing to give themselves over to the government of it; when we found we were subject to it, we had joy in believing, before we attained the end of our hope; it was gladness to us we found ourselves willing; and I am persuaded that every one of you would be glad to find yourselves willing to part with that which you cry out against.

What a cry is there of our bondage and corruption, and of our being led captive by our lusts. We may hear such a cry from one end of the kindgom to the other: People cry out of the bondage of corruption, and of their subjection to sin and satan: I would they were in earnest; there is not that earnestness and reality in men and women that God looks for, and so there comes nothing of it. There is no redemption, and no deliverance; the Lord doth not hear them, though they come now a-days into his presence, to offer up their prayers. I would have you to be in good earnest, I wish well to you all; and it would be hard to say that you do not wish well to yourselves. Here lies your welfare, that you find yourselves willing to be subject to the power that made you; you have been subject doubtless to the power that destroyed you; that power that never gave you life and breath, and would be instrumental of your destruction: The power of the God of this world never did men good, but destroyed them, deceived them, and deprived them of their lives.

Now if there was but a willingness in every one of us, freely to give up ourselves to that power that created us, to obey his will, I am sure there is never a man or woman among us should long be without the knowledge of it. If I am but willing to be subject to the law of him that made me, it will not be long before he discover it to me, and reveal his power in me in the glory and excellency of it; that power which is more able to preserve me, than all the power of men on earth, or all the power of the devils in hell is able to destroy me. When the Lord shall discover and reveal his power in you, you will be willing to be subject to it.

But methinks the sound and noise of flesh and blood grows loud here: I would be subject to God, but I would
not

not have him cross mine interest, and deprive me of that I love and thirst after; I would not have him imbitter my carnal delights and pleasures, and undo me as to my reputation in the world.

You may see whence this comes, that you would make a bargain, and draw a contract with the God of your lives about these things; this is a nonsensical thing; because of all people in the world, you are a people that have had a veneration for the holy scriptures, the scriptures of truth, and have been acquainted with them as familiarly as with any book in the world, wherein you find articles drawn, long ago fixed and sealed; and no new ones are to be drawn. If any one will be my disciple, *John* or *Thomas*, *James* or *Peter*, or whosoever he be, he must take up his daily cross, and deny himself, and follow me. Now here is a contract made, therefore turn aside from all kind of reasoning and consulting with flesh and blood.

If you will become spiritual, and partake of spiritual blessings and benefits, I would advise you to turn from all kind of reasonings that come from the pit of darkness, that hath thus far deceived you, and will ruin you forever, if you hearken to them. For assure yourselves, new gospel-terms no man can make; and if any come to preach new gospel-terms, count him a deceiver; for there is no possibility of being a disciple of Christ, but by taking up a daily cross, and denying ourselves, and following him as our leader and guide. To him I must go, and go in no other way, speaking nothing, and doing nothing but what is holy and pure; he must conduct me in my walking, guide me in my way, and justify me in it. This is to be a true disciple of Christ.

As soon as he comes to adhere, and join to the power of God revealed in his soul, he sees the coming of the kingdom of God; he sees it at a distance; he saith within himself, and makes this conclusion, I will follow my captain; I will become subject to the kingdom of Christ. If I obey this divine principle of the grace of God, and the gospel of Christ, I shall be his disciple. I read in his blessed book, *that as many as are led by the Spirit of God, are the children of God.* I am not to propose new terms,

terms, but to accept of the old terms of the gofpel of Chrift. I fee that the kingdom of God is to be fet up, and the kingdom of the devil to be brought down in me; if I follow this divine principle, I fhall never follow the devil more; if he would have me lye, I fhall refufe, and fay I cannot; if he would have me run into vain and corrupt communication, and foolifh jefting, that will be a bridle to me, that I cannot do it.

I fpeak now to perfons that live under the light of the gofpel of Chrift, and that are fubdued by his grace; I would fpeak that which all the logic in the world cannot overthrow; that which the moft cunning logician, with all his wit and quirks, cannot refute and prove erroneous. If a man be led by the Spirit of God, he cannot lye; this is a common cure for all men; if I be led by the Spirit of Truth, and hearken to the principle of truth in my own foul, this will cure and heal me of the wounds and maladies of my corrupt nature, and fet me at liberty from my old mafter; I do not like his fervice.

I hope if any of you like the fervitude and bondage of fin and fatan, you will defire liberty before you die: Why do not you defire it now? It may be thou thinkeft to enjoy a little liberty, and reputation, and pleafure in fin for many years, for fix or feven, nine or ten years, and then break off from it, and repent and turn to God: How doft thou know that thou haft ten days to live? It is of high concernment to every one of us to wait for a difcovery of gofpel liberty, and an ability and power in his foul, to enable him to break off from the fervitude and bondage of fin and fatan, that he hath fo long lived under; and to wait upon God with patience, for the fetting his foul at liberty, and fetting up the kingdom of Chrift within him, and pulling down the kingdom of fatan, that he may be brought into the kingdom of Chrift, that confifts in *peace and righteoufnefs, and joy in the Holy Ghoft*. Thefe are the things that follow one another; when righteoufnefs is fet up in me, I fhall not be difturbed, I fhall have peace; and if I have peace I fhall have joy, and this joy is in the Holy Ghoft; the apoftle faith the kingdom of God confifts in thefe things.

Now

Now that every one might be perfuaded that God hath given a meafure of his grace to them, as well as to other folks, let them confider and fay within themfelves, God hath not fhut me out of the number of his people: He hath knocked at the door of my heart, to bring me to repentance; he hath waited upon me fo long, furely he hath a mind to fave me: Would he call upon me, had he not intended I fhould repent and turn to him?

But where is the power? you will fay; knocking at the door of the heart, and checks of confcience, we underftand them; but we underftand not where the power is, to be conformable to the will of God.

People will never underftand it while they are in the kingdom of fatan, and under the power of the prince of darknefs; the apoftle tells us, *that the God of this world hath blinded the minds of them that believe not, left the light of the glorious gofpel of Chrift, who is the image of God, fhould fhine upon them.* If men faw the beauty of the gofpel, they would run after it, and embrace it; therefore the devil blinds their minds, that they fhould not fee the beauty and amiablenefs of the gofpel, and like the terms of it: He hath the rule and government of the children of difobedience. So long as I live in fubjection to that devilifh, hellifh power, which leads me forth into fin, I fhall be a ftranger to God's power, that would enable me to break off from it.

You never read in fcripture of any that ever came to be faved by the power of God, but there was faith mixed with it, that came to join with that power of God. Our Saviour faid to the impotent man, *thy faith hath made thee whole*; thy faith joining with that power of God: *We fhall be made ftrong in the Lord, and in the power of his might,* and be able to withftand temptations.

As foon as the foul of man joins with the grace of God, he doth forfake the fervice of his old mafter and governor: Sin fhall no longer have dominion over him; though he may meet with the fame temptation, it fhall not have the fame power over him, but he will be enabled by the grace of God to withftand it, and overcome it. If you ask fuch a man, how it is that he overcomes that temptation that formerly

prevailed

prevailed over him, he will tell you, I have now an helper, I am now joined to the grace of God in my foul, therefore do I withstand temptations, and have power over them. Thus comes the kingdom of Christ to be set up in the foul, and this is that which will fit and prepare us for the everlasting kingdom of God. They that do wait upon God, shall see this work wrought inwardly in them, they know more by faith than they can see by sense.

I know, and am certain, that the power the devil hath in the world, shall be broken down, and righteousness shall be exalted, and justice and equity shall prevail in the nations. I shall not perhaps live to see it, but I may see it by faith; I have seen enough for my generation, and they that live in the next generation, shall see it also; for the church of God is the same from one generation to another. Now unto us it is given to see the things that in former generations were prophesied of, God having (faith the apostle) *provided some better thing for us, that they without us shall not be made perfect.*

The church of God from one generation to another, have their measure and degree of service, and bear their proper testimony, and leave the rest to succeeding generations: It concerns us in our generation to see a change made inwardly in our souls, and the kingdom of Christ set up within us, and the kingdom of satan brought down in ourselves. This doth not concern my son or grandson only, but it concerns me, and when they grow up to mature age, in their time it will concern them: Therefore that which is most profitable to us, is, that we have such a station, and stand in such a place in our time, where we may see the work of God carried on.

I have considered, many a time, that there are many brave men and women in this age, that might have been eminent witnesses of God in this world, and borne their testimony to his truth, but their faith hath been weak and ineffectual: They have discovered their unbelieving hearts, and have joined with the common herd of the world, because they thought such great things could never be done, that the kingdom of satan could never be pulled down and destroyed, and the kingdom of Christ set up within us,

but

but I would hope better things of you, things that accompany falvation; and that he that hath begun a good work in you, will carry it on to perfection; that living praifes, and joyful thankfgivings, may be rendered to him who alone is worthy, who is God over all, bleffed forever; to whom be glory and dominion forever, and ever. *Amen.*

SERMON XV.

The UNDEFILED WAY *to* ETERNAL REST.

Preached at DEVONSHIRE-HOUSE, *July* 29, 1691.

My Friends,

THE Lord will be with all his people, that are undefiled in the way, that are fpiritual travellers walking in that undefiled way, that leads to an undefiled reft. There are fome that by this way are entered into reft, that reft which God hath prepared for them. We cannot apply to ourfelves that promife that is made to us of *entering into reft*, unlefs we be real and true travellers in the way that leads to it, for if we do, *we deceive our own fouls.*

Therefore you that have had a fight and vifion of the way everlafting, that leads unto a holy reft, you are an engaged people to make ftrait fteps therein, and to have it your daily care, and make it your continual bufinefs, to look that your goings and foot-fteps are of the fame nature and kind that the reft is that you defire to enter into: For it is an undefiled reft, that we all are, or ought to be travelling after; therefore every one of us muft be undefiled in the way, and every foot-ftep muft be of the fame kind and nature, and feparate from all that which defileth it and polluteth it; that fo it may have a tendency to the bringing of the foul nearer to its reft.

This holy reft many travellers have attained by this holy travel, and many are ftill in hope to attain it.

But now they that are full of hope of attaining this reft, their foot-fteps and goings are not of the fame nature and
kind;

kind; they are not holy and pure, they are not undefiled: Thefe have not their faces truly *Zion*-ward, though the face of their profeffion may ftand that way; but the Lord looks at the heart of every one, and he knows which way the heart ftands; they who have their hearts truly turned to the Lord, they have the mark of holinefs in their eye, and the mark of purity and righteoufnefs in all their undertakings, becaufe they know there is no attaining to that divine reft, but by a holy way and travel; therefore their truft and reliance is alone on the Lord, that is to keep them in all their way; for if they be ever fo clearly convinced that holinefs and righteoufnefs is their duty, and is the way whereby they may attain to the kingdom of God, though they are ever fo fully convinced of it, yet there lies an impoffibility of any walking therein without the divine affiftance of the grace of God; for though they have been convinced by the appearance of his grace, and have had a light that openeth to them a fight of thefe things, it is not this fight and vifion that will enable them *to run the race that is fet before them.*

For the manifold impurities and hindrances which are in our way, between our coming out of Egypt's land, the bondage of corruption, and our entering into the kingdom of God, are too mighty and too great for any man with his knowledge and ftrength to overcome. The children of *Ifrael* might as well have gone through the Red Sea, without the help of God, as the Chriftian traveller can go through the many difficulties, and the many impediments that he is to meet with in his way, without the affiftance of God's Holy Spirit.

My friends, it hath been a labour and travel at this time upon my mind, that all whom God hath fo fignally bleffed with the knowledge of the truth, that you may fee your way, and moft clearly know and underftand, that your way leads to life eternal; that all and every one of you in your particular meetings, are to have a dependence upon that which can help you in your way.

For I have feen too many that have had a wrong dependence, after they were rightly convinced, and after they have had a true knowledge of their way wherein they fhould walk; they have too much trufted to openings and fights
which

which they have received; they have thought their mountain so sure, and that their *feet have been past sliding*, that there hath grown up a state of presumption, that they have thought they should never turn aside, and have not had due regard to the renewing of the Divine Power of God in their souls, that God's children always must have. They have (as I may so say) forgotten what our Lord said, *without me ye can do nothing:* They have passed a sentence upon that doctrine in their minds, and they have thought they could do something; that they could withstand temptation; that they could do some work for God, and service to God, without the Divine Assistance of that power that did beget them; and alas! the least they have sustained hath been, that they have run into evil, and they have defiled their way, and run into temptations, though it hath pleased the Lord, whose mercy is infinite, to pull them many times back again out of the snare which they were fallen into, and to take them again, and to wash them, and cleanse them, and purify them, and set their feet on a sure place. This was more than they deserved; but his mercy, and goodness, and tenderness, is over all his works.

This he hath wrought for many a one; and not only once, but many times; it is hard venturing; it had been better if such a one had never fallen, or that their footsteps had never slid from the ways of the Lord, than after *they are fallen, to be renewed again by repentance.* It hath caused sore judgment, and condemnation, and anxiety of spirit; and they have given their old enemy an advantage to whisper in their ears; thou hast lost thy ground; thy sins are gone over thy head, and thou shalt never find repentance. These are the words of the wicked one, who seeks occasion against us; and through our carelesness, and not being watchful, we put an advantage into his hands. Now seeing you know he is vigilant, and seeks occasion that he may turn you out of your way, before you attain to the end of it, you ought to be vigilant to keep occasions from him.

But some may say, how may I keep occasions and advantages from the enemy? I answer, the way hath been often told you, and I dare say most of you have tried it,

and

and found it to be true, that so long as you have remained in a watchful state and posture, and have had your minds exercised by the grace of God, by which you were convinced of your sin, and by which your duty was manifested to you, so long you gave the enemy of your souls no occasion; but the truth preserved you wherein you trusted, and wherein you hoped and waited for the virtue and power of it. Did you find want of ability then? Did the enemy prevail then? He did not cease to tempt when you was in the most watchful state of a Christian; the devil did not then cease to tempt you, but you found in you a power that resisted him, and said, *get thee behind me, satan.*

So long as you are upon your watch; so far as you keep your mind fixed upon the Divine Power, so long you are in a sure place; and whosoever turns aside from this, they suffer great harm and prejudice; and if ever they be restored again, it is with loss and damage, and sore exercise; and if they be not restored, they are lost to all eternity: *Then it had been better for them not to have known the way of righteousness, than after they have known it, to turn from the holy commandment delivered to them.* And then they said within themselves, this must be the way.

Sirs, these things pertain to your everlasting welfare; I speak to you as a people that God hath abundantly loved; and it hath been far beyond any thing of desert. He hath made known his ways to you; the Lord may say, concerning you of this city, as of old, *what could I have done more for my vineyard, that I have not done?* So he may say concerning you, what could I have done more to make them a grown people, a holy people, an entire people, that *they may bear my name, and walk before me in holiness and righteousness, all the days of their lives?* What should have been done more for them?

But this is an exercise to us, whom God hath blessed, and set as watchmen, to behold and see the state of his people, and to feel and bear the burdens that are to be borne; and this is a great burden, that after all that God hath done, and that we do in the hands of God, all that is necessary for the welfare of the people, there are some
that

that turn aſide, and defile their way; and we teſtify in the name of the Lord, that whoſoever walks in a defiled way, ſhall never come to an undefiled reſt; therefore that you do not attain to that undefiled reſt, it is becauſe ye have been defiled: Seeing the holy converſation of the people of God is the effect of the working of his own power and Spirit.

Here comes the reſt, by and through a Mediator, even Jeſus Chriſt the righteous, who is the Mediator between God and man, and the leader of all his people in the way of holineſs and righteouſneſs, which he hath made manifeſt to them that believe and obey the power: And *he hath purchaſed eternal ſalvation for all that believe and obey the goſpel*: But the tranſgreſſors do not obey the goſpel; the Spirit of Chriſt doth not lead you to tranſgreſſion; and the power and light that comes from Chriſt, doth not lead you to pride, vanity, envy and bitterneſs: Wherever theſe things are led into, there is another ſpirit, and that other ſpirit hath another tendency, it leads into the wrath of God.

And my friends, this is that which my ſoul deſireth at your hands, and it is for your good and advantage; it is my duty to diſcharge my conſcience, and to ſpeak plainly as the Lord ſhall give me utterance, to warn you that you abide in the truth; for if ſo be you be not ſaved, but will turn aſide after your own hearts luſts, after your pride and the vanity of the world, and the luſts thereof, you may blame yourſelves, and your *iniquity will be your ruin*. We that have given up ourſelves to God for your ſakes, and the churches ſake, we ſpeak theſe things which we have learned of God, and we earneſtly preſs you that are convinced, that you walk in the truth which you have believed: There is no great need of more knowledge, and of the viſion of heavenly and divine things; for abundance of you have ſeen more of the things of God, than ever you have travelled and come up into. I would to God, that every one of you that are convinced, would come up *to the meaſure of the knowledge you have received.* O! that you would anſwer the Lord's power, in opening and diſcovering his mind and will concerning your travel, and the things that belong to his everlaſting peace, that your foot-ſteps may be directed thereby. If you will walk in this undefiled way, you may lay down at night, and rife in the morning with peace, and in the favour of the Lord, and have the anfwer of a good confcience in his fight.

The means that muft help and conduct us in this way, muft be that familiar converfe that the foul muft have with fomething greater than itfelf; the familiar converfe that the foul muft have with the Divine Power, with that manifeftation of Divine Light and Grace, which, through Jefus Chrift, God hath given unto you. For if a man prize and efteem the truth ever fo much, and fuffer ever fo much for it, and love the minifter ever fo much, if he keep not a familiar converfe with the truth, notwithstanding all his profeffion of love to the truths of the gofpel, and the preachers of it, he will reproach it: Though he profeffes and fays, I love thee, I love thee; though he hath fuffered much in the way, yet if he love not the truth in his own heart, and defire not to feel the excellency and virtue of it, that man will certainly difhonour the truth, and grieve the Holy Spirit of God.

We warn you to take heed of your way, and to your feet in your Chriftian walk, that you may come to have an *abundant entrance into the kingdom of God.* Pray to God that the work of regeneration may be wrought upon you, that you may be born into another feed, and partake of the divine nature: Then, though the devil affault you, he cannot overcome you; he will find nothing in you whereby to betray you into his hands, when that change is wrought, and when God hath made an alteration, and hath brought you out of the love of the world, and the love of earthly things, *and fet your affections above, where Chrift fits at the right hand of God.* Now you can fay, here comes a temptation with this inftrument, and the other inftrument, and the devil lays things before me that he would have me to do, but I have no inclination to it, I have no mind to be fucking at the world's breafts; but my mind is fet upon this, that I may reach acquaintance with God, *who will be a prefent help to me, and tread down Satan under my feet.*

There is need of your continual care and vigilancy, and
that

that you watch and pray that you may not enter into temptation. It is not so easy a thing for a man or woman while they are in this world to do any thing without sin; but God hath called you to a holy profession; which is, that you should do all you can do, to do every thing you do without sin: *For whether you eat or drink, or whatsoever you do, you should do all to the glory of God.* This spirit we would have in you, and we would have all you *that have received Christ Jesus, the Lord, to walk in him as you have received him*: Then you shall be kept undefiled in the way, and delivered from temptation.

To this end you must be still, waiting upon the Lord, that you may have acquaintance with him from day to day; you are in the world, but you should not be of the world: The prayer of our Lord Jesus Christ, to his heavenly Father for his disciples, was not that he should *take them out of the world, but keep them from the evil.*

Merchants, tradesmen, and shop-keepers, have always something to do in the world, but they should pray earnestly that they may *be kept from the evil of the world.* There is nothing can be done in the world, but there is evil in it, which we shall be overcome by, if we do not keep our watch. In the government of a family, there are occasions and provocations given to be passionate and furious; many occasions are given to men and women; but we should not be transported and overcome: Our profession obliges us, that when a child or a servant gives a provocation, we are not to behave ourselves unseemly, and unbecoming our holy profession; for it is not in their power, nor in the devil's power either, to kindle your wrath and anger into a flame: If you are upon your watch, and wait upon the Lord, he will give you wisdom and strength to stand against all temptations whatsoever, and *to order your conversation according to the will of God, and as becomes the gospel of our Lord Jesus Christ.*

In merchandize, buying and selling, there are snares, and there is evil we may run into; but this is our comfort and joy, there is no coercion, we cannot be forced to sin, the devil can only lay a temptation before me; if thou wilt tell a lye, equivocate, dissemble, here is an advantage
for

for thee; but the devil with all his subtilty, power and allurements, cannot say, thou shalt run into this sin, and be overcome by this temptation; for though of ourselves we can do nothing, yet in the name and strength of our Lord Jesus Christ, *we can do all things*; we can do that which is just, and stand over the temptation, and trample upon it, and *not be overcome of evil, but overcome evil with god*. When we have bought and sold, we may look back upon what we have done with pure minds, and clean consciences in the sight of God, and we may come off victors, and *more than conquerors* (over temptations) *through Jesus Christ that hath loved us.*

The more a Christian keeps himself unspotted, and the more watchful he is in his walking, he may go on from day to day, and see the snares of the devil, that lies in this vanity, and this and the other vanity and temptation, and yet escape it.

I would I could say of some of you, that when the devil laid a snare for you, you did not run into it when you saw it. I have known some that have had understanding enough, that they need not be told where the snare of the devil lies; yet so hath it been, the devil and their own hearts lusts have agreed together, and they have run into the snare. This is from the old confederacy that men have had with God's enemies; *you are my friends*, faith Christ, *if you do whatsoever I command you.* If you are the friends of Christ, you will be his subjects, and yield obedience to him; when he shews them a snare they will keep out of it: This is the proof of a true Christian, that he will be true in a time of trial, and will trust in that divine power that keeps him out of the snare.

One thing more I would say, that divine fellowship that you have with Christ Jesus, it consists in holiness of life and conversation, and the exercise of a good conscience towards God, and towards man. It is in vain to tell me that you will walk in unity with the truth, unless you have unity with the truth in your own hearts; you cannot deceive the Lord, nor long deceive his people either. Here is the fellowship that you are to live in all your days, to live in fellowship with the people of God, and communion of saints; can the saints have communion in any thing but holiness? and holiness is a blessed, sacred thing, *it becomes the house of God forever;* they that are saints, are sanctified and made holy; and *he that sanctifieth, and they that are sanctified, are all of one; for which cause, he is not ashamed to call them brethren,* Heb. ii. 11. They that are sanctified are become saints, they bring forth the fruits of holiness and sanctification, and they are come into fellowship with God and one other. *Every branch in me,* saith Christ, *that beareth not fruit, he taketh away; but every branch that beareth fruit, he purgeth it, that it may bring forth more fruit.* That branch which beareth not fruit, is cast into the fire and burned.

There are some that bring forth fruit, but it is fruit to the flesh, and the wicked one, but I hope you are not of that number: These separate themselves from the life of the true vine; these have no fellowship nor true membership with the church of Christ, while they walk as captives to the devil, and sin; these are of the world, and not of the church. If you would have fellowship with the church, do not think to have it by outward conformity: Do not think that this will maintain your fellowship with Christ, without a life of inward holiness and righteousness; for that day you break with the truth in yourselves, you break off your fellowship with the church of God, and break your peace with God, and can no way be restored again to the favour of God, but by an unfeigned repentance; *for the mystery of faith* is to be kept in a pure *conscience:* How is my conscience defiled, if I wrong not this, or the other man or woman? Some can hold the mystery of faith; so far as it consists in a profession, they can profess it, and they preach it; but they have not held the mystery of faith in Christ, so as to receive life, and virtue, and comfort from him. You have got the history of words and doctrines; but as soon as you defile your conscience, by doing evil things, and depart from the principle of grace, you make shipwreck of faith.

But, my friends, as you have a mind to continue and abide in the faith, and in this travel and heavenly journey,

I would give you this as a certainty, it may do you good when my head lies low: The way to continue in the church of God, and communion of faints, and to retain your peace with God, is to keep a familiar converfe with the truth in your own fouls, and it will keep you from falling, and lead and guide you in your way, in your travel and journey to Heaven. As the mother, when the child cries after her, but cannot go, takes it by the hand and leads it, fo if you keep clofe to the truth, it can lead you through all difficulties, through great bufinefs as well as little, and deliver you from fnares and temptations, and when you are affaulted, it can bring you off clear. As for communion with God, and communion with the faints and people of God, it ftands in that peace, and purity, and keeping a holy frame of mind in your heavenly travel, in the undefiled way, that will at laft bring you to the undefiled everlafting *reft that remains to the people of God.*

SERMON XVI.

The DAWNING *of the* DAY *of* GRACE *and* SALVATION.

Preached at GRACE-CHURCH-STREET, *Auguft* 2, *1691.*

My Friends,

YOU cannot but know and be fenfible, that a gofpel-day, a day of grace and falvation, hath dawned upon you, and that the light of it hath broken through many clouds of darknefs, which fometimes you could not fee through. This is an ineftimable and unfpeakable mercy of God unto us, that the light of the gofpel of falvation fhineth upon a people, that without it muft be miferable.

There hath been a very dark and cloudy day upon our fore-fathers, and alfo upon us, in the days of our ignorance. We are apt to wander hither and thither, and to

be

of GRACE *and* SALVATION. 175

be turned afide with the wind of mens' doctrine, that we could not find a reft, a home or a fettlement for our fouls, in order to eternal life. And there are many that have cried unto God, that he would pleafe to reveal his way, and to make it known unto them; and they have been apt to covenant with the Lord, that if once they come to a certainty, they would walk in it. Unto fuch as thefe the Lord hath bowed his ear, and hath anfwered them; and in his anfwering the cry of the foul, he hath brought falvation near, and hath revealed the power by which he would bring it to pafs, in every particular foul that receiveth the gofpel of his Son.

But now friends, you that are fenfible of this bleffed and glorious vifitation of his gofpel-day, in which *falvation is brought near*, it is needful for every one to examine their own hearts, whether they have really received the gofpel; whether they have received and embraced the great bounty, and unfpeakable bleffings of the gofpel, with which the Lord God of life hath vifited us, or whether they have rejected it. For though it is our happinefs to know the vifitation of life, yet it doth not follow that every one that is vifited will be made an heir of it; for *there are many that fall fhort through their unbelief*. There are many that have received the gofpel, who do difobey the gofpel of Chrift, and fo have not eternal life by it.

When people come to this ferious examination of themfelves herein, then the light and grace, that comes from Chrift unto every one of us, both to him that rejects it, as well as to him that receiveth it, that will make known to them their ftate and condition, with refpect to the gofpel of Chrift. For there are a great many, that by an alienation of their minds from the light of Chrift Jefus, are apt to be miftaken in their ftate, and to make a better judgment of themfelves, and of their ftate inwardly, than really it will amount to in the day that the Lord fearcheth and trieth them. But they that make a judgment of themfelves, by the openings and difcoveries that they have through the light of Chrift Jefus (for fo we are to do in this weighty matter) they make a judgment of their ftate and condition, according to the evidence that the Spirit

of

of God bears to their spirits; and this I hope you will all say is a most certain way. For if we go to compare ourselves one with another, and say, I am better than thee, and that man is better than I, here we are liable and subject to a great many errors, where there ought to be none. But if we come to measure and determine our present state and condition, by the evidence of the Spirit of God, bearing witness with our spirits, here we have a foundation to place an infallible and certain judgment upon. And they that are obedient to the gospel of Christ, are capable of giving a sound judgment of their state, because they are made partakers, through Christ, of that grace, and light, and truth, which they should be obedient to; and they are brought into a kind of knowledge and understanding of their duty, whether they do it or no. And this knowledge, and this understanding that God hath given them, makes them capable to pass a right judgment upon their own state. They will not call it a good state, if it be an evil state; and they will not call it an evil state, if it be a good one. They know it is good by the principle of truth in their judgment.

Therefore since there are so many uncertainties in the world, and that men are so apt to take hold of an uncertain way of judging and determining, even in matters relating to their souls: There is a greater aptness in people to take hold of uncertainties, in judging about the matters of their souls, than in those things that relates to their bodies. Seeing people are so liable to it, it can do none of us harm to exhort one another, and move and stir up one another, to make a calculation of our states, by something that will not deceive. There are abundance deceived in this country, as well as other countries; we shall not need to go into foreign parts to find people deceived and deluded. It will not be amiss to say, the drunkard, the swearer, the liar, the oppressor, the proud, and the malicious, are deceived: If they were not so, they would never be overcome by the wicked one; the author of all evil, he hath deceived them, in that they should think to go on in these things, and cry *peace, peace,* to one another, and in their own souls: This is a great delusion; and the devil is the
great

of GRACE and SALVATION.

great deluder that they are deluded by : And it would be worth the while to find out *that* which would make a man think himself in a happy state, and hope to enjoy eternal life, with God and Christ; and when he goes on in sin and iniquity, it would be worth the while to find out the delusion.

There is nothing so proper to turn every one to the grace of God, as *to search their own hearts, and try their ways*. This is that which will discover their thoughts, and make them known to themselves: This is God's grace and gift to men while they are yet sinners and disobedient; he doth not withhold his grace, but gives his grace, and light and truth, *even to the rebellious: He gives gifts to men, even to the rebellious*, that he might have a place and dwelling among them, that they might know there is a God *that searches the heart, and tries the reins*, and judges all unrighteousness. If God hath given thee so much grace, that he might have a dwelling in thy heart, should not that restrain thee from sin, that the devil, by his temptations, might not defile thee, and unfit thee for the kingdom of God? When the Lord comes to search the heart, it is in order to the purging of it, and the taking away of iniquity and sin, that would unfit thee for his kingdom. This is a better way, and more excellent than living to the flesh, and fulfilling the lusts thereof. Let people live ever so much to their own corrupt wills, in pride, wantonness, looseness, and the vanity of their minds, they will not find so much true satisfaction and delight, as in living a holy life, living in the fear of God, and avoiding sin, and keeping themselves from the temptations and snares of the devil.

This is a more excellent way; and it is our work and business to declare to people this more excellent way, which all, one time or other, will confess. This is irksome, some will say; this will abate my pleasure and delights in the world, and spoil my secular interest. If it were not for this reason, they would grant it were better to live a holy life, and to live in the fear of God, than live in the service of the devil; and their carnal interest lies in the way, and weighs down the scale, but it is because thou joinest with it, otherwise the devil, and all the powers of hell, could

could not weigh it down. If people would confider thefe things ferioufly, they would fay, it is better to ferve God, that made them, and gave them life, and breath, and being, than him that would deftroy them; and then when they meet with the pleafures and delights of the world, that the devil lays before them, they would never weigh down the fcale againft a Divine Reafon: If thou wilt give thy heart to it, and ferioufly confider it, it will weigh down the fcale againft all temptations to live in fin, and pleafure, and jollity. If thou wilt but join with this Divine Reafon, that tells thee thefe carnal pleafures and enjoyments are not neceffary for thy foul, but it is neceffary to live a holy, heavenly life, and to ferve the Lord that gave thee life, and breath, and all things; that hath vouchfafed thee manifold prefervations. If thou wilt but join with the Divine Reafon, and hearken to that which opens the truth in thine own heart, all the devil can do, cannot make thee ferve him; for the devil hath no coercion, no power to force thee to commit fin; he cannot make a man work wickednefs againft his will; he muft cloud the underftanding, and work upon the will, and allure and entice the affections by earthly things. So thou canft not be forced by the devil againft thy will, to yield to his temptations, to commit any fin; but thou muft fay, I will do it.

I confefs, when the underftanding is bribed, and the will allured and feduced by the devil's temptations, there is no withftanding them. But on the other hand, if men would give up themfelves to the power of God, they would have Divine Affiftance; and joining with that power, they would *be more than conquerors.* Therefore we cannot but be encouraged to keep in the way of the Lord, and have acquaintance with the power of God, which will preferve you, and give you victory over all the temptations and affaults of the devil; and without this power you cannot overcome; but if you have the affiftance of this power, nothing will be too hard for you. When you are in ftraits, and in a helplefs condition, you fometimes are ready to cry out, I fhall not overcome my fpiritual enemies; I fhall never get victory over fin and the world, the flesh and the devil; and I shall never be able to withstand his temptations, but they will prevail over me all my days. No wonder you make this conclusion, when you have parted with your trust and dependence on that power that is able to overcome the devil, and baffle him in your thoughts, words and deeds.

You may be ready to say, alas! of myself I can do nothing; I am not able of myself *so much as to think a good thought*; yet by Divine Assistance, I do many times think good thoughts. *In me, that is, in my flesh, there dwells nothing that is good.* Not in my flesh abstractly; separate from the power of God, and the Divine Assistance vouchsafed unto me. *In my flesh dwells nothing that is good.* But if you take me as one that hath faith in Christ the Mediator, this faith embraceth the tender of the love of God in the Redeemer. And when I have this faith, there dwells a good thing in me; and from this good thing that dwells in me, there flows forth good words and good actions; then you come to be acquainted with a power greater than your own; and if you trust in it, you will be able to withstand temptations. When you are tempted to any sin, you will not only be able to withstand the temptation, but to overcome it too, and to be more than conquerors in your spiritual warfare. This relying upon, and trusting in the power of God, is that which we call faith; and this faith is the operation of God.

To speak in plain words, God will operate upon thy mind, and make thee know, that this is his power, light, truth and grace, by which he would save thee. And after God hath wrought and opened unto thee in this manner, it is thy duty then to belive in it, to put thy trust and confidence in it, to be delivered. But though faith be offered unto me, yet it is not forced upon me; God hath offered faith to all men, but he doth not force it upon any. All have an opportunity offered to them; if they will but join with it, they may have faith wrought in them, and be fitted and prepared for the kingdom of God.

There are many that are convinced of the truth of the doctrine that we preach to them, but they do not get into the

the power of the truth; they will hear us preach of the power of truth, and will hear what this man faith, and what the other man faith; and this will ferve their turn, that they may talk of religion, and make a profeffion: But they do not feek after that power that fhould enable them *to work out their own falvation.* Thefe perfons grow in knowledge, but they do not grow in grace; they will embrace truth as far as doctrine and words will go; they have profeffed it, and they have fuffered reproach for it, and yet they have not received the truth in the love of it; they cannot reach to the power of it; they glory in their knowledge and in their underftanding, but they come not to that which fanctifies them; they are not able to refift the devil, and to ftand againft his temptations; when a temptation comes, they join with it, but they cannot withftand it: They come to the knowledge of truth in words, but they come not to the knowledge of the power of it in their hearts and minds, fo as to make them prepared veffels for God's honour; God is more difhonoured by them than by thofe that never profeffed his name: They fall into the temptation of the devil, and never difcern the operation of God's power in their own hearts.

Secondly, There is another error as great as this; there are a great many that when the Lord's power hath wrought in their hearts, and they have truth opened to them in the power of it, yet they have not believed in it, they have not had faith wrought in their hearts, they have not trufted in it, nor relied upon the power; fo they are weak and feeble, they have little faith, which is next to none at all. If they have ever fo much knowledge, how eafy can the devil tempt them to fin, if they have no faith; *this is the victory,* faith the apoftle, *that overcomes the world, even your faith.* This is not my victory, that I fee the fubtilty and wiles of Satan, and know much; but that which is my victory is my faith: My truft is in the power of God, and my reliance upon him who is God, mightier than all the ftrength of men and devils; that God who knows my heart. If I be faithful to him, and rely upon him by faith, I fhall refift the devil, and withftanding his temptations, obtain victory over them.

This

of GRACE *and* SALVATION.

This power you may have by the gospel; but then you must be true to the power of it in yourselves; for I do distinguish between the gospel, as it is a doctrine and word preached, and an invisible, divine power working upon men by the preaching of the gospel; you will all hear the gospel preached, though you be ever so proud and high-minded, and you will say it is true; but you can never come to the saving knowledge of the gospel itself, till you find it working inwardly upon yourselves.

We do not pretend to any power of opening mens hearts, as God opened the heart of Lydia; but when people come to wait upon God with a serious and religious mind, you will find the power of the word working effectually upon you, and so the gospel *will become the power of God to your salvation.* This is, and shall be my prayer, for all religious assemblies, that the Lord will be pleased to teach them, by his invisible word, and beget living desires in them towards himself, and bring them to an esteem of holiness and righteousness, that they may adorn the gospel of Christ, by living gospel-lives; for want of this, what dishonour have men brought to God, and what reproach upon the gospel. O! that people would come to hear the word preached, with desire to profit by it, and say, Lord, do me some good this day, give me a powerful refreshing visitation at this time; give me some living experience of thy Almighty Power working upon my heart, that I may not be led by this man's word, or that man's opinion; for if they mistake, I shall be mistaken: But if I build my faith upon what God in his word reveals to me, I shall infallibly know what I am to believe and practise, and I shall receive from God some good thing, and I shall *know what is the good and acceptable will of God*; I shall find that there is power in the gospel *for building me up in the most holy faith,* and that *it is mighty, through God, for the pulling down of the strong holds of sin and Satan,* and I shall *see the salvation of God brought near to me.*

When the gospel becomes the power of God, and worketh upon the hearts of men by the operation of the Divine Power, they may distinguish between that faith that is built upon the declarations of men, and that which is

wrought

wrought by the revelation and discovery of the mind of God in their souls; this is that which we may bottom upon, and have an anchor sure and stedfast in our own souls; when I depend upon Christ, *the rock of ages*, both of this age, and all other ages, my faith must be placed upon him; and when I hear the word of a man, I must have an eye to God, that he will reveal his power in my heart; this will make me believe in the Lord Jesus Christ, and *receive that ingrafted word which is able to save my soul:* I shall not only hear the word, but live in obedience to it. What signifies it to make a profession that I have the light within, if I do not give obedience to it? For without that, it is all hypocrisy; all pretence to holiness, or righteousness, all mortification, is but hypocrisy, any further than we find the power of truth making an impression upon our hearts and minds, bringing us to the obedience of faith.

Let them therefore that profess righteousness, live righteously, and they that hear the gospel, live in obedience to it; and those that profess to be Christians, let them live like Christians indeed: When every one comes to know within himself, so far as the gospel hath shined upon him, that they have received the truth in the love of it, and love the truth as it is in Jesus, and are obedient to the gospel, they shall know the salvation of it. There is a discovery of God's power in the gospel, and there is a believing of it, and trusting in it; this is that which belongs to a Christian, this is the beginning and the first step to a Christian life; we must believe in Christ; *for without faith it is impossible to please* God. He that believeth, should be careful to walk in the truth that he hath received, and then he shall have a testimony of the power and virtue of it in his own soul. This virtue and power, if he joins with it, hath the government of his heart and life, and gives him victory over the world, and the temptations of Satan.

You know in the primitive times there were believers that not only held the faith, but *lived by faith;* and by that faith they got victory over all the allurements, and pleasures and vanities of the world. *I have fought a good fight,* saith the apostle, 2 *Tim.* iv, 7, 8, *I have finished my course, I have kept the faith, henceforth is laid up for me a crown*

of GRACE *and* SALVATION.   183
of righteoufnefs, which the Lord, the righteous Judge, fhall give me at that day, and not to me only, but unto all them alfo that love his appearing. I have got the victory, and there remains an eternal weight of glory for me.

My friends, this is our ambition, and all our labour among you, that you may be built up in the moft holy faith; that you may be brought home to Chrift, in all your meetings and gatherings together: You fhould defire to be enriched with faith, and to have your own ftorehoufe filled with all the fruits of the Spirit, and not only feek for the knowledge of the truth, but be fubject and obedient to what you know, otherwife by your religion you will but hurt yourfelves. And the apoftle *Peter*, 2 *Peter*, i, 12, fpeaks of knowing the truth, and of being eftablifhed in it, and of fome that *after they had efcaped the pollutions of the world, through the knowledge of our Lord and Saviour, Jefus Chrift, they are again entangled therein, and overcome, and the latter end with them is worfe than the beginning; for it had been better for them not to have known the way of righteoufnefs, than after they have known it, to turn from the holy commandment delivered unto them.* There is a power goes along with the preaching of the gofpel, that will enable you to do what you know; the gofpel is a powerful doctrine, whether you know it or not, or whether you fubmit to it or not, yet pray remember that God's *people are a willing people in the day of his power,* they are a certain fort of people that are devoted to God, and fubmit all their worldly honours, interefts, profits and pleafures, to the pleafure of God, and defire no other pleafure or happinefs, but to enjoy his prefence and favour; they are fatified with this, and they are a happy people, being made *a willing people in the day of God's power;* they are willing to deny themfelves, to take up a daily crofs and follow *Chrift*, and have *falvation* upon his terms.

There are a great many profeffors that have notions, and out-fide appearances, but they want that virtue, and life, and power, that fhould fettle them in religion, and a love of the truth. The Lord that knows our hearts, knows that our labour and travel among you hath been defigned for your good, and *that our hearts defire is, that you may be*
                                                                            faved

saved in the day of the Lord Jesus. We would have people consider, and attend and hear what God speaks, and remember what he hath taught you by the ministers of the gospel: We have all ears to hear, let us thank God for that; blessed be God that there is a power and an ability of hearing with an outward ear; but there are many that will not so much as give the hearing to what might be spoken to them from the Lord: *He that hath ears to hear, let him hear what the Spirit saith to the churches;* and what he saith to his own soul; hear what the Spirit saith of your own state and condition; if it be good, bless God for it; are you in so good a condition, that you have no trouble, no distress to lament, no wants to supply, blessed are you that have none; but if you find that you have done amiss, and if the Lord should call you this night to give up your account, the Lord hath a great deal against you, I am sure; and I tell you it is your duty to turn to the Lord with unfeigned repentance, that through Christ Jesus, you may receive pardon and remission of all your sins, and hear what the Spirit saith to yourselves, and in yourselves.

Pray come and make it your work and business the rest of the time you have to live, *to work out your salvation with fear and trembling*, that when Christ comes, you may say, *come Lord Jesus, come quickly,* purify me and sanctify me, and prepare me to be presented to the Father *without spot, and blameless;* the day is coming that this will be the desire of every one of you.

And it is the earnest breathing and desire of my soul, that every one of you may have an eye unto the Lord, and he will look down from Heaven, and have regard to the cry and the sighing of the needy soul. God will arise, and find out the people that breathe after him, and that desire to be reconciled to him, through the Mediator Jesus Christ; the Lord loveth to find out such a people, and I am glad to preach to such a people the glad tidings of the gospel, and to teach as God hath taught me; *good and upright is the Lord, therefore will he teach and guide you in the way which you should go. Walk humbly with* God; *he will resist the proud, but he will give grace unto the humble.* Walk uprightly

before

before the Lord in this gofpel-day that fhines upon you; love the appearance of God, and prize it, though it hath not been fo glorious to you, as to fome others, yet defpife not the day of fmall things: live in fubjection to that grace that the Lord hath given you, and the Lord will give you more grace, and pour out his Spirit, and multiply his bleffings upon you; the Lord hath *begun a good work in you*, and he will *carry it on to the day of Chrift*, and will vouchfafe to bring the glorious day of his vifitation upon you.

To the Lord I leave you, to his favour and protection I commit you; remember that there is no falvation but by Jefus Chrift, and none to be had by Chrift, till you come to believe in him; to him that fearcheth the heart, and tries the reins, that pardoneth iniquity, tranfgreffion and fin, for the fake of Chrift Jefus, the Mediator, to him I do commit you, not doubting but that he that hath begun a good work in you, will at laft complete and finifh it to his own praife and your falvation.

SERMON XVII.

The EXCELLENCY of PEACE with GOD.

Preached at DEVONSHIRE-HOUSE, *Auguft* 5, 1691.

My Friends,

IT is man's great happinefs in this world to have acquaintance with God, with the Lord that made him, from whom he hath life and breath here, and his eternal welfare hereafter; this doubtlefs every one will acknowledge one time or other, that peace with God is a great jewel, and the beft eftate and riches. It is the great defire of every one that they may attain to this one time or other; and there is a great neglect of happinefs among the fons and daughters of men, in not feeking of it, and not labouring to attain it while it is to be had; Oh! how many trifle away their time about fading and perishing objects, and they know at the same inftant that they are yet deftitute of the favour of God, and peace with him. Oh, friends! the very thoughts and confideration of the worth of this jewel, and of the mifery of being without it, and the uncertainty of our time while it is to be attained, might put every one upon a ferious, diligent enquiry after the way and means whereby they might attain it, that fo they might have a refting-place for their fouls, and fatisfaction to their inward man, that it fhall go well with them, when time fhall be no more.

And they that come to this confideration, and are refolved in their hearts and minds, that they will labour after this, and fet their whole endeavour after it, they will in the firft place feek *the kingdom of God, and the righteoufnefs thereof*: Thefe do need a daily encouragement in their way to Heaven, and there is nothing on the Lord's part wanting to fuch fouls, but that they may attain their defire.

But alas! this hath been, and is ftill the mifery of thoufands, they are feeking after peace with God, but they err in the way to it, they do not feek in that way, nor take hold of thofe methods, by and through which God hath promifed peace; you fhall fcarce meet with any body, but they would have eternal life and peace with God; we fhall not need to perfuade people to wifh for, and to defire to have peace with God when they fhall come to die, and lay down their heads in the duft. There is not a *Balaam*, but he defires to *die the death of the righteous, and that his laft end may be like his*: There is not a *Scribe*, or a *Pharifee*, or any that profefs religion, but they are feeking eternal life. The Lord Jefus did witnefs concerning them, that they were an envious, proud, perfecuting people, yet that they did feek after eternal life, and they pitched upon fome methods and ways whereby they thought to get and enjoy it; but all this was error ftill, they where out of the way of attaining it, and fo are a great many people at this very day; they are in a ftate and condition wherein they are never like to enjoy it; the methods and the ways that they have chofen to themfelves, to find eternal life by, and to obtain peace with God, will never anfwer the end. And God hath been pleafed to difcover to us the many by-ways that people have chofen, and feek peace with God by; therefore we are willing at all times, to fhew people their error in thefe great matters of higheft concernment to them. If they did err in their way of feeking to obtain fome earthly good, and miffed their end, they know the price of it, it is but a lofs of fo much, which if they had taken a right courfe, they might have attained; but it is an unfpeakable lofs, an ineftimable lofs, if they lofe peace with God, and all the pains and labour they are at to obtain it.

I befeech you, friends, confider thefe things, they are of great weight, and you will fay fo one day or other; for, faith our Saviour, *what will it profit a man to gain the whole world, and lofe his own foul? Or what fhall a man give in exchange for his foul?* O! How fad is it to confider, that a man hath not made provifion for his foul, that he hath not a place of reft for his immortal foul, and that the arms of the Lord Jefus Chrift are not open to receive his foul, when his body can retain it no longer! If this be a man's ftate when he comes to die, it had been better for him that he had never been born: Men may live and gather riches, and enjoy a plentiful eftate; but if they be deftitute of the favour of God, and peace with him, what will they do with thefe perifhing enjoyments? They cannot poffibly fatisfy themfelves with thefe tranfitory, vifible things; but if thefe perfons only mind their bodies, and neglect their fouls, do they not *live like the beafts that perifh?* The beaft feeks after his meat, and when he finds it, he eats it with delight and pleafure, and in a little while he lies down and dies, and there is an end; fo it is with carelefs fouls, that have no regard to their future ftate; but they fay, *let us eat, and drink, and be merry, for to-morrow we fhall die.*

Oh! that every one of us did apply our hearts ferioufly to the confideration of the weight of thefe things that concern our eternal ftate; if perfons did this, then they might come to an enquiry into their own fouls, what method and way is moft fafe for the attaining of fo bleffed an end. For you know there are abundance of people, if you look up and down in the world, you will fee

188 The EXCELLENCY of PEACE with GOD.

every body almoſt hunting up and down in ſome way of religion or other, and are engaged in religious performances: What is the matter? what would you have? We would have peace with God here, and everlaſting reſt hereafter in the kingdom of Heaven; that we would have. Thus have the nations been ſcattered and driven up and down in the purſuit of happineſs and ſatisfaction.

There is a general belief amongſt people, that there is a Heaven, and a Hell, and that they muſt have their part in one of them; there are none that deſire a portion in the *lake that burns with fire and brimſtone.* Thoſe prophane wretches that cry to God to damn them, they do not mean what they ſpeak, they would be ſaved for all that; every one will cry at laſt, Lord have mercy upon me, if he hath but time to ſay ſo: Let us cry, Lord have mercy upon me now; Lord beſtow thy favour upon me; *Lord lift up the light of thy countenance upon me;* Lord touch my hard heart, and ſoften it and break it, by the power of thy Spirit; *open mine eyes, that I may ſee the wonderful things of thy law;* open mine ears, that I may hear thy voice. It is good for people to make uſe of time while they have it; whoſoever calls upon the name of the Lord ſhall be ſaved, and God will *pour out his wrath upon thoſe that call not upon his name.* He that calls upon the name of the Lord, ſhall be ſaved; and God gives great encouragement to people to ſeek after him.

What mean you by ſeeking after God? I have gone to church, and ſaid my prayers; I have gone in the way which my fathers have led me, and directed me, I hope I ſhall find mercy at laſt; I am a believer, I believe in Jeſus Chriſt that died for my ſins, and roſe again for my juſtification; I hope, through the merits of Jeſus Chriſt, I ſhall be ſaved. What mean you by ſeeking after the Lord? Do not we all hear of him, and pray to him every day?

Is there any thing more common than this, that people ſpeak to one another generally about? as for the general knowledge of God, you and I may ſee to our ſorrow, that a great many cry, Lord, Lord, that are never like to enter into the kingdom of God. If all that take the name of God in their mouths, ſhould enter into the kingdom

kingdom of Heaven, it would be a very foul kingdom: If all the drunkards and whoremongers of *England*, and all prophane ungodly perfons, that will take the name of God in their mouths, fhould enter into the kingdom of Heaven, it would be a very unclean and impure kingdom; there is *nothing enters* there *that is unclean, that is abominable, that loveth to make a lie.* So that there muft be fome more peculiar people that fhall have an abundant entrance into the kingdom of God; and there muft be fomething that will entitle them to it. For you may remember our Saviour faith, *no man knoweth the Father but the Son, and he to whom the Son fhall reveal him.* So much as may be known of God by works, you and I may know, without the revelation of Chrift; we need not wait for this knowledge, we can have it by books; we can have it by Chrift's revelation. Nothing would ferve fome in our Saviour's time, but eternal life; and our Lord Jefus bids them *fearch the fcriptures, for in them* (faith he) *you think to have eternal life, and they are they which teftify of me.* Yet for all the profeffion they made, he tells them, *no man hath feen God at any time, neither feen his fhape, nor heard his voice;* they were ftrangers to God, though they had a general knowledge of God.

So it is at this day; there is a general knowledge of God, and people hope to obtain peace with God, and eternal life. Their parents and their tutors have inftructed them in the principles of Chriftianity, and about the attributes of God; but all this will not bring a man to a faving knowledge of God, and reconciliation with him: For a man that is as wicked as the devil can make him, knows thefe things, and yet may be a fervant of the devil, and do his work; he is not born again, and become a child, by all his external knowledge. Now he that defires to come to the true, faving knowledge of God, our Saviour hath told us, *that none knows the Father but the Son, and him to whom the Son will reveal him;* this is a fure way to come to the true knowledge of God, by Jefus Chrift; he hath the key that openeth the heart, and he will bring us to the true knowledge of God the Father. *Chrift hath* the key of David, *which openeth, and no man shutteth ; and shutteth, and no man openeth.* He can bring us to behold the glory of God in his own face; without him we are never like to come to the saving knowledge of God.

Poor man is in a lapsed, fallen state, he is fallen into sin, and is in a state of alienation from God, and therefore he cannot come to him but by a Mediator ; *there is one Mediator between God and man, the man Christ Jesus*, and he must make peace for him, else he will never have it : How then shall we come to Christ, if he is the only means, and there is no other by which we may come to the knowledge of God, as the scripture speaks? Hearken to it, how may we come to Christ? I answer, you will never come to him; if he first come not to you, you will never be able to do it. It is not coming to Christ, when you say, you do believe that Christ died and rose again, and ascended up into Heaven, and sits at the right hand of God, and lives forever to make intercession for his people, and to read those words and doctrines which he preached up and down at meetings, and solemn assemblies ; but if you believe that he is *the eternal Son of God, and the author of eternal salvation to all that obey him*, you must come to him, and entirely give up yourselves to his glory and service; without this, you cannot come to him, nor will he bring you to the Father : Christ is come near to us, he stands at the door of our hearts, and he stands and knocks : *Behold !* that is a word that calls for attention, for people to take notice of. *Behold, I stand at the door and knock ;* what dost thou knock for ? saith Christ, that thou mayest open the door of thy heart; *for if any man open, I will come and sup with him, and he with me, and my Father will come to him, and we will make our abode with him.*

Now people are loth to be at this pains and trouble, to open the door of their hearts to Christ, for they will not believe it is Christ that knocks, and that rebukes and checks them, when they refused to open to him ; when they find something within that reproves them for their sin, and doth condemn them that they cannot be at quiet, they will never believe that this is Christ: How can this be Christ? they say, He is ascended up to Heaven, and he is at the right hand of
God

The EXCELLENCY of PEACE with GOD

God the Father: Will you make me believe that this is Chrift knocking at the door of my heart? I cannot believe it: But what faith our Saviour, *unlefs you believe that I am he, you fhall die in your fins*: For there is nobody elfe can help you out of them.

There is a two-fold confideration that we are to have of Chrift; one is, as he was *made of a woman, made under the law*; and another confideration of Chrift is, as he is the eternal Son of God. Men have very grofs thoughts of Chrift, to think, that becaufe he is in Heaven, therefore he cannot be here too: They meafure him by themfelves; they know becaufe a man is at London, therefore he cannot be at York at the fame time. Thus thefe men object, if Chrift is in Heaven, how can he be here? His doctrine and precepts are here, let us make ufe of them all; he will come again at the day of judgment; but this is a day of judgment: Doth not he judge you now? *He is the judge both of quick and dead, and he is the fearcher of hearts, and the trier of the reins;* fo that thou canft not think an ill thought, but he will tell thee of it; he is nearer to thee than the wife of thy bofom, or thy hufband that is near to thee: Hufband and wife may think an ill thought, but they cannot tell one another of it; but Chrift is one that comes fo near thee, that thou canft not conceive an ill thought againft thy neighbour, but he will tell thee of it.

This is the Lord Chrift, as a Spirit, a quickening Spirit, who is made manifeft in the flefh: *He hath given to every man a meafure of the Spirit to profit withal:* The grace of God which bringeth falvation, hath appeared unto all men. Notwithftanding the diftinction of learned men between common grace and fpiritual grace, this grace *that brings falvation, hath appeared unto all men.* This manifeftation of the Spirit and light within, we have from Chrift. Thefe are the ways and methods that the Lord Chrift hath taken to approach near to us. Now your own reafon will tell you, if this be the way and means that Chrift takes to approach near to us, we cannot take another way to approach to him: If Chrift hath taken, I fay, this way to approach to us, by the light and manifeftation of his own Spirit, which convinceth us of fin: If this be Chrift's way of coming to us,

there

there can be no other way of our coming to him, but by the fame method of his grace. He faith, *if you have the light, believe in the light.* I have the light, I am enlightened, there is fomething that difcovereth my evil thoughts: Why muft I believe in the light? That you may be children of the light, as our Saviour fpeaks; they that are the children of the light fhall have it for their inheritance; and they that are children of darknefs, muft have darknefs for their inheritance: While we have the light, we muft believe in it, and we fhall be made children of the light: God hath fent his Son, and the Son hath fent his Spirit and his heavenly grace into our hearts, that we may draw near to him, and be directed how to attain acquaintance with him, and to do that which pleafeth God, and come to be in union with him, and do the works of God. This is that which God requires of us, *that we will believe on him whom he hath fent;* that we may embrace the light, and believe in the light, in the Lord Jefus Chrift.

Pray what do you mean by believing? There is fomething within me checks and reproves me for fin, and calls me off from it, and bids me turn over a new leaf: Muft I hearken to this? Is this that which you mean by believing? As to this degree of believing, they that reject it now, fhall believe it hereafter; for all the world at laft, and the damned in hell fhall certainly confefs that there was grace, and light, and means afforded to them, and they might have gone farther, and efcaped that mifery that they are fallen into.

But there is a more precious faith that I would have you partake of, a *faith that worketh by love.* Since the Lord hath been fo gracious as to extend his mercy and love to me, I am fo taken with the love of God, that I will be obedient to him; this faith that worketh by love, is the faith of God's elect; that by which we may obtain victory over our paffions and lufts, and over fatan and the fnares of the world; when we are come to clofe with the grace of God, and to believe in Chrift, this is well: But we muft alfo yield obedience and fubjection. Yet when faith hath brought forth obedience, you cannot be juftified by it, you cannot be faved by your obedience, but Chrift alone: *He is the*
author

author and finisher of our faith, and a Mediator from first to last.

Now all that come to close with the appearance of Christ in their own heart, they have laid hold of the method appointed for their coming to him. It is Christ they must hear; he is come so near to men that they may hear his voice, and hear him tell us our very thoughts. Why should not I hear him when he checks me and reproves me for sin? He comes near and tells me that I have done amiss; Lord, I have done iniquity, I will do so no more. Thus Christ converseth with his people, and doth not only check and reprove them, when they do that which is evil, but persuades them and enables them to do good. He is a Mediator, he is a middle person, and hath taken flesh upon him, that he might reconcile them to God, that do believe in him.

Now, when we come to have acquaintance with God, and have chosen him to be our God, he teaches us to do what is good, and reproves us for what evil we have done. Who can choose a better guide, to lead him into acquaintance with God, than Christ that is conversant with us, piercing into our thoughts, and speaking to us? I may hear him with the inward ear of my heart; when I do evil he checks me for it, and tells me the thing I should seek is of inestimable value; and if through my unbelief and carelesness I miss of it, it had been better for me that I had never been born; now we are in the way of coming to receive the end of our faith, the salvation of our souls, *let us not neglect so great salvation.* No man can save himself, nor save the soul of his brother, nor find a ransom, nor procure an offering for the expiating of his sin; therefore let every one that would have his sin expiated and pardoned, and cannot be satisfied and quieted, till he hath peace with God; let him come to Christ, the Mediator, and come with faith and truth in the inward parts, and submit to him, and be willing to be ruled by him, then Christ will save him, *and present him without spot and blemish* to his father.

Consider that those that are the people of God, are led by the Spirit of God. They miss their way to reconciliation with God, that love any other way, or think to come to God any other way than by Jesus, the Mediator, their labour

bour will be loft: Therefore I muft exhort and perfuade you that are out of the way, that you would take God's method, and come into God's way. The terms, I have told you, are made already; the bargain is not to make now; I will give fo much to be at peace with God, or I will part with this or the other thing that is dear to me. No, the agreement is made between God and Chrift, and his *covenant is ordered in all things, and fure;* and his covenant ftands fure with none, but thofe that are in Chrift Jefus. There was a covenant made with *Abraham; in thy feed fhall all the nations of the earth be bleffed.* The promife is made to the feed, that is, to thofe that are in Chrift; the faithful are counted the feed; now the faithful are thofe that are obedient to Chrift, who is the feed of the promife, *in whom all the families of the earth are bleffed.* They muft come to Chrift the feed, they muft not rebel againft him; they muft come to him, and believe in him; be there never fo many nations and families in the world, the promife is not to them, *but to as many as the Lord our God fhall call.*

Here is the way for people to lay hold of, for their coming into acquaintance with God, which is of fo great neceffity before they die; they muft come to Chrift himfelf by his Spirit in their own hearts. We need not go to this and the other learned man, and enquire of this and the other fort of people; but we muft cry to God for help and direction, and come unto him, and give up all the powers and faculties of our fouls to him, to be governed by him: God will have fervants that will be obedient to him; if ever we come to obtain falvation, we muft have another mafter, *one is your mafter, even Chrift;* I muft come under the government of Chrift, and he muft lead me, and rule me, if I will be a child of God.

When people come to fee there is no effectual way, but fubmitting to the grace of God in their own hearts, and yielding themfelves up to the dictates of the Spirit of Chrift in their fouls; when they come to this, there are many hazards and difficulties to be encountered with; there is the appearance of the crofs of Chrift, and we muft

The EXCELLENCY *of* PEACE *with* GOD.

muſt take up this croſs if we will follow Chriſt, and be obedient in all things unto him. This is that which will kill all my pleaſure, lay waſte all my religion, and deſtroy my hopes; I muſt be like a man that built a houſe without a good foundation; I muſt pull it all down again, and I muſt come to build up again upon a new foundation.

Here many have turned aſide, the croſs of Chriſt hath ſeemed to them ſo ſharp, and hard and intolerable, that they could not bear it; they would not be at the charge of ſuch a religion; what, muſt I part with all my delights, and my beloved luſts and pleaſures, and all my intereſts in the world for Chriſt? I cannot part with theſe, theſe things lie in my way, I muſt rather loſe my ſoul than part with what is ſo grateful to me, and join with the light of mine own conſcience, and the truth in my inward parts; what, muſt not I have ſo much as liberty of thought? What, muſt my thoughts be regulated by that which is ſo croſs and repugnant to my mind? Muſt I throw out all evil thoughts out of my heart, and ſuffer none but good thoughts to remain there? Who can ſtand here? Who can bear ſuch ſtrictneſs as this? Rather than endure this, I will chooſe to loſe my ſoul; many have loſt the truth on this account, and many are in danger to loſe their ſouls.

If there be in you any deſire of peace with God, that you may not go hence before you have attained it, take hold of the preſent opportunity; hardneſs of heart is a deſperate plague, it comes from a long obſtinate continuance in ſin; when we have *withſtood the day of God's patience and long-ſuffering, and grieved the Holy Spirit of God; then* God *giveth us up to our own hearts luſts,* becauſe *we will not hearken to the voice of the charmer, charm he never ſo wiſely ;* when we ſtop our ears, and will not attend to the calls of God; when men will go on, and nothing can ſtop them, in the career of their luſts and pleaſures, but they will retain their carnal delight and friendſhip with the world; this hardneſs of heart is a deſperate plague; take heed of it, that it doth not overtake you, and bring ruin and deſtruction upon you: *Conſider the patience and long-ſuffering of* God, *and*

let

let his goodness lead you to repentance: Confider God hath waited to be gracious to you, he hath exercised much long-suffering and patience towards you; whereas he might have cut you off long ago, and given you your portion with the damned in hell; but he hath hearkened to the Mediator that hath pleaded for you; he hath extended his patience and long-suffering to *the wicked and rebellious alfo*; and for this reason, the apoftle tells us, that Chrift is *the Saviour of all men, especially of them that believe.*

Now the patience and long-suffering of God hath been lengthened out to all, and we have not improved it. Confcience hath been fenfible of the inward ftrokes and rebukes of God for fin, and of the inward calls of his grace to bring us to repentance; but we have not regarded thefe calls, nor hearkened to the voice of God, fo as to hear, that our fouls might live; O! let us not put off our repentance any longer; but *to-day, while it is called to-day, let us hear his voice, and harden not our hearts*, but be of a tender heart; let our hearts be foftened, and tendered under the word of God, and under the ftrokes of his judgment. If ever the Lord bring you under a tender frame, you will receive the word of God with meeknefs, and mix it with faith; then it will work effectually to the amendment of your lives; it will work faith in thofe that are unbelievers, and ftrengthen the faith of thofe that believe. Then we fhall have caufe to blefs the Lord, and praife and magnify his great name for his patience, long-suffering and mercy, which at this day he hath lengthened out, and gracioufly extended to us.

SERMON XVIII.

TRUE CHRISTIANITY.

Preached at GRACE-CHURCH-STREET, *April* 10, 1692.

THE inftitution of the Chriftian religion was for this purpofe, that holinefs and righteoufnefs might be brought forth in the earth; that God, through his Son Jefus Chrift, might take delight in the fons and daughters of of men, that they might be reconciled to him; *for that which the law could not do, by reason of its weakness, God hath had a purpose to do by his Son, and to him he gave all power in Heaven and Earth*, that thereby he might be enabled to perform the great work of God, in establishing righteousness, and in bringing forth a holy people, to serve a holy God. This is the great blessing that is come to us, and to all mankind, through our blessed Lord and Saviour, Jesus Christ, that came *to turn every one from the evil of their ways*. That is the way and method by which our Lord Jesus accomplished the end of his coming, and the will of his Heavenly Father; *Moses* and all his washings, offerings, and sacrifices, could not make clean and purge the conscience; and by all his offerings and sacrifices, he could not reconcile us to God: But *Jesus, by his once offering himself, did forever perfect them that are sanctified; and by one offering, reconciled us to the Father*, and so brings forth a holy generation unto God, through regeneration and the sanctification of the Spirit.

And seeing the Lord hath been pleased in the riches of his grace to open this new and living way, for man's returning again into unity and fellowship with his Maker, the question, my friends, that I would put to you on the behalf of God, is, for all of you to consider, whether it is not best for every one of us to lay hold of salvation, to lay hold of that blessing wherewith the Lord hath blessed us, that so the principal institution of Christianity might not only be named and spoken of, but might come to be enjoyed and witnessed in every one of our own souls; and that all might wait with expectation on the Lord Jesus Christ, for fulfilling of this great work in themselves.

There is a general notion among people, that Heaven is a holy place, and that nothing that is unclean can enter into it, to have a habitation there, when time in this world shall be no more with us; and that time which we have given us, I am sure is given us of God, as an opportunity of fitting and preparing us for his dwelling-place; and every day and hour of it ought to be employed in that great work, that so we might draw nearer and nearer to that state and condition that suits and befits that holy dwelling where saints and angels, for evermore, praise the great and glorious God: So that I am persuaded you believe, that you and all of us, are to be accountable to God for all the time he hath bestowed upon us, whether we use it to the purposes for which he hath given it, or whether we mispend our time upon those things that are not profitable to us; and upon these considerations, we had need all of us to take heed to our present state that we are come to, and are arrived at in the present time; as for the future time, that we all know we are not sure of; and the future state that we may hope to come to, there is no certainty of it, unless there be an improvement of the present time, and the opportunities of our present state: Therefore every one should apply their hearts unto the seeking of wisdom and understanding, and unto God, that he may give us to understand our state, and our present fitness or unfitness for the kingdom of glory and happiness, and of that holy dwelling we hope to enjoy forever.

If I will but turn my mind inward, to the serious consideration of my present state and condition, I can tell whether I am fit or unfit to approach God's presence; and if I find I am unfit, I must have recourse to the divine working of that great power, which God hath ordained and appointed for this purpose; I must come to him to work all my works in me, and for me, according to his good pleasure; and that he will never do, unless it be by crossing me in my carnal pleasures and corrupt inclinations; for that which pleaseth man, doth not please God: And God will not revoke the holy scriptures, that tell us, *that they which live in pleasure, are dead while they live;* they that are indulgent to their own affections, and their own delights, and their own humours, they are not at all ready to please and glorify God; they are not fitted for it, therefore he never sanctifies, nor brings any into a true Christian state, but through a daily cross; so that if I am not already fitted and prepared to do that which is pleasing to God, I may be fitted by taking up a daily cross, to glorify God here, and enjoy him forever.

What those things are that you are to do, I need not tell you, nor what you have done. I judge no man: There is one that judgeth, he will tell you if you ask him, what your state and condition is; he will tell the drunkard, if he ask him, whether he is fit for Heaven; and alfo the proud and haughty perfons whether they are fit for Heaven: Let fuch as are guilty of thefe or any other fins, enquire of the oracle in their own bofoms, am not I fit for Heaven, notwithftanding all this? He will tell thee no, there is *no unclean thing fhall enter there, nothing that defiles,* nothing that hurts or oppreffes; the proud, peevifh, malicious perfon, that is hurtful to others, that hurts his neighbour, is fhut out. *There fhall in no wife enter into Heaven any thing that defileth,* Rev. xxi, 27. *For without are dogs, and forcerers, and whoremongers, and murderers, and idolaters, and whofoever loveth and maketh a lie,* Rev. xxii, 15. None fhall enter into the holy city of God, but thofe that are purified and purged from all iniquity: Therefore God hath fent his fon Jefus, feeing none elfe could do it: *Mofes* and the Prophets could not do it, therefore he fent Jefus to *blefs us, in turning every one of us from our iniquities,* and from our evil ways; one man hath this evil way, another that evil way: It is all one to him; his work is to turn every one of us from our evil ways.

But why then (you may fay) are fo few turned from their evil ways throughout Chriftendom, where Chrift is believed in, profeffed, read and heard; that yet fo few are converted and turned?. for we fee great numbers of liars, fwearers, drunkards, and unclean perfons among us, where Chrift is cried up at a mighty rate, and yet people are not turned from the evil of their ways; there is fomething fure that is the reafon of it.

I would have all of you confider what the reafon of it is, that thofe that profefs to be Chriftians, are not turned from the evil of their ways; for Chrift *hath all power in Heaven and Earth committed to him,* and he is able to do it, and he was fent from God on purpofe to do it; but this is a certain truth, it is not done; and what is the reafon of it? *He came to his own, and his own received him not;* what is the reafon? He hath caufed his grace to appear to every man in the world, and yet they are not taught by it. Here is an object of faith for all, and God hath offered faith to all men, *fince he hath raifed up Jefus from the dead*, yet men have it not: What is the reafon that this nation, as well as other nations, have been puzzled about it, to find out things that are fo plain in fcripture, in relation to the love of God to mankind, and in relation to Chrift Jefus the Saviour, and fo little of this work is wrought among us?

Some fay there is never a man in the world turned from the evil of their ways; they live in fin, and they are under a fixed neceffity of continuing in it, and lying under it all the days of their lives, for all this belief of the love of God, and the power of Chrift, and the profeffion of it: Some fay there is never a Chriftian in the world can live one day without fin, but will defile himfelf with one thing or another; that the devil will prevail over men, and fin mix itfelf with our prayers and alms, and all our holy duties; fo that there is nothing clean; nothing pure that we can perform to God. There are others that are not fo rafh in their judgment, and not fo inconfiderate, but they will believe fome men and women may come to a power and ability to withftand fatan, and refift him in his temptations; and that there are thofe that have been turned from the evil of their ways, but they are not; What is the matter? You have fpent time about this, what is the reafon you are not turned from the evil of your ways? The devil hath told the people in former days, that the reafon why men live in fin, is, becaufe God hath appointed it fo to be: And that hath ftopt the mouth of many a plain-hearted tender Chriftian; they have cried unto God under the weight of their fin, and they fee no deliverance after all their prayers and tears, becaufe they have been told they cannot do it, and that God hath appointed it fhould be fo, and required them to do what they cannot do; and with fome the cuftom of fin hath taken away the fenfe of fin, and they go on to perdition in their fecurity.

I hope, my friends, that God hath opened your eyes, and that you have better thoughts of God, than that he hath fet you a work and a labour to do, and by his eternal power and decree, hath ordained that you fhould never do it, but damn you after all. Confider, there are men and women in
bondage

bondage and captivity, and God hath sent his Son into the world to redeem them from all iniquity, and turn them from their evil ways; we are not turned, what is the reason of it? I beseech you in the love of God, be serious in this matter; serious you must be, one time or other; when you come to the tribunal of God, there must be a reason given, or if not, you must be speechless; therefore find it out here. What is the reason that I am not turned from my evil ways, since God hath sent his Son Jesus to do it, and given him power to do it; why then is it not done?

Some persons upon enquiry, and after their search, have brought forth this reason: They have alleged the great power the devil hath: The devil is so strong, and hath such a power to darken their minds, and enchant their affections; he injects and brings things into their minds before they are aware of it. I confess this, and I will say a little to it, I will confess as much as the argument will bear, that the devil hath great power, and a way of injecting things into the spirits and affections of people: He is God's enemy and ours too, and he lies in wait, and will do as much as he can against us, that no one shall get to Heaven; if we come thither, it shall be against his will: I have heard some magnify the devil's power to such a degree, that he hath such power over a man or woman, that he is able to keep them in sin all their life, though God hath put forth the exceeding greatness of his power for their redemption: This is hard to believe, that the devil is stronger than Christ Jesus: Well, as great as his power is, we are in a capacity of knowing a greater power; the apostle did comfort the Christians, notwithstanding all the power the devil used with them to defile them, and keep them from inheriting the kingdom of God, 1. John i. 4. *You are of God, little children, and have overcome, because greater is he that is in you, than he that is in the world.* I would have you believe this; I do believe it heartily, the devil only *rules in the hearts of the children of disobedience;* and he that hath the Holy Ghost in him, hath one greater than he that is in the world: If you believe this, then the question is thus far answered, that we have a Saviour, a Deliverer, that is more able to redeem us, than the devil is to keep us in bondage: I hope we are pretty well, now we know we have a keeper: We are aſſaulted with the devil's temptations, and they are powerful; how powerful? He hath ſo much power, as he finds in us an inclination to yield and join with his temptations: If he comes with a temptation to a man or woman that hath no inclination to that thing he tempts them to; if they hate that thing, then there is an end of it: The devil's power lies in this, when he brings a temptation that I have an inclination to, then he hath a party within me; if that be rooted out, what ſignifies his power, let him bring ever ſo many temptations?

There are many of you that underſtand what I ſay; if a temptation comes to a man to commit an act of uncleanneſs, if he be a chaſte man, there is no inclination in him to yield to it, or join to it, he hates it, it is an abomination in itſelf, and grievous and provoking to God, if he doth it; a man abhors it, then what powerful temptation is it? If it light upon a man of an unclean mind, that is defiled in his heart, he hath not only the devil, but his own luſt and corrupt inclination to contend with; but if a man believeth in Chriſt, he relies upon him, and he will ſay, Lord, thou ſeeſt I am under temptation; here is a great and powerful temptation, I can never withſtand it, but I truſt in thy name and power, do thou ariſe and deliver me from it: Thus when God doth ariſe, his enemies will be ſcattered; tho' the devil's power be great, yet there is a deliverer that is ſtronger than he: The reaſon of mens being overcome, doth not lie in the greatneſs of the devil's power, but in the frailty of our nature.

Some will ſay, that our natures are ſo frail, weak and depraved, that we can do nothing as as we ought to do; this is given for another reaſon, and there is truth in it, but that truth is but a deluſion; they would excuſe themſelves when they have yielded to a temptation, I am weak and frail, I cannot reſiſt the devil; though the devil is not ſtronger than Chriſt, yet he is ſtronger than I, he worketh with all his might, power, and ſubtilty to deceive me, and enſnare me, and overcome me; I am a poor, frail creature, therefore I muſt yield to him: This is a carnal reaſon; as tho' I were to grapple with the devil in mine own ſtrength, and to deliver my ſoul, as if God hath left me to myſelf: If thou ſay,
Lord,

Lord, thou haſt ſet me to grapple with the devil, and to withſtand his temptations, Lord I am not able to do it myſelf; God will anſwer thee, *I have laid help upon one that is mighty, that is able to ſave to the uttermoſt, all that come unto me by him;* ſo that thou art not to overcome the devil by thine own power and ability: If any man reaſon thus, his reaſon is out of doors; for we are ſaved by Chriſt, therefore I cannot plead my own frailty, ſeeing God hath provided a *rock* for my defence *that is ſtronger and higher than I*, that I may truſt and rely upon.

So that you ſee the frailties of our nature is not a ſufficient reaſon, we muſt ſeek further for it yet; and when we come to ſearch narrowly, and to the bottom of our hearts, I will tell you here it reſts; it hath its centre in the perverſeneſs of the will that is in man, that is contrary to the will of God; it is the oppoſition of our will to the will of God; we may talk what we will of ſalvation and Chriſtianity, that we have a mind to be ſaved, and go unto God when we die, and to enjoy the happineſs of Heaven to eternity: We may talk thus; but as long as the perverſeneſs of the will continues, I am the cauſe of my own ruin; if I grow in a profeſſion, this perverſe will, will grow up with me under that profeſſion, and under any profeſſion; change your judgment and opinion as often as you liſt, this will go along with you; the reaſon and the bottom of things will come to this, none can overcome the devil, nor be a diſciple of Chriſt, without a daily croſs. When people come to this, to ſee a neceſſity of taking up the croſs of Chriſt, and denying themſelves; when it comes to this, there are ſuch ſhifts and evaſions, and arts that men have to cover themſelves, to make themſelves and others believe, that ſuch and ſuch a thing is conſiſtent with the will of God, and that they may do it, and ſave their own ſouls; but they boaſt of their own deceit, and are glad that they can make a ſhift to deceive their own ſouls; ſo that there is no hopes of their ever being purged and cleanſed, and of having any holy work brought forth by them; but when a man comes to be ſenſible of his ſpiritual condition, and is ſincere and honeſt, he will be ready to ſay unto God, if I

be

be deceived in any thing, open mine eyes, Lord; if I indulge myself in any thing that hath a contrariety to thy holy will, Lord, I beseech thee difcover it to me; fuch a man will lay afide his own will, if it be contrary to God's will: Now here is one that is a very fit object for Chrift to work upon; he will not be long before he be favingly convinced. When a man comes to the word, he is convinced of fuch an evil in his confcience, where nobody but God and himfelf were privy to it, or had any knowledge of it. It is difcovered that he liveth in fuch a practice as is contrary to the mind of God. God hath convinced thee, that thou lovest it, and livest in it, and if thou wilt but break off that evil practice, that he hath fent his Son Jefus Chrift to turn thee from every evil way, and to *redeem thee from all iniquity.*

This truth hath a favour in it; and if thou art fincere and upright, there is nothing for thee to fay or do, but to fet thyfelf againft every thing that is contrary to the mind of God, and thou wilt have light from Heaven fent to guide thee and direct thee in thy way thither; if thou wilt but receive that grace that is freely given of God unto thee through Jefus Chrift, he will certainly purge thee and cleanfe thee from thy fin, and turn thee from every evil way, notwithftanding the perverfenefs of thine own will and the power of fatan; and he will work in thy heart by his grace, till it hath brought thee off from thine iniquity, and wrought iniquity out of thee, and fo bring forth a holy work to God.

Without faith it is impoffible to pleafe God: We cannot pleafe God without faith, nor with it neither, unlefs it be the gift of God. There is a great deal of faith in this nation, and in this city; but do you believe all their ways are pleafing to God? We muft diftinguifh of faith here; when the apoftle would give a defcription of faving faith, he tells you, that *it is the operation of God*; if I have not that operation, and a regard to it, how can I have that working? But fince it is the difpenfation of the gofpel of Chrift, and defign of Chrift, to turn people to the operation of God in their own hearts, we would have them believe it.

If

If there be a drunkard or a prophane perfon, if God work faith in his heart, he will be convinced and fay, what a ſtroke hath the Lord given upon my conſcience, and he will fee it is the Lord's work: Then believe, whoever thou art, and lay hold of this, for this is *the operation of God* upon a believing foul, the ſtroke of God's hand and the power of God, and then thou haſt the work of faith, by which faith thou art enabled to keep thyſelf from that thing that God fmote thee for, and before he gives thee over, the fame hour thou wilt find the fame hand fmiting thee for another ſin; this will be like fire in thy bones, kindling up thy zeal and hatred againſt thy ſin, and will kindle in thee a high fire of love to God, that hath not let thee lie in thy mifery, but minded thy condition, and had compaſſion on thee: This love God will ſhed abroad, which will run over thy heart, *he hath ſhed abroad his love*, faith the apoſtle, Rom. v. *upon our hearts by the Holy Ghoſt*, to conſtrain us to yield obedience; when thou falleſt into the way of faith, which is the operation of God, the devil comes and knocks and bounces on this ſide and that, but God will not fail to give thee power to withſtand temptation.

The Lord Jeſus Chriſt worketh in people's hearts, to turn them from the evil of their ways, that ſo he may bring forth holineſs and righteouſneſs, and redeem a people from under the bondage of ſin, and fit them for the kingdom of his Father, and to uſe the apoſtle's words, *preſent them before the throne of God, without ſpot and blameleſs; he will purify them, and ſprinkle them from an evil conſcience;* their bodies being waſhed with pure water, he will ſanctify the creature; his word is nigh them, and in their hearts, he begins a work in many, and will carry it on in one, and in another.

Here lies the chief work, it is the good hand of God muſt *work all our works in us, and for us, according to the good pleaſure of his will:* Work in you a willingneſs to bear the croſs of Chriſt, and to deny yourſelves; he will operate for you for this purpoſe, therefore you muſt commit yourſelves to him.

It is not our preaching which will convert men to God, but it is the work of God that is pure, which converts the
foul

soul to God, and that cleanses, fits and prepares it for the kingdom of Heaven, *Psalm* xix. 7. We must come to the word of God, that will convince us, reprove us, strengthen, encourage and illuminate us, and do in us and for us all that we stand in need of: To him be all the praise that worketh all in you, and prepares you *to be a peculiar people to himself.* The word of his grace I commit to you all, take heed of doing any thing contrary to it; if you do, that which would be your comfort, will be your condemnation.

His PRAYER after SERMON.

BLESSED God, and Father of Life! thou art glorious in holiness, infinite in power, the eternal God; thy dominion is an everlasting dominion, thy kingdom is without end.

O Lord! we bless and praise thy glorious name, that thou hast made known thyself among the sons and daughters of men; thou hast revealed to us in thy word the manner of thy kingdom among us, in setting up righteousness and truth, and throwing down iniquity.

Powerful God of Life! subject the minds and hearts of all thy people to thy divine power and pleasure, and let the dread of thyself rest upon our spirits, that every one of us may fear to sin against thee, and to do despite to thy Spirit, the Spirit of thy grace, that we may every one of us turn from our iniquities, the evil of our hearts and ways, that we may praise thee in the land of the living, and may become faithful witnesses of that salvation which thou hast wrought for us, and for all them that believe.

Powerful God of Life! the souls of thy people which thou hast gathered out of the world, do praise and magnify thy name for what they have seen, and for what thou hast wrought; thou hast wonderfully appeared in thy love, and brought salvation near, and gathered many into it, it is become a wall and a bulwark to them, that they are defended from the evil one, and from the evils of the world.

O dearest God of Life! raise up poor and needy souls out of the dust, that they may serve thee, and obey thee, and do thy

His Prayer *after* Sermon.

thy will, and shew forth thy power and strength in their weakness and infirmity, that they may trust in thee, and rely upon thee in the time of their distress.

Blessed Father of Life and Power! give grace to the humble and meek, and teach them in thy way. We have had experience, O Lord! of thy fulfilling thy promises; thou art still fulfilling of them to all that truly wait upon thee; thou hast begun a good work, carry it on to the praise and exaltation of thy great name.

Blessed Father! reveal thy power more and more in the nations round about, that they that long after the life of the Living God, may come and find thee, and behold thy divine appearance, through the Son of thy Love, in their own spirits, that so they may receive thy word, and thy word may quicken them, that they may stand up from the dead, and live; for it is the living, the living, O Lord! that praise thee, that honour thy name, that offer praise, and glorify thee.

O blessed Father of Life! carry on thy great work with power throughout all the earth; gather a remnant of thy seed that are scattered, and bring them home into the kingdom of thy dear Son, that we may praise thee together, and rejoice in thy name.

Dear Father! thou hast saved this nation, the land of our nativity, to this day, by a wonderful power, by thy powerful arm; our souls are deeply sensible of the stretching forth of thy Almighty Hand in our preservation at this day; so Living Father! if it be thy heavenly pleasure, lengthen forth our tranquillity, and the enjoyments of thy mercy and goodness to the inhabitants thereof, that they may learn to fear thee, and turn to thee with their whole hearts, and break off, by true repentance, from all those sins that grieve thy Holy Spirit; that so, Living Father of Life! they may come to walk in love and in union with thy heavenly power, and have concord one with another, and shew forth the power of thy grace manifested to them, and magnify thy love and power, and give thee honour and renown for that great salvation that thou hast wrought for them; that so thy great name may be exalted, and thy will may be done on earth as it is in Heaven; that the souls of thy people may be refreshed

freshed with thy love, and the joys of thy presence, and the revelation of thy heavenly power; for this, we offer up to thee living praises, and Christian thanksgivings, in and through the Lord Jesus Christ; for thou art worthy of all praise, and glory, and dominion, forever, and ever. Amen.

SERMON XIX.

The MIGHTY WORK of MAN'S REDEMPTION.

Preached at GRACE-CHURCH-STREET, *Feb. 8, 1687.*

My Friends,

WE are met upon the most weighty affair that can be to every one of us, even to wait that we may have a true knowledge of the beginning, carrying on and perfecting the mighty work of redemption, that people may know that redemption is wrought in their souls; for every ones soul hath been lost and captivated, and led away from the pure presence of God; all have been alienated by reason of sin, which hath been an universal wall of partition and hath excluded and shut out unholy souls from the Holy God; all that have been defiled and polluted, they have been excluded from his dwelling-place, they have been driven out into the world, and the world hath become a world of misery, and of distraction and confusion to the sons and daughters of men; there hath been *anguish, tribulation and wrath* upon all their souls, and an insensibility hath happened unto many, that they have not been apprehensive of the great depravation they have lain under, and they have not been sensible of the glory of that state and condition which they were to have enjoyed; and in that state of insensibility they have not sought after the Lord, but have been *captivated and led away by divers lusts and pleasures*, by which they have wounded their own souls more and more.

And

And in such a state as this it is, that the Lord hath found us; he hath sought us out, and he hath found us *cast out into the open field, and wallowing, as it were, in our own blood*; and yet this hath been a *time of love*; and he hath manifested his love to us in this respect, in that he hath awakened us and brought us to a sense of our depraved and deplorable condition, and given unto a remnant to perceive, that there is a *more excellent glory*, a more excellent enjoyment to be had, than any this world can afford.

But a great many of those whose eyes are so far opened, that they can see and discern a more excellent glory, yet they cannot receive it, for they are not in a capacity for the enjoyment of it; many have the glimmerings, and some little sight of heavenly things, but they themselves are earthly: Many perceive there is a holy life, but it is not theirs, for their own life is unholy, and yet they know there is a life that is holy and pure. Hereupon desires are begotten, by the word of life in the sons and daughters of men, through the Lord Jesus Christ, the Mediator; by him desires are begotten in people that they might come to enjoy that life of holiness, that they might not only see a better state than what they do enjoy, but that they might come to enjoy it, and have it for theirs.

There is a universal desire in people that they might have eternal life, and they believe there is an eternal life to be enjoyed; but every one hath it not, and the reason is, because they are not fitted and prepared for the enjoyment of it; for it is a kind of treasure that is never put into an unclean vessel; there must be a cleansing and purifying, that so earthen vessels may come to retain and hold this heavenly treasure; and when it comes to this, that people must be cleansed and purified, here the world turns out to divers means and methods; some have gone to outward washings, outward cleansings and observations of this and the other ordinance, and when all that hath been done, themselves being judges, they were yet unclean; when they have done all that lies in their power and ability, towards their washing and cleansing, and towards preparing themselves, they

they have found some secret testimony in their own consciences that their hearts were still unclean, and that there was defilement still abiding and lodging in the secret of their souls; and this hath put a great many to a stand, what they should do; when they have come to the end of all, they know not what to do: Many have cried secretly, what shall we do to be saved? For all that we can do, cannot save us. We have retained this, and the other doctrine, followed this and the other way, and made many observations; but all this doth not cleanse our soul, nor *purge our consciences from dead works*, this will not bring us to the inheritance of that immortal life that will give us satisfaction. We hear many speak of satisfaction, and of *joy unspeakable and full of glory*; but here is a weight and burthen still lies upon our souls.

Therefore, my friends, that all such who are brought so far, as to be under such a burthen and oppression, might be informed and come to understand, where the true rest is, and where that power can be found, that is able to answer those tender desires that are begotten in them; for this cause hath the Lord our God communicated and given the dispensation of the gospel of his son, unto a remnant whom he hath sanctified, that they might *speak a word in season to the weary soul*. This is not a day to *make a mock of sin*, this is not a day to make *a covenant with death and hell*, and to resolve to go on in a wicked life, and to continue in it all their days.

But yet there are a sort of people that desire to have a *word spoke in season* to them when they are weary. How many are there in our age and generation, that one may reckon of this number, that are sinners, and overcome by their lusts and corruptions, and by the temptation of *satan* and his instruments. But they are weary of it, it is a burthen to their souls, it costs them many a bitter tear, many a sigh, and many a sad and sorrowful thought in secret, that they should have a sight of a *more excellent glory*, and of a better life than that of their own, and yet know not how to get into it.

My friends, that same divine word of life, by which any of the people of the Lord, in any age, were ever restored,

redeemed

redeemed and purchased again to the Lord; that word of life muft have been at work in their hearts, and hath been at work in them, or elfe thou hadft never been fo far opened; there hath been fomething that hath unftopped thine ears, that thou mighteft hear; and the reafon of thy continuance in thy bonds, after thy knowing fomething that might have freed thee, is, becaufe thou haft not heartily clofed with that which hath begun the work, which God, by his redeeming power, hath effected in the hearts of them that believe in Chrift, and thereby an inclination is raifed in people to feek after the Lord.

You know what the apoftle faith, *it is not of us fo much as to think a good thought*. But this all people will grant is a good thought, when a finner thinks of turning to God, and leaving his evil ways, if he had power and ability, and cries out, if I knew how to ftand againft temptation, I would never fin againft the Lord more; this muft be a good thought in thy mind: How came it there? Who is the author of this thought, you will fay? This ought to be attributed to the love of God in Chrift, that he hath convinced and perfuaded us; and that though there is fin and pollution, yet he hath not fo forfaken us, as utterly to caft us off, he hath fent forth his *quickening Spirit, that is, the Lord from Heaven*, that he might ftir up and quicken people to confider their condition, and bring them to a fenfe of their prefent ftate, that they may come into a better ftate than they are in at prefent.

If this may be granted, that the Spirit of God, and the grace of God, is the author of thefe defires, then it will be granted at the fame time, that every one of you ought to be fenfible, that fuch fpiritual defires ftirring you, are from the motion and operation of the Spirit of God that hath raifed them in your fouls; and then I hope you will grant, that if you had but joined with that Spirit, and with the affiftance of that Spirit, all things would have been poffible thereunto.

So that here is the firft thing that I would have every one fatisfied about in their underftandings, whether they are totally exempted from any fuch touches and operations of God or no; for it is faid by fome ignorantly, that a great part of mankind have never had any fuch divine workings of the Spirit of God upon them, in order to their converſion; therefore it is not in vain for you to conſider your ſtate and condition; for if you, or I, or any here, be under ſuch circumſtances, that they never had, nor are ever like to have any ſuch divine operations or touches of the ſpirit of life, in order to converſion, then I am ſure you and I had better never have been born.

· If you will conſider with yourſelves, and lay aſide the diſputes of doctors and learned men, you may know the things pertaining to yourſelves. Things relating to others, I may let diſputes alone about them; but as for things relating to my ſalvation, I muſt have a certain knowledge of them. It concerns you, my friends, to know within yourſelves, by an infallible evidence of the Spirit of God, whether you have had ſuch divine touches, workings and operations upon your hearts, as have inclined you to ſeek the Lord. I hope I may believe there are none here but have in their hearts an anſwer; I have had ſuch touches and operations in me: This is great love from God; more than any tongue can ſet forth. You will be ready to ſay, I have not deſerved this; I have not ſo behaved myſelf towards my Maker as to deſerve that he ſhould wait upon me, and call upon me. *When wilt thou turn, and amend thy life, and hearken to him that made thee? When wilt thou leave ſerving God's enemy, and ſerve him that is thy rightful Lord?*

So that now this is a great aggravation of our ſin to continue in it, and yet to have a belief that God is ſtill waiting upon us, and that he hath ſuch a kindneſs for us, as now and then to touch our hearts by the inward operation of his ſpirit and grace, in order to converſion.

Now when this is agreed, and men ſettle themſelves in the belief of this, you know what the conſequence will be. When I conſider with myſelf, I that have been under theſe workings, have been rebellious, wicked and diſobedient to God, yet the Lord is not ſo angry as utterly to call me off, but is ſtill waiting to be gracious, by the operation of his ſpirit, to gather me to himſelf, in order to ſanctify me, and heal my backſliding, to cure my weakneſs nefs and infirmities, and at the laft to fave me, and make me an heir of his eternal kingdom, what is the confequence of this love? Why, the next refolve muft be this; I will either rebel againft his grace, and refift his power, or I will fubmit to him; which of thefe is the beft way, the fafeft way?

Are there not a great many in this age, that are as fenfible of the workings of God's grace for their converfion, as ever you and I were; that are as fenfible that God hath called them to holinefs and righteoufnefs, as any of us can be, and yet they have refifted the grace of God? They have faid in their hearts, we will not fubmit to this power, that will make us fo holy, and fo watchful, and fo careful, diligent and obedient, for this very reafon, becaufe it will crofs my intereft, it will crofs my pleafure, it will hinder my preferment in the world, and my reputation among men; and for this reafon I will not bear this yoke. I would be glad to hope there are none fuch here, that have made fuch *a covenant with death and hell*, and yielded themfelves up to the devil, to ferve him all their days.

Let us, who are at this time, and at this meeting, under the operation of God's grace, and feel the Lord calling us by his grace, and working upon us by his fpirit; let us enter together into a holy, folemn refolution, that we will obey this good Spirit, and take him for our leader, and fubmit, though it fhould be to a crofs: Thus people will think, they will come to this refolution, when the work of redemption is begun in their fouls, and when they are convinced of their fin, and their eyes are opened to fee the way of holinefs; and though they never take a refolution to walk in it, yet every one fhall be convinced, and fee there was a better way than their own, and be convinced by the grace of God one time or other, that in refpect of God's working of it, it is beginning; but in refpect of men that fhould join with the operation of God, it is not beginning, for he hath no defire to thofe things which he doth not know, he ftill depends upon himfelf; but when the foul comes to be fatisfied, that it is the vifitation of God, and joins himfelf to him in a holy refignation of his own will, and faith, this is the Lord, he
is

is come to work upon me, he is come to change and alter the frame of my mind: It is the Lord, let him do what he will; here is a mind brought to submit to the grace of God, God is able to do that for him which he cannot do for himself.

When people come to the right object of their faith, and act their faith upon that object, they every day find a progress, a going forward in the work of grace, according to the work of grace in their souls; and there is a power that inclines them to believe; it is not for such to cry, if they had power, they would do more; he that hath the spirit of grace, the Spirit of Christ, that had *all power in Heaven and Earth given* to him, to put it forth on purpose for the bringing back of men and women home to God; he that hath this object of faith before him, he will not look for power in his own will and affections to redeem him, he expects a power to be daily ministered and dispensed to him, as he hath need of it, through the Lord Jesus Christ, who is present with him, in all his trials and temptations: He cries, here is a temptation that will carry me away, O Lord help me, *put forth the arm of thy power and save me*, plant thy fear in my heart and deliver me, *their eyes shall see their Saviour*, saith the prophet.

Thus when a man comes to be joined to the right object of faith, and doth exercise and put forth lively acts of faith upon Christ, his eyes shall see his Saviour; the light that shines into his heart, discovers to him the temptation, and it also shews him a Reedemer at hand; his Saviour is nigh him, and he trusteth in him, and relies upon him, and says, this word of God is in my heart, and I do really believe, that although the temptation that assaults me be strong, yet it shall not prevail; whether it be the profits, the pleasures, or the honours of the world. If I put my trust in this power, I cannot go near the evil; I am a Christian; I have entered into a covenant in Christianity, that I will join with nothing but what God approves of: Now when I have represented to my mind the temptation of the devil, and that evil which he sets before me, and I know it is contrary to the mind of God, how can I go into that evil, and break my covenant with
God,

MAN'S REDEMPTION.

God, after I have entered into covenant with him, to love him, serve him, and obey him? The power of grace upon such souls, the operation of grace, is so powerful, that the temptation comes and goes, and they are saved and delivered out of it, because God helpeth them; but if they comply with the temptation, then *tribulation, wrath and anguish*, pursues all such as are rebellious and disobedient to the will of God.

Now this redemption is carried on gradually from day to day; the truth that thou believest, it operates by degrees; thou art delivered, first from one evil practice, and then from another evil work: But there is a great deal more; thou rejoicest and art glad, that thou art delivered from one sin; but thou wouldest be more glad to be delivered from them all. I speak to those that are serious for their immortal souls; when they see themselves delivered out of one evil, that they were ready to run into, they would be glad if they were redeemed out of every evil; that their crossness and peevishness, their frowardness and wantonness were removed: They should be glad to be delivered from all their sins.

What do you think, say some, that a man, while he liveth here, may come to see all sin, all evil and corruption brought under, and nothing but holiness, righteousness and truth remain in him; and that there shall be nothing but simplicity and innocence? Do you think that such a thing can be?

Why should not I think so? You will grant me, that the power of grace is able to get such power and victory over sin and corruption, that you may come to hate it as much as ever you have loved it; if you grant me that, the consequence will follow, he that gave me victory over sin, can give me power over all sin. All Christians believe, that God's power is infinite; the scripture testifies, *all things to be possible to God, with whom we have to do.* If all things be possible to God, sure this is possible; there is nothing so contrary to God as sin; and God will not suffer the devil always to rule his master-piece, man. Mankind is God's master-piece, the most eminent creature in this lower world, made after God's likeness; and though
the

the devil hath brought men into his own likeneſs now, yet nothing can be more contrary to the mind of God, than that the devil ſhould have the rule of us, for God would have the government of us himſelf.

When we conſider the infiniteneſs of God's power, for deſtroying that which is contrary to him, who can believe that the devil muſt ever ſtand and prevail ? I belive it is inconſiſtent and diſagreeable with the true faith, for people to be Chriſtians, and yet to believe that Chriſt, the eternal Son of God, to whom all power in Heaven and Earth is given, will ſuffer ſin and the devil to have dominion over them; *there is no other name under Heaven by which I can be ſaved,* therefore I have put my confidence in him : If the devil muſt have the rule of me here, then I cannot be ſubject to Chriſt in all things ; I may go to meetings, but can never maſter the devil and his temptations ; this is as inconſiſtent with the faith of a Chriſtian, as light with darkneſs, and Chriſt with *Belial.* If Chriſtians think themſelves true believers, then let them ſee how far their faith will reach, whether it be like that faith, *which was once delivered to the ſaints,* for by that faith their hearts were cleanſed, and they became free from ſin, *Rom.* vi. 22. *But now being made free from ſin, and the ſervants of God,* ſaith the apoſtle, *you have your fruit unto holineſs, and the end everlaſting life ;* you were ſervants to ſin, but now you are free from ſin ; ſo that this faith is but one, and if men have got another, it will do them no good : Take heed thou art not miſtaken about thy faith.

I have heard ſome learned men ſay, that a believer is a ſervant of ſin, and he is ever like to be ſo ; but he is not at the ſame time free from righteouſneſs, for he hath the righteouſneſs of Chriſt imputed to him, and God looks upon him as righteous in his righteouſneſs ; there cannot be a more anti-apoſtolical doctrine, I may be a ſervant of ſin, and yet have the imputation of Chriſt's righteouſneſs ; I may be a ſervant of ſin, ſay they, yet Chriſt is righteous, he is the righteouſneſs of God, and he *hath fulfilled the will of God, and hath purchaſed ſalvation* for me, and he is the object by which I am made righteous.

Conſider this, the imputation of Chriſt's righteouſneſs
will

will never do me good, till I come to partake of his righteousness, till his righteousness be made my righteousness, in me and for me. Chrift is made *to us of God, wifdom, righteoufnefs, fanctification and redemption ;* fo that if a finner, one that was a finner the other day, come, through faith in Chrift, to have his heart cleanfed and purged, and true righteoufnefs planted in him, where fin was planted, there fin, through the blood of Chrift, is cleanfed and purged away.

So that Chrift is made righteoufnefs to me, and not his righteoufnefs barely imputed and reckoned to me; *Chrift is my wifdom,* I am a fool without him; Chrift is made *righteoufnefs to me;* for my good deeds and holy living cannot be acceptable to God till they be done in him, and commended to God by him; the proper work of faith is, to fix the foul on him that *worketh all things in us and for us, that worketh in us both to will and to do, according to his good pleafure;* and it is the good pleafure of God that we fhould live in all righteoufnefs.

They that come to receive this faith at firft, have to receive it from an inward feeling; they have the operation of the word of God in them; fo the apoftle reckons faith, not becaufe fuch a man heareth, and fuch a man believeth what fuch a man preacheth, but *faith is the operation of God;* you may hear me, and a thoufand preach, and you may die unbelievers for all that, except you come to this, to know the operation of God, and the work of faith in you. How doth my heart clofe with this? How doth my foul join with this? What virtue and power do I feel in myfelf? it may be others that preach, feel the power, but do I feel it? if not, I come but to a noife and found: If people feel not their hearts joining with the word preached, there comes no advantage to them; you read in fcripture, that *the word preached did not profit, becaufe it was not mixed with faith in them that heard it:* This is your cafe, you come to meeting, and you love to hear the doctrine of truth preached; I tell you, and I will fpeak plainly to you, unlefs you come to feel the operation of the word of truth in your hearts, you may hear the gofpel, and the word of life preached to you, but it will not profit you much.

How is it possible for a man to have a testimony against drunkenness, and yet be drunk? a testimony against uncleanness, and yet be unclean? How can a man hear such a testimony and believe it, and yet commit the sin? He heard it, but did not feel the virtue of it within himself, and so he did not mortify the sin that he was inclinable to; but they that come to join with truth, and *with meekness receive the ingrafted word*, they find the power and ability of it, they find how able it is to save their souls, they find how it worketh, not only just when they hear it, but it goes along with them, and dwells with them, and they find the virtue of it overshadowing their souls, with the dread and terror of the Lord, not with the words that a man speaks; I do not trust to them, but here is the power and the fear of the Lord, which will preserve my soul, and keep me in safety; this is that which will keep my mind fixed upon him, and keep my mind inward, that I do not gaze about me; so that every one may have an infallible testimony of what they have heard and known.

I have known the doctrine of several sects that have been among us, and the main thing that many have gone from one people to another about, is this, that they might know what such a man holds forth more than such a one, and they think the truth is more perspicuous among such a people than other people; if you examine the matter, it is this, who preached and proved his doctrine best. Alas! if they did all concur together, and did preach as certain and infallible doctrine as ever Christ and his apostles preached, this will all do thee and me no good, unless we know the power. You know there were thousands that heard Christ preach, as you now hear me, and there were some so taken with him, that they went away, and said, *never man spake like this man.* But were they all Christians? Did they partake of life by him? No, some of them were ready to stone him.

Now bring this home and consider with yourselves, whether you are not some of you in the same state; when you hear truth preached, there is an assent and agreement with it in your minds; but when a command comes to be obeyed, and a cross to be taken up, and self-denial to be shewn, or some encrease of trade lies in the way, let truth go where it it will, you muſt follow your intereſt ; there wants ſomewhat to fix you in the principle of truth, which is able to ſanctify you and perfect you, that you may be reconciled to God through Chriſt.

They that are reſigned and given up to truth, it is poſſible for them that they may be ſatisfied ; they have an infallible teſtimony *of the ſpirit of truth witneſſing with their ſpirits,* that ſuch a thing is bad, and if they might get the whole world to do it, they will not. What is profit and pleaſure to me ? My pleaſure is at God's right hand, and my profit is to get grace, and to *have an abundant entrance into God's everlaſting kingdom.* Thoſe that have the true knowledge of Chriſt, they have profit and advantage, pleaſure and delight enough, which is hid from the world, and ever will be. They are for profit and pleaſure, which they may have with a good conſcience. Thoſe things which God affords them as bleſſings in this world, they deſpiſe them not, but take them with thankſgiving, and uſe them for his glory : But if they cannot have profit or pleaſure without ſinning againſt the Lord and their own conſciences, let thoſe who will, take profit and pleaſure.

They that come thus to cloſe with truth, they have an infallible evidence within them ; they do not conceive it is thus and thus, becauſe ſuch a man ſaith it is ſo ; but they have an infallible evidence in themſelves. This is the mind of the Lord ; God hath ſignified it by his Spirit, and ſealed it upon my ſpirit, and I cannot but know it.

What, do you profeſs infallibility ? Yes, elſe I would hold my tongue ; if I did not know what I aſſert infallibly, I would never preach more ; truth may be many times concealed. A man may have wronged and cheated his neighbour, and he not know of it ; this man goes away, and his neighbour doth not reproach him ; but when he comes to lie down in his bed, he hath a ſting and a reproach in his conſcience, I know I have done him harm. Is not this infallible ? Let me conſult ſome learned men, that I may know whether I have told a lie. I need not go to learned men and logicians, to know whether it was a lie ; I am infallible in this, I know certainly it was not a lie; I have a certain evidence, and if a thoufand men tell me to the contrary, I will not believe them. If there be infallibility here, is there not then infallibility in the word of truth? Shall I queftion it, or doubt it, if I have an infallible teftimony of it?

Tho' men have ever fo little proficiency, if they have it upon fure terms, and lafting foundations, let a thoufand men come with all their logical skill and fophifm, yet they can never remove a man from the witnefs in himfelf. The remnant that God hath brought to this foundation, they have a certainty and infallibility in their obedience, that they pay to the will of God, and in the comfort they have to the obedience of the law of God, *which he hath written in their hearts*. Let what will come, they can never be removed; for this exceeds all the precepts and doctrines of men; it is the precept and doctrine of Chrift and his apoftles. Let people read them, and endeavour to practife them: But here comes the teftimony, the divine power by which the precept was given forth to them, and is now given forth again to thee and me, with the fame livelinefs and power. Let us perform them as did the primitive Chriftians.

Here now, comfort comes to flow forth from a fettled foundation that fhall never be moved. The winds have come and blown upon religion; let what wind will blow, that can blow, God hath built his church upon a rock, and it will remain unmoveable againft all oppofition; bleffed are they that are founded thereupon. Hath God fixed and eftablifhed us in our fociety with one another, and with our Lord Jefus Chrift? this is the foundation that God hath placed it upon. We defire that all men may come to the fame ftability and fettlement, and never more to be *toffed with the winds of doctrine, but be built upon Chrift Jefus, the Rock of Ages,* the rock of our ages, the rock of us and our children. That God will carry us on in this fociety, is the defire of our fouls, for ourfelves, and all our friends and countrymen. The way for you to be bleffed, and to have an advantage for your immortal fouls, by the teftimony that hath been raifed up, is, to have regard to the working of the fame power, that

you

you may come to partake of the benefit of those gifts and graces which God hath bestowed upon his church.

His PRAYER after SERMON.

MOST blessed and glorious God and Father of Life! how wonderful art thou in thy appearances to thy people in the day of thy power, in which thou hast stretched forth thine arm, and hast gathered a remnant of those that were scattered, and art yet gathering and bringing to thyself, those that have been driven away; and thou hast made known thy power and goodness in the hearts of the sons and daughters of men, that they might love thee. That thou mightest beget love to thyself, thou hast made known thy love to their hearts; if thou hadst not loved us first, we had never loved thee: But thou hast been shedding abroad thy love in our hearts by the Holy Ghost, to constrain us to love thee. Thy love is manifested to all that are breathing after thee, and none do breathe after thee, but through the life that thou givest them; and those that were dead in sins and trespasses, hast thou quickened, and we would send forth thy praises and thanksgivings for the great things thou hast done for us in Jesus Christ. All thy works praise thee, and thy saints bless thee.

Holy Father of Life! encrease and multiply those graces and holy desires which thou hast begun to work in us, and pluck up every plant that thy right hand hath not planted. Let spiritual Sodom be burnt up, and all that are corrupt; let those things that thou hast planted spring up to the praise of thy name, and the salvation of the souls which thou hast gathered.

O powerful God of Life! let thy blessed presence and living fear be among us, that all thy children may offer praises, and the sacrifices of humble thanksgivings upon thy holy altar.

Arise, O Lord! more and more in the greatness of thy power, and dispel the clouds of darkness that hath been upon the sons and daughters of men, and raise up in every one of us more and more holy desires and breathings after that life that is eternal. Those that have been scattered, let them be now gathered, and let those that have been driven away in a cloudy

and

and dark night, be brought to a glorious and blessed day, wherein they may enjoy the gospel that brings light to dark souls, that praises and thanksgivings may be offered up in thy house for thy holy presence with us, that we may be fed there, when we are assembled together in thy name, according to thy promise. Continue to be in the midst of us, that living praises and thanksgivings may be offered up to thee, through Jesus Christ; for thou alone art worthy, who art God over all, blessed for evermore. Amen.

SERMON XX.

The WORD of GOD, a CHRISTIAN'S LIFE.

Preached at GRACE-CHURCH-STREET, *March* 14, 1687.

IT was the doctrine of the great master of the Christian religion, the Lord Jesus Christ, while he was preaching and publishing, and making known the way of salvation among the sons and daughters of men; he then preached and declared, that it was *not bread only by which a man lived, but by every word that proceedeth out of the mouth of God*. Now the way and means of man's preservation in life, in a living state, the method and course that the God of Heaven doth open to keep the sons and daughters of men alive, is by this word: *Every word that proceedeth out of the mouth of God*, hath a ministration of life in it; and, therefore, all that are desirous of the enjoyment of the immortal life, and of the preserving and encreasing of it, they are diligently to wait to be made partakers of this divine ministration. Outward bread is for outward preservation, but man is made inward as well as outward, he hath a soul as well as a body. Now Christ, to signify to us, what the inward man is nourished and fed by, tells us, that *man liveth not by bread alone, but by every word that proceedeth out of the mouth of God*.

So now in this our day, as well as in former days, it hath pleased God to give unto a remnant an experimental knowledge of the truth of this; that they have been
quick-

quickened and made alive by the word of God; that is, they *have heard, and felt, and tafted of the word of life that was with the Father before the world began,* that hath been divinely miniftred to them, by the mercy of God, through Jefus Chrift; many *that were dead in trefpaffes and fins, he hath faid unto them, live.* He hath given unto many an inward fenfe of their ftate, who fometimes had it not; he hath brought many a one to feel fin to be a burthen and an oppreffing load, who fometimes before have taken pleafure and delight in it. This is a great change that is wrought in a man's mind, that he fhould come to be laden with that, burthened and oppreffed by that, which was before his pleafure and delight; yet this great change hath been wrought in many a foul, by the operation of the word of God, of that inward word, that inward voice, when the Lord hath taken men in hand himfelf.

There are many have taken finners in hand, and have gone about to convince them and convert them, but they were not able to do it; but when the Lord hath taken men in hand himfelf, when his Creator hath undertaken to deal with him himfelf, then the man cries out, *I am a worm, and no man;* then he cries out under the fenfe of the judgment of God, then he cries out under the indignation of the Lord, which he hath kindled by his fins, he cries out for mercy, then he prays for remiffion, then he wifhes that he had never provoked the Lord; for the word that goes out of the mouth of God, hath a mighty force and power upon the fpirit of a man, fo that he is converted and changed by it; as the prophet faid of old, *the word of God is pure, converting the foul.*

Now where any come to an experimental knowledge of the word of the Lord, of this inward voice, whereby God fpeaks to the fons and daughters of men, they have received thereby an infallible feeling of their own ftate and condition; this is the firft leffon learned by it. They come to have a certain, infallible knowledge of their own ftate, and they are fure that they cannot be deceived; for it brings an evidence with it in their confciences, fo that whatfoever this word of life fignifieth to a man, he hath the knowledge of the fame thing evidencing it in his own confcience, as the apoftle

tle faith, *if our hearts condemn us, God is greater than our hearts, and knoweth all things*. Now here is a way found out for men to obtain divine knowledge by a divine means; for the Lord speaks by his Spirit, and if men come to hearken to that voice, unto that speaking, they perceive readily what it saith unto them: The Lord tells people as well now as in former ages, what he hath against them; and this every one in the closet of their own hearts, come to understand. We read in the book of *Revelations*, what our Lord Jesus Christ appointed *John* to write to the seven churches in *Asia*, that he had *few things* against some, and *many things* against others.

Now that which is the design of our meeting when we are assembled together, is, that we may know what the mind and judgment of God is, concerning ourselves: How shall we know that, unless we ask him, and come to wait upon him, and enquire at the oracle of counsel, that God hath appointed in the bosom of every man? For he signifies his mind unto the children of men, by that light and grace which Jesus Christ hath planted in them, he hath *enlightened every man that comes into the world*, with an undeceiving light, and he *hath ministered of his truth* and grace to every man; though the man be bad and untrue, and in the dark, and there be darkness in him, yet *the light shineth in darkness*. The man may be a false man, yet there is true knowledge in him; if this man hearken to the voice of truth, when the God of truth signifies what his mind and judgment is concerning him, and his present state.

So that there is an opportunity offered, and if a man believe the word of truth, which is administered to his own mind, he cannot say such a man hath deceived him, for it is truth itself which is signified to him which he believeth: For the truth is the object of his faith, and he believeth it of himself; he believeth that while he remains wicked in his unrenewed state, he is out of the covenant of God, and in the high road to destruction, if he doth not get out of it, and return to God, and mind his duty: He believeth this, and he believeth the truth: It hath been so with many, it hath been so with us all; this is the first kind of faith and belief that ever we receive; for when truth signifieth to us

our

a CHRISTIAN'S LIFE.

our fallen ſtate, our alienated ſtate, when truth ſignifies and diſcovers to us the partition wall of ſin and iniquity which we have builded up, whereby the glory and favour of God was hid from the ſoul, we believed this to be true; we would have been looked upon as heirs of God's kingdom, yet when we are come to hearken to truth, we find that we are children of the devil and do his works; ſhall a man believe this after he hath been forty years a profeſſor of Chriſtianity? If a man believe truth, there is no danger in believing it, tho' it be his own deſtruction that is threatened.

Now the great thing that I would have uſhered into the hearts of men, is, that they may believe the truth for truth's ſake. If men will believe the truth, they muſt believe many things againſt themſelves, which they are not willing to believe; but ſaith Chriſt, *no man can be my ſcholar, my diſciple, but by denying himſelf*. I muſt deny myſelf, my pretenſions to Chriſtianity, my ſuppoſed ſaintſhip and title to the kingdom of God; now if I would be convinced that I am a wicked man, a prophane man, one that doth not live as becomes the goſpel, I muſt believe truth, the voice of truth being of infallible certainty; it is ſignified divinely, by the immortal word that cannot deceive us; this ought to be the reaſon why people ſhould believe the teſtimony of it, tho' it be againſt themſelves; they that do ſo, preſently come to find the effects of it, for they were in their ſins and treſpaſſes before, and ſo are ſtill; they were before in a kind of liberty, in a kind of eaſe and indulgence of themſelves, and ſtill their ſin remains in them, and they remain in it; but they are now under a ſenſe of ſorrow, under a weight, under a burthen, under an oppreſſion, which ſignifies they are alive, and quickened; for (if you take an outward compariſon) they remain not ſenſeleſs and dead; now lay what load you will upon a dead man, he will neither groan, nor grumble at it; but if he comes again to life, he cries take off the burthen, the weight and oppreſſion, that lies heavy upon me.

This is the difference between being *dead in ſins and treſpaſſes*, and being brought to life and ſenſe again; this word of life that comes from the mouth of God, begets a ſenſe in every one that receiveth it; it is of great ſervice and uſe to all people to be acquainted with it, that desire to be *heirs of life eternal*, that desire to be *inheritors of the kingdom of God*: But how should they come by it? They think by this and the other duty, and temporary performance, to obtain it; no, but if they will have life, they must have it from the God of life that created them, he must *create* them *again to good works:* They can have it but by one way, all must be brought to it that way; it cannot be by hearing a man preach; unless the spirit doth co-operate with the word of God, there is no possibility of being quickened, and necessity binds me to hearken and have regard to that one means: *Now I say to you*, saith Christ, speaking of people's way of living to eternity, *man liveth not by bread alone, but by every word that proceedeth out of the mouth of God*; now when we come to understand this text, as spoken by our Lord Jesus Christ, we did conclude there was a possibility of understanding and hearing that inward voice and word of truth in our own hearts, that God did speak to us by his Son, Jesus Christ, who enlightened us. Hereupon meetings were appointed at first, that the word should minister life in them, and life to them that attend them; and to this day our meetings are appointed for this purpose, that we may have the ministration of life and virtue, from Christ, the fountain of life and virtue, by whom we were to be quickened and strengthened, and by whom *those that are dead in sins and trespasses were quickened.*

Therefore I would have every one always to have a reverence to the word of life, that speaks in themselves; for, if we speak as we are *moved by the Spirit of God*, and utter those things by verbal testimony, which God hath made known to us; if you have not an oracle in your bosoms, if you do not at the same time perceive an echo of truth in your own souls, this will do you no good, but be an empty sound which will pass away again; but the mind that is serious and settled, in waiting upon God with an earnest desire, that it may receive benefit in going to this and the other meeting; such a one will say, I pray God bless this opportunity to me, that so I may receive benefit to my soul. Where people meet in this manner, they have not only an administration of doctrine from without, from this and the other

other inftrument, *but they have a miniftration of the word of God in themfelves, by which a man liveth.*

Let us not be led and hurried away with the grand error of the times, the great error of this age, and of the ages bypaft, that there is no poffibility for people to underftand and hear this voice of God, this inward voice. There are, fay they, no immediate teachings now-a-days, no infpirations now-a-days; they might as well fay, that there are no converfions now-a-days. I will prove it from the holy fcriptures, that there is no man in this age, is like to be converted to God, or redeemed from his iniquity, and brought to the knowledge of his Maker, unlefs he have it by the inward working of the eternal God: Not by man's preaching and inftruction, nor by reading all the good fermons that ever were preached, without the co-operation of the holy fanctifying Spirit, which begets life in them that believe ; and if thefe men fay none can be converted, then we muft all go headlong to hell, even they and all.

Thefe Quakers may fay what they will, there is no immediate teaching now-a-days, no man can know the mind of God, nor underftand the fcriptures ; none can open them to you.

But, bleffed be God, this darknefs is removed ; this veil is gone over and taken away ; the brightnefs of the glory of the gofpel hath expelled this darknefs, and thoufands now-a-days do not only hear the minifter reprove them, but they hear a voice within that doth reprove them for iniquity ; and they find and feel a judgment and tribunal within themfelves, and that God hath an immediate way of counfelling and inftructing them if they will hearken to him.

You that are under any fenfe of this, that are come to fuch an inward fenfe of the operation of the word of God, if you have heard it reprove you, exhort you, judge you and condemn you, confider that this *word* proceeded *out of the mouth of God,* and not out of the mouth of any man. You hear the fentence of God upon you in your own confciences: Whence comes it ? This is out of the mouth of God. Every word that comes out of the mouth of God, adminifters life, fenfe and conviction; and you feel it and receive it, and
you

you may have a more familiar acquaintance with it. There is not a day or hour that paffes over your heads nor mine, but if we attend to this inward voice, we may know what it fpeaks to us, by its counfels, doctrines, reproofs, convictions and illuminations; *for the Spirit fpeaketh exprefsly*, with an' exprefs fignification, unto the fpirit of man; and if he be under a temptation to tell a lie, and he comes to a little paufe or queftion, whether he fhall tell it or no; if he hearken to this inward word he will not paufe long about it, but fuch a fentence will arife in him, as that in *Jofeph, how can I do this great wickednefs, and fin againft God?* How can I fpeak a lie, tell a lie, when in fo doing I fin againft God? Here is a fentence of truth, wilt thou receive it or no? No fayeft thou, I will venture to tell a lie; then fhalt thou come into the rank of them that do *defpite to the Spirit of grace, and trample under foot the Son of God, and count the blood of the covenant an unholy thing.* What fentence fuch fhall have at the latter end, you may read at large in the holy fcriptures.

Now there is a great neceffity that every one be perfuaded to hearken to this voice, not only at a meeting, but on all occafions they have in the world. I hope I fpeak to many ferious and religious perfons that are enquiring about their immortal fouls, what may be beft for their fouls, whether it is better to go on in wickednefs, or leave off; and that refolve and fay, I would be glad to leave my fins as well as you, if I had power, and to live a holy life. As for the want of power, (that you have not power) I do not wonder at it; for until you come to an exercife of faith, in that which hath empowered the people of God, in all ages, I wonder not that you have not power. You fay I am fo weak, that I am overcome before I am aware; the devil is fo fubtile and cunning with his temptations, that I am furprized and fnatched into temptations, and overcome with evil before I am aware: *He is like a roaring lion, going about continually, feeking whom he may devour.* But whom can he devour? Can he devour thofe that hearken and fubmit to the word of God? If he could, then none could efcape him; if the devil could pluck out of God's hands, then nobody would go to Heaven, nor never fhall, if he have power. Where

Where the devil finds any in their own hands, as suppose a religious person of this and the other religion, who never experienced any thing of this power of God, but trusteth to his duties and performances, this man is in his own hand; now such a one the tempter hath power over: He can make him cheat his neighbour, and lead him into drunkenness and uncleanness sometimes, and into the greatest abominations; but if a man come into the exercise of faith and dependence upon God, and hath left trusting in himself and faith, I see I cannot preserve myself from sin, I see a necessity of putting my trust in the Lord, and of waiting upon God's power to keep me: If the tempter come to such a one, he cannot prevail, all the devils in hell cannot stir him one jot; the devil may tempt him, but he stands in the power of faith; he knows his name, and faith, *get thee behind me satan;* when the devil comes before him, and lays a temptation before him, he casts it behind him; if the devil rise up against him, he can chain him down, he can say in the name of the Lord, *get thee behind me satan.*

This is the reason why many are tempted, and not overtaken; why many are tempted to sin and not overcome: How comes it to pass that we do not do every thing that we are tempted to?

There is something that keeps us; the devil is not so bad to tempt, but we are as bad in our own inclinations to yield to him; *the heart is deceitful above all things, and desperately wicked; who can know it?* There is more wickedness in it, than can be uttered. If people be tempted and not overcome, something must preserve them; if there be something that preserves a man from any evil, it can preserve him from all evil.

The reason why some people are led into temptation sometimes, and resist it, is because sometimes the temptation suits not their inclination; sometimes the reputation lies in the way, sometimes one thing, sometimes another: But when a thing they are tempted to, suits their profit and pleasure, then away with the fear of God, and nothing shall hinder them; I will have my pleasure.

But they that understand the *keeper of Israel*, and come to know his power lying in their hearts, these always bring their
deeds

deeds and temper before him, and they come to him for a verdict and judgment, and they ask, doth this tend to the honour or dishonour of God? Is it good or evil? The oracle of God in thy heart says do it not, it is evil, thou wilt *kindle the indignation of the Lord against thee; what will it profit thee to gain the whole world and lose thy own soul? or what wilt thou give in exchange for thy soul?* Here is one at hand that can give counsel to all of us, at all times; this is he that we must advance; our labour and work upon the stage of this world, among the sons and daughters of men, is to advance the virtue and great authority of the mighty Counsellor, Christ Jesus; we do say and affirm, in the name of God, that the same light by which God *hath brought us out of darkness into his marvellous light, and from the power of the devil into the kingdom of his dear Son;* the same power is extended to you, *that you may be sanctified and saved from your sins.*

One sect will say, my tenets are so and so, and our ordinances are so and so, will you come over to us? You shall be a member of our church.

Our duty is to come over to the grace of God that shines in our hearts; now we are witnesses for God, *that he doth not desire the death of them that die, but rather that they would turn and live;* for his word is gone forth, and his light shines, and his glory is risen upon the nations, that they that inhabit the earth may fear him. *Fear God, and give glory to his name, for the hour of his judgment is come:* Do you know that to be true? That you may not be deluded, you shall certainly know that the hour of God's judgment is come.

Thus when any one suffers himself to be led away with the evil one, when he feels after that a remorse upon his own heart, he finds a secret judgment and tribunal set up in his own bosom, against whoredom, lying, drunkenness, fraud and other sins, he knows he hath done amiss; he is not going to a confessor, that will take off and remove the guilt from his conscience; he hath offended the majesty of the great God, and God hath signified it to him, is not judgment come, and hath not God set it up in his own heart? If through custom in sin thou losest the sense of his judgment, it is not because God hath determined to take advantage against thee,

but

but becaufe thou acteft againft thyfelf, and comeft to be *paft feeling*; thou waft once under a fenfe of thefe things, and thou waft not *paft feeling*; if thou at any time told thy parents a lie, thou hadft remorfe; but now thou canft tell a lie, and not feel it, thou art *paft feeling*; whofe fault is this? The Lord would have brought thee to love the truth, but thou choofeft lying; if thou perifh, *thy blood will be upon thine own head,* the Lord is clear from it.

They that receive the word of God have life. *For man liveth not by bread alone, but by every word that proceedeth out of the mouth of God.* You are fenfible of God's fpeaking this word to you: I exhort you all in the love of God, that you would prize this manner of fpeaking, and look upon it as the greateft mercy that ever you enjoyed, that God hath not given over fpeaking to you, and that confcience hath not given over fpeaking to you, and that the Spirit of the Lord doth yet *ftrive with you; he will not always ftrive;* you may be of that fort of fools before you die, that *make a mock of fin,* and be *as trees twice dead, and plucked up by the roots.* You that are fenfible of this inward voice, prize it above all your mercies; health and wealth, and all other mercies; are not worthy to be compared to this voice of God fpeaking in you: They that prize this, will never complain for want of power; they will find power in it; all the power in Heaven and Earth is contained in this truth that fhines unto you. They that come to be exercifed in this word, receive power from God, for God gives it to them; he gives them power by degrees (from being fons of *Belial,* fons of the devil) to become *fons of God, even to as many as believe in his name.* They that receive this truth, grow tender of a lie, of a vain word; they find themfelves grow tender, feeling and fenfible. Here is a token that the God of life is quickening them; I am now tender of fpeaking a lie to my neighbour; I will not do that thing to another, that I would not have another do to me; when you come to a tender ftate, which is far better than a hard-hearted ftate, you will have an evidence in yourfelves, that *man liveth not by bread alone, but by every word that proceeds out of the mouth of God.*

Bleffed

Blessed are they that God hath brought into acquaintance with his word; of all nations and people upon the earth, they are a blessed people; though there are manifold blessings that reach indifferently to all, *the sun shines, and the rain falls on the evil and the good, and on the just and unjust*; yet this is a blessing that can only make the soul happy, that an intercourse between it and its Maker is open; that there is an open intercourse for the Lord to hear a man cry, and he to receive his word; all those that God hath brought into covenant with himself by Christ, he hath made sensible of this intercourse and way of God's speaking to his people, which he spake to them by in former days: Take heed that this way is not stopt up; you know by what it was opened, and what will stop it up again; when you were in much trouble and grief, you cried to the Lord, and he delivered you: But if *I regard iniquity in my heart*, said *David*, *the Lord will not hear me:* You cried to the Lord again, it may be, and he did not answer you; and the Lord cried to you and you answered him not, but hearkened to your lusts.

Yet the Lord by his *long-suffering and patience* hath won upon a remnant, and hath brought them over to believe and trust in his power, to remove out of the way that which hindered the intercourse between God and their souls. What a great stir was there in removing out of the way the pride, corruption, enmity, loosenefs, wantonnefs, and abundance more of evil things, that made the soul like a wildernefs? What hacking and burning up was there? God's word, *like a hammer*, and *like a fire*, did break up and *burn up thefe* things; and the same word of God, like a sword, did cut down those sins and lusts which prevailed over you before: By this means God hath opened a way for you, to have accefs to him, and for his word to have accefs to you: When you come to the Lord in this way, you know you live by this word, and if you hear the word of the Lord spoken immediately to you, your joy and consolation encreafeth, and you have sweet communion and fellowship with God and Christ, and with one another, by this covenant of life. How came you

into

a CHRISTIAN'S LIFE. 233

into it? It was by removing a great deal of rubbish out of the way. If you should let this rubbish grow up again, which kept you from the joy of the Holy Ghost, will it not do it again? If your pride, corruption, enmity, prejudice, loofenefs and wantonnefs, if thefe be fuffered to grow up in any of you, they will do as they did before, they will feparate you from the Lord and from one another: As the truth brought you to God and this heavenly fellowfhip with him, fo if a wrathful mind and wanton fpirit get up again, it will feparate you from God, and fcatter you from one another, then you will live in the outward life, and die to the inward one and perifh: Remember you were told fo.

Every one that goes from this living word, and fuffers any thing to arife of the old nature, fo much as that rifeth, fo much will your way of intercourfe with God be ftopt; fometimes men cry to God, but they have a bar in their way; and they come for comfort to the throne of grace, but they cannot receive thofe miniftrations of joy and peace, which they defire; *their foolifh hearts are darkened, and their minds blinded,* and they will go on in darknefs, and be left out of the holy covenant which God hath called his people to.

You that God hath engaged to be his, by the operation of his power, O live in a holy fear and watchfulnefs; and know this, that let your underftandings and gifts be what they will, you have nothing but what is given you; and what God hath given you, he can take away. *Thou haft decked thyfelf with my flax, and my wool, and with my filver and gold, and other ornaments, and followed thy lovers, therefore will I take them away from thee, and ftrip thee of all thou gloriest in.* Thofe that forget God, of whom they had thefe things, that forget their brokennefs of heart, and the fubjection of their fpirits to God; if they forget this, let them know, that let their parts be what they will, they will certainly wither, and their inward life will fail: You that have regard to your own fouls, and do defire heartily, at this time, to be quickened, and find that the Lord hath removed your deadnefs, and quickened and raifed you to fuch a degree and

G g meafure

measure of life, that you can say, I find communion with God, and fellowship with my friends and brethren in that one eternal life, I pray God you may continue in it long, and lay down your heads in this blessed, heavenly life. Now that you may so do, keep yourselves low and humble, and in the fear of God, and keep your ears always open to his word, and live as becomes those *that are born again* and begotten of God, and are brought to partake of the divine life. Let temptations surround you, that life will preserve you; he that never sinned is with you, to keep you from sin; and he that never deceived any, will keep you from being deceived. To his counsel and conduct, and to his divine care and protection, I now commit you.

SERMON XXI.

The NECESSITY of a HOLY LIFE and CONVERSATION.

Preached at St. MARTIN'S-LE-GRAND, March 26, 1687.

O How happy are they that have bread in their own houses! and that can draw water out of their own wells! These have a blessed, glorious dwelling-place; these are the children that their father provides for: All the divine treasures and the riches of heavenly things are laid up for these; O that all that have a sight of this blessed state, were got into it! that their minds might not more wander; that people might not be scattered in their thoughts, that when they meet together, they might have their expectations entirely from that God whom they profess to worship. *Lord, thou hast said that thou wilt teach thy people thyself;* here a cry goes up to the Lord, and their expectations through faith pitched upon God; they never meet in vain, but *a well springs up, and the water of life comes to them,* by which they meet with divine

refresh-

refreshments; for you know the promise that our Lord made to his disciples, *he that drinketh of the water that I shall give him, shall never thirst more.* Why, will once drinking serve, because I have tasted of the living water that the Lord Christ gives me; will that serve? No, but he giveth me a substantial river, that is the reason why I shall thirst no more; it shall be in me *a well of living water, springing up to everlasting life;* blessed are the witnesses of it; these are they that are satisfied concerning religion and doctrine; they are satisfied concerning worship; they are looking after no new things; when they meet together, they meet in the name of the Lord, and they have their eyes to him, who is a fountain, and they discern a brightness and a glory that is unspeakable; and the glory that is speakable, that appears many times thro' instruments, will not satisfy them; there is something beyond that, which must satisfy; this will never do it; such as these will never be satisfied with hearing and seeing, till they come to hear and see *that which is unutterable*, and then they are satisfied: Christ had preached many sermons in the hearing of his disciples, and there were a great many said, *that there was never any spake like him*, or preached like him; yet one of them that was the nearest to him, and most acquainted and intimate with him, after some years meeting and hearing of his sermons, he cries out, *shew us the Father, and it sufficeth us.*

My friends, this comes near to many of your states; many of you have heard long, and have heard the speakable word of God, that which could be uttered, that which could be spoken forth, by the demonstration of the Holy Ghost, by them *that have received it of the Father;* this you have heard long, and yet there are many of you, that if you come to a serious search, you will find a want; you will still find that you have not that satisfaction that puts you beyond doubt, beyond fear; there is something that stands in the way, that hinders your enjoyment of the unspeakable glory of the unspeakable word, and this will never be removed, but by your innocent submitting to the work of the power of God in your own hearts, that so you may not only be believers, but come to be really

really baptized, and then all is out of doubt; for our Lord faid, *he that believeth, and is baptized, shall be faved*; he doth not fay he may be faved; but, he shall be faved,

Woful experience hath told us in our days, that a great many have believed the truth, and yet they are never like to be faved, they *have made shipwreck of their faith*; but if they had been baptized, if they would have endured the baptifm, if they would have been buried with Chrift in baptifm, they should have been faved, every one of them; and now there are a great many that remain in the belief of the truth, and yet they are not baptized, they are not dead, not buried, notwithftanding *they have received like precious faith with us*, that *faith which is of the operation of God*, and that *is like precious* in its nature to all that do receive it, and would work the fame effect in all too, if it were not obftructed; but notwithftanding they have received faith towards the faving of their fouls, yet their fouls are captives, their fouls are fubject to lufts, and pleafures, and vanities, and unto empty and foolifh things, and to paffions and corruptions, after they have received faith.

For if you take one that is a believer of truth, that is overtaken with his luft, and paffions, and corruptions, he will commonly own that he believeth the contrary, he believeth that thefe things should not be, that it ought to be otherwife: This is the fignification of truth againft untruth; if it should be otherwife, why is it thus then? Why, he finds a life to fpring up in that which is corruptible, that is always contrary to the life of God, and at enmity with it: What fhall I do? I believe the truth, I know it is an holy thing, it leads all that fubmit to it to a holy life, and there is this and that unholy thing, this and that corrupt thing remains, what fhall I do?

It is an evident demonftration that thou wanteft the baptifm of him in *whom thou believeft*; thou haft believed in Chrift Jefus that cometh after *John*, and was before him; and now having believed in him, thou wanteft to be baptized by him, and for want of that, the pollution and corruption that was in thy nature in the time of thy alienation,

alienation, prevails still upon thee, contrary to thy faith; and there is no coming to obtain this baptism, but by sinking down into that which will slay thee, that which will kill thee: But there is such a shifting to save ones life, there are so many twistings and twinings of people to save their lives, that at last they lose them; but there are none that could ever find that life that is eternal, but those that are willing to be given up to the dead, and submit to this baptism, that is, by the Holy Ghost and by fire: These only do come to life, they come to the resurrection, for you never knew any that died this death but they rose again; it is as impossible for death to hold any one down that is buried in this baptism, as it was impossible to hold Christ down, when he was in the grave; *the same power that brought again our Lord Christ from the dead, the same power it is that quickens us*, while we remain in these mortal bodies, after we have sustained this death and crucifiction.

But who can believe this saying? For *this is a hard saying, who can bear it*? Is it not enough that I am a believer, which makes me a Friend, and entitles me to a community among you; and as long as I hold the truth, and profess the truth, I am looked upon as one of your society? This is very true; this doth entitle people unto the outward privileges of the Church of Christ; but there is another inner court, that lies under the angel's reed (the measuring-reed) that is to be measured; the temple is measured, and every worshipper in the temple is measured; there was an outward court, that was for representing the Church of God in general, from the particular; the outward court was not measured, that the Gentiles might come in; the unbaptized people, which were never regenerated, they might come so far as the outward court, but this did not entitle them to the privileges of the house of God, nor to any worship or sacrifice that was accepted upon God's altar.

It concerns you and me, my friends, to be serious about matters of this moment and importance, and not spend our days, and, as it were, speak by rote, under an airy profession, though of truth itself, without considering what

progress

progress you have made, what benefit you have obtained, and whether you are come not only to *the shadow of good things to come*, but to the very substance of the heavenly things; *for the comers to the outward worship could never, with those sacrifices they offered, be made perfect; the comers thereunto were not made perfect, as to the things pertaining to the conscience*, speaking there of the outward worship, *Heb.* x, 1; but coming to the heavenly things, whereof the other was but a shadow, they made people perfect, as to the conscience, and did bring them to salvation. The apostle alludes to this baptism, for he speaks in a figure of the *eight persons that were saved in* Noah's *ark*; then he brings down the allegory to christian baptism, not only the baptism of *John*, the fore-runner of Christ, that preached of Christ, but to the christian baptism itself; *by the like figure whereof baptism now saveth us*, saith the apostle; *not the putting away of the filth of the flesh, but the answer of a good conscience*. What doth he mean by baptism saving us? He means, *the answer of a good conscience towards God, through the resurrection of Christ from the dead*; so that christian baptism did bring along with it the *cleansing and putting away of all sin out of the conscience*, that might bring them under doubts and scruples; and then there is an arising of Jesus; the Saviour, in the conscience, the Mediator that brought them to answer for them in the sight of God; for if people be conscious of sin, and do leave off their sin, this doth not yet cleanse the conscience; for there still remains a conscience of sin; tis not the leaving off our sin that makes our atonement with God, or that expiates our guilt, or doth away the guilt of the sins that we have committed; but there must be a forsaking and a leaving off sin by the virtue and power of the spirit, by which we are enabled, not only to leave off sin, but are guided and directed to the Mediator, *whose blood alone reconcileth us to God, and cleanseth us from all sin*. If I should never commit a sin while I live, it is not this simply in itself that will make me have the answer of a good conscience in the sight of God; for there remains the guilt of sin contracted in the days of unbelief, which is a bar and hinderance, that

none

none can approach the Holy God, but in the atonement and falvation that comes by Jefus Chrift; for all that believe and obey the gofpel are accepted in Chrift, and that upon the account of Chrift's precious blood, that cleanfeth us from all fin and unrighteoufnefs. Whom doth it cleanfe? Thofe only that forfake their fins, and by his power are brought to a holy life; they, by the virtue of his power, and the cleanfing of his blood, come to have their former fins removed from them, as far as the eaft is from the weft.

But what is this to them that remain in their fins? what is this *to them that are not baptized for the dead? that have not put off the old man, nor put on the new man,* but have only put on the name and profeffion of Chrift, and put on the outfide of him, his garment, but have not put him on, they are not *created again in Chrift Jefus unto good works, that they might walk in them?* No wonder there remains a confcience of fin in them, there is a bar that hinders them from the fight of the glory of God, and from real and true fatisfaction, concerning their atonement and reconciliation with God, and this hinders them from the enjoyment of *that peace that paffeth underftanding;* and it is no wonder, becaufe they are not come to this baptifm that brings the *anfwer of a good confcience in the fight of God;* they are not rifen with Chrift; how fhould they? for they are not buried with him. *Know ye not that fo many of us* (faith the apoftle) *as were baptized into Chrift, were baptized into his death; therefore we are buried with him by baptifm into death; that like as Chrift was raifed from the dead by the glory of the Father, even fo we alfo fhould walk in newnefs of life,* Rom. vi, 3. Here is a change figured out between them that had partaken of the fpiritual baptifm, and were come again to the participation of life in the refurrection of Jefus Chrift, and thofe that were not baptized.

So it is now with every one that cometh to believe the truth, and make a profeffion of it; there is a way caft up, and there is a door opened for falvation; but the grand queftion that every one ought to enquire about, and put to themfelves, is, what progrefs they have made in this way? Whether they are baptized yet or no? whether they have *put off the old man with his deeds, and put on the new man and the new man's deeds, which are righteousness and holiness?* They that find, that though they are believers, they are short of this, they do also find that their shortness is their hinderance, their shortness in not coming up to the pattern that hath been shewed them, is their hinderance, so that they enjoy not the things here spoken of; the being under this sense, and really sitting under this sense in a meeting, though there should be no man speaking to them outwardly, yet being come to this faith, and made partakers of this baptism, people would find in their own bosoms the hidden word of life ministering to their condition; they would have enough, there would not be a famine of the word unto them, nor they should not need to be in expectation of going out to this or the other instrument, but they would be satisfied when they are met together with the presence of the Lord, that the Lord is in the midst of them, ministering unto them the word of life, in his operating and working, speaking in a tongue that every one can understand, speaking with a kind of voice and language, that every one may understand his own state and condition; and this is the way that God brought up people from the beginning, to the knowledge of heavenly things, and opening of the mysteries of salvation; we had it not of men, but of Jesus our Lord; he was our great minister, we waited upon him, and trusted in him, and he taught us himself; he hath ministered to us at our silent and quiet waiting upon him, those things that were convenient for us; we might well say, *he gave us our food in due season*; he hath not only given *strong meat unto men*, but hath ministered of the *sincere milk of his word unto babes*, that lived in sincerity and self-denial, loving God above all things; and he taught and conducted us in our way, this way of simplicity, until our understandings came to be opened, until our souls came to be prepared to receive the mysteries of his kingdom.

In those days there were some that started up in knowledge, and that *built their nests on high, and took flax and wool,*

wool, and gold and *silver*, and decked themselves with them ; but the Lord found them out, and brought them down, and took the crown from their head, and cloathed them with dishonour. So God doth from age to age ; his judgments will begin at his own house : If you would *grow in the grace and in the knowledge of our Lord and Saviour Jesus Christ*, then grow in humility and self-denial, and keep a constant watch upon your hearts ; examine your hearts, and *commune with yourselves upon your beds, and be still* ; take heed left you sin against the Lord, and provoke him. *There were some that provoked the Lord of old, and they committed two great evils* : What be they ? *They have gone away, and forsaken the fountain of living water* ; as much as to say, they have not their dependence upon an invisible power, as they ought to have : For I am a living fountain, and it is by an invisible power that I am able to counsel, teach, direct, purify, and open their understandings ; but they have forsaken me, that is one great evil ; and the other is, they would not be without somewhat ; *they have forsaken the Lord*, and they would have somewhat instead of God ; *they have digged to themselves broken cisterns, that will hold no water*. And how many in this age have committed these two great evils !

My friends, examine yourselves ; are there not many that have been guilty of these two great evils ? They do not keep their close dependence, trust and reliance, upon the invisible power of God, as they profess they ought to do, but are hurried away from it ; some by the love of the world, some by lusts and pleasures, some by passions, and others by worldly interests, are drawn away from the power, to do and say that which the power is against : Is not this a forsaking of the Lord the living fountain ? What do they do then ? Are they not for this and that, and the other man ? for hearing this and the other man's word, and *digging to themselves broken cisterns* ? And have they not their trust and confidence in going to meetings, in commending this and the other way ? Have they not their trust in their profession outwardly, when it ministers nothing to their souls, so that they secretly wither for all this ?

this? If you had all the men and angels that were ever sent of God, appointed to preach to you, they could not minister life to you, unless there be that faith that stands in the power of God. The faith that stands in any man's words, will not overcome your lusts; but the faith that stands in the power of God, *purifies the heart*; it will not suffer any unclean thing there. As for preaching, let a man preach against this and the other lust and corruption, there it will remain for all his preaching, unless men know God's power and life, in which there is righteousness; for words and knowledge, and sight and speculation, will never give people victory over their sins.

Therefore you know, every one who is settled must be settled where the foundation of religion is; it is not coming to meetings, and owning this and the other doctrine which is the foundation of our religion; God hath revealed his power to every one of us; God hath not given his Spirit to preachers and prophets only, for then there would be a *famine of the word*, as was in *Israel, the priest's lips only preserved knowledge.* If you did take away the priest, you did take away their knowledge. The prophets had the word of God, and they only spake the word of God. If the prophet was taken away, then the word of God was taken away. The Lord threatened to send a famine among them; they grieved and vexed, and killed and destroyed, the priests and prophets; therefore, saith the Lord, *I will send a famine among you, not of bread, but of the word; and they shall go from city to city, and enquire for the word of the Lord.*

Thus it was in the Jewish church; if there was a prophet they would go thirty, forty, or a hundred miles to him that had the word of the Lord; *they shall go from city to city, to enquire for the word of the Lord:* But blessed be God we are come to another day, for now the word of the Lord is manifested in the hearts of all that believe; they know the word: I do not say all that believe do preach the word, or ought to preach; but the word preacheth to them; they are not as *broken cisterns that can hold no water;* when they find the word and hear it, they speak it presently; what is ministered to

their

LIFE and CONVERSATION.

their own condition, that they tell to other folks; when people come to the blessing of this dispensation that God's word revealeth in their hearts, they then know what the signification of it is, they understand the doctrine of it, the doctrine preacheth holiness to them; not that they should preach holiness and yet remain unholy; not that they should preach humility, and yet remain proud: it preacheth holiness, humility and singleness of heart to a remnant, that like good scholars and disciples learn the lessons and doctrine of the word of God.

Now when thou hast learned them well, and art come to see the effect of the word, and dost bring forth the deeds and works which are the fruits of holiness, *perfecting holiness in the fear of God, and with humility known and witnessed in Christ Jesus*, and art not only meek in show, but *meek and low in heart;* when people come to be meek and lowly, and of a clear conscience, *purged from all dead works to serve the living God;* then if the Lord gives them a word of exhortation, of doctrine or counsel, it is very welcome, and it hath a favour through the blessing of God, and they come by it to be *built up in their most holy faith*, and this word is brought forth in holiness and righteousness in their lives, and shews itself in a life of holiness; then thou wilt shine in thy conversation to all that thou converseth with, so that they may see thee to be such a man or woman as hast been with Jesus, and learned of Jesus, and received *a word engrafted;* when thou dost receive the word into thy heart, there is the engrafting of it: If it hath not root there, then, saith Christ, *my word doth not abide in you.* If you feel something of this invisible word in your hearts, it brings you to a resolution to serve God, and to keep yourselves from sin, and to answer the profession which you make of God; this is the effect of the word of God, if it doth abide in you. Doth it abide? You shall know anon or to morrow, so soon as a temptation comes to stir you up to pride or passion, to fraud or deceit, then you will see whether the word abide: If it abide, you sin not.

This is scripture, a certain fundamental doctrine, that may be as safely preached as any doctrine: If the word abide
in

in you, you sin not; what of that? let the word go, and you will sin, when ever you are tempted to it. *I write to you young men, becaufe you have overcome the wicked one, you are ftrong, and the word of God abides in you, and you have overcome the wicked one.* We shall fee as foon as a temptation meets with thee, whether the word abides in thee; if it abide, thou wilt not fin, but refift the tempter. Set thy foot upon the temptation, and go over it, and thou wilt have the dominion; and this will make thee a free man or woman, and thou wilt *ftand faft in the liberty wherewith Chrift hath made thee free.* The apoftle fuppofeth them free, and that they have got dominion; then *ftand faft*, faith he, *in the liberty wherewith Chrift hath made thee free.* It is a liberty not of luft and fin, but a liberty of the foul; the foul now is not at the devil's will and call.

For it is a fhame to the doctrine of Chriftianity, that we profefs things, and yet deny them in practice: We profefs that there is a power in Chrift to keep and preferve us out of fin, and we profefs to believe this power is communicated to them that do believe in the Lord Jefus Chrift for their prefervation; that is, he will not withhold it from them: We profefs thefe things in the face of the whole world; and yet when the devil calls one man to covetoufnefs, and another to defraud his neighbour, and another to defile himfelf, he is drawn away thereby; what hypocrify is here to profefs this, and act the contrary? I do not wonder that they that profefs they cannot live a day without fin, that they fhould fall; but they that profefs to believe there is power enough in Chrift, and that it is offered to them, to live in fin and yield to temptation, this is horrid wickednefs. They that are of an upright, fingle mind, would die before they would fin, knowing that God is Almighty, and gracious, and willing to beftow his power, and wifdom, and grace, upon them that ask it; they would die rather than fin againft God prefumptuoufly: let it coft me my goods, my eftate, my liberty, or my life, *how can I do this great wickednefs, and fin againft God?* They love God above all; you never heard them complain that they wanted power, *for the Lord is at their right hand, and they shall-*

shall not be moved. They cannot fall; though they are tempted, they will not fall into temptation. They have power when they fee the devil before them, to put him behind them; the nobility of their extract, of their new birth and regeneration, puts such a temper and disposition into their souls, that they scorn to be at the devil's command, as if they were his children.

Oh! it is a noble and honourable thing to be a child of God, a very high dignity to be in such an honourable relation to God, and to have a right to the heavenly mansions, *to sit down in heavenly places in Chrift Jesus.* I would to God you were all ready for it, that you had the wedding garment on, that you might not be *bound hand and foot, and cast into utter darkness.* What is the reason that you do not sit down in this heavenly frame and temper, and draw the waters of salvation out of your own souls; could the Lord do any thing more than he hath done, and could his servants do any more than they have done for your help? Are not their labours demonstrations of it? We have been *as epistles of Chrift written in your consciences.* We have been testifying that there is something wanting in too many, the want of resigning up themselves to the baptism of the cross. People are willing to be counted friends; but they are friends of God, *that do whatsoever he commandeth them;* that is the Christian lesson, not to say, I will be a friend to you, and a friend to the church, and to such a sort of people; but I will be a friend of God, and do whatsoever he commandeth me; whatsoever command God lays upon you, either to take up a cross, or to deny yourselves and follow him.

Learn this lesson, and you will be disciples indeed, and members of the church too; not members of a church privileged outwardly only, but *members of a church of the first born, and you will have your names written in Heaven;* when one comes to have his name written in Heaven, he comes to know his name, it is a *white Stone,* not a speckled one; they that have it, they know it, they are not ignorant of one another's names, that are written in this book; they have a fellowship that nobody can declare; their communion is in that bread and that cup: This is a cup of blessing fing indeed, and this hath bleffed us, and will blefs us. God will preferve a people in this fellowſhip. You that are at a diſtance now, you muſt come nearer to him; God will chooſe a people by whom his name ſhall be magnified; becauſe *the love of God is ſhed abroad in our hearts*, we cannot but defire this for all, *eſpecially for the houſhold of faith*; we cannot but defire their perfection, their growing up in the grace of God, that they might come to be partakers of Heaven. And in the next place, our love is to all people, every where; we would be glad *that all were ſaved*; they that defpife us, when we are ſpeaking of heavenly things, ſpeaking like a child, like a ſtammering child, ſpeaking of the glorious excellencies of God, of the loving kindneſs of God, ſpeaking of thoſe things which God hath ſpoken to our fouls, they that defpife theſe things, we would be glad that they might be ſaved: If they were partakers of theſe things, they would be glad as well as we, and they would be more really happy in reſpect of this world, for the time that they are to live here; they would live a happier life, even in this world, and they would *have everlaſting life in the world to come*.

The love of Chriſt conſtrains men thus to judge, that every one that hath received like precious faith, ought to anſwer that grace and faith which God hath miniſtered to them in a holy life and converſation, and every one who is a ſtranger to this thing, ought to be of an enquiring mind, and an open heart, to wait for the day when God will viſit them with the ſame grace; when you give up yourſelves to a daily croſs, as Chriſt's diſciples, you will not be running after any one to teach you to know the Lord, for you will all *know the Lord, from the leaſt to the greateſt*; I that have been but a little convinced, ſhall I know the Lord? Thou ſhalt know the Lord, thou that *art dead in thy ſins and treſpaſſes*, thou that haſt not *known the blood of cleanſing*, thou ſhalt know *the Lord* to be thy *judge*, and thy *law-giver*, to teach thee how thou muſt live, walk and act; and is not that a good knowledge? This is the way they reckoned upon in old time, it is a notable expreſſion, *the Lord is our judge*; there is the beginning, he began there, judgment began *at the houſe of God*; thoſe

he

he brings into his houfe, he brings them under the difcipline of his houfe, *the Lord is our judge, he is our king and law-giver, and he will fave us;* this fame exercife of difcipline under judgment brought to them the faith and experience of his being their law-giver, and this brought them to a faith of the laft fentence, we fhall be faved; and the Lord anfwers fuch a people, that he will bring falvation to them, *falvation fhall be for walls and bulwarks:* Did the people of this nation but know falvation was brought near to them, and that it was their bulwark, there would not be a crying up this and the other rotten thing for a bulwark.

We talk of a bulwark as well as others; we have a bulwark, bleffed be the God of Heaven, made of better ftuff than theirs; for it is the falvation of God which hath kept us from the pollution of fin, and from a running *into all excefs and riot* that others have run into; it hath kept us from the evil, it hath kept evils out of us, and we have found that certainly true, that *all things work together for good, to them that love God, and fear God;* that all the providences of God together, have all wrought for our good; and this is the bulwark that we have trufted in, and it hath ferved hitherto, and it will ferve us and our pofterity to the end of the world: This is a bulwark that will never be ftormed, that will never be thrown down nor laid wafte: Though all the powers on earth, and all the potentates in this world fhould agree together, they fhall not prevail againft it; we have *falvation for walls and bulwarks;* if I be within thefe walls, falvation is round about me; if I am got into this eternal bulwark, I am fafe from the devil and his inftruments; here is a bulwark to be relied upon.

Many wonder we differ with them in fome opinions; we have that confidence in this bulwark, that we defire not another; God will laft and abide forever, fo will this bulwark; all the care that I take, and all the care that you fhould take, is to keep within thefe walls: Do not fally out, if you go out, the devil is watching, and *feeking continually whom he may devour;* he will catch ftraglers; if people will go out for profit, or for pleafure, or intereft, tereſt, the devil will catch them; how can ſuch people talk of ſalvation for walls and bulwarks? the devil hath got them in his ſnare, and they are caught in drunkenneſs, uncleanneſs and other ſins; the reaſon is, they have gone out of their bulwark, they have ſallied out of their walls, for the devil could never have forced them out.

O take heed, ſays the apoſtle, *leſt there ſpring up in any of you an evil heart of unbelief, in departing from the living God;* as if he had ſaid, you are Chriſtians now, you are a people come to a good ſtate in Chriſt; but conſider you have no ſtrength to ſtand but in him; no power to keep yourſelves but in him; *take heed,* at all times, *that there ſpring not up in you an evil heart of unbelief, in departing from the living God;* take heed leſt there ſpring up in you ſuch a thought as this; I may take this pleaſure, and the other profit; conſider that thou dieſt and withereſt if thou depart from the living God; take heed of taking liberty above the fear of God: It is not our talk of ſalvation for walls and bulwarks, that will do us good, but our keeping within theſe walls.

I remember a notable ſaying of the apoſtle, which hath a great emphaſis in it, and a great deal of doctrine; he writeth to the church, after they were become a people of profeſſing Chriſtians, *take heed leſt you come to be beguiled by the ſerpent, as he beguiled Eve;* he did not ſpeak of *Jezabel,* a wicked woman; but he ſpoke of *Eve,* a good woman, *created after the image of God, in righteouſneſs and holineſs;* they were come to a life of ſanctification, to a life *that was hidden from ages and generations.* You muſt look to yourſelves, and look upon yourſelves as in the ſtate of your mother *Eve,* a woman brought forth in righteouſneſs and holineſs, that might have ſtood in that primitive ſtate, notwithſtanding all the ſubtilty of all the ſerpents in the world; but having hearkened to this old ſerpent, ſhe was beguiled; there grew up a conſultation in her reaſoning part; it may be ſo as he ſaith, I will try.

So I ſay to you that are come to a ſtate of ſanctification, and in ſome meaſure to know the cleanſing power of God, that you have not believed in it in vain, but

it

it hath effectually wrought some change and alteration in you, and is still carrying on the work of your salvation. Many temptations will attend you, and many snares will be laid in your way; but God hath preserved you to this day: I know the devil's wiles and temptations are manifold; they are fitted to every one's inclinations, fitted to every opportunity, and to every occasion in this world: Men are tried every way by the tempter, to see which way he may ensnare them; he tries every way to *ensnare and entangle the simple,* that he may turn them to the right hand or to the left, that their souls may be destroyed and perish.

I cannot speak to you by a more emphatical word, by a more familiar exhortation than this, *take heed you be not beguiled as Eve was:* Many will be tempted as she was, but I would not have you do as she did, and yield to the temptation: Take heed that you do not defile yourselves, but *keep your garments white;* you that have been washed and cleansed, labour to *keep yourselves unspotted from the world; this is pure religion and undefiled,* that which hath enlightened many a nation, and shall enlighten many of those whose religion is to be undefiled, and to *keep themselves unspotted from the world.* I pray God encrease the number of them, that so the blessed work of sanctification that hath begun in this way, may be carried on to his praise, and the salvation of our souls, to the spreading forth of his glory, and the exalting of his name; that the strangers which are scattered and desolate, may be brought into his holy way, and walk in it; that we all, in a fellowship together, walking in that holy way, may through the eternal Spirit, offer praise and thanksgiving to God, who is worthy to receive glory and honour, power and dominion, forever and ever. *Amen.*

SERMON

SERMON XXII.

BAPTISM *and the* LORD'S SUPPER *aſſerted.*

Preached at GRACE-CHURCH-STREET, *April* 15, 1688.

If any man hath not the Spirit of Chriſt, he is none of his.

IF I ſhould ſay no more, there is that in every one's conſcience that will make application; if he that hath not the Spirit of Chriſt, is none of his, you may ſay, whoſe is he then? If they be none of Chriſt's that have not his Spirit, whoſe are they? They are all his whoſe Spirit rules them, every one of us doth belong to him whoſe Spirit ruleth over us, unto whoſe power we are ſubjected. You know this diſtinguiſheth people in the world, one king knoweth his ſubjects from another king's ſubjects; they are under the obedience of this, that, and the other king or prince, his law is over them, they are ſubject to it; ſo here is a deciſion of all the people in the world, whom they belong to.

We, all of us, I hope, do expect there will be a deciſion at the day of judgment, and believe the things we read concerning it, that there will be a deciſion, and ſome will be placed on the right hand, and ſome on the left; ſome will have the ſentence of, *come ye bleſſed*, and others the ſentence of, *go ye curſed;* but now there is a way of finding out the deciſion of the matter before we go out of the world, before the day of judgment, when there will be no remedy, what then is, muſt be and abide ſo; now there is no need it ſhould continue ſo; if it be amiſs, it may be mended; if I do not belong to the right prince, if I be not under the right power and ſpirit, I may be, for now it is a day of grace, a day of mercy; I have been a rebel to the right prince, I may be pardoned and taken into favour; it is far better for people to know their state now, than to know it then, because then there will be no remedy.

The apostle, in laying down fundamental, apostolical doctrines, that were to be believed and taken notice of, and are in our age, so that we may say, *things written of old time, were written for our learning;* he makes this affirmation and position of doctrine, *he that hath not the Spirit of Christ, is none of his,* he doth not belong to him; tho' he be called a Christian, he is not a Christian, if he hath not the Spirit of Christ; it is but a name he hath got, he hath not that which makes him essentially so, for nothing can make a Christian, but having the Spirit of Christ; therefore when they would vindicate their being Christians, they prove it thus; *for he* (speaking of God) *hath sent the Spirit of his Son into our hearts, and we know the mind of Christ; we know him that is true,* or we are in him that is true; these things, if they were right, if they were true, were evident demonstrations that they were a sort of men who depended more upon the Spirit and spiritual teachings, and spiritual guidance, than upon all the rules and methods of teaching that were in the world.

I speak of this, friends, because you know as well as I, how averse this age of ours hath been, to have any thing spoken of spiritual dispensations, or about spiritual teachings; though a man hath been counted formerly a wise man, a learned man, or a man of parts, if once he come to smatter out a little about inward teaching, it is enough to spot him, and make him ridiculed of his acquaintance, as if there were no such thing in the world: We have a book, called the *bible,* it is from one end to the other full of such expressions, of being led by the Spirit; *you have an anointing which teacheth you all things*: The whole tenor of the New Testament is about spiritual teachings and divine operations, and of *faith* being *the operation of God;* and the Old Testament hath abundance of expressions by way of prophecy, that in the New Testament days, if people would look for the law of God, they must look for it *in their hearts;* and if they would know God, they must look to *the Mediator, the Lord Jesus Christ:* The
New

New Testament also directs us that way; Christians should be the most spiritual people in the world, that is the guide, the rule.

But, say they, the scripture is the foundation of faith and manners, belief and practice; this is too often but dissimulation, and I am afraid it is to be found in some; what, is the scripture the rule of faith? and may people believe what they find in scripture? Yes, but say some, it is best be aware for fear of error. What is in the scripture is serious, sound and orthodox, and did Quakers, think you, never find in scripture that people were to *wait for the Spirit,* and *pray in the Spirit,* and *serve God in the Spirit,* and that all religion that is not in power, is not available, did they not find it in scripture? And you that are not Quakers, did you ever read the New Testament? How came it to pass that ye never found these texts? But some people read and read the New Testament twenty times over, and mock and deride, and persecute a man that shall speak of the Spirit's teaching.

I have admired at it, how intelligent men, to whom God hath given a competent understanding, should be so blinded; they have learned to read English, and they have read the New Testament over several times, and the Old Testament too, and they have read those sentences of Christ's doctrine, that do so currently and unanimously speak of divine teachings and spiritual operations, spiritual worship and spiritual religion, that must have some motion and stirring of the Holy Ghost to be the original of it, and that all others are not acceptable to God; doubtless they have read these things, but I have often desired and do still desire that they would read it again once more, and try and see what God will do; he hath oftentimes made use of the holy scripture as a means to awaken people and to open their understandings, and let them see the mind of the spirit by which the scripture is written, and the next time if they can find scripture text and apostolical doctrine, to teach people to wait upon the Spirit, I hope they will leave scoffing and mocking.

It hath been hitherto looked upon as an invention, to speak of the *teaching of the Spirit,* and *waiting upon the Spirit,* and being moved by the Spirit. This apostolical doctrine, prayer and worship, hath been looked upon as an invention

that

that we have brought in: To look for the Holy Ghoſt in that way that was never known to our fathers, is a fantaſtical conceit of the Quakers, ſay they: To tell people they muſt be led by the Spirit in divine things, as in prayer and worſhip, and the like, that in theſe things they muſt wait for the Spirit, was there ever any man that was counted good for any thing that ever preached ſo, before they came? Do we read any ſuch kind of thing in ſcripture?

O! the blindneſs that hath happened to this nation! I have conſidered, not without admiration, how the devil (he is a Spirit too, and a wicked one) how he ſhould have power to prevent our acknowledging the belief, ſenſe and feeling of the Spirit of God now-a-days; there are thouſands in this nation that have formerly believed that it was as impoſſible for a man to believe the divine motions and ſtrugglings of the Spirit of God in this life, as to raiſe their fathers and mothers out of their graves; ſome of their learned teachers have told us it is a whimſy and fancy, and that there was no inſpiration of the Spirit now-a-days, but that it was a fooliſh fancy in us to wait for ſuch a thing, it is needleſs, ſay they; there was an immediate teaching in the apoſtles days, and they had the ſenſe of the Spirit of Chriſt working in them, to teach them to write letters and epiſtles to the church, which letters and epiſtles were written by the moving of the Holy Ghoſt, but we have no need of it now, the Holy Ghoſt hath brought order and government into the church, we have it now in black and white printed in our books, therefore ſay they, there is no need of the Spirit, and people need not be acquainted with the operation of the Spirit now-a-days, in regard they have it in their books what manner of worſhip they muſt perform.

I grant them their due, that they have the direction of the ſcripture; I am able to underſtand that people are to worſhip God, and pray to him, and are to meet together and to obſerve this and the other doctrinal precepts there laid down; I confeſs I can make ſhift herewith to frame out a form of religion, and if I do not miſtake in the opening and explication of the doctrine, I could make a right form too, but I am liable to miſtake, another man that underſtands Greek better than I, ſaith that the Greek word ought to be tranſlated ed so, and the form ought to differ in such a respect; some say the only way of government is by bishops, and the word bears it in the original, and another saith he hath stretched the word, for the word means presbyter; another saith presbyter signifies no more than choice of church elders and deacons, and such like, and this is all out of one book, the settlement of bishops, presbyters, and elders.

Here a number of form-makers all fall out about the meaning of the word; what remedy can any mortal man provide for this? We must not be killing and slaying one another about words; if I be an episcopal man and say the word signifies bishops, I may be a wicked man still; and if another say it must be presbyter, he may be a wicked man too, and if another say it should be pastor, elders, and deacons, he may be a wicked man notwithstanding.

Thus they have rent and torn one another about church government; what remedy shall we have for this, that these quarrellings and contentions about terms and words may come to an end? Could a man prescribe a more certain remedy for all these mistakes than this, if they had a measure of this Spirit which did work in the apostles when they wrote down these words, which the apostles had in writing them, then I say they could tell you what the Spirit meant, for the Spirit is the same and not changed, and the words are the same to a small matter, so that if a man had that, he might end all the controversy; but where shall we have a man that hath this Spirit to end the controversy? There is none now-a-days say the Protestants, and say the Papists there is none but one that hath this infallibility; and many will not suppose that neither, for some of them say, that one man is as infallible as another man; there is a great dispute whether any one man be infallible, or a great many men together are infallible about doctrine and worship: This might be cured all at once if we could come to this conclusion. Papists, Protestants and Quakers, here is an end of all out-side worship, *he that hath not the Spirit of Christ is none of his*: If there be not Spirit in it, it is not Christ's religion and worship.

So that they that jangle and bark and bite, are without, among *dogs and sorcerers*, that are strangers to the Spirit of Christ;

Lord's Supper asserted.

Chrift; there is a fpirit in them that denies the Spirit of Chrift, there is a Spirit that rules in them that are without the Spirit, for nobody that I know of, acts things without a fpirit, and without being moved. What, are good and bad all moved by the Spirit, and yet are there no motions? I have fometimes turned the queftion upon people, and asked them if there were no motions of the evil fpirit, hath it no fuch kind of influence that it can move upon our fpirits, that we can fenfibly feel ourfelves thruft forth to fuch an action? I never met any man that would deny it, they are fo generally favourable to the wicked fpirit; no man will deny but the devil hath a way of moving and ftirring upon the fpirit of a man, and to fuggeft to him fuch an evil thing, and as I have fometimes faid, it is fo received an opinion, that when the malefactor comes to be arraigned at the bar for fome grievous crime, they lay the foundation of the indictment, fuch a day he was moved and inftigated by the devil to do fuch a thing; here is a fettled motion for the devil, for him to influence peoples fpirits, but no way for the good Spirit of God to influence mens fpirits; here is nothing left us but a bad inftigation; but to know inward motions to good things, it is not to be expected now-a-days.

How fhould ever the cunning ferpent, that would have power over the beft of us all, be faid to winnow us? Chrift fignified to *Peter*, a bold and refolute difciple, *fatan defires to have thee, and winnow thee as wheat*; if the devil had power over every one, to make them his fervants and flaves, what remedy have we but we muft all perifh and go headlong to hell with him, unlefs there be fome way of refifting him? That is true, fay people, the devil muft be refifted; we find it in the New Teftament, *refift the devil*; this is a good exercife; but tell me one thing, when I go about to refift the devil, muft I refift him in my own power? If I was to fay you might do fo, you would fay I was an erroneous preacher, and well you might: This is an old free-will doctrine, that a man may refift the devil by his own power, and efcape his fnares, and do the will of God: This hath been cried down by the doctors of the Church of *England*, and by moft of all forts of Chriftians; and for our parts, fince the

Lord

Lord hath opened our mouths, we did never speak a word in favour of it, as if we went about to resist the devil in our own strength; if we did, the devil would make fools of us : He that goes about to resist the devil in his own strength, will be entrapped and ensnared by him, in that men have a propensity to sin, and by his cunning and subtilty, may be led into a snare before they are aware.

Thus it is agreed on all hands, that our power, as men, is too weak to resist satan's temptation, so that you see we must have the assistance of the divine power, or all go to hell; there is no medium between those two extremes, some extraordinary power must assist me, or else the devil will have me. If you will not admit of a supernatural power to come in to help me and you, we must all go to hell, there is no remedy : I will say my prayers, saith one; do so, yet in the best of your prayers there will be sin ; and *if I regard iniquity in my heart, the Lord will not hear me*: I will go and hear sermons, say you ; the very man that preacheth will tell you, that hearing of sermons will do you no good at all, unless there be motions of the Spirit of God, so that you will be wrapt from one thing to another, and have diversity of doctrines, and come to no fixedness ; and while you concern yourselves about doctrines, all the while the devil prevails upon you; as for the tongue, he hath the rule of that, and as for the hands, he hath the rule of them, and makes you do those things that by his perpetual suggestions he moves you to; so that your going to church and saying your prayers signify nothing to bring you from under the wrath of God, and from the captivity of the devil : Hath not the devil those in captivity that go to church, and say their prayers, and give alms? These are things that you can do by your own power, the saying of your prayers, and fasting, and giving of alms, these things thou mayest do, the devil will not hinder thee, for he knows that these will not bring thee out of his clutches, nor out of his chains and fetters.

There is but one way and means by which the devil may be effectually resisted, that is by taking to our help one stronger than he; I have gone for help to many stronger than I, in my young days, that I thought to be stronger

Christians,

Chriſtians, and many of them did afford their help in the work, by counſel, by perſuaſion, by exhortation and by doctrine, but all this did not do; and the reaſon was this, becauſe the devil was too ſtrong for me, and ſo he was for them. As long as you go for help to this and the other place, until you find one ſtronger than the devil, expect no deliverance or help from any thing in the world, but lay aſide *all confidence in the fleſh*, in any many man on earth, or in all the doctors words and beſt preaching you ſhall hear, lay aſide your confidence in them, they will never do you any good in this reſpect, for they will never break your chains off; many are loaded with them, but ſome, I hope, are *weary and heavy laden*, and feel the weight of ſin, I pray God increaſe the number; though it be a ſtate of ſorrow, it is better than the ſtate of *fools*, that *make a mock of ſin*; I would have you weary and heavy laden with your ſins, and brought into this ſtate, to ſee yourſelves captivated by the ſtrong power of darkneſs, and to ſee you are unable to deliver yourſelves out of it by your own power.

For me to fall into the hands of a tyrant that is ſtronger than I, and no man to deliver me, how ſad would it be. If I could find a man ſtronger than this tyrant, and that would kill him, I ſhould be his ſervant, and have a better maſter: No man can kill this tyrant, that hath led me captive and made me a ſlave; if he ſay, be drunk, I muſt be drunk; if he bid me ſwear, I muſt ſwear: This is the ſlavery that the devil hath got his ſervants into, that whatſoever he ſaith, that they muſt do, if he bids them do it: *O! wretched man that I am, who ſhall deliver me?* I cannot deliver myſelf, and no man can deliver me; I would be acquainted with all Chriſtians, if they could help me; I would try all religions that are this day in the world, to ſee if there be help for me: Many are oppreſſed with ſin, and they go to and fro, to ſee what help can be given them, to free them from the bondage that the devil hath them in: This ſort of people are to be pitied, and the ſouls of all good people will pity them, for ſuch as theſe ſeek the living among the dead; they ſeek that to redeem them that cannot redeem them: We have fought, ſay they, for power and ſtrength from them that had not enough for themselves, they were captivated as well as we, and all this because we came not to him that is stronger than the devil. You will take the same course, and stay till grey hairs come, and you go down to the grave with sorrow, unless you come to one stronger than the devil, and then trust in him, believe in him, and expect deliverance by him. The reason why people do not expect deliverance is, because these two things are shut out of their belief.

I. They believe not that a sinful life will carry them to destruction.

II. They think there is not any possibility in this world to live any other than a sinful life.

The devil hath brought men to this pass, that they live as easily in a sinful life, as a fish in the stream: We are in the way, say they; when we were baptized, we were initiated into the Christian church, we were baptized with the sign of the cross, that shews we are soldiers of Christ and bear his badge and banner upon us; and the man said at that time, I was made a child of God and an inheritor of the kingdom of Heaven; if this be not true, then I am cheated and deceived, for I am to believe this to be true; the church hath affirmed that these things are to be believed; and to question the veracity of the church, is to question all.

I would question whether thousands find the truth of it. When thou wert baptized, there was a kind of covenant and bargain made for this child of God and heir of eternal life, that he should forsake the devil and all his works, and the pomps and vanities of this wicked world, and the sinful lusts of the flesh: And there is security given that this child shall never serve the devil and sinful lusts, and never be proud, but serve God and keep his commandments: Now this security being taken, then they suppose that this child will certainly be an heir of the kingdom of God. It is very true, stand to thy church; if this security that is taken for a child be but effectual, then there is no doubt of being a child of God, and an inheritor of the kingdom of Heaven. But if this security fail, is the church to blame if men's hopes to eternal life fail? Was it not my condition, that thou shouldest

forsake

devil and all his works, and the pomps and vanities of this wicked world, and the sinful lusts of the flesh, and if you break the bargain, and thy part of the covenant, and lose eternal life, who is to blame? Look to the security, that thou forsake the devil and all his works, and the pomps and vanities of the world. But thou mayest rather say, I have enjoyed as many of them as I could; and for the lusts of the flesh, I have enjoyed as much of them as I can; and what, dost thou believe thyself to be a child of God, and an heir of the kingdom of Heaven, notwithstanding?

If I promise to deliver a man any particular kind of goods, upon the payment of so much money, if I fail in delivering the goods, he will not deliver the money; a man must forsake the devil and all his works, and never lust after the pomps and vanities of this world; that is a child of God, let us see him grow up, and if he goes on to be faithful in this covenant till he die, I do not at all question but he will be an heir of eternal life; but when all this is broken, and the security signifies nothing, and the man is given up to serve the devil, breaks all God's holy laws, erreth and strayeth from the way of God's commandments like a lost sheep, and grasps at the pomps and vanities of the world, as much as he can, and thinks he gets no more than comes to his share; and when he shall indulge the lusts of his flesh, this is a child of the devil; he is a child of that Spirit that was a liar from the beginning. Never talk of being a child and an heir of God's kingdom, such a man is in fetters, he is to go along with the devil and his angels, and there is a kingdom prepared for them, and a kingdom of darkness, and he must have his portion with them in everlasting misery: *Tophet is prepared of old for all the workers of iniquity.*

What for those that are baptized? Yes, but do not you deny baptism?

No, not I, I would have men and women baptized with a baptism that will do them some good. Some have seen the vanity and weakness of this kind of baptism, and called it baby baptism; and therefore would go and be baptized and plunged in the water over head and ears, but they came up again with the same heart and mind, and the same polluted soul. *John* baptized in *Jordan*, and all *Jerusalem* and *Judea* came

came to be baptized or him: There were a fort as well as
perſons then that crucified the Lord Jeſus Chriſt, a ſtronger
did them harm in his life, but much good. ſtay till

This baptiſm had never an apoſtolical patron, but orrow,
another baptiſm that is ſo infallible a baptiſm, that if a truſt
were ſurely baptized withal, he was ſure of Heaven, he wothe
never need any other aſſurance of Heaven than to be baptized with the baptiſm of Jeſus Chriſt: The lip of truth ſpeaks
of him, *he that believeth and is baptized, ſhall be ſaved*: He
ſhall be ſaved in ſpite of the devil and all his temptations,
in ſpite of perſecutions and the ſtumbling-blocks laid before
him. Here is a baptiſm worth a man's while, worth all his
labour, if he could obtain it. *he that cometh after me*, ſaith
John the Baptiſt, *he ſhall baptize you with the Holy Ghoſt and
with fire*; here is a baptiſm belongs to Chriſtians, an ordinance ordained. Far be it from us to deny baptiſm; but
we would light of the right, ſince there are ſo many ſorts:
This baptiſm is ſo right and certain, that it aſcertains a
man of his ſalvation, but it is done by *the Holy Ghoſt and
with fire*: If it be by the Holy Ghoſt, then it is far
enough off from us; for there is no Holy Ghoſt in our days,
ſay ſome, ſo this baptiſm is ceaſed, and inſpiration is ceaſed.
If the *Holy Ghoſt* and *fire* be the matter of baptiſm, the thing
being failed and ceaſed, the conſequence cannot follow;
thou and I cannot be baptized becauſe there is no working
of the Holy Ghoſt in our days; ſay ſome, this baptiſm is
with the Holy Ghoſt and with fire; with fire for burning
up our corruptions, and purifying our hearts. But the Holy
Ghoſt hath done working upon men, ſay they; why then
there is an end of baptiſm: A man is hungry, and when his
time comes to eat, he hath no victuals, yet he ſits him down
as if he did eat; will this feed and nouriſh him? So men now-
a-days, they have a baptiſm wherewith they are baptized; but
baptiſm with *the Holy Ghoſt and with fire*, is the right baptiſm, therefore do not baptize until you find the Holy Ghoſt,
this will be far better; this is the baptiſm that they which
come to know it, are ſure of ſalvation by it; for by this
baptiſm, they are borne up and tinctured in their ſouls with
the Divine Spirit of Chriſt Jeſus, proceeding from the Father
& the Son, till they receive his likeneſs, and ſo die unto
ſin:

LORD'S SUPPER *asserted.*

sin: As ma[ny] as were baptized, were baptized into Christ's death. The [apo]stle openeth it, in that he died he died unto sin [o]nce, but in [tha]t he liveth he liveth unto God; so that they that were bapti[zed] were baptized into Christ's death; and you that are dead [u]nto sin, how should you live any longer therein?

These that were ba[pti]zed lived without sin; can that be true, that no one lived [w]ithout sin but Christ only? Yes, saith the apostle, *you that* [we]*re* free from sin, are alive to *righteousness;* their life stood [...]d they are alive to Christ, life is taken away by baptism, [...] He that comes to be and he that liveth he liveth to G[od...] he live ten, twenty, partaker of the first resurrection, [...] God, he liveth no forte, or a hundred years, he li[veth?] [unto?] the world, and the more in the pomps and va[nities?...] *liveth unto God*. This baptism, sinful lusts of the flesh, but h[...] tized with it, [sh]all be saved; tism, whoever comes to be b[aptized...] baptism.
ed; so that we do not deny [...] deny the Lor[d's] Supper.

But we hear say, that yo[u...]ght, God knows; thei[r...] is We have never had such a thou[ght...] more; but people have nothing that our souls long aft[er...] their own, they have lost been making a kind of work of [...] children do, who when a reality, and make shadows, a[re...]e for service, they will they see things made in the ho[use?...] People do not not see make the like in sand and clay[...] to the supper of the what a great thing it is to atta[in...] vangelical opening, we Lord; as things come into an [...] of things. *Behold I* spake then more lively and freshl[y...] *y man open to me, I stand at the door and knock, if a*[*ny...] *he with me.* For the will come in and sup with him, and [...] mine, and search all understanding of this text, go and ex[amine?...] see what the learn- the commentators you can find, and [...] apply this to the ed men say of it; see if they do no[t...] Christ, to let him inward call of the Spirit and grace of [...] at those that wrote into our hearts; and would one think th[at...] l dispensation of these things should be against the spiritu[al...] the door of the things? They say that this knocking at [t]he door of the heart signifies the call of God's Spirit at [...] God knock- heart. There are two sorts of sinners that [...] a man that is eth at the door of their hearts; one is, weary

BAPTISM *and the*

weary of his sin: For his part, he wisheth that he might never sin more. As soon as he perceives he knock, and is called upon to let in the grace of God, to help him against temptation, he freely opens his heart to receive it, and faith, with all my heart I will entertain and welcome the grace of God; glad I am that God hath had so much patience towards me; and since God offers his grace, I will embrace this grace of God above all pleasures, and I will take it into my heart; the grace of Christ is the greatest jewel that I know. Honest *Paul*, he took this course, and prayed, Lord take away this tempter; here is a temptation that troubleth me, and I am not willing to yield, for all the devil follows me with it; *he cried unto the Lord, and besought him three times, earnestly,* to take away the temptation; What the Lord answers him, *my grace is sufficient for thee*. What matter if the tempter buffet thee, and trouble thee, hast thou not received my grace into thy heart? Thou art a believer, and thy trust is in me, and *my grace is sufficient for thee.* Let the tempter do his worst, keep thou to the grace of God, and thou wilt withstand and overcome the temptation when it comes.

If a man openeth his heart and receiveth Christ when he comes, then you shall find such an alteration in that man, that go and try him with the same temptation which prevailed over him the last week, it will not do so now; though he be as weak as water, and as prone to corruption and iniquity as before, yet now having a faith begotten in him, that the grace of God will defend him, he keeps out of the devil's snares. Now this man trusting in this grace till his sin and iniquity be purged out, now is the time to spread the table; there is a clean heart, and the heavenly guest is now come, and the dainties of the kingdom are brought to him for his nourishment. *Now,* saith Christ, *I will come in and sup with him, and my Father also will come, and we will sup with him, and he with us.* This never happens to any body so long as the table and heart is foul; for the table must be clean, and the devil and sin thrown out, and then will the Lord confirm and ratify, and seal the covenant; so that here is a seal with a witness. When a man hath this testimony of the love of God, that God is

reconciled

Lord's Supper asserted.

reconciled to him in Christ, then Christ will come in, and he will bring his Father, and they will sup with him; and this is that which will give complete satisfaction to such a soul.

All the tongues of men and angels are too short to speak of these things, as they are in themselves, but they are all manifested by the Spirit. All the mysteries of the kingdom of God, are manifested by the Spirit of God; now to say there is no Spirit to be regarded now-a-days, that is as much as to say, we must never regard the kingdom of God, *for no man can discern the things of God but the Spirit of God*, no man can tell what they be; *as no man can know the things of a man but the spirit of a man.*

But I must look to this and the other form, and mark, and methodize them, for we can know nothing of the things of God themselves.

I hope you are all of another judgment, and believe that this is a trick and cheat of the wicked one; people do find the Spirit and will feel it if they will wait upon the motions of it. I do not only mean when you are here together, but when you are separated one from another; when you feel the motions of this good Spirit, embrace them, and make them yours. This Spirit is a gift that is given; so may a shilling or a piece of bread be held forth to a poor creature, but if he receive it not, he may perish for all that; it is not his, tho' I have appointed it to be his, and have seperated it from my other substance to be his. If he receive not what I offer and would give him, he may perish for all that.

Here is *grace and truth comes by Jesus Christ, and God hath offered it to all men, in that he hath raised up Christ from the dead; the grace of God which bringeth salvation, hath appeared unto all men;* but all men have not received it, therefore all men have it not; and they that have not the grace of Christ, and the *Spirit of Christ, are none of his;* but it doth not follow that they never will be more of his. When they have received the gift by Christ, and say, I will be his sheep or lamb, they will come into his favour by that gift, and shall partake of the good things of his Father's kingdom; but till they have received this gift,

gift, they are not the better for it, they have not any benefit by the death of Chriſt; they have no help, no benefit by it, except it be the patience and long-ſuffering of God, who for Chriſt's ſake bears with their weakneſs, and waits to be gracious, and for Chriſt's ſake offers them favour; but they are not come to the poſſeſſion of it, till they open their hearts, and receive the grace of Chriſt; then they are convinced of Chriſt's end, and that there is a poſſibility of enjoying the Spirit of God, and of being taught and led by it.

Take this along with you, that it is your abſolute and indiſpenſable duty to wait from day to day upon the great God of Heaven, *the giver of every good and perfect gift,* that you may have that bleſſed gift, that you may have the aſſiſtance of a greater power than your own to lead you out of ſin into righteouſneſs, that through Jeſus Chirſt you may be acceptable to God.

SERMON XXIII.

CHRIST the WAY, the TRUTH, and the LIFE.

Preached at GRACE-CHURCH-STREET, *April 18, 1687.*

I Fear the high places are not taken away; it hath been ſo in all ages, and it is manifeſtly ſo in this day; where the heart is not rightly prepared for the Lord, there the high places are not taken away: For all the high places in the time of *Iſrael*'s idolatry, they were ever ſet up when they departed from the Lord, and all the high places now they are up in a time of ignorance of God; when people have forgotten the Lord, then they exalt themſelves, then pride, and arrogance, and every evil way prevails upon us; but when men come to ſeek the Lord with uprightneſs, that brings down their high conceits, that brings every one into humility; for every one comes to be convinced in themſelves that none can find the Lord, but as they are brought to be humble; nay, indeed, none seek after him aright but such, none have the promise of finding him but the humble.

Therefore it is the duty of every one that is a real enquirer and seeker after God, to know the right preparation of mind, to know themselves in such a frame of spirit, that they may seek in hope, that they may have a right and just expectation of finding him whom they are seeking after; for this hath been the reason that a great many have been frustrated in their endeavours, and in their purposes of seeking after the Lord, they have not been rightly prepared for him to manifest himself unto them, they have not known the *preparation of his sanctuary;* there was a peculiar preparation that was requisite, to those that drew near unto the sanctuary of God, they were hallowed, that is, made holy, ere they drew near to the holy place; but alas! this hath been greatly neglected in our days, unholy people with unholy minds have been seeking after the Holy God, they have been enquiring after a holy way, and were not prepared to walk in it, there was nothing raised in their minds, that was fit to walk in that way.

For so long as men or women stand in unity with their lusts and concupiscence, with the spirit of this world, and the way of it, they are not capable of receiving that which should lead them into the way of holiness; nay, if it appears to them, they cannot receive it, for it is with them as with other guests, there be other lovers already let in, which employ the powers and faculties of their souls, so that if the most beloved of all, the most excellent, if *the chiefest of ten thousand* do appear, they cannot *see a comeliness in him.* The prophet speaking of this state and condition of men, did prophesy concerning our Lord Jesus Christ, *when we shall see him there is no comeliness in him why we should desire him;* and so it hath happened to a great many now-a-days, though the truth hath appeared to them, yet they have not looked upon it as a pleasant way, as a way desirable, but a way to be shunned if possible. What shifts have a great many people made to keep themselves, if possible, out of the way of truth, arguing for this and that, and disputing for one way and another that was out of truth's way, out of the way of holiness. What was the meaning of all their arguments, but to tell us they might be happy, they might be saved, though they did not come into truth's way, and walk in truth's way? And though they did abide in those things, that were contrary to the testimony of truth in their own hearts, yet it might go well with them.

This is the strength of the arguments of all sorts, of all persuasions in the world, that have been arguing themselves out of the truth, and would argue us out of the truth too, and would take the liberty to do those things which are not agreeable therewith; but now the reason of this is because the preparation is wanting, they are those that have no need of truth, and that have no need of God, and of a Saviour; but think they can make shift without them; he is not become the chiefest to them, they can abide in the high places, they can *call upon the name of the* Lord, and they can *worship in the groves, and in the high places* both together, like those nations that were brought to inhabit the kingdom of Israel when the ten tribes were carried away, they sent for priests to teach them, they sent back to the king of *Assyria* to send them some priests, to teach them to worship the God of their country, and when the priest came to teach them, he taught them the ceremonies of the law, and the divers observations that the Jews used to practise in that country, and so they grew into a formality of serving the God of *Israel, they called upon the name of the Lord, and every nation worshipped their own Gods.*

How is this nation, and the nations of Europe, now inhabited with such a people that are called by the name of the Lord, but every one worshipping their own Gods; one makes gold and silver his God, another makes his pleasure his God, another his honour, another this, that, and the other lust, and they bow down to them, that is, they yield themselves to their lusts, concupiscence and corruptions, that they stand in unity with, but they call upon the name of the Lord too; they do apply themselves to some kind of form of worship, which they say is unto the immortal and invisible God; but alas! they come not to the knowledge

ledge of God by this. All that the priests could do that the king of *Assyria* sent back, could not bring the *Samaritans* to the knowledge of the God of *Israel*, they only brought them to a report of such a God, that had set up such a law: They had the report of it, and for fear that the lions should tear them in pieces, they would enter into that form, but they worshipped their own Gods still.

So it is now, people do not come to the knowledge of the true God, the living God, by entering into any form of religion; for instance, prayer, hearing of any ordinance or church-fellowship, these give not men the knowledge of God, there is but one way to come to that, but one only. Men have found a great many, it is past your skill and mine to reckon up the many ways that men have found out upon the face of the earth, how they might come to the knowledge of God, and to peace and reconciliation with him; but they have only played the fool, and spent their time in vain, especially they that own the scriptures of truth to be a true and faithful record of the mind and will of God, they play the fool abominably; for the scripture that they give so much reputation to in their profession doth testify the way is but one, and there is no other way for people to be reconciled to God, than by coming into Christ; to be found in him, to be regenerated and born into his nature, and have his qualities put upon them, *that as he was pure, they may be pure; that he that sanctifieth, and they who are sanctified by him, may become both one, and so be reconciled to the Father through him.* This you know is the common profession of Christendom, or at least of our nation. And in other nations, the common profession is, there is no Mediator but one, no Reconciler but one. Indeed some others hold there may be other Mediators, and that there are others that may contribute to them by their mediation, and by their prayers and merits, but the generality of the nations are otherwise.

Now for people to fall out, and say, my way is best, and thy way is not best, and to fall into contests about many ways, when the scripture concludes there is but one way, is not well; we had better all agree about this doctrine, that there is no possibility of reconciliation with God, since we are

fallen

fallen out with him, and since sin hath made a separation, there is no way of being reconciled again to God, but by and through our Lord Jesus Christ; nor by him neither, unless we receive of his Spirit to quicken us; nothing can quicken us, enliven us, or recommend us to God, but the Spirit of Christ operating and working in our hearts, that he may prepare us for the Father's kingdom.

If people would agree upon this, there would be an end of all labour, and toil, and jangling about the right way, for the consequence and conclusion would be this: That the man who doth not know himself the sanctifying power of the Spirit of Christ Jesus, he is out of the way to reconciliation with God, let his form and profession be what it will: If therefore he be reconciled to God, it must be by and through the Mediator, and he will never recommend him to the Father till he hath made him a temple to let in the Spirit of Christ, to work in his heart, to fit him for the kingdom of God: And men have no other way to come to it; for though they be zealous in every prayer and form, it signifies nothing to any great purpose, their hope will be frustrated; *there is no other way,* faith Christ, *of coming to the Father, but by me; I am the way, the truth and the life.* If I am out of the truth, I am out of the way; and if I am out of the way, then I cannot come to the end of the way. This is plain reasoning among men: If I tell a lie, that is out of the truth: If I have vain communication, or deceive or wrong my neighbour, that is out of the truth; if I am in that which is manifested in my conscience to be contrary to the truth, I am out of the way; though I be strict in that way, as to profession, yet I am out of the way to God, I am out of the truth; there is no way to God but by Christ, who is the way, the truth and the life; whoever is out of him, is out of the way; which made the apostle say, *that his labour, endeavour and desire was, that he might be found in Christ, not having his own righteousness, but having on the righteousness of Christ Jesus.*

Many men think to recommend themselves to God by their righteous, just and honest dealings, and doing wrong to nobody. This is good in itself, but doth not recommend us to God, unless it be done by the righteous and

holy

the TRUTH, *and the* LIFE.   269

holy Spirit of Christ Jesus, unless it be of his working; he must have the working of righteousness and truth in us; he must plant it, and it must grow by his working, if it be acceptable to the Father; *for without me*, saith Christ, *you can do nothing*. A man out of Christ, a stranger to his Spirit, may do something, but nothing available to the well-being of his soul, 'till he have reconciliation by Christ Jesus: If he be reconciled to God, this Mediator must be the Reconciler, and he must fit and prepare him for reconciliation with the Father.

All the divisions, sorts and sects of religion, must all come to an end; if this measuring line be laid to them, they all appear too short; and there is nothing will do a man good, but that religion that obligeth and ties him to the good pleasure of God, through the Spirit of the Mediator, which he feels working in him, by which he is raised from death to some degree of life: When he is sensible what a burthen sin is to his life, that godly life which he hath, he is burthened with every sin, and oppressed with every vain thought, and every vain word, if he be not in some measure quickened, he is not sensible of this burthen; but being quickened, he is sensible of the burthen that lies upon his life, by reason of his sin; and then, being under the weight of his sin, he calls to God for his assistance; he cries to God to help him; he now knows that he hath striven and laboured in vain. O God of all grace, if thou vouchsafest not help to my soul, if thou dost not interpose by the assistance of thy grace, I cannot overcome this sin. There is a continual cry to God for divine assistance, and as they cry to God for assistance, he ministers assistance to them, by which they are able to overcome the enemy of their souls, and all temptations when they come: And when a man finds such divine assistance, his faith is strengthened and confirmed, and so he *fights the good fight of faith*, and at last gets the victory; victory over his sin, and his own lusts, and concupiscence, and victory over the assaults and temtations of the adversary, and at last he comes, through the grace of God, *to deny all ungodliness and worldly lusts, and to live righteously, soberly and godly in this present world.*

Now

Now when people do thus, it is by the grace of God. This life of righteousness, sobriety and godliness, is not the effect of their labour and exercise, and of their endeavours herein, but it is the effect of the holy Spirit that hath been the teacher. When you see a man has become a good scholar, eminent in all sorts of learning, you will conclude he did not attain to all this of himself, he did not learn this and the other language, this and the other art and science of himself; no, he had some judicious and able master and teacher, who communicated of his learning and knowledge to his disciple and scholar: This is the efficient cause of his improvement. Now if a man, by the grace and the Spirit of God, and the teachings of it, live a holy, godly life, this is the effect of something; he did not always live such a life, how comes he to live such a life now? Is it by his own industry, labour and exercise? No, it is by being exercised, taught and led by the Spirit of God; so that it is the effect of the grace of God that he should live such a holy life, this is the meritorious cause of it, as he is a creature, and by this only acceptable to God in Christ the Mediator.

Thus a man comes to be justified and accepted, not because he is a godly man, but is made so by the Spirit of God: *You are not under the law,* faith the apostle, *but under grace* : You are under the teachings of it, under the directions of it: Grace can reprove people; for that grace and that truth that comes by Christ, and manifests itself as a light in the hearts of transgressors, reproves their sin, and calls them out of it ; it reproves them for it, and exhorts them to leave it, both at one time ; so that we must acknowledge all our righteousness, holiness and obedience to be of God, and all that we do in order thereunto, as it is done by the teaching, by the influence and operation of the grace of God given us in Christ Jesus ; it is the effect of him who is our Mediator, he worketh it in us, and for us, of his good pleasure.

If we be justified, we are not justified for a righteous, holy life, and for our obedience ; but we are justified through Christ, who worketh a godly life in them that believe, so that a man is not justified by any other way or means ; and all
other

other ways a man takes of being reconciled to God, are vain and fruitlefs, and have been fpoken againft by all that were moved by the Holy Ghoft in the New Teftament. Saith the prophet, *what, fhall I come before the Lord withal?* I am fallen under death and fin, and in a feparation from God, I would fain be reconciled to him ; what fhall I do to be reconciled to God ? He goes about to reckon without Chrift, and without faith and holinefs. *Shall I take a thoufand rams, and ten thoufand rivers of oil?* Shall I come nearer ftill ? *Shall I make an offering of the fruit of my body, for the fin of my foul? Shall I offer my firft-born to God*, that I may not be rejected and brought to a feparation from him ? Thus men when they come to be fenfible, do feel in themfelves that all this is to no purpofe : The anfwer comes, thou mayeft live, but all thy contrivances about making an offering are vain : *He hath fhewed thee O man ! what to do*. It is not thy finding this way and that way, viz. thy rams, and thy oil, and thy firft-born ; it is no way of thy devifing and imagining that can reconcile thee to me, *I have fhewed thee, O man, what is good.* What is this that is fhewed ? It is comprifed in a fhort compafs, *it is to love mercy, to do juftice, and to walk humbly with thy God*. Will this ferve without offering rams and oil, and offering my firft born ? This will do if thou canft but *love mercy* when it is fhewn thee; that is, embrace mercy, and love it. He hath fhewed mercy to all men ; then love it and receive it ; *do juftly*, leave every thing that is unrighteous, and do that which is juft in the fight of God, but do not boaft of thy juftice and righteoufnefs, but *walk humbly with thy God;* here is the whole duty of man. Here is no dependence on dead works, or my own exertions, in order to my juftification.

Indeed the confideration of thefe kind of leffons do corrupt fome men, and put them upon doing this or that, and upon forbearing this or that, and hath brought many to confeffion and great abftinence, and put them upon great doings, thinking this would anfwer the juftice of God; I have loved mercy, and given all I had to the poor. If I do juftly, and abftain from this and the other liberty, if I walk humbly, that is, if I humble myfelf by

this

this and the other manner of pennance and contrition, then I do what God requires, and then I have pleafed God.

Now all that have gone this way to work, to do juftly, and love mercy, and to make themfelves humble, and humbled themfelves in fuch a low manner, they have miffed the mark. *He hath fhewed thee, O man! what is good;* that it is impoffible for fallen man to anfwer this himfelf; he may be convinced of his duty to do juftice, but by his own power and ftrength he cannot do it; there are fo many temptations from without, and fo many from within, fuch a propenfity in nature, that will prevail againft all the bonds of charity that he can make.

Therefore is *help laid upon one that is mighty;* without the grace of God that comes by Chrift Jefus, a man can never do right, though convinced: Tho' the Lord hath fhewed him what is good, he fhews us that we are unable of ourfelves; he hath taken care to fend his Son: *God hath fo loved the world, that he hath fent his Son into the world,* that he might help thofe that have need of help, that every one that is in diftrefs might have an eye to Chrift, *the author and finifher of their faith;* when men have a reference to their faith in Chrift, this makes their duty acceptable; I cannot do it except the Lord ftrengthen me; therefore I will have refpect to the Mediator, Chrift Jefus, who was fent for a light into the world. God fends forth his grace for every one to lay hold on, who generally believe, that tho' they are unable to do what God requires, yet he will enable them to do it; *for as many as received him, to them he gave power to become the Sons of God,* tho' they were the devil's children before; *he is the fame yefterday, to-day, and forever.* He abides always the fame in his grace to men, he is in his operation to them the fame; he offers grace to them that are in a frame of mind to receive it; they may know that his power will give them ability, and that whatfoever they do of themfelves will prove fruitlefs, becaufe it is not done in Chrift's name and power, and fo not acceptable to God.

The greateft thing that we are to be concerned about, if we will be religious, and concern ourfelves about divine matters, about the kingdom of God and the world to come, is, is, to see what frame of mind we are in at present, whether the high places are taken away, whether we are not exalted in our own conceits of knowledge and wisdom, and reckon not to be beholden to him for his grace. If we be highly conceited, and think we can stand upon our own legs, the high places are not taken away : Men are not in this state prepared to seek the God of their fathers ; therefore, let every one turn to God, and see how it is with you ; see whether there be a mind brought low enough to be subject to Christ, and to the gracious teachings of his Spirit.

A man may say, I can make a sermon, I can make a prayer and exhortation, and I can make a book, and send it abroad, I can do all this by my own parts and abilities ; so thou mayest, and mayest make it all full of good words, but thou canst never make it acceptable to God ; for *without me*, saith Christ, *you can do nothing*. Thou must have the assistance of the Spirit of Christ, else thou canst not make a good prayer, nor a good book, nor any thing good ; God esteems *the very plowing of the wicked to be an abomination* to him. Where the mind is not exercised by the Spirit of God, if he should pray from morning to night, and spend all his days in pennance, it will do him no good. *If I*, saith *David, regard iniquity ;* you may think I am a man in favour with God, a man after God's own heart ; *yet if I regard iniquity in my heart, the Lord will not hear my prayer*. What signifies prayers and sermons, made of good words, if they come not from a heart separate from iniquity ? If it be not so, it will do no good at all, in point of acceptance with God.

O let the fear of the Lord enter upon every heart ! wait all to feel the Divine Power of the Lord, that brings down every high thought, that so you may look to the preparation of your hearts, that is a right preparation ; when the people are so low, so broken and so tender, that they are nothing in their own eyes, but what the Lord will make them to be ; then they are as clay in the hands of the potter, they are fashioned by his hands, and made the *workmanship of God in Christ Jesus*, the *one Mediator between God and man.* They must bear the likeness of Christ Jesus, bear his Heavenly image, they must have his qualities, and have the same mind in them that was in him: *I do always that which pleaseth my Father,* faith the Lord Jesus Christ. Indeed he hath the doing of things in the hearts of men, and God is pleased with him, and where men have the doing of them themselves, they are thrown back as dung in their faces; where any rightly desire justification, where men have a right preparation of heart, so to seek the God of their fathers, as to find him and be accepted of him, it is through Jesus Christ, in whom he is well pleased.

In all your assemblies, prayers, exercises and meditations, you must be separated and drawn off from your former lovers, and you must be joined to him that God hath sent to be a leader and a guide unto you, then you will find daily his assistance; and as you have assistance from him, you will find acceptance with God, and he will shew you the Father, and that, and nothing else, will satisfy the soul hungering and thirsting after God. *Shew us the Father, and it sufficeth us.* So when Christ, the Mediator, comes to have wrought so far as the purifying of the soul, and the sanctifying thereof, and thereby fitted it for his glory, such holy souls shall behold his glory; *for the Lord will give grace and glory, and no good thing will he withhold from them that walk uprightly.*

That you may be brought to this state, and kept and preserved in it; that the Heavens may rain down fatness upon you, and that you may feel the living virtues that flow from Christ to every member, is the labour and travel of the servants of God, for their own souls, and the souls of others that are in unity and fellowship with the Holy Spirit.

SERMON

SERMON XXIV.

CAPTIVE SINNERS *set free by* JESUS CHRIST.

Preached at DEVONSHIRE-HOUSE, *April 29, 1688.*

THERE is nothing will make people live to God, but that which they receive from God. For as all men are by nature in a state of death, so there must be something beyond nature to make them alive again; and this is what every one ought to wait upon God for, that you may feel something that is supernatural, and that you may be acquainted with God's gift; *the gift of God,* saith the scripture, *is eternal life.* Many find a life in this world, that is not the gift of God. The life that people have in sin, it is not the gift of God; the delights and pleasures of this world are become a life unto them. The world is that to which every one must die; they that are not dead to that, they all live to themselves, they do not live to God, for none can live to God, but by the life that comes from him. That which people receive of man, gathers them unto man; that which they receive of God, carries them to God.

So men have made gatherings, and have communicated of what they have to one another, and by virtue thereof, have made them a people: Many men have gathered many people, many churches, and they live to them that gathered them; they do not live to God, for want of receiving something from God, but all they that come to receive the gift of God, they die to the world, and they come to live such a life as the world doth not love, doth not care for, and hath no pleasure in: *If you were of the world,* saith Christ, *the world would love you; but because you are not of the world, they hate you.* How should this be understood, were not they some of the men of that generation? How doth he mean they were not of the world? *Why, I have taken you out of it,* saith he; and yet they were there still, and they were named by certain names, the sons of such and such men; yet for all that, they

they were not of the world; and that which differed in them was, being made partakers of that life which the world knew not.

And so there will be an enmity in the world against the life of holiness; they will hate any body that lives in it; and as it was then, so it is at this day, they that are of the world, they hear and receive those things that are of the world, from the men of this world; but they that are of God, they hear them that are of God, and they receive the things of God, and their greatest comfort and joy that they have is in their communion with God in Christ Jesus, through whom, as through a conduit, the blessings of the father are ministered to them, and through whom, as from the fountain of life, their life is renewed from day to day.

But these things are hid from the world, *from the wise and prudent of it;* they cannot dig into the depth, nor ascend to this height; they cannot *comprehend the length and the breadth of the things of God, which are in Christ Jesus;* they may reach unto something of the love of God, that is in the creation; they can tell when the sun shines upon them, and when the rain falls upon their fields; and when it falls in due season they call it a blessing; and while the covenant with winter and summer remains, they look upon it as comfortable, and perhaps sometimes will bestow a saying, *I thank God for it.* All these things are beneath us, and *there is neither love nor hatred known by them all. I saw the wicked, saith one, I beheld his dwelling place, and he flourished like unto a green bay-tree,* and was wicked still, notwithstanding all this.

But now, they that see where they live, that live to God, they can say, that their leaf never withers, but they *bring forth their fruit in due season;* but he did not so. But the wicked man *that flourished like a green bay-tree, behold I looked, and he was removed, and his place was no more to be found:* There came a blasting upon all his blessing and his flourishing came to an end; his riches perished, and his good things passed away from him. But the man *whose delight is in the law of God,* and makes it his pleasure both night and day, he is *like a tree planted by the rivers of water, whose leaf never fades, and brings forth his fruit in due season.* But *set free by* JESUS CHRIST. 277

But this is hid ; there is no body in the world but would have something of this life too ; they would be sure of eternal life, but they would not die to the other life, they would not be crucified to the world, they would not be separated from their lovers; if they could get into the state of a righteous man, an hour or two before they die, when they are sure they shall die, it would please them ; but to live that life that is to God, is to die to the world, and to part with that they have, their comfort, their joy, their peace and honour, and all their worldly enjoyments in it, before they can come to receive the gift of God, they think is hard : But they that look after it, and have a mind to find it out, without parting with the world's life, they deceive themselves.

Do not you see how men have deceived themselves in these days? They have sought after the kingdom of God till they are scattered in their own way ; they are quarrelling about their own way, as if they never had any scripture to be their rule : They cry the scripture is their rule ; this is the way to eternal life, saith one ; and this is the way, saith another ; and the one and the other say all these ways are false saving their own ; and all these contenders about the way to eternal life, they all say the scripture is the rule.

And yet the scriptures speak of the way too, and tell us the way plainly, the way to rest, peace and life eternal. If the scriptures had been silent in it, and had said nothing but of genealogies and histories of armies and wars, it had been something; but the scriptures of the Old and New Testament speak of a certain way to eternal life, and say it is the way of holiness, *a way shall be cast up for the redeemed and the ransomed of the Lord to walk in, and the wayfaring man, though a fool, shall not mistake in it.* Though he never took a degree at the university, he shall not err in it; though he be a fool in the account of the world, and never understood Greek or Latin, yet he shall not err in this way.

The way that leads to the kingdom of God, is called the way of holiness ; but while many have been reading in their books, they have been contending for a way of unholiness ; no wonder then they have been quarrelling about
it,

it, and have all missed it, and that in the main point of all: Let them make a way, which way they will, and frame it ever so wisely, according to the best wit they have, be it a way that hath all material qualifications that should make it a way of holiness, these men may walk in it, but they will never find the way to the kingdom of God, though they have sought it out : Go to one place and another place, and ask them what is your way? Our way, say they, is the right way, the most sure and certain way that can be found for people to walk in : But whither will it lead me? It will lead thee to the kingdom of God: That is it I would have; but will it lead me to holiness? No, never in this world, thou must never come to holiness; do the best thou canst do here, it is but sin; the best day's work thou makest is but sin; the best child of God on earth cannot live a day without sin : Do you hold out that in your way? Yes; then I have done with that, and must go to another people.

So many have gone many ways to the kingdom of God, and when the upshot is come, they have found every way a polluted way, a sinful way; I know this way will never lead me to God; sin first led me from God; I had been well enough as I was created at first, if I had never sinned against God; a sinful way will lead me from God. It is against common sense, and against rationality, to say we did first go from God by sin, and must go to God again by a sinful way. Who will believe that such a way will lead men to God's kingdom? and that any way will lead men to God, that will not lead them to holiness?

The Psalmist saith, *if I regard iniquity in my heart the Lord will not hear me;* though a man keeps close to meeting, and ordinances, and duties, and performances, iniquity it seems remains still; there is no rooting it out in this world. This continuing and remaining with a man, makes all his performances, and duties, and prayers unacceptable to God; they are all turned back again upon him, and cast as dung upon his face, and true enough too; so that here is no coming unto God in this way; the comers thereunto know well enough they are not reconciled to God, if they are men that are conscientious.

There

There are a sort of people so stupid and sordid in their judgment, that if a man tells them they are reconciled to God, they will believe him though conscience reproves them an hundred times a day. If the parson of the parish say, that he hath made *this child an heir of the kingdom of God and an inheritor of eternal life*; I know some have believed it forty years after, and have born themselves up upon this man's word all their life: Do you think there is any danger of me, that in baptism was made an inheritor of eternal life, and an heir of the kingdom of God? God hath not appointed ordinances in his church for nothing.

I speak not of such sordid hard-hearted people, that never entered into themselves to know how it was with them, whether they are converted; but I speak of sober conscientious people, that do not desire to be cheated in a point of salvation, though they have been deceived a great while, they may be undeceived: Then they must take this for certain doctrine, that nothing can reconcile them to their Maker but that which takes away sin. *God hears not sinners*, he will never be reconciled to a man in this world, as a sinner; but there are many thousands (blessed be God) in this age, as well as in other ages, that were sinners, and reconciled to God through Christ, and had remission of sin; but never any man in his sin was reconciled to God, though he did believe the truth, if he did not come to the sanctification of the spirit, he could never be reconciled to God.

So that there hath been, in all ages, a way of the working of the Spirit of God in the hearts of them that believe, to prepare them for the sinless kingdom, for that glorious kingdom, into which nothing that hurteth, defileth or corrupteth, can enter. And because we cannot enter with corruption and defilement, he hath appointed the ministration of his Spirit to work out that which might hinder the cleansing of us from sin, that we might *have an abundant entrance into his glorious kingdom*; so that whilst they say there is an impossibility of living without sin, I had as lief they had said, there is an impossibility of entering into the kingdom of God; for never any shall come into the kingdom of God, but those that are without sin; for there is no purgatory after death. The

The Papists have a better conceit than the Protestants in that respect : The Protestants conceive sin to be expelled at the point of death ; and they say, all the sins of believers, all the guilt of sin, after we are believers, is pardoned, forgiven and done away, by the death of Christ upon the cross ; we will have it, if we can get it. If men can imagine a way into the kingdom of God, they will have one. They believe that a man may sin and contract no guilt; and that he may sin till his dying day, and then all sin shall pass away, and he shall enter into God's kingdom. The Papists say none can come to Heaven till they be purged from sin ; and they say God hath appointed a place for that purpose, and persons must go into purgatory, and they must lie there till they are purged, and purified, and fitted for Heaven. Now, say the Protestants, truly ; there is no such thing, we find no such thing mentioned in the scripture, therefore such a thing as this cannot be ; for the apostle said, *we have declared to you the whole counsel of God*, and he speaks not a word of purgatory in all the New Testament. The Protestants have got a way to help themselves, and the Papists, also, to help themselves, and both lie under danger : As for the Papists, if their priests mistake, and there be no such place as purgatory, then they must be brought back to the doctrine of the scripture, which declares, *that as death leaves us, so judgment shall find us ; and as we sow so we must reap ; if we sow to the flesh, then of the flesh we shall reap corruption.* Then the Protestants, likewise, if they mistake in saying, a man may act sin and yet contract no guilt, then they must be brought back to the doctrine of the scriptures, that tell us, *the soul that sinneth must die: If a righteous man forsake his righteousness, and doth that which is evil, his righteousness shall be remembered no more, but in the sin that he hath committed he shall die.*

This is sound doctrine : I had rather trust the doctrine of the prophets and apostles than the doctrine of all others, either Protestants or Papists ; and had rather depend upon their doctrine for salvation, that were inspired by the Holy Ghost, than upon those doctrines that say, there is no inspiration now-a-days. Some conceive this scripture *set free by* JESUS CHRIST.

may be interpreted thus and thus; and others conceive it means so and so, but we must, say they, submit to better judgment: I am a fallible man, I submit it to better judgments. Now when people are concerned for immortality and eternity, to have such things dished out in such a manner, what souls are so dull but they would bestir themselves, and consider and look about them before they go hence, and how it shall go with them when they are gone?

We are now to work out our own salvation, that is on our part: None ever have wrought out this salvation, it is wrought out on God's part already, and it is to be made ours; he that is our Saviour, he *hath suffered for our sins, and rose again for our justification; he was made to us, of God, wisdom, righteousness, sanctification, and redemption.* Now wisdom signifies the opening of the counsel of God; righteousness signifies the subjection of our wills to the will of God; sanctification signifies obedience to the Spirit of Christ. Sanctification signifies obedience to something; to what? what shall we be obedient unto? what is our rule? *He that is led by the Spirit of Christ, he is his; but he that is not led by the Spirit of Christ is none of his;* so that it is plain, sanctification signifies obedience to the Spirit of Christ, and redemption signifies buying again, or setting free from bondage.

We know when our friends are in captivity, as in Turkey, or elsewhere, we pay down our money for their redemption; but we will not pay our money if they be kept in their fetters still. Would not any one think himself cheated, to pay so much money for their redemption, and the bargain he made so that he shall be said to be redeemed, and be called a redeemed captive, but he must wear his fetters still? How long? as long as he hath a day to live.

This is for bodies; but now I am speaking of souls, Christ must be made to me redemption, and rescue me from captivity. Am I prisoner any where? Yes; *verily, verily, he that committeth sin,* saith Christ, *he is a servant of sin,* he is a slave to sin: If thou hast sinned, thou art a slave, a captive, that must be redeemed out of captivity; who will pay a price for me? I am poor, I have nothing,

I cannot redeem myſelf, who will pay a price for me? There is one come, who hath paid a price for me; that is well, that is good news, then I hope I ſhall come out of my captivity. What is his name, is he called a Redeemer? So then I do expect the benefit of my redemption, and that I ſhall go out of my captivity. No, ſay they, you muſt abide in ſin, as long as you live: What benefit then have I by my redemption? I could have been in captivity no longer; if I had not been redeemed, I muſt wear my ſhackles and fetters ſtill, and be ſubject to my old maſter and patron, and when he will have me be drunk, I muſt be drunk; and when he will have me be unclean, I muſt be unclean.

Thus many profeſt Chriſtians there be (you ſee it with your eyes) that will tell you they believe all the articles of the creed, and they have been baptized into the Chriſtian faith, and can rehearſe all the principles of the Chriſtian religion, and perform the duty of Chriſtians in going to church, ſaying their prayers, and giving alms too it may be; they are ſuch as would be called Chriſtians, they would be called ſo, yet they *are not redeemed from their vain converſations;* for what makes their ſhackles and fetters about them? When their old maſter bids them be drunk, they will be drunk; and when he bids them commit whoredom, or lie, or cheat their neighbour, they will do it: You do believe the devil leads you to this; you will not ſay the Spirit of God led you to it. If one demand, how did you do it? You ſay, the devil prevailed upon me: What, hath the devil power over men after they are redeemed? What ſort of redemption is this? Then comes in the old ſhift again, we are redeemed from the puniſhment of our ſin, but not from the act of it.

Now if thoſe that are called ranters had told me this tale, it had been like them; but when doctors of divinity tell us this tale, it is ſo unlike divinity, that it is *carnal, ſenſual and deviliſh*. To tell believers they are redeemed from the puniſhment of ſin, but not from the act of ſin; that this is the benefit which we receive from Chriſt's ſufferings; that we may ſin on, free coſt; that there is no guilt contracted by it; will any man or woman, that underſtand they have a ſoul, venture their immortal ſouls on this divinity? I hope

hope not. They will not venture their foul on this foundation-doctrine: I hope God will awaken the confciencies of people, that they will not hazard their fouls upon fuch a carnal, devilifh foundation; that if the devil fhould preach, he could not preach a worfe doctrine than this, to perfuade Chriftians they may live in fin, and fin will not hurt them, nor impair or break their peace with God, and reconciliation with him.

I will tell you how it hath been with me; in my childhood, if I had fpoken a vain word, or a falfe word, I had contracted fuch a guilt thereby, that I was afhamed to draw near to God, to pray to him; I knew he would not hear liars, I knew there was no way to be accepted without repentance and amendment of life. I believe others have met with the fame dealing from God, by the fecret ftrokes of conviction that have come upon their hearts, when they have finned againft God.

So that I am ftill of the mind, that the perfons that depend upon this kind of doctrine, do at fometimes, efpecially when ficknefs comes, and death looks them in the face, or in times of common contagion or peftilence, at fuch a time they have a weight of guilt upon their confciences; for this doctrine will not fupport them at death, but that then they believe they have contracted guilt, or committed fin.

I have wifhed many times that the Lord would open the eyes and hearts of the people of this city and of this nation, to fee how miferably they have ventured their fouls. Will merchants in this city ever venture their goods at fuch a rate as men commonly venture their fouls? What, will they venture their goods in a fhip without a bottom, before fhe goes to fea? Now this doctrine hath not a foundation; fhall I believe a perfon that tells me I do not contract guilt, when I feel it upon my heart; when I commit whoredom and drunkennefs, and cheat my neighbours, fhall any one perfuade me that I do not contract guilt?

O friends! we are fpeaking of great matters; it is about eternity, that we are fpeaking, it is about the hazard of eternal happinefs; therefore I pray, let every one be ferious, and confider what I fay, for I fpeak in God's name, and on your behalf: Men are to come to a true search in themselves, what a life it is that they live. Many support themselves by the *doctrines and precepts of men*, and they buoy themselves into conceits of salvation; let them examine whether it be a life that hath its support from the Spirit of God; this is material for every one to consider. There are none can live to God, but by the life they receive from God; *the grace of God, which bringeth salvation, hath appeared to all men.* Now here is an universal doctrine.

There are a sort of men in this city and nation that tell us, that saving grace is given only to the elect. Saving grace is given to *all men*; but you must construe those words, *all the elect*, where they are somewhat injurious, and would cast off the condition of the text, if they make a distinction in the latter part of the sentence, for it will not be good sense: *The grace of God that bringeth salvation, hath appeared to all the elect, teaching us to deny all ungodliness,* &c. Here is *us* taken out of the *all*. The same grace, that is our teacher, appears to be the teacher of others, though they *turn it into lasciviousness*. The grace is the same, though they make many school-distinctions between common and saving grace. The apostle explains it, by telling what grace he means; *the grace of God, which bringeth salvation, appeareth to all men*, and that is *by teaching us*; what doth it teach? I pray consider it; it teacheth us *to deny all ungodliness and all worldly lusts, and to live soberly, righteously and godly in this present world*. Where is sin now, if a man be taught by this grace, and the dictates of it. Can a man live in sin, and yet live righteously, soberly and godly too? Can a man live in sin, and yet deny all ungodliness at the same time? Where have men's understanding been, that cannot understand their mother tongue, and consider sense? Where are men's understandings that will say, I may *deny all ungodliness and worldly lusts*, and yet follow the lusts of my own heart? You would think I speak nonsense if I should speak thus; and yet we have been put off with such nonsensical stuff as this. We must pray to God to send *his holy Spirit into our hearts, to enable us to live godly, righteous and*

and sober lives, and at the same time believe that we shall never do it, but that it is a business of impossibility.

Now when men come to lay these things together, and when they consider between God and their own souls, how it is with them, many are amazed to think they should ever be put off with such incongruous, disagreeing, and dissonant things, that are not consistent with one another.

But do you think it is possible for any man to live without sin? Yes, or else I would say it is impossible for any to be reconciled to God; for God will never be reconciled to sinners, as such; for his bargain and covenant is made of such kind of articles. *Wash ye, make ye clean, put away the evil of your doings from before mine eyes. Cease to do evil; learn to do well,* &c. Then *some and let us reason together, saith the Lord; tho' your sins be as scarlet, they shall be as white as snow; tho' they be red as crimson, they shall be as wool,* Isaiah i, 16, 17; still these are the terms, *put away the evil of your doings,* then patience, mercy and long-suffering, shall be extended to you; *God will give grace and glory, and no good thing will he withhold;* what, from those that say their prayers, or go to the church or meeting? No, but *but no good thing will he withhold from them that walk uprightly;* Psal. lxxxiv, 11. These are the men.

And when the Lord distinguishes by his prophet whom he would have among them, he speaks of a sort of people that called upon the name of the Lord; *those that feared the Lord, and spake often one to another;* that is, of the goodness of God; they were a sort of people *that trembled at the word of God*; a sort of people that did not do as others did, hunt after pleasures, riches, and the honours of the world, but to be acquainted with the inward word that wrought upon their hearts; *in that day that I make up my jewels, they shall be mine, saith the Lord.* Whose shall the others be? Thou wilt own these for thine, but whose shall the others be, that think not upon thy name, and tremble not at thy word? There is a place for them too: *Tophet is prepared of old, made both wide and large; the fuel thereof is fire and brimstone, and much wood,*

wood, and the breath of the Lord kindleth it. This is for all that are wicked, and that work iniquity.

This is in the Old Testament; then comes the New Testament, in *John's Revelations*; there is a separation again: There are a sort of people which are called the true worshippers, and the angel was commanded to go and measure the temple, and those that worshipped therein: The outward temple was not measured, but left for the *Gentiles* to tread in, and left without the measure; *for without are dogs and sorcerers, and whoremongers, and murderers, and idolaters, and whosoever loveth and maketh a lie.* And then the Lord speaks to his prophets in the Old Testament again; *if thou put a difference between the precious and the vile, then thou shalt be as my mouth unto them*; but if thou huddle them altogether, and *few pillows under elbows*, then thou shalt not be as my mouth.

So that in all ages God aimed at a separation of the state and condition of his people; and one sort of people were purified, through the sanctification of the Spirit, and belief of the truth; and another sort were unsanctified and unpurified, and remained in their sin; and the end of Christ's coming into the world, it was to call people to repentance; *he came not to call the righteous, but sinners to repentance*, and to leave off their sin. *To as many as received him, to them he gave power to become the sons of God, to as many as believed on his name.* Whose sons were the other? They made as high a rattle of profession as the other: He tells them who is their father, *you are of your father the devil;* and he did orderly prove it, and that was thus; that they did the devil's works, *ergo*, they were the devil's children. It was Christ himself, the greatest doctor of divinity that ever was in the world, that spake these words: And this is the manner of logic whereby he argues with the *Pharisees*, to make them believe that they were the devil's children; they that do the devil's works are the devil's children; but *you do his works*, therefore you are his children; so they sought to kill him, they could not bear such arguments.

If one should go and search out a people in this city and nation, and see one man of this religion, another of
that

that religion, and pick them out, and ufe this argument with them: There is a man profeſſeth high, he profeſſeth a light within; if you look upon his deeds they are dead and dark, why then he is one of the devil's children: If you put me to prove this, I ſay he doth the devil's works, he is an extortioner, a deceiver, and a drunkard and unclean perſon, and doth the devil's works, and ſo is none of God's children. And ſo go to another ſort and uſe this argument, it is fafe enough, you can never fail in this kind of argument which Chriſt uſed; and if people would uſe it with themſelves, and think themſelves no better, then we ſhould have people confeſs themſelves the devil's children.

None come to be God's children, till they come to acknowledge their loſt eſtate, their deplorable condition; that they are fallen from God, and through ſin and iniquity are got into a nature that is at enmity with God; then they will cry out, *who ſhall deliver me from this body of death*, and childſhip of ſatan, this heirſhip of wrath? I am an heir of an inheritance; I am an heir of wrath, and I would fain part with this inheritance and heirſhip, and have an *inheritance with the ſaints in light:* We ſhall never know this, till we come to divinity without ſophiſtry, and without tricks and quirks, and come to Chriſt's reaſoning. He that doth the devil's work is the devil's child; then they will confeſs this is of the devil, and the other is of the devil. This is an evil work; and I ſee that I have need to be brought into another condition.

When people come to an acknowledgment of the truth, and of their own condemnation, then they are one ſtep towards redemption and ſalvation. No one ever took a ſtep towards their ſalvation, till they acknowledged their own condemnation. *He that ſanctifies, and they that are ſanctified, are all of one; and they that are joined to the Lord, are one Spirit. An evil tree,* faith Chriſt, *cannot bring forth good fruit*. When Chriſt ſpake this, he ſpake it to men and women, and he ſpake it of men and women, and not of trees: And when he ſaid, *no man can gather grapes of thorns, nor figs of thiſtles*, he ſpeaks of a generation of men: As if he had ſaid, this thorn muſt be tranſlated and changed into another nature before it can

bring

bring forth grapes; and this thistle must be changed into another nature before it can bring forth figs.

There must be a change in the nature of man before there can be a change of the fruit and effect of his doings; *whatsoever he sows, that he shall also reap; whatsoever a man doth in the body, he must give an account thereof at the day of judgment; for the books will be opened, and men judged according to the things written in those books.* If there be a book for thee and me, I will warrant thee there is a great deal in it; there is a recorder and a clerk for the book, which God hath opened in every man's conscience; and there is set down every man's transgressions and his sins: Saith one, *thou hast written my transgressions as with the point of a diamond;* thou hast engraven it so deep, that it seems impossible that it should ever be blotted out again: Some have had their sins so deeply engraven in their conscience, that they have thought they would never be blotted out, they were written as with the pen of a diamond.

When people see and consider that they have ventured their souls upon such slight grounds, I hope they will be awakened to seek after righteousness; when they see there is nothing good in them: Where there is any thing good, it is God that hath given it to them. Some will say, if I be perverse, corrupt and wicked, I cannot help it, therefore I must be beholden to my Maker to help me, else I must never be helped. Now, because God knows that we are helpless, *he hath laid help upon one that is mighty*, that is, our Lord Jesus Christ; and Christ *hath sent forth his Spirit into the world to convince the world of sin, and to lead his people into all truth:* And this grace that comes by Jesus Christ hath been so universally shewed, and so universally extended to all men, that I never met with a man yet that had none of it: But let them be as bad and as dark as they could, yet the light of Christ shined in that darkness, into the darkest heart, that ever I met with in all my life: He sheweth men, that *his light shineth in darkness, and the darkness cannot comprehend it.*

Therefore the work that God hath set us about, and the service which he requires at the hands of many of us, *set free by* JESUS CHRIST.

us, is to turn men from their own darkness unto the light of Christ their Saviour, and from the devil's power, that hath enslaved them, to the power of God that can redeem them; and yet we are far enough from that which they call *free will*; it is God's will *that every one should be saved*: But some will not be saved, they will keep their own wills and not resign them up to God; they have a free will to go to destruction. As for salvation, if they will obtain it, they must part with their own wills, and they must take a yoke and burthen upon them, before they can be saved: If people can have their wills, they will not take Christ's yoke upon them: He that will be Christ's disciple must deny his own will and take up his daily cross; these are the terms of the gospel.

But you will say, no man, by all the power he hath, can redeem himself, and no man can live without sin.

We will say amen to it: But if men tell us, that when Gods power comes to help us, and to redeem us out of sin, that it cannot be effected, then this doctrine we cannot away with, nor I hope you neither. Would you approve of it if I should tell you, that God puts forth his power to do such a thing, but the devil hinders him? That it is impossible for God to do it, because the devil doth not like it? That it is impossible that any one should be free from sin, because the devil hath got such a power in them, that God cannot cast him out?

This is lamentable doctrine: Hath not this been preached, this doctrine of impossibility of living without sin? It doth in plain terms say, though God doth interpose his power it is impossible, because the devil hath so rooted sin in the nature of man. Is not man God's creature, and cannot he new-make him, and cast sin out of him? If you say sin is rooted deeply in man, I say so too; yet not so deeply rooted but Christ Jesus is entered so deeply into the root of the nature of man, that he hath received power to destroy the devil and his works, and to recover and redeem man into his primitive nature of righteousness and holiness; or else it is false, that *he is able to save, to the uttermost, all that come unto God by him*. We must throw away the bible, if we say that it is impossible for God to deliver man out of sin. Is not Christ entered into the root of our nature? And hath he not taken upon him the seed of *Abraham*, after the flesh? Hath he not entered into the root of all men's natures, and *tasted death for every man, that he might quicken every one that is dead in sins and trespasses?* All these things speak the love of God to mankind, in order to their salvation.

Much might be said to these things, these clouds of error and darkness that have overspread the nation; yet, this I say, if one were to speak of it ever so long, it must be by the eye that God gives you, that you must see it; it is he that opens the hearts of men as he did *Lydia*'s: If there had not been the power of God that reached her heart, *Paul* could not have opened it.

When all is said that can be said, the counsel of God which hath sounded in your ears, is recommended to you, that every one may retire in quietness and stilness of mind to wait for the feeling of that quickening power of the Spirit of Christ that is sent into the hearts of men; that it may open your eyes to see your present state; then you will see a better state, a further state, and when you see with your inward eye that your state is not so good as you would have it to be, then trust and rely upon the all-sufficient and powerful operation of God's Holy Spirit to mend your state, and give you power over your corruptions, and to go on from one step to another, towards the cleansing and sanctification of your souls, so that you may receive something from God to enable you to live to God; for all that you receive from men will only make you live to men, but that which you receive from God, will help you to live to God; that will purify you and sanctify you, *and make you clean through the word*: So through the word you will come to cleanness, purity and holiness: And when you are come to the way of holiness, you may believe you have got into the way of God's kingdom, and never till then.

It is not enough to make a profession, but we must live up to the profession of that religion that we make; it is not holding this tenet and the other tenet, and saying, this minister, I am sure, preacheth the truth; thou mayest be

a

a child of the devil for all that. I now speak indifferently to all people, without respect to any sort: They that believe they are walking towards the kingdom of God, and yet their way is not a holy way, they have cheated themselves, and deceived their own souls, and they had need look about them and take heed what they do; the glass is running, and time is hasting away, and our life may end we know not how soon. It is good to prize and improve time, while you have it, and bring your deeds to the light; see what reproofs, instructions, counsels and openings you have met with from the Lord, and see how you have answered and been obedient to them, and so you will come to take a sound and infallible account of your condition; and if it be not so good as it should be, wait upon the Lord to mend it; he that made you can mend you, he that made your ears, must unstop your ears to hear the word of God.

To that power that carries on the works of sanctification and redemption by his word, to that word I must leave you, and to his spirit I commit you. This word will be with you, and if you part not with it, it will not part with you; it will go with you to your houses, and to your shops, and to your beds; it will lie down with you at night, and rise with you in the morning: To that end, Christ is a leader and governor, and the captain of our salvation, to lead the van, and carry you on in the way of salvation; and *as many as follow Christ, and are led by the spirit of God, they are the children of God.*

SERMON XXV.

The SHEEP of CHRIST *hear his* VOICE.

Preached at DEVONSHIRE-HOUSE, *May 10, 1688.*

My sheep (faith the true shepherd) *hear my voice.*

THE sheep of the true fold hear the voice of Christ, the good shepherd, and know the voice of strangers too: But, faith he, *the stranger they will not follow.* This scripture hath been a mark of distinction in all ages, that
hath

hath been peculiarly beftowed upon the people of God, that they have had a difcerning knowledge to make a certain diftinction between them that were of God, and thofe that were of the world : *Now they that are of God hear us*, faith the apoftle.

Now, that you may all find in yourfelves this peculiar gift of God, to be able to underftand and *difcern between the precious and the vile*, that you might know the miniftration of life from the miniftration of death, you muft all be gathered inwardly into that which you have received of God; for they that are only exercifed with gifts and parts, and acquirements that appertain to this world, they have been always fubject to delufions, apt to be led away into a bypath and crooked way, *that leads to deftruction*: But they that are under the government and direction of the gift of God, they have been able thereby to make fuch a diftinction of voices, and of founds, that they have been preferved from the delufions of the age.

This was the difference of old between the prophets of God and the falfe prophets, between the apoftles of our Lord Jefus Chrift, and the falfe apoftles; the difference was not fo much in their words, for they had in a great meafure the fame words; if the true prophets ufed to fay, *thus faith the Lord*, the falfe prophets would fay fo too; if the true prophets declared againft fin, the falfe prophets likewife would do fo; for the falfe prophet ftole his word from his neighbour: But the greater matter by which the people of the Lord were preferved, was, that hidden and divine wifdom they received of God, by which they difcerned the voice of the fpirit from the voice of ftrangers, from the voice of them that were of the flefh; and that was the caufe that the Chriftians in the primitive days did not adhere to, and follow thofe falfe apoftles that came to them in their own names, and held *a form of godlinefs, but denied the power of it*.

But they among them in whom their witch-crafts did enter, they went away from the fpirit, and fought to be *made perfect in the flefh*; they went to the outward obfervation, and to the *beggarly rudiments of things that perifh with the ufing*, and from *the law of the fpirit of life in Chrift Jefus*.   And

And as it hath been in thofe ages of which we have read, fo it comes to pafs in this our age, in which a difpenfation of the fpirit of truth is manifefted and revealed unto the children of men; there is a remnant that have received the teftimony of eternal life, and have believed the teftimony, and waited on him of whom the teftimony is born, not to have life by the teftimony, but *to have life in him*; fo they receive their life by the miniftration of the Spirit of Chrift, and they live to God, and others who have received no life from him, but have a life in the words, and founds, and noifes and terms, and diftinguifhing phrafes of things, their life lies there, they live not to God but to themfelves, their glorying is not *in the crofs of Chrift*, but in the words and outfide of things; fo that every one had need, at fuch a time as this, to approve their hearts unto the Lord; who knows the infide of people's profeffion, the infide of their religion, that knows how the heart is concerned towards God, and what they fay and do upon the account of his fervice, fo that all that are met together might come to receive more and more of the life and virtue that fanctifies the foul of him that receiveth it.

For, alas! my friends, it is not the gathering together of the moft excellent words about religion, and about worfhip and fervice, which will approve any man in the fight of God; that is but the painting of a fepulchre, and covering the rottenefs that is in many; but the Lord fees into the infide of every profeffor, and whofoever *names the name of Chrift and departeth not from iniquity*, they do but take his name in vain, and contract a guilt upon their own fouls; fo that every one that feemeth to be religious, ought to enquire whence their profeffion fprings; if it fprings from a real pofeffion of a meafure of that which fanctifies the life, and fhews itfelf forth, in its working and operation, many times abundantly more, than it doth in word and profeffion; it manifefteth itfelf in holinefs and righteoufnefs, to the honour of God; it is the aim and defign of all fuch to exalt the name of him whom they profefs, by holinefs and righteoufnefs fhining forth in their works, for it will never fhine through words alone; many good words may be fpoken, yet God not glorified, but his name

name may be dishonoured by them; but whosoever comes to feel that which is life in themselves, they know what will honour God, they feel the birth immortal that is of God, of his own begetting by the word of truth.

This living birth is that which brings forth living praises; the other is but flesh, *that which is born of the flesh is flesh*, and it glorifies the flesh, and when the flesh is most of all glorified, most of all exalted, it is then but *as the flower of the field*, it is then *cut down and withereth*; the *sun of righteousness* shines with the beams of the everlasting glory of God, and causeth it to wither and come to naught,

So friends, let your minds be gathered inward, that you may be able in your own selves, by virtue of the divine gift of God, to distinguish between the voice of the true shepherd, and the voice of a stranger, so that your minds may not follow a strange voice, that you may follow the Lord with your whole heart, *with a full purpose of heart;* for there is a real word of prophesy discovered in the inward parts, which doth *distinguish between the precious and the vile* in every one's particular; and that which is precious in one, it answereth to that which is precious in another; and that which is vile in one, it answereth to that which is vile in another.

For there is an inward and secret *mystery of iniquity*, as well as a mystery of godliness. The *mystery of godliness* is when *God is manifested in the flesh*; the mystery of iniquity is, when the wicked one is making himself manifest, and appears and discovers himself in the flesh, that he may rise up and glory in the flesh.

Now the eternal truth, which never changeth, this is that which giveth a discerning, this hath always put a difference between the true and false prophets, the true and false apostles, and between the true and false ministers; the difference hath not been so much *in words as in power*, as the apostle speaks concerning some in his days, that had endeavoured to deceive, and to draw men aside from the simplicity of the gospel; *when I come*, saith he, *I will know.* Now, he does not assert, that he will pay particular attention to their words, whether they were judicious or no;

for

for he fays, I will not know their words, but their power. How fhould he know their power if he were not in the power himfelf? Now this divine power, as every one acquaints himfelf with it, it worketh unto the fanctification of them, when they have fellowfhip with the ftirrings and movings of all others that are partakers of it: This is that which will eftablifh and confirm your minds in the true faith and fimplicity of the truth, that you turn not afide to the right hand or to the left. If you have regard to the principle of divine truth that you have received from God, then you can receive confirmation from any one that hath a meafure according to it. There is a *meafuring line*, and the *reed of the fanctuary*, that *meafureth the temple and all that dwell therein*, that meafures them with one reed and one meafure, and every one anfwereth to that meafure, according to the ftature and degree of growth of the grace of God they arrive to; and now they are come to a fixed foundation.

Others there are in the world, that have laid their foundation upon this creaturely help, and the other creaturely help, upon this man, and the other man; but now true Chriftians come to have their foundation, their rooting and building upon Chrift Jefus, upon that word of life that firft of all gathered their minds into a defire after holinefs, into a defire after acquaintance with God that made them.

You that are true Chriftians can remember, how you were begotten, and that which did beget you; that word of God that is incorruptible, that is immortal, that was not of a dying quality, that need not be fupported by this, and that, and the other means, but it hath its fupport in itfelf, it hath its nourifhment in itfelf, and it grows up in itfelf, and every one that receiveth it they grow up in it, until they come more and more to partake of the life and qualities of it; *that as he is, fo they may be in the prefent world.*

But this is never known, but where the word of God hath its free paffage: Many have *tafted of this word of God*, and by tafting of it, have been acquainted with the *power of the world to come*; they knew well enough the power that would bring forth another world, a *new Heaven*,

ven, and a new earth, and righteousness in it; many have felt the power that have never continued to see the working of it, never continued to see and witness what this power would work; going aside from the power of the world that was to come, they have never seen the coming of it, but *their foolish hearts have been darkened again, and their imaginations have grown vain*, and they have conceived to themselves a false liberty to the flesh, and their wills have been strong, and have prevailed over them; that though they had tasted of the powers that did belong to the world to come, they never saw the working and operation of that power to bring to pass that which by sight and vision they did behold.

Therefore it is needful for every one of you, in every state and condition the Lord hath brought you into, to keep yourselves in a deep humility; to know the afflictions, temptations and trials you are under, and to exercise your minds, not only on account of what you have got over, but let every one know the state and condition in which at present they are labouring; for when some come to look at what sufferings and difficulties they have got over, they are apt to be exalted above measure, and lifted up in their minds; let every one consider what is their present state and work; their help lies in that condition. Some have always a foundation of their faith present with them, that they may feel the object of their faith where they hope for help, where they hope for comfort and strength to be present with them.

Now every one that believeth in the word of God, their care is, that they may know this word of God, that they may hear it, feel it, and behold the beauty of it under the exercises of it; how it conducts and leads, how it counselleth and adviseth, that so, in all things they are to pass through, they may not be as those that have run into it; as those that do this and that of their own wills, but may be properly followers of something.

I go into this, or that, or the other thing, not to do mine own will; I do not run into it, but I am led into it; my leader goes before me, the word of God, that hath conducted me and led me: I am a follower of God

in

in all his difpenfations, and in all his leadings and guidings; I am to follow him, for he teacheth me his way, he inftructeth me in the true way: The beft of all his fcholars and difciples, they are to be led and guided into that work and fervice they are to do, that they may run into no irregularily or abfurdity, for he will lead you into holinefs, righteoufnefs and humility, where all become the fervants of God in Chrift Jefus, and fervants to one another: There is a mutual concord and harmony in the work of this fpirit, in the fervice of this power, where every one finds what they are appointed and directed to, and all the members of the body of Chrift know they ought not to be disjointed and rent, and feparated one from another, but *tied together in joints and bands, to edify one another in the love of God;* fo that here is one fpirit that hath been the guide of this one people in all ages.

Many people have been guided by many guides, and they have been fcattered, divided and feparated one from another, and have been under this, that and the other name; but all God's people have been guided by the Spirit of Chrift, that univerfal Spirit that is one with God. In the Old Teftament times, and the New Teftament times, they were all led by the univerfal Spirit of Chrift, and they were *of one heart, and of one mind, ferving the Lord;* there was a concord and unity among them; and if at any time any difcord or divifion happened, it was becaufe the *roaring lion that goes about continually feeking whom he may devour,* had found fome or other that he might devour, and draw into his fnares and gins; for there are fome that he may, and fome that he may not. Who are they that this roaring lion may deftroy? The devil knows who thofe are that he may prevail upon; he knows that thofe which are in the hands of God are out of his reach: *My Father,* faith Chrift, *is greater than all, and none fhall pluck them out of my Father's hands;* yet doubtlefs thofe that are in the Father's hands are tempted and tried, the roaring lion goes about feeking to devour them if he might; a man that he devours, he fwallows up with prejudice, enmity, covetoufnefs and pride, and he will lead him into any evil thing; he hath many gulphs to fwallow men up in, in, but if he meet with one that is kept in God's hands, he knows such a one is out of his reach, and he is not able to catch him.

If he meet with a man that he can prevail over, as he did over our father *Adam* and mother *Eve*, such as are in their own hands, that stand upon their wit and parts, and knowledge and eloquence; those that stand upon these things as their foundation, they are in their own keeping; these are they whom he may devour and catch, and ensnare in one or other of his gins, and swallow them up in one of his gulphs and temptations: But seeing God hath opened and manifested these things by his Spirit, and seeing the secret wiles of *satan* are discovered and made known by the shining of his light, how ought every one that is a believer of the truth, to depend upon God for his protection, and be careful that he goes not out of his Father's hands, that he never trust himself to his own keeping for his security and preservation, lest he meet with a temptation that may swallow him and devour him.

I remember our Lord Jesus Christ when he was upon earth, he put his disciples in mind of what happened long before, *remember Lot's wife*: You may take notice of her, the power of God took hold of her and brought her out of *Sodom*, and was leading her to a place of safety, but she had something of *Adam*'s apostacy in her nature, she looked back, and was turned into a pillar of salt. Our Saviour was pleased to make use of this passage that happened some hundreds of years before, to shew how she failed of coming to the place of safety, though she was led out of *Sodom* by the hands of one of the angels of God. O! remember her, she was turned into a pillar of salt, and this remains instructive to this day.

If we remember where our safety is, and from whose hands we must expect it, we need not go to look at *Lot's* wife. We have seen many in our days that have stood fair for redemption, they have had a power revealed to them, that is able to redeem them, and save them to the uttermost; but afterward by exalting themselves above this power, and taking the government of themselves into their own hands, they have robbed God of his glory, and he

hath

hath withdrawn himfelf from them, and then it was with them as with *Saul*, when the Lord departed from him, *the evil fpirit entred into him.*

We have before our eyes from day to day, thofe that have known the beginning of the redemption of God's power, and have been in a great meafure brought out of *Sodom*, and out of the way of *Egypt*, and they have had opened to them *the myftery of the kingdom of God* for their encouragement, but at laft they have taken and arrogated thofe gifts to themfelves, and looking upon themfelves as far excelling others, magnifying their parts as if they were their own, when they were the gifts of God. Then the Lord hath left them, to let them fee whether they could ftand of themfelves, and they have fallen, and been taken in the gins and fnares of the devil, who, *like a roaring lion, is going about continually, feeking whom he may devour.*

Now, my friends, it greatly concerns us all to know what refuge we have to fly to, in a time of trial; we have a time of trial now, tho' not a time of external fuffering and perfecution, and enduring hardfhip yet upon us, to try our faith and truft in God; yet we have no reafon to be fecure, carlefs nor remifs in our prefent duty, *nor to put the evil day far from us*, but to be in the exercife of humility and watchfulnefs as becomes Chriftians; for there is now as much danger and peril in this time of liberty and tranquillity, as there was before.

If any one in the time of perfecution and fuffering hath faid within himfelf, I had better give over and part with the truth, and forfake the ways of the Lord, and give over my teftimony for his name, for I fhall be undone and ruined in the world; this man by his carnal fears hath loft his teftimony.

So likewife if a man in this time of liberty and freedom of ferving the Lord, and bearing teftimony to his name, if he fhall not entirely truft in the Lord, to carry him on in his work and fervice, and continue his dependence upon him, and wait for the affiftance of the Holy Spirit of God to work in him *to will and to do of his good pleafure*, this man fhall lofe his teftimony, as well as the other: Therefore, let every one of you keep up a dependence upon God's

Holy

Holy Spirit for carrying on the work which he hath begun in your fouls; confider what work it is that Chrift is now at in every one of you; I know what his work was when I was firft convinced, he was burning up and hewing down every thing that hindered his carrying on the work of fanctification and redemption, and firmnefs and ftability in the covenant of life and peace.

And now our meeting together ought to be in the name of Chrift; I hope it is fo with moft of you: I hope it is not to fee and hear what this or 'that man faith, but to know within yourfelves what part of the work of redemption the Lord Jefus Chrift is carrying on, that you may join with him, and *be a willing people in the day of his power*, and fay as *Paul, Lord, what will thou have me do?* If thou wilt have me part with my all, Lord here it is, I offer it up; and if thou wilt have any fervice done, Lord here I am, *fpeak, for thy fervant heareth*; let there be in every one of you an attentivenefs, and an humble waiting upon the Lord, and fay as the Pfalmift, *behold, as the eyes of fervants look unto the hands of their mafters, and as the eyes of a maiden unto the hands of her miftrefs, fo our eyes wait upon the Lord our God until he have mercy upon us.*

Whenever a Chriftian hath his dependence upon God's wifdom and power, fuch a one fhall never want wifdom, the Lord will give him wifdom to preferve him againft all the wiles of fatan; and he fhall never want power, for the Lord will enable him to fulfil and perform what he requireth of him; he fhall be replenifhed with judgment and underftanding, ability and power, to direct him into the good ways of God, and to enable him to walk in them.

It is the earneft defire of my foul, that every one of you may be exercifed in thofe things which are profitable for you, and which may be comfortable to your friends and brethren; that you may all grow up into a ftability and ftedfaftnefs in the good ways of the Lord, that you may not be fhaken and toffed with every ftorm and tempeft; that when there comes a time for the trial of your patience, and fortitude and courage, you may not be toffed to and fro like children, but *be ftedfaft and unmoveable, always abounding in the work of the Lord*, that fo living in all holy obedience

obedience *and patience, and continuing in well-doing,* you may have a constant supply of strength and power from God ministered unto you by his Holy Spirit.

SERMON XXVI.

No TRUE WORSHIP *without the* RIGHT KNOWLEDGE *of* GOD.

Preached at GRACE-CHURCH-STREET, *May 24, 1688.*

My Friends,

THERE is no man can truly worship God, till he comes to a measure of certain knowledge of him; for all the worship in the world where the veil of ignorance still prevails upon the mind, is all abominable; there is no acceptance with God: There must be a knowledge of God before there can be a true worshipping of him; for they that worship before they know God, *they worship they no not what;* they worship a God they have heard of, but do not know; so every one that would be a true worshipper, must first come to that which giveth a true knowledge, that raiseth up a certainty in the mind, *this is the Lord, we will trust in him; this is our God, and we will serve him.*

And that all people might come to this certainty of knowledge, therefore it is that *God hath sent forth his Spirit,* that the things of God might be communicated by the Spirit of God, for without the assistance of this Spirit, men seek after the knowledge of God in vain; if they seek after the knowledge of God, they cannot find it, and if they seek after the worship of God, and after acceptance with God, they cannot find it; so that all religion, and religious performances, that people are exercised in, where the spirit of truth hath not the beginning, they will all prove fruitless in the end.

There are wise men in the world, who have employed their

their wifdom to find out the true God; but God in wifdom hath ordained, that the world by all their wifdom fhall not know him; fo there is an end of all their labour: How fhall they know him then? As *none can know the things of a man, fave the fpirit of man that is in him, fo none can know the things of God, but the Spirit of God;* fo that they that refift the guidance, direction and counfel of the Spirit of God, are like unto thofe that would enter into a houfe or palace, and remember not the door that leads into it.

People would fain come into the divine knowledge and into the underftanding of divine myfteries, but they would come by it another way; they would ftudy for it, they would learn it by arts and fciences, they would attain it by their own induftry; and herein they labour to excel one another. If there comes a man among them that tells them, friends you are all out of the way, then they are angry, and inftead of enquiring what is the way, they are angry that their way muft be rejected. Friends, you will never come to the knowledge of God but by the Spirit of God; then they mock, and then they fcoff and fcorn the doctrine of the Spirit, for the teaching of the Spirit hath been the common fcorn and derifion of our age.

It is fo in our day with many; if they cannot come to the knowledge of God any other way but by the Spirit, they would deny to make ufe of that, to be fubject to that, and thefe put their truft in their own power and induftry, to find out the myftery of the knowledge of God; *fo they are ever learning, but are never able to come to the knowledge of the truth:* How fhould they? How can a people come to a knowledge of the truth, without the *fpirit of truth that reveals it?* Can any come to the knowledge of Chrift unlefs *he that fent him reveals him?* Where are people's books? where are their bibles? where is their rule (they call it fo) that all their endeavours for many ages have proved fruitlefs in refpect to the knowledge of God?

This is but your fay fo, fome may fay; how doth it appear that we have not attained to the true knowledge of God? and to the true worfhip, and to the true religion?

I will tell you how it appears; for all, in all ages, that have

have attained to the knowledge of God, they have been *made partakers of his divine nature* and his divine qualities; they have brought forth a sort of fruit in their lives and converfations, that hath been of the fame nature, it hath been holy and divine. They have known the fanctifier, and they have been a fanctified people, fo they have become one with him, and have fhewn forth the beauty of holinefs in their lives, that is a demonftration that may fhew the knowledge of God, for without it they live another life, an unholy one, a corrupt one, a life of felf-love, a life of pride, vanity and enmity, and that they never had from God, but from another root; a life of iniquity and fin, it came from another feed; fo that they are ftill without the knowledge of God.

And again, all that have come to the knowledge of God, they have trufted in him; that people cannot do now-a-days, except here and there a few that do know him; the generality of the age they cannot truft God; they muft have fomething elfe to rely upon, and truft to, for in him they cannot truft. Now the Lord faid by the prophet of old, *they that know my name will truft in me*; that is enough if people know God, *whom to know is eternal life, even to know thee the only true God, and Jefus Chrift whom thou haft fent*: This is life eternal; if people were come to this divine knowledge, they would never take care or ftudy for any refuge, or fet up this, or that, or the other thing to lean upon. A rich man he trufteth in his riches, one trufteth to one thing and another to another, but they would truft in the living God, and he fhould be their God and their rock, and they would venture their concerns upon him, both in this world and that which is to come, if they did but know him. People may talk as much as they will, but he can never, properly, be faid to be my God, and thy God, till we caft our care upon him, and can venture our concerns upon him, both in this world and that which is to come; and can fay, he is our God, and our reliance and dependence is upon him.

Now this is the effect and confequence of this knowledge of God; fuch as come to partake of it, they fhall have no need to be bid to worfhip him. You fhall have no need to make a law, that this people shall worship the God that they know; there needs no law to command the people of God to worship him; his *law is written in their hearts*; and they that know him, will worship him. There was never any man on earth, that had the knowledge of the true and living God, that needed be put upon worshipping him, that needed a law to oblige him to it; for the very knowledge that is given of God through Christ, this brings forth naturally an adoration of the invisible power which men put their trust in; it produceth an adoration that is true worship; it causeth an humble reverence of that power; it brings the soul upon its knees, as it were; it brings the soul to stoop and bend, and bow upon all occasions to God, as his God: It raiseth his expectations to receive counsel, and judgment, and understanding, from him, as the fountain of wisdom; and hereby people are taught to worship in the right divine knowledge.

But to tell men of the worship of God before they know him; though you make as many laws as you will to force them to worship that God they do not know, yet you can never do them any good, nor make their worship acceptable, nor make them devout; you can never bring devotion, nor divine adoration into their hearts, by all the laws that you can make.

But there is a spirit of life that sets the soul at liberty from its former bondage to sin and satan; and when this law comes to be revealed in my heart, what saith this law? Worship God, give honour and glory to him. This law saith, submit thyself to him that redeemed thee, thou art his, thou art no more thine own; this law being written in the heart obligeth a man to a true worship, and to *worship God in spirit and truth*, for this man hath done imagining among the Heathen, that there *are Gods many, and Lords many*: He hath done imagining what God is, and where he is, for he is now come to know him; he is instructed beyond the best scholar in *Athens*, let him be ever so mean and despicable in the world; if it be ever so poor a lad or lass, they are beyond the best scholar in *Athens*; for the best scholar there came only so far as to contradict their fellow scholars: Some of them were for *Mars*,

and

the RIGHT KNOWLEDGE *of* GOD.

and some for *Jupiter,* some for one God and some for another : These scholars, by some beam of divine light shining in them, had come to perceive that the influences that were in *Mars, Jupiter* and *Venus,* and the *Sun* and *Moon,* and other planets, they received them from an higher power, that is, God. They denied not that these plaets had power and influences given to them; sometimes they are called heavenly bodies; the sky, or canopy of Heaven ; and sun, moon and stars are called heavenly bodies, they have power and influences; but this was given them, and that power must be greater than theirs from whom they receive their power, virtue and influence, even that God who is the maker of all things. The scholars at *Athens* understood so much, as to see there was a God greater than the planets which the nations worshipped; they thought that God was to have an altar as well as *Jupiter* and *Mars,* and those other Gods, and therefore they built an altar *to the unknown God,* whom they ignorantly worshipped.

If thou and I are come to the knowledge of the true God, then we must know more than these scholars of *Athens,* who erected an altar *to the unknown God :* When the apostle came to preach divinity among these scholars of *Athens,* who were masters of arts and sciences, he preached to them, saying, that *unknown God, whom ye ignorantly worship, him declare I unto you ;* we do not need to declare to you the Gods of the nations, for you worship them, but to declare to you the unknown God whom ye ignorantly worship; these were the great scholars of *Athens* that the apostle spake to : What dost thou declare of God? *He is the God that made the world and all things therein, seeing that he is Lord of Heaven and Earth, and dwelleth not in temples made with hands, neither is worshipped with mens hands, as though he needed any thing, seeing he giveth to all life and breath, and all things, and hath made of one blood all nations of men to dwell upon the face of the earth, and hath determined the times before appointed, and the bounds of their habitations, that they should seek the Lord, if haply they might feel after him, and find him, though he be not far from every one of us ; for in him we live, move and*

Q q. *have*

*have our being; for as certain alſo of your own poets have
ſaid, for we are alſo his offspring; for as much then as we
are the offspring of God, we ought not to think that the
Godhead is like unto gold, or ſilver, or ſtone graven by art
and man's device.*

Here is a way of learning, you need not turn over books any more; if I would know the true God, I muſt know who gave me life and motion, and who created me, he is not far from me; and how ſhould I find the knowledge of him? *feel after him, if haply you may find him; for he is not far from any of us; in him we live, and move, and have our being;* we cannot live without him one moment; he giveth life, eſſence and power, to all creatures in Heaven and Earth; we muſt have him with us, or we cannot live; I die as ſoon as my life departs from me, ſo do you; if my breath and life continue with me, it is by the power of him that giveth it, in whom I live, and move, and have my being; ſtill it is in him that firſt gave it.

Here all the great ſcholars and philoſophers were counſelled to feel after him; ſo are all people now-a-days: This is our buſineſs, when we go to preach the knowledge of God to them that want it; our commiſſion runs not, that we muſt read ſuch a book, ſuch an author, and turn over ſuch a leaf, and there you ſhall have a diſcovery, and a fair demonſtration of the attributes of God, of his wiſdom, power, goodneſs, mercy, omnipotence and omniſcience; our commiſſion runs not that way, but our commiſſion runs thus; that we *turn people from darkneſs to light; and from the power of ſatan to God;* to turn their minds from that which may hinder the knowledge of Chriſt, from darkneſs, blindneſs and ignorance; God is not far from them; perhaps they might find him, if they did ſeek after him.

There are a ſort of men now-a-days (ſuch as were in former times) that *ſay unto God, depart from us, we deſire not the knowledge of thy ways;* ſuch a ſort of people are dark, and blind and ignorant, and are like to continue ſo, that ſay to God, depart from us; God is come to them, but they bid him depart from them: We are

ſent

sent to these people that are dark and ignorant, and have not the true knowledge of God, though they have abundance of notions, hear-say knowledge, learning and speculation; our business is to convince them of their ignorance, *and to turn them from darkness to light.*

There are a people that have mocked and scoffed at us many years; what, say they, is there a light within? Must we go to the light within? Hath every body a light within?

Yes, I believe so; and you must believe so too, if you will believe the scriptures. *Christ is the true light,* and he hath *enlightened every man that cometh into the world.* If he did light them, how did he do it? I will tell you, say they; he spake a great many gracious words, and somebody hath writ them down. What, will this prove the light within? Because we have got a New Testament, and Christ hath spoken a great many gracious words, and they are written down and recorded, doth this prove the light within? No, people might have been in darkness still, for all the books of the New Testament, and the Old Testament too, and for all the books in the world; for they would never have conveyed light into the hearts and consciences of men, if God had not placed it there.

Indeed these books may be instrumental, and God doth make use of them as a means for the conveying of light and grace, and working of true conversion; but the holy scriptures cannot do it of themselves, unless there be a co-acting and co-operation of the Spirit of Christ with them; without this spirit they cannot convey saving light to us; how prove you then a light within? The apostle tells you, if you will believe him, 2 Cor. iv, 6; *God, who commandeth the light to shine out of darkness, hath shined into our hearts, to give the light of the knowledge of the glory of God, in the face of Jesus Christ;* so that every one that retireth into himself, will know quickly, and understand his error, and confess that there is a light within, and that by this rule, because there is something in the heart, that makes manifest that which is reprovable; if they do or say a thing reprovable, that which manifesteth a thing is light; that which manifesteth dark words or works, is light. Now

Now when they have found this *light within*, the next queſtion in controverſy is, whether this will give men ſufficient light for the true knowledge of God; whether this be ſufficient to bring a man to life and ſalvation?

I am of that judgment, that it is ſufficient; and I believe it heartily, and preach it boldly in the name of the Lord, that the light that ſhines in your hearts, ſhines there to give you the true knowledge of God, in the face of the Mediator, the Lord Jeſus Chriſt. You cannot believe this, you will ſay, for you have had this ever ſince you was a child, and you know not the leaſt good it hath done you; all our learned men and miniſters, go to what ſort you will, they ſpeak very ſlightly of it; this light within is nothing but natural conſcience, a poor light, it is but an *ignis fatuus*, that will miſlead us. But let me tell thee, the reaſon why it doth thee no more good, is, becauſe thou haſt been looſe and wanton, and vain, and wouldeſt not receive the reproofs of it; reckon up the time, and call to mind, when thou didſt receive the reproofs of it, then it did thee ſome good, and brought thee to remorſe, and brought anguiſh and ſorrow, and trouble into thy mind, and brought thee to a right ſenſe of what evil thou hadſt done; but if thou didſt not regard it, no wonder it did thee no good; its reproofs and counſels were like the ſeed ſown by the high way, *the fowls of the air gathered it up*, and it did not grow; that is, the devil plucked it up, and then the ſoul lay as ſeed that brought forth no fruit to God, and the devil might have what advantage he would.

I will tell you the reaſon why ſo many learned men, men of great abilities, ſpeak ſo ſlightly and meanly of it, becauſe it hath done them no good, inward nor outward, that they know of: How ſhould it do you good when it hath done them none? The reaſon why it doth them no good, is becauſe they do not believe in it; and did Chriſt ever do any body good that did not believe in him? *He gave* men *power* indeed *to become the ſons of God*, the greateſt good that they are capable of; but it was *to thoſe that believed on his name*: Were all they the ſons of God that heard Chriſt preach? No, ſome were the

the RIGHT KNOWLEDGE *of* GOD.

the devil's fons; our Saviour tells them, that they were of *their father the devil, and they did his works;* they came to meetings and heard Chrift preach; he difcourfed to them, but it did them no good, for they did not believe on his name.

And then it appears in the next place, that if this light be taken heed to, and if men come to be taught by it and receive inftructions, they would then have it all for nothing, they would have it all for God's fake; all the counfels and underftanding of divine myfteries, all the openings of God, and all their knowledge of God would be obtained without charge: What then would become of the trade of preaching Chrift, and the attributes of God; then their filver-fhrine-trade will be fpoiled, and then their *Diana* is gone; and this light hath done them no good inwardly becaufe of their unbelief; and it doth them no good outwardly, becaufe it fpoils their preaching trade, becaufe it teacheth men for nothing, but teacheth them, for God's fake, the *light of the knowledge of God, that fhines in the face of Jefus Chrift,* wherein are the openings of the myfteries of the kingdom of God.

So that if any come to know the virtue and the power that turneth men from darknefs to light, they are come to another ftate, and *turned from the power of fatan to the power of God;* aud when the power of God is revealed in them, then they fay, *this is my God;* now I know the true God; they fpeak as thofe that are acquainted with him; *this is life eternal to know thee the only true God, and Jefus Chrift whom thou haft fent:* It is not to know him at a diftance, but as always prefent: The foul comes to be acquainted with God, as familiarly as a man is acquainted with his friend, and better too: A man that is acquainted with his friend, only knows fome things pertaining to him; but thofe that are acquainted with their Maker they know *the whole counfel of God,* fo far as belongs to their peace; therefore it was not in vain faid of old, *acquaint thou thyfelf with him, and be at peace:* Be but acquainted with that inward power that knows thy thoughts, and then nobody need to preach a fermon to thee of the omniprefence of God; nobody need make thee

thee a doctrine of it, and offer reasons and motives for thee to believe it; it is all foolish labour; I know that God is with me, and near me; I feel him in me, and with me, at my down-lying and up-rising; when I am in my shop and about my business, he is with me in all places; and such a man is also well instructed about the omniscience of God; God's knowing every thing; I have learned that since I came to know him, all the doctors in *Europe* can tell me no more than I know in that point; *the Lord observeth all my goings, and numbereth all my steps; Lord, thou makest manifest the thoughts of my heart, thou searchest my heart, and tryest my reins.* Here is God's omniscience and knowing all things. Here is divinity growing out of the life.

Then the wisdom of God is infinite; so are all God's attributes infinite, incomprehensible and unspeakable, they are all so in him, but he makes manifest a measure of his wisdom; he brings a man from being such a fool as he was before, to become a wise man; he was such a sot and fool as to become drunk and tumble in the dirt; he could not stand upon his legs, but now he is become wise and sober: Another was so foolish as to defile himself and wallow in his uncleanness; now such a man comes to true wisdom, it begins in the fear of God, *the fear of the Lord is the beginning of wisdom:* What doth his wisdom do? It keeps him out of the dirt; it makes him live, first as a man then as a Christian, *to live righteously, soberly and godly, in this present world:* It leads him into the knowledge of the mysteries of the kingdom of God; *to know and comprehend with all saints, what is the heighth, and length, and breadth, and depth, and to know the love of Christ which passeth knowledge:* This is more than bare sobriety and moderate living; such are taught to live soberly, righteously and godly, to live by faith, and to be led into the *knowledge of the mystery of the kingdom of God;* to know the Lord Jesus Christ to their justification. This is the learned and the wise man; he hath got the substance as well as the shadow; he hath the marrow as well as the bone; he is reconciled to God, through Christ; he hath *remission of sins through Christ Jesus, that died for him and rose again.* When

the RIGHT KNOWLEDGE *of* GOD.

When you come to be partakers of this, it will do you good; notions will not do it; when you come to know God for yourselves, and understand him for yourselves, to know him as your Saviour and Redeemer, that hath rescued you from the snares of the wicked one; whoever doth this, they will worship God; when they have this knowledge of him, they will bow to him, they will be like those of old that said, *he is our judge, he is our law-giver, he is our king, and he will save us* : There arose a testimony in the hearts of good people of that age, that God was their judge that judged them, their law-giver that directed them, how they should make their way to him; that he was their king, and ought to rule them, for he must save them.

So when people come to know God for themselves, to be inwardly acquainted with God for themselves; when a company of these souls meet together, when they have been at this school, and learned this lesson of divinity, they then sit down and wait upon the Lord, that God *that searcheth the heart and trieth the reins*, and observeth how they do service for the honour of his name, and they receive spiritual gifts from him to their edification and comfort, and they receive judgment from him when they do any thing contrary to his mind.

The Lord Jesus Christ is the Minister of the Sanctuary which the Lord hath pitched : If men have a church, as they call it, they must have *John* or *Thomas* for their minister : We know who is the minister of such a place; but here is a minister set up in God's sanctuary, this *priest's lips shall preserve knowledge.* All that come to God's church are taught of this priest, he is a high one, *the high priest of our profession*, we have not such another; he is not set up by a carnal commandment; his induction came not from any priest in this world, but his induction came from the God of Heaven and Earth; his Father set him up for a priest; he comes by a Heavenly induction and commission, *he is a priest forever, after the order of Melchisedeck*, not after the order of *Aaron* : If you come to God's church, you may hear this minister.

Some have called a house of stone, or wood, a church, but

but that will not do now, therefore there are people that know better than they, who see churches gathered of living stones; men and women are gathered to these churches. Now the apostle saith, the church is in God, the Father of our Lord Jesus Christ: If you will come to church you must come to Jesus Christ, the church is in God, the Father of our Lord Jesus Christ, the general assembly, the congregation of his faithful people. What do you mean by a church? Ask a learned man, that understands Greek and Hebrew, what is the meaning of the word? A church, saith he, is the congregation of the faithful, it is an assembly of the faithful people congregated together. Where must they meet? *they must meet in the general assembly of the first-born, whose names are written in Heaven.* The *Hebrews* were come to that church, though they lived many hundred miles asunder, in *Asia*, *Cappadocia* and *Bythinia*: *You are come to the general assembly of the first-born;* there is a priest, there is *the high-priest of our profession, the Lord Jesus Christ, who is a priest after the order of Melchisedeck, not after the order of Aaron.* How long is this priest like to stay in his priesthood? Forever; *he is a priest forever, not after a carnal commandment, but according to the power of an endless life.*

The priests that were after *Aaron*'s order, they could not continue: Death snatched one away, then they must have another priest; but here is one that hath a priesthood higher than the Heavens, by the power of an endless life: Here is the priest of God's church, and the teacher of God's people; so that when God's people come to church, that is, to God the Father, there Christ teacheth them, according to the old prophesy, *I will teach my people myself.*

We have laboured to bring people to this teaching, that they might come to the knowledge of the living God. Now there needs none to teach them, *for they are taught of God;* blessed be God, *our labour hath not been in vain, we see the fruit of our labours, and are satisfied.* We have been labouring to bring men to know the Lord; now *all shall know the Lord, from the greatest to the least,* and bow before him, and worship him; they hear that *their*

high

the RIGHT KNOWLEDGE *of* GOD.

high priest's lips shall preserve knowledge. If they do amiss, he chastiseth them for it; if they do well, then he comforteth them by his Spirit: Now our labour is, that all may be brought to this, and that every one may know the Lord, and may fear him and serve him, and worship him in his temple: Our bodies are a temple for that use, to worship God in; *know you not that your bodies are temples of the Holy Ghost?* you must worship in yourselves, you must go into yourselves, you must know the exercise of the grace of God in yourselves, and the workings of the spirit of truth in yourselves, and that your souls in your bodies may be bowed to the power of the spirit, and that your worship must be in the spirit; you must pray in the spirit, and give thanks in the spirit.

Though those that set up worship in the church, talk of divinity and religion in every part of it, yet the substance of all the shadows of the law are fulfilled in the gospel; the substance of all the modes, and rites, and forms of religion, are fulfilled in the gospel-way: So then let every one compare and examine their state, and consider how the case stands between them and their Maker, what knowledge they have of God, and what trust they have put in him, that so they may be persuaded and prepared to come within the pale of this church. But you must first come out of the world, else you can never come into that church that is in God; if you be in the world, you must go to the world's church, and be the members of the world's church; and you shall have this for your pains, the world will love you; but if you come out of the world's church into God's church, the world cannot love you.

Be as good as thou wilt, thou canst never be so good as Christ Jesus, and they loved him not, because he was not of the world; *if you were of this world,* saith Christ, *the world would love its own; but since you are not of the world, I have taken you out of it, therefore the world hates you; if they do so to the green-tree, what will they do to the branches? are you better than I?* saith our Saviour; *the servant is not greater than his Lord:* Those that are the disciples of Christ must be content to *be persecuted, reviled, and hated for his name's sake;* for thus they treated him who *was holy, and harmless, and undefiled*, who gave them a good example, and who did them no hurt, but did them good; yet the world hated him, and it is but reafonable to expect that you fhould fuffer from the world in the fame manner, and bear it at their hands.

If you come to this church that is in God the Father, and *Jefus the Mediator, the church of the firft-born that are written in Heaven*, and come out of the world's church, then the world will be about your ears; all the world will fet themfelves againft this church, againft the woman that fhall bring forth a birth, that fhall rule over the nations: *There appeared a great wonder in Heaven, a woman cloathed with the fun, and the moon under her feet, and upon her head a crown of twelve ftars, and fhe being with child cried, travelling in birth, and pained to be delivered. And there alfo appeared another wonder in heaven* (a terrible thing) *and behold a great read dragon, having feven heads and ten horns; and the dragon ftood before the woman that was ready to be delivered, to devour her child as foon as it was born: And fhe brought forth a man child, that was to rule all nations with a rod of iron, and her child was caught up to God, and to his throne.* When the dragon was ready to devour this birth, God took it into his own care, in fpite of the devil and all his inftruments, and he will fave the child and preferve the woman; *he that fits in Heaven will laugh* at his enemies and defeat them. There is a place appointed for the woman in the wildernefs, where fhe is preferved by the Almighty Power; where fhe is nourifhed for a time, and times, and half a time, from the face of the ferpent; but fhe muft come out again after fome time, in fpite of the devil and all his inftruments, of all his dragons and ferpents: The woman muft come out of the wildernefs, and the man-child muft come down with great power, to rule the nation.

This hath been accomplifhed, fay fome, above fourteen hundred years ago; and if you will take their word, the church hath been come fo long out of the wildernefs. But the church that they fpeak of, hath it not wanted holinefs and righteoufnefs? Hath it given *glory to God on high*, with *peace on earth and good will to men*? No, their

their church hath lived in tyranny and barbarous cruelty, and shedding of blood. They say the church was in the wilderness in *Dioclesian's* time, and when *Constantine* came to the empire then she came out of the wilderness.

If it had been a holy church, we should have seen the man-child come down from God, and holiness and righteousness would have *run down like a mighty stream*, and truth would have filled the whole earth. All these things have not yet been fulfilled, for we have seen the professors of truth fallen in the streets; they have been persecuted and troubled, and thrown into prisons and dungeons; but there is a better church somewhere to be found.

I read of the holy church, the lamb's wife, the spouse of Christ that hath been hid somewhere, a great while, in some corner or other in the wilderness; but she will come forth again out of the *wilderness, leaning upon her well-beloved*: She doth not come leaning on this prince and the other potentate: She comes not out of the wilderness leaning on captains, generals and armies, but leaning on Christ her well-beloved, the immortal, invisible power of the Son of God; she trusteth in it.

All the other churches, I have read of, they have leaned upon one prince or potentate, or one emperor or another, and they have relied on these great men as on their bulwark; but this church that comes out of the wilderness, will come leaning only upon her well-beloved, the Lord Jesus Christ, who is the author and finisher of her faith; she will put her trust in him, for he will deliver his church from all her enemies: And though the serpent cast out of his mouth water as a flood, after the woman, that he might cause her to be carried away of the flood, yet the Lord will cause the earth to help the woman, and the earth shall open her mouth and swallow up the flood which the dragon cast out of his mouth. Let the dragon do what he can to destroy the woman and her seed, she knows what her beloved can do, he will command the earth to open and swallow up the flood, and she shall go dry through it.

How happy are they that lean upon Christ their well-beloved! The church of Christ in all ages hath leaned upon him, and he hath founded his church upon a rock, so
that

that the devil and all his inftruments, and the very *gates of hell fhall not prevail againft her.* The members of this church have Chrift Jefus for their teacher, and they receive counfel and direction from him: He is their prieft and teacher, and he teacheth them by his fpirit and his word, which he hath placed in their hearts, and given them an underftanding to know him that is true: Chrift's word you muft keep to, if you will be true fcholars. This is true divinity; if you will have the myfteries of the kingdom of God communicated and opened to you, *give heed to his word,* and that truth *that is in your inward parts:* Attend to that light and that grace that is manifefted in your hearts, and the Lord will fhew you more of the power and efficacy thereof; and *if you be faithful in a little, he will make you rulers over much;* live anfwerable to the underftanding and knowledge that God hath given you, and if you be faithful in a little, he will communicate more and more of his mind and will to you; and if you be led by the fpirit of truth, you will truft in it, and hearken to it, and underftand the language of it in your own hearts; and if you be *a willing people in the day of God's power,* God will work all things in you and for you, and work in you both to will, and to do, of his good pleafure.

SERMON XXVII.

GOD's WONDERFUL LOVE to MANKIND.

Preached at St. MARTIN'S-LE-GRAND, *November* 9, 1690.

IT is our great concern, while we are in this world, to promote the glory of God, and to *work out our own falvation,* to endeavour, as much as in us lies, to be fenfible, and to help one another to be fenfible of the love of God to us: This is the only thing that can give us true comfort, to have a fenfe of the love of God to us in Chrift Jefus:

Jefus: There is nothing more certain than that all of us are partakers of the love of God, which is imparted to us daily, and we live not a day without it; but we may, if we have not a care, live many days without it, and without the comfortable fenfe of it; and that is the reafon, that a great many of the fons and daughters of men, do fhew forth in their lives, fo little love to God, becaufe they have fo little fenfe of his love to them; for the apoftle *John*, that had attained to a great knowledge and experience in Chriftianity, plainly declareth, that the reafon of that love that we have to God is, *becaufe he firft loved us;* and I do not believe that any man can have any true love to God, that is not fenfible of the love of God to him.

And as for thofe temporal bleffings that we enjoy in this life, as health and ftrength, and our very breath and being, and well-being, that every day and hour are continued, they are from the love of God to us, and the lengthening out of our lives and vouchfafing us opportunities for the good of our fouls, are evident tokens of God's love and good-will to us. Where thefe things are not confidered and regarded, men live *like the beafts that perifh*, and regard not him that made them, but go on in difobedience to him, and difhonouring of his great name, and heaping up wrath upon their own fouls: And thus doth every man, while he remains in his natural ftate and condition; for there is in every man by nature the feed and root of all fin and rebellion againft God, which makes him return evil to God for the good he doth to us.

And I believe we are all of us fenfible, in fome meafure, of the depravity that is fallen upon all mankind, and of that enmity to God, and that averfion that is in men to the doing the will of God, and that impotency and inability that is in every man to the reforming of his ways, and the changing of his heart, and leaving off his corrupt and vicious inclinations, without the divine help and affiftance of the grace and Spirit of God.

Now they that are thus far fenfible of their alienation, by nature, from the Lord, and are alfo fenfible, that the time they have here, is the only time they have for their preparation and being fitted for that everlafting kingdom,

which

which we all would enjoy; how ought this to affect the mind of every one, that while they have time, they might prize it and improve it, and come to an inward fenfe of the love of God, that fo they might have a love raifed in their hearts again to God? For people will never be obedient unto God, till they love him, nor ever love him, till they are fenfible of his love to them.

Therefore, that which is the means and way of God's making himfelf known to the fons and daughters of men, that means, and that way, every one ought to embrace; every one ought to be acquainted with it, and have the exercife of their minds in it, that fo we might come to the knowledge of God, and might know, by an experimental and fenfible feeling, the kindnefs of God to us.

And truly friends, they that are minded to fpend their time, and exercife themfelves, in the confideration of the mercy and kindnefs of God, they have work enough for their whole life-time, to confider and contemplate the manifold mercies of God beftowed upon them; for we have our life and breath from him, whom the whole world obeys, and ferves; God, that made all living creatures, hath created us, and preferved us; he hath had long-fuffering and patience towards us until now, and he is yet mindful to do us good, which is evidently manifeft by the invitations and promifes he hath made us, and the workings of his Holy Spirit that he hath made us acquainted withal.

For who is there in this affembly, that God hath not made fenfible of the tenders of his grace, and invitations to repentance and reformation, that they that live loofely and vainly in the world, might turn to the Lord with all their hearts, and confider their ways and doings? God *hath waited to be gracious* to the fons and daughters of men, and his mercy and patience hath been beyond all human patience, beyond the patience that ever you did beftow upon any, this the Lord hath beftowed upon you; therefore I entreat you, in the love of God, let this confideration fink deeply into your fpirits, that you may be affected with the kindnefs of God, and his *patience towards you*, and his *long-fuffering*, while you have been finning againft him.

But

But some will say, how shall I know this? After what manner may I experience this love of God to me? How may I be sure that the Lord hath a love for me?

My friends, it is not only temporal kindness that we enjoy from God; it is not only the lengthening out of our days, that is an evident token of the love of God to us; but there is a demonstration and manifestation of it, that is universally extended to the sons and daughters of men, in that he hath sown his word in them, and hath sown his truth and his grace in their hearts, that every man, tho' he may be ever so wicked, ever so foolish and vain, yet he hath many times checks and reproofs in his own heart: I know it, and I doubt not but you do.

Pray whence comes that principle which doth stop you in a course of sin, and check and reprove you for sinning against the Lord? If you attend to it, and consider it, you will find it proceeds from God; it comes from him, from him comes our life and breath; then people should be incited to receive the grace of God; the favour and mercy of God which he hath bestowed upon them, in order to their salvation. The scripture tells us, that *grace and truth came by Jesus Christ*. If thou hast any good, it came by Jesus Christ; and if thou hast any truth, it came by Jesus Christ, who is the fountain of truth, and the fountain of the grace of God; it is he by whom God hath made himself known to the sons and daughters of men; it is Christ alone, that *God hath ordained to be a Mediator between God and man, that so he might be the minister of an everlasting covenant*, which we are brought into with God; so that now people should come to the consideration of the way and means that God hath ordained for their redemption, namely, that he hath given Jesus, that great and unspeakable gift of his love and kindness, to the sons and daughters of men; here is *grace and truth*, that came by Jesus Christ: How is it come? It is come into my heart. Tho' sin, and lusts and corruptions, perhaps, have a place in many, yet Christ hath a place too: *he hath made his grave with the wicked, and was numbered with the transgressors;* he was like the seed that lies under the clods, and is the least of all seeds, yet when it comes

comes out of the ground, it rifeth high, and fpreads abroad its branches, and brings forth fruit; this love of God, this unchangeable holy truth, is in every one ; why then fhould not every man be ruled and governed by it ?

But fome men will fay, is truth better than falfhood, and grace better than luft and corruption ?

You may fee that, by the light that is difcovered in the inward parts : Let every man turn inward to the grace of God, turn to that light that fhews itfelf in the creature, and fee what it will do for us : This is the doctrine that the apoftle was fent withal ; he was fent with a commiffion *to turn men from darknefs to light, and from the power of fatan to God :* Why did he do it ? It was for this end, that men *might have remiffion of fin, and that they might come to an inheritance among them that are fanctified by faith in Chrift Jefus our Lord ;* fo that this gofpel is the fame that it ever was, though men have divers ways of preaching, and feveral methods and ways of declaring the truths of the gofpel ; bleffed be God the apoftolical doctrine is preached again, and the bleffed gofpel hath the fame power attending it that was in former days, and may have the fame effect ; and that this may be the portion of every one of you, is the end of our labour. And we have in our eye but two things.

Firft, to difcharge a good confcience in the fight of God, who hath given us his word to preach, and *to turn men from darknefs to light, and from the power of fatan to God ;* that we might keep ourfelves free from the blood of all men.

Secondly, another end is, the defire that God hath placed in our hearts, *that all men every where might be faved ;* this is God's will ; if any be damned it is their own will, and the devil's will ; this is God's will, *that none fhould perifh, but that all fhould come to repentance* and be eternally faved. Now in this work of your falvation, we would have regard to him that fent us to preach the everlafting gofpel, and we would difcharge ourfelves faithfully, and *be made manifeft in your confciences,* that the benefits of the gofpel might come to be yours ; that you might anfwer the purpofe of God, in fending Chrift to be

the

the Saviour of mankind; you muſt turn from ſin to God, and then you will find the bleſſing that comes by Jeſus, which is *to turn every one from his evil ways.*

You may read this in a book, and you may alſo plainly read it in your hearts: The Lord Jeſus Chriſt hath given you light to diſtinguiſh between good and evil; if you do good, you may make a comfortable reflection upon yourſelves, and this will be your rejoicing, *the teſtimony of your conſcience* on that account; but if you do evil, though all men do juſtify you and commend you, yet you will be condemned in yourſelves; ſo that you have that in yourſelves which diſtinguiſheth between things that differ in their nature and kind, and you have a little enlightening by the knowledge and underſtanding you have received concerning the things that are pleaſing and diſpleaſing to God; if after you know this, you will go on in a way diſpleaſing to God, he will at length be too hard for you, and plunge you down into the abyſs of his wrath to all eternity.

After perſons are ſatisfied and enlightened with the light of Chriſt, and come to the experience of things in themſelves, they will love the light and walk in the light; but there are many in this age that have read the ſcriptures plentifully, and yet ſtill go on in a way of ſin, they cannot love the light that reproves them; *he that doth evil he hates the light, and the dawning of the day is as the ſhadow of death to him*, and it brings nothing but condemnation upon ſuch perſons, ſo that they do not love the light, though it is evident they have it and enjoy it; and it ſhall be their condemnation whether they will or no; if they do not love the light and embrace it, it will never be to their ſalvation.

God hath given Chriſt *to be a light to the Gentiles, and his ſalvation to the ends of the earth. He is the light that enlightens every man that comes into the world;* the apoſtle John tells you the genealogy of the word of God; *in the beginning was the word, and the word was with God, and the word was God; and the ſame was in the beginning with God; all things were made by him, and without him was not any thing made that was made; in him was life, and the life was the light of men;* the life of the eternal word was the light of men; what men do you mean? I answer, *he is the true light that lighteth every man that cometh into the world.* He extendeth his light to every man, but it is condemnation to every man so long as he continues to be a sinner against God: *This is the condemnation, that light is come into the world, and men love darkness rather than light, because their deeds are evil.*

Now all men are by nature dead in sins and trespasses; after our first parents fell into sin they were dead to God; *in the day that thou eatest thereof thou shalt die;* when they had eaten the forbidden fruit, they did not die as to outward appearance, but they died as to that communion they had with their Maker; in this dead state lie all the sons and daughters of Adam; but, as our Saviour speaks, *though they be dead, they shall live again; Christ is the Lord from Heaven, a quickening Spirit;* this is the object of our faith that hath been extended and offered to mankind ever since the fall; *there is no name under Heaven,* no other power or spirit *by which a man can be saved;* this great Mediator, the eternal Son of God, is *the light that lighteth every man that cometh into the world:* Faith in Christ is the same that ever it was, notwithstanding the many forms of worship among the sons of men; some of God's setting up, and some of men's setting up; yet among all these, the object of faith is the same, and faith the same.

In the 11th chapter of the *Hebrews,* that little book of martyrs, the apostle there gives you a catalogue of the mighty things that have been done by the faith of God's people; he begins with *Abel; by faith Abel offered a more excellent sacrifice than* Cain, *by which he obtained witness that he was righteous, God testifying of his gifts; and by it, he being dead, yet speaketh; by faith* Enoch *was translated that he should not see death, and was not found, because God translated him, for before his translation, he had this testimony, that he pleased God;* and so the apostle there goes to *Noah, Abraham, Isaac, Jacob, Joseph* and *Moses: And what shall I say more,* saith he, *for the time would fail me to tell of* Gideon, *and of* Barak, *and of* Sampson, *and* Jeptha, *of* David, Samuel, *and of the prophets, who through*

through faith subdued kingdoms, wrought righteousness, obtained promises, stopped the mouths of lions, and quenched the violence of fire, escaped the edge of the sword, out of weakness were made strong, turned to flight the armies of the aliens. All these great and noble things were done by faith; it was the aspect their souls had upon Christ the Mediator between God and man; it was their trust and reliance upon God through Christ the Mediator that did support and uphold them in all they did and suffered. This faith is still the same.

There are many faiths in the world beside, but they will prove but the faith of hypocrites. Some have a faith, that if they do this and the other work, they say you may trust your souls upon these good works; but this is not the faith of *Abraham*, the father of the faithful. But some called Christians are gone so far in the doctrine of merits, that they think they can do enough for their own salvation, and for their friends and relations too; that there may be more merit still over and above, that others may have benefit by the merit of their works of supererogation: But this is not the faith of *Abraham*, and other saints, by which they wrought such wonders in the world. I would not have men trust at all in their own works for salvation, but trust in Christ alone, who *is able to save, to the uttermost, all that come to God by him.*

But some will object that we are taught the doctrine of faith in Christ, and justification by him.

Well, for my part, my tongue shall as soon drop out of my mouth, as oppose the doctrine of being justified by faith in Christ. But, let me tell you, this may be misapplied: If a man believe that he is justified by faith in Christ, and yet knows, in his own conscience, that he is condemned, he believeth a lie; he is seduced and deceived. A man cannot be justified by Christ, when the Spirit of Christ condemneth him: Such a one, when he comes to lay down his head upon his dying pillow, all his faith will fly away. I have met with some instances, lamentable instances, of those that were called Christians, that have made a profession of religion, and at last have laid down their heads in sorrow. If this be your mistake,

take, consider, while you have time, that you may die in peace.

Now the proposition and tender of the love of God to mankind, hath always carried that limitation with it, that every one in the world ought to observe; if a man hope to be saved by Christ, he must be ruled by him: It is contrary to all manner of reason, that the devil should rule a man, and Christ be his Saviour: The whole tenor of the New Testament is against it (pray read it as oft as you please, for it is a good exercise) you will find the true Christian's faith to be this, that he that hath faith in Christ hath an operation upon him for the cleansing his heart, and purifying and purging his *conscience from dead works, that he may serve the living God*; though he hath been a servant of the devil, it will make him leave his former servitude, and bring him under the influence of another law, *the law of the spirit of life in Christ Jesus, which will make him free from the law of sin and death*. The apostle sets down the several conditions he had passed through; *I was alive without the law once*; he thought himself a man, a brave man, a man of understanding, that had profited among the Jews; I was alive, having respect to that law which should have been my governor; *but when the commandment came, sin revived and I died*. He had read the law, the commandment, many times, and had been at the reading of it in the *synagogue*; but there was a comming of the commandment which he had not been acquainted with; there was a writing of the law of God in his heart; when he came to this inward work upon him, where was then the life he lived? *When the commandment came sin revived, and I died*: There was a professing life he formerly lived, but he was slain by the power of the commandment, it laid him in the dust as a slain man; when he was in a slain condition he found out that law in him that was the law of sin and death, and this caused a combat and a war in him; *I find a law*, saith he, *that when I would do good, evil is present with me; for I delight in the law of God in the inner man; but I see another law in my members warring against the law of my mind, and bringing me into captivity to the law of sin,*

which

which is in my members : Now this brought him to a poverty of spirit, into a sense of his miserable condition, and then he cries out, *O wretched man that I am, who shall deliver me from this body of death!*

Now some people in this day, they are like the apostle, they have a *law in their members warring against the law of their minds; the good that they would do they do not,* and they can go no further : But the apostle *Paul* did reach further, though he did not in that state know deliverance, yet he had a faith that he should be delivered, and that he should not be miserable all his days. Thus having led the *Romans* into the several states through which he passed, he brings them to a further state, *the law of the spirit of life in Christ Jesus hath made me free from the law of sin and death : and now there is no condemnation to them that are in Christ Jesus.* How shall we know this? *They walk not after the flesh, but after the spirit.* Now *Paul* was come to that sanctified state, that state of freedom and liberty which Christ Jesus will bring all those unto that believe in him.

Holy men, in former days, did experience and find a great strife and warfare in their own hearts, they would all do well, and *exercise a conscience, void of offence, towards God and towards man;* but there is a law of sin that wars in their members; if we yield to it it leads to sin and death; but if we yield ourselves to the *law of the spirit of life,* there is a power that is derived from the Mediator, that will translate the soul *out of the kingdom of darkness* and sin, which the devil is the prince of, and bring it *into the kingdom of God's dear Son.*

There must be a real change wrought in us before we can come to God, and to fellowship and communion with God, which alone can make the soul happy. Let this be the exercise of every one of us to adore and magnify the great mercy and the kindness of God, that he hath not withdrawn his spirit from you, but hath placed a monitor in your bosoms that calls upon you to *cease to do evil, and learn to do well,* and to consider that *the wages of sin is death :* Here is a sin, I may commit it; there is a temptation before me, but I know there is a bait and a hook; I may swallow it if I will, but if I do, it will be my ruin: Would I come to eternal death, and have my portion with liars and wicked persons in the kingdom of darkness, *where the worm dieth not, and the fire is not quenched?* Or would I have my portion with saints and angels? If I would have my portion with the blessed in the kingdom of God when I die, I must walk in the way that leads to it; but the *gate is strait and the way narrow, and few there be that find it*; labour then to be one of those few.

But what signifies our labour (some may say) if we can *do nothing that is good, not so much as think a good thought?* What signifies our labour? All the labours and endeavours in the whole world cannot make a man happy.

I now speak to a people to whom God doth vouchsafe the help and assistance of his grace and Spirit, and the visitations of his love and power; you must now endeavour to do something; if a man endeavour, with the help of God, he may do a great deal of good, and shun a great deal of evil: Though all our endeavours, in our own power and strength can signify nothing, yet they are required by God, and by joining them with his grace, and laying hold of opportunities, by divine assistance, we may do what God will accept. But if a man do any thing in his own power and strength, whether prayer, hearing, reading, meditation, or any other duty, he had as good let it alone.

I would consider you as those that God hath followed with his grace and the manifestation of his spirit; this is given to every man *to profit withal*, and every man hath opportunity to work with it; but he must *work while it is day, for the night cometh when no man can work.*

Let every one of us that are now met together, labour to be sensible of the love of God to us, and love him above all, and express our love by a willing and persevering obedience, that we may have the *love of God shed abroad upon our hearts by the Holy Ghost*, and offer up living praises to him through Jesus Christ, *who hath loved us, and washed us from our sins in his own blood, and hath made us kings and priests unto God and his Father: To him be glory and dominion forever and ever.* Amen.

SERMON XXVIII.

SALVATION *from* SIN *by* JESUS CHRIST.

Preached at DEVONSHIRE-HOUSE, *Auguſt 9, 1691.*

IT is a general doctrine in the world, that no man by any means can ever be ſet free from ſin in this life: This is univerſally received among almoſt all Chriſtians, in all churches; and though they differ ever ſo much in other things, yet they agree in this; ſo that this doctrine hath got a ſway in the world, and it is accounted a great deluſion and a hereſy, and a grand error for any to queſtion the truth of it.

Now while a man is of that belief, that there is an impoſſibility of living without ſin, and of breaking down the kingdom of ſatan in any one ſoul in the world, how can men hope or believe that righteouſneſs ſhould prevail in the heart of one man? There is neither king nor beggar, nor biſhop nor a goſpel miniſter, but the devil muſt have a rule and government in him, ſo long as he lives in the world. As long as this is believed, it is not poſſible that the other belief ſhould take place; it is madneſs to think that I muſt be under the rule and government of ſatan if I am under the government of the Son of God. And it is ſtill greater madneſs to ſay, that Chriſt and the devil are both my governors and rulers: It is prodigious folly and madneſs to ſpeak after this manner.

This belief prevails over all men; over the wiſe, and mighty, and noble, and learned, that they can never be freed from the power of ſin in this world, but that the devil will lead them into ſin every day; let men be ever ſo ſober, ever ſo abſtemious in their lives; let them ſpend ever ſo many hours in prayer every day; let them come to meetings and hear ſermons, and write them, and repeat them, and do what they will, here is a bar of unbelief that lies in the way, that makes men *depart from the living God*, and his power, and loſe the benefit they ſhall receive from Chriſt: And therefore they go to obtain

tain it another way, that is, to have the righteoufnefs of Chrift imputed to them, and they fhall be pure and holy in the fight of God, when they are polluted in their own eyes; and when they fee their daily failings, infirmities and corruptions, yet God may not fee them; but that he fees them holy, juft and righteous in his Son.

What ftrange kind of doctrine is this? I muft prefume that God will fee me in his Son, Jefus Chrift, when I never was in Chrift: How can this be? *He that is in Chrift, is a new creature; old things are done away, and all things are become new:* But if there be old things remaining ftill, and I am not become new, fhall I prefume that I am in Chrift, and that God will fee me in his Son? When people come to ufe the underftanding that God hath given them, they will look upon themfelves as barred out by their unbelief, that the nations have drunk in; and it is as fweet to them as the honey and the honey-comb.

But, bleffed be God, many have vomited it up already; If they would have placed this doctrine upon man's natural ability, I would have faid *Amen* to it. I know there is none of us all have a natural ability and power to deliver his own foul from fin and fatan; but when they come to place it upon God, that though the *Lord make bare his arm, and reveal his power;* though they come to have the grace of God, that ftill they could not be delivered from fin, this hath blafphemy at the bottom of it. The other reflected upon man's power; this reflects upon the power of God Almighty: That the devil hath got fuch a power over us, that God hath not power over us, nor can have power and dominion over us, fo that of a whole nation he cannot have one man to ferve him.

Much might be faid in anfwer to this: When men are once willing to ferve God, they will be willing to leave the fervice of the devil. There is no way to anfwer that good wifh, but by wating upon God for the revealing of his power: I pray God that when you come to a meeting, you may fay, Lord, let thy power go forth upon my heart; let thy arm be made bare, and deliver me from the power and dominion of fin. Some will fay they feel God's

power

power in a meeting; I feel the power of God working upon my heart, in order to the taking away sin and transgression, and giving me victory over it, through the Lord Jesus Christ. If they feel this power of God upon them, it is their duty to believe it and depend upon it: If I believe it, I must wait for the dictates of it, and believe that I shall be able to do *all things through Christ that strengthens me*: Then faith will come forth into works, and appear to be a living faith.

You may remember what the apostle *James* saith, *as the body without the Spirit is dead, so faith without works is dead also*. As soon as a man comes to join with the mighty power of God, he will be able to withstand temptation: If he comes into evil company, he will deny them and not comply with them; he will find then something of a power and ability to serve God; though he is not come to perfection, yet he is walking in the way of holiness, and *pressing forward towards the mark of the high calling of God in Christ Jesus*: He will say, I have got a little nearer than I was towards the place where I would be, towards that life which I would live and die; then let death come when it pleaseth God, it shall be welcome.

This is the wickedness of many in the world, they will not live such a life as they would be willing to die in. They cannot come at it unless it be given them to believe, for it is the gift of God; they must come to their governor and leader, which goes before, to the gift of God, which is eternal life; then let death come when it will, if I have the gift of eternal life.

It is a miserable thing to think that there are many that have not laid hold of eternal life: It is manifested, that we may lay hold of it, there is a hand of faith joining with it. When a man comes to lay hold of eternal life, this life will purify him and sanctify him, at least by degrees, till he be wholly sanctified in body, soul and spirit: This is that which the apostle writes in one of his epistles, *your salvation is nearer than when you at first believed*. When they first believed, their salvation was a pretty way off. He describes salvation to be the end of their faith and hope.

When a man comes to be delivered from his sins, he shall serve God without fear; but when a man comes to live

live by faith, he shall overcome; he is a good soldier of Jesus Christ, and he must fight valiantly under his banner, till he gets a victory over all his enemies, and then his salvation is much nearer than when he at first believed.

I would I could say so of some of you; for I fear your salvation is farther off: Some go straggling here and there, as sheep not having a shepherd; this is that which my spirit is exercised with. You that are travellers towards the kingdom of God, it is the wonderful grace and mercy of God, that ever it should come into your minds to seek the kingdom of God, and the righteousness thereof. They that have obtained this mercy from God, shall receive and enjoy other mercies, better mercies; *blessed are they that hunger and thirst after righteousness*: That is one mercy; but there is another mercy, they shall be filled; they shall be satisfied: When a man comes to this, he must take up a daily cross, and exercise self-denial; but if he follow Christ, he shall be satisfied; he shall then have nothing but peace and joy; he shall then sing praises and glory to God in the highest, and to the Lamb forever.

There is none can understand the glory that is laid up for those that take up their cross and follow Christ, and love his appearing. This is the greatest blessing that God doth give unto his people, *he hath sent his Son Jesus to bless us, and turn us from our iniquities*. This is a blessing indeed. Take heed that you do not admit of any new terms: Do not think to bring God Almighty to new articles, the terms are declared and concluded on already: If you will obtain the blessing, you must be turned every one of you from your iniquities: The terms are already made, the law of God must be *written in the heart and inward thoughts*, and you must close with that power that will write the law in your hearts, and by travelling towards the kingdom of God, you will see the coming of that kingdom in you.

It was the joy of my soul, that I saw the kingdom of Christ would be set up in my heart, before it was set up there; then I saw the Lord's wonderful work, and there was a great alteration in me, when the Lord was pleased to wean me

from

from the world's breast, and take off my heart, and wean it from worldly lusts, from the world's joys, and pleasures, and fashions, and the world's honour and reputation: I say the Lord was pleased to wean me from these things, and brought me to a holy resignation, to give up my heart to him: If I have joy, it must be from the Holy Spirit; if I have pleasure it must be in the presence of God, who *in the multitude of my thoughts within me* made his comforts *delight my soul*; and if he bring not comfort to you, you will never have it; you cannot expect it till you do believe; and when you have faith, you can feel the kingdom of God within you: There must be the new birth, the work of regeneration, for *except a man be born again he cannot see the kingdom of God*; there must be a translation from death to life, there must be a turning out of the old bottom and a fixing upon a new bottom, upon *Christ Jesus the rock of ages*; there must be a subjection to his holy power and government, else you cannot see the kingdom of God.

Many have gone on in a profession many years, and never saw the beauty of it; and every little trifle in the world hath diverted them, and drawn them away. This and the other pleasure hath drawn away their hearts, they have seen the glory of the world, which hath captivated them: But those that make a profession of the truth, and have seen the beauty and glory of the kingdom of Christ, they should be shy of returning to the world again, for the apostle saith, *it happened to them according to the true proverb, the dog is turned to his own vomit again, and the sow that was washed to her wallowing in the mire; it had been better for them never to have known the way of righteousness, than after they have known it, to turn from the holy commandment delivered to them:* They made a profession, and were members of a visible church, and had a name to live, but they were inwardly dead, the sight of the kingdom of God is not given to such, but unto babes, that have a divine birth, and *that desire the sincere milk of the word, that they may grow thereby. God hath hid these things from the wise and prudent, and revealed them unto babes.*

I speak to those who are here this day, that would receive some kindness from God, and that desire the knowledge of his ways, and that the myſteries of his kingdom may be revealed to you, let your minds be retired and you ſhall find the great things belonging to your peace made known to you. We have ſpoken much of this, but I would not have you know it only by our ſayings, I would have you go into yourſelves, to ſee whether God hath not beſtowed this grace and bleſſing upon you: If God hath given you grace, do not *turn it into wantonneſs*; do not abuſe the grace of God. What is it that you do when the grace of God hath convinced you, that ſuch and ſuch a thing is ſin, and if you do it, it will turn to your ruin? Dare you venture to commit ſin after you are convinced of it? O take heed of doing *deſpite to the ſpirit of grace*, and of *grieving the Holy Spirit, whereby you are ſealed to the day of redemption.*

I wiſh that the weight of this conſideration might lie upon you, and that a holy dread and awe of God might be wrought in your hearts, that you might be kept from ſinning againſt God. You know there is a general outcry againſt preſumptuous ſinning, ſinning againſt light: Why ſhould not we all cry out againſt it? It is a moſt dreadful thing for any man to ſin againſt his knowledge and conviction; if any of us have been guilty of ſinning aganſt light, let ſuch a one ſay, I have done iniquity, I will do ſo no more, but enter into covenant with the Lord, and ſay, O Lord, ſo far as thou haſt revealed thy will unto me, I will obey it; I will delight to do thy will, O God, tho' I croſs mine own will. Whatever I croſs I will not croſs God's Holy Spirit, by which I may be ſealed to the day of redemption; I will never do this though I hazard my chief intereſt in the world: This is the temper of a true Chriſtian, and I pray God make you all of this mind.

And now my friends, you that deſire to ſee this great work wrought in yourſelves, commit the whole work to God, and trouble not yourſelves about it. I am ſure God will carry on his own work, and bring down the devil's kingdom, and rebuke that unclean ſpirit that is gone forth over the whole nation, and pour out abundantly of his Holy Spirit to carry on a glorious reformation. This I believe

believe God will certainly do, from what he hath wrought in my own foul. I know not what inftruments are to be employed in the work, I leave that to the Lord; but the kingdom of Chrift fhall be advanced, and it fhall be outwardly, and a befom of deftruction fhall fweep away all his enemies from the earth, and the wrath of God fhall burn againft them; but there is an obduration hath been upon the nations of the world, and fomething hath ftood in the way in all generations.

But, however, I am fure we all may well fay, that Chrift is the *Saviour of all men, but efpecially of them that believe.* He hath faved this city and nation from the plagues and vengeance that hang over us. Many years the Lord hath fpared us, and waited to be gracious for a long time, to fee if we will at laft turn to him. How long the Mediator will intercede on our behalf, we cannot tell; there is a time when the long-fuffering of God will come to an end. God hath brought a fcourge upon the nations round about us, and the flames of his wrath hath kindled upon them, and deftruction hath overtaken them; how foon it may be our lot, we know not; all our money, our filver and gold, and valour and courage, will not be able to ward it off, if the Lord but blow upon us. It is even at the door; there is but one way to fave us, and that is turning to the Lord, and crying to the Lord for the continuance of his mercies and long-fuffering, and patience towards us. In this cry to the Lord, let us all unite, that are lovers of the nation, and let us join our earneft fupplications in this work, feeing the Lord hath made us the monuments of his mercy and preferving goodnefs.

We have been continually furrounded with war and blood, and flames and deftruction; and the cry of the orphans hath been heard from other nations. And while they have been confumed with flames, and deluged in ftreams of blood, we have fat under our own vines and fig-trees; but judgments hang over the nation, and whether they will fall or not, the Lord knows: But what fhall we do for the good of our nation, and cities and families, but labour every one, in the fear of God, to reform our lives,

and

and to take heed that we fin not againſt the light, leſt we die, and periſh in the middle of thoſe terrible judgments that hang over us.

Let us turn from our evil ways, and depart from all iniquity, that the kingdom of Chriſt may be ſet up in ourſelves. It is the righteous in the nation that the Lord looks at, and for their ſakes he will ſpare a nation. If there be a people among us that walk in humility, and lament and mourn for the abominations committed in the midſt of us, God will have regard to them, and he will hear the cries and the ſupplications of a praying people.

Friends, you that cannot make uſe of ſword and ſpear for the ſaving of a nation, you may do good by your prayers, and turning to the Lord with an unfeigned heart, and let your ſincerity appear before him. If I would take a common prayer-book in my hands, and pray ever ſo devoutly and ſolemnly, if I be not ſincere, what will that do? Or, if I pray without a book, or if I pray without a form, or reject the form that others have made for me, what will this avail? But the *cry of the poor, and the ſighing of the needy, and the effectual fervent prayer of the righteous,* hath availed much for the ſaving of this nation many years.

Therefore, I exhort you all, as you love the nation, and as you love yourſelves, and your families and relations, ſin not againſt the Lord; for he is now ſetting up righteouſneſs, equity, and juſtice, and it ſhall prevail in the nation. God hath been pleaſed to gather in many, that have been enemies, that are now turned from ſin to God, and led by the truth: And it is their greateſt joy, that now they are no longer ſervants of ſin, but are now become the ſervants of God.

Now truth will prevail, and righteouſneſs go forth as the morning ſun, and we hope the Lord will ſhew mercy to us for the glory of his own name, though we are an unworthy people: It will be matter of joy and gladneſs to us, if the kingdom of God be come; then we may ſay our prayer is anſwered. We have often prayed, *thy kingdom come, and thy will be done in earth as it is in Heaven.* If the will of God be done, then I can do mine own will no longer, then I can be led away by ſatan no longer; the devil will

have

have little power, if I do God's will on earth, as it is done in Heaven; then praises will arise in the hearts of every one that delights to do the will of God, and God will carry on his work for the glory of his own name, and for the redemption of his people, that Chrift may be *preached for falvation to the ends of the earth.*

SERMON XXIX.

The ACCEPTABLE SACRIFICE.

Preached at GRACE-CHURCH-STREET, July 3, 1692.

ALL people that would worfhip God and meet together for that purpofe, they had need have a great reverence upon their minds, and a holy fear upon their fpirits, that when they enter into the houfe of the Lord, and draw nigh to the living God, they might not *offer the facrifice of fools*, but may offer to God that which may be acceptable to him. For all worfhip, and all religion, and all offerings and oblations that ever were offered to God by any people, they have had a return unto the offerers and worfhippers, either of acceptance or rejection. Many you know have been rejected tho' they have offered, and many have been accepted of God, and their offerings have been *a fweet fmelling favour in his noftrils*; and, I hope, we are all of that mind, that we would be glad to have our worfhip, and fervice and offerings to God, accepted in his fight, and that our prefent affembling together might be for the better, and that every one might have an anfwer of peace, and of acceptance in their bofoms; but that can never be unlefs men be qualified and prepared in their drawing nigh to God, and in all our offerings and worfhip that we perform, our hearts be prepared *according to the preparation of the fanctuary*, the preparation of God's dwelling and holy place.

The worfhippers muft be holy; there muft be the fear of God, and a reverence of the great God upon their minds, before people can offer an acceptable sacrifice unto him, as the holy apostle faith, *Heb.* xi. 6 : *He that cometh to God, must believe that he is* ; which signifies, that a preparation ought to be in the minds and hearts of people that would draw nigh to God ; or perform any service or worship to God, they must have the knowledge of the God whom they worship, they must first *know that he is, and that he is a rewarder of them that diligently seek him.* Here is a qualification for worshippers, for religious persons ; as they expect when they meet together to find the Lord in the midst of them, they must be qualified accordingly, there must be an awe upon their minds.

I am in the presence of God, I have an expectation from God, that he will open his abounding treasury, and minister some good unto me, or else to what purpose do people draw nigh to God ? It is because they would have something of him ; but they must come in an humble petitioning frame ; *he giveth grace to the humble.* It is the lofty, the proud, those that exalt themselves, the fat and the full, that want nothing. *These,* faith the prophet, *the Lord beholdeth afar off.* A proud man or woman cannot draw nigh to God, the Lord looks upon them afar off ; nor do they partake of those divine and heavenly comforts and blessings, and counsels and instructions that the humble mind hath the promise of and will certainly enjoy, *the humble, God will teach, he will instruct the meek in his way ;* but what is this to the lofty mind ? What is this to one that is exalted, and conceited and puffed up, and reckons himself full and wanting nothing, while he is swimming in the streams of pleasures of this world, and favours only the things of the earth, the pleasures of a sensual mind ? These persons are not hungry, and so they are not fed ; they are not thirsty, and so they never obtain that which can satisfy the soul. Our Lord Jesus Christ pronounced a blessing upon them that hunger and thirst ; but what is that to them that are full and lack nothing ?

So my friends, in this and all other religious assemblies, a great care ought to be upon every one, that their coming together to wait upon the Lord may be in that reverence and fear, and that hope and expectation at the hands

of

of God, that they might be bettered by it, or elfe they all lofe their labour, as *Cain* did; he would be an offerer, he offered facrifice, but was not accepted; becaufe his mind and heart was not right before the Lord, his facrifice was rejected. It was before he had killed his brother; he had great guilt upon him, before he had killed his brother; he wanted the qualification of well-doing; *if thou doft well, fhalt thou not be accepted? But if thou doft not well, fin lies at thy door.* He was got into evil doing, and an evil mind hindered his acceptance with God; fo it doth with all men and women in the world that meddle with religious worfhip, and facrifice to God, if they meddle with evil doing. There muft be a taking off the mind from the evil of fin and corruption, and the mind muft be brought over to fomething that they have received from God before ever they can be accepted.

You know the general doctrine of all Proteftants is, that we have no acceptance with God but through Jefus Chrift; we have no way to pleafe God, nor can do any thing that fhall be acceptable in his fight, but thro' one only Mediator. Now if I fhould go to worfhip God, or perform any religious duty without refpect and deference to the fenfe and participation of the virtue and power of that only Mediator, how can I be accepted? And it hath pleafed God out of his infinite love to mankind, to fend this great Mediator into the world, that every man that comes into the world is made a participant of fomething of the life and virtue of that Mediator. So you read, *John* i. 4. *in him was life; and the life was the light of men, the true light that lighteth every man that cometh into the world;* and that with refpect to men whether they are good or no, both good and bad, though all men are bad by nature: So that tho' they are children of wrath, and heirs of eternal damnation in their natural ftate, by reafon of fin, yet for all that this one Mediator, in whom this light hath fhined, hath fent forth his light among the fons and daughters of men, that is, the light of men, that enlightens every one. So there is an offer made of fomething that prefents itfelf to the view of every man that is good; if he apply his mind to it, he may have that good

U u   that

that comes by Jesus Christ; he may draw nigh to God; as bad as he is, he hath some good, that God hath bestowed upon men good and bad. There is no man such a liar, but he hath some truth in him; there is no man so ungodly, but he knows that which is pure and holy, that which hath reproved him, checked and convinced him of his ungodliness. This presents itself to the view of every man and woman, and calls them to repentance.

Now for men to make a shew and pretence to worship, and not have regard to the glory of God, how can they draw nigh to God, or God draw nigh to them? Our Lord Jesus Christ saith, *that where two or three are gathered together in my name, I will be in the midst of them;* but if people meet together in their sin and wickedness, if they have a loose and vain mind, and intend to go on in wickedness and sin, if they meet, they meet not in Christ's name, but in the devil's name, and he is in the midst of them, and he works and *rules in the hearts of the children of disobedience.* So that this hath been the ground and reason why abundance of meetings upon this account have been fruitless as to the benefit of their souls, and the expectations of people have been frustrated as to their salvation; they have not met with that in which the blessing is, and to which the promise is made. The promise is not made to people that the devil rules; there is no promise to such but the promise of eternal wrath to be executed upon them, with the devil and his angels to all eternity; if you can make that a promise.

The promise of life and salvation which is recorded by the prophets and apostles, it hath always relation to the seed that are in covenant with God. In this the covenant stands, saith God to *Abraham,* Gen. xvii. 7. *I will establish my covenant between me and thee, and thy seed after thee in their generations, for an everlasting covenant, to be a God unto thee, and to thy seed after thee.* The covenant is made to *Abraham* and his seed, that is, with Christ Jesus the Mediator. It is he that brings to God, those that trust in him and come to him, *he that cometh to him, he will in no wise cast out;* they that do not come to Christ, are cast off already. All men, by nature, are cast away

away already; if any of them will be faved, it is by coming to Chrift, *who is able to fave, to the uttermoft*, and to make peace for them, and of twain to make one new man; and to make peace between God and the foul.

There is a neceffity for all people, that have any fenfe of their natural ftate and condition, that according to nature have no title to the kingdom of God, to be reconciled to God. By nature they cannot make a claim to righteoufnefs and life; they connot reconcile themfelves to God by all their works; faith the prophet *Micah, will the Lord be pleafed with a thoufand rams, or with ten thoufand rivers of oil? Shall I give my firft-born for my tranfgreffion, the fruit of my body for the fin of my foul? He hath fhewed thee, O man! what is good: And what doth the Lord require of thee, but to do juftly, and love mercy, and walk humbly with thy God?* They that will be faved, muft lay hold of falvation in that way and method that the Lord God of Heaven and Earth hath prefcribed. He hath prefcribed a way for every body to be faved; he would not have any one to perifh, but that all fhould come to repentance, and obtain everlafting life. God hath made a way that will ferve every body alike; thoufands as well as ten; and all the world as well as one man. Now the way that God hath made, is turning out of the ftate into which they are fallen, and forfaking that governor that rules in the hearts of the children of difobedience, and clofing with Chrift, whom God hath appointed to reign in every ones heart. People in Chriftendom will fay, they have clofed with Chrift. Do not you hope to be faved by Chrift, on the terms of the covenant? It is not crying, *Lord, Lord*, but doing the will of God; the terms are, *all men muft believe in Chrift, the eternal Son of God*; and through the power of that faith they have in him, he comes to rule over them, and they become fubject to him. And if a beliver be not fubject to Chrift, he is all one as if he was an unbeliever; *circumcifion, or uncircumcifion, avails not any thing, but a new creature; and faith which worketh by love.*

The covenant doth not ftand in meer words; if I conform to fuch articles, then I am a Chriftian; if I believe

lieve all the articles of the creed,' then I am a Chriftian, and a child of God. If a man will fay, I believe, his fay fo is not fufficient. The condition of the covenant that God hath made, is, that Chrift fhall rule and have the government of thofe fouls that he prefents to God: How fhould it be otherwife, feeing he is not to prefent any to God that are unclean? Chrift hath no commiffion to prefent any to God in their uncleannefs and wickednefs. He that believeth, muft be cleanfed and purified by him: If fo, then that cannot be done, but by ruling over them. If they had the rule of themfelves, they would be polluted, and be like water, whofe current is ftopped with dirt and mud, not running in its own proper ftream. People will commit fin, when they have the rule of themfelves; but when Chrift prefents people to God, and when they come to be led by him, they are cleanfed and purified.

When the apoftle defcribes true faith, he doth it by this quality and property of it, *it purifies the heart*. All other faith is *but the hope of the hypocrite*; but real faith is *the operation of God*, faith the apoftle; and that faith worketh in an unclean heart to the cleanfing of it, and in an impure heart to the purifying of it: If the heart comes to be purified, then it muft needs follow that the converfation muft be pure alfo. No one doth an ill work, or fpeaks an ill word, but it is from an evil heart. Now if the *axe come to be laid to the root of the tree*, and the word of the Lord operate in the heart powerfully, if ever fo much evil be in it, the axe when laid to the root of the tree will cut it down; the power of God will execute judgment upon every thing that is contrary to him; Chrift is *holy, harmlefs, and undefiled, and feparare from fin and finners;* and though he extend his life and virtue to the life and foul of the moft wicked man in the world, it never joins with their uncleannefs, but keeps immaculate and undefiled in the heart of the worft of men.

Now this immaculate power that comes from Chrift, it will *purify the hearts* of men, and preferve them from evil thoughts, words and actions. This is the manifeftation of the one Mediator that they muft be governed by, elfe they

cannot

cannot be prefented fpotlefs to God the Father. There is a neceffity of coming to a Saviour otherwife than by words and profeffion; we muft come to him and heartily join with him; we have all joined with the devil, he hath fuggefted, moved, and inftigated, and people have followed his inftigations and motions; there is no man but is fenfible of a devilifh motion, why not then of a divine motion? Though now it is become a bugbear to fay, we are moved by the Spirit of Chrift, why not by that Spirit, as well as by the fpirit of the wicked one? No man doubts but that there are motions of the devil which they are fenfible of, that fometimes they have joined with him, and fometimes they withftand him. What is the reafon that men fhould join with evil motions? There is no juft reafon for it. The reafon why you and I withftand the motions of the devil, is becaufe we find another motion conveyed into our hearts by the Spirit of God; if a man hath one motion to commit uncleannefs, he hath another motion to keep himfelf pure; if he hath a motion to fpeak a lie, he hath another motion to fpeak truth; there are two movers at the fame time, in the fame heart, which fhall we join with? Shall I join with the devil's motion? If I find any thing of the love of God in my heart, it will conftrain me to mind the good motion, and make me withftand the evil motion; fo that the moving of the Spirit of God is not fuch a wonder.

There are none who have not had bad motions in them, and they have alfo motions of the Spirit of truth; they have met with evil motions, and they have admired them too much, then it is time to repent; if there be a diftinction between a motion of the Spirit of truth, and a motion of the fpirit of error, then I may boldly fay, it is our duty to join with the Spirit of truth, and not with the fpirit of error; if there be a defire in us *to be faved from the wrath to come*, then the way to be faved from God's wrath is to be faved from the caufe of it; take away the caufe and the effect ceafeth. The caufe of God's wrath being kindled againft man is fin, for God had no wrath againft man when he firft made him; for he made him after his own image, and gave him power to continue in

that

that holinefs and righteoufnefs, wherein he created him; but he fell, and was caft out of paradife, and an angel was fent *with a flaming fword that turned every way, to keep the way of the tree of life.* Thus man fell under the wrath of God by his fin; but how fhall I have the wrath of God allayed? By breaking off from fin, and returning to God again.

This looks like a covenant of works, fay fome; do you fay I muft break off from fin, and fo efcape the wrath of God?

Yes, I do; but no mortal man can break off from fin but by joining with the Mediator, *he is the author of eternal falvation, he worketh in us to will and to do, and enableth us to work out our own falvation;* it was fin that drove man out of paradife, and brought upon him the wrath of God. Sin is the devil's work; now that Chrift might be a Saviour to us, he will deftroy the devil's work; *for this purpofe,* faith the apoftle, *the Son of God was manifefted that he might deftroy the works of the devil.* Now the devil was not the deftruction of man fimply in himfelf, but by tempting him to fin, which is the devil's work; and Chrift *was manifefted, to deftroy the devil's work;* that propenfity to fin that is in the nature of man, which makes him rebel againft the mind and will of God. Chrift the eternal Son of God became man; he took the nature of man, that he might bring man again to his primitive ftate, wherein *he was created after the image of God.*

Now how doth the devil perform his works? doth he do his works coercively? No, he ufeth no irrefiftible force. But doth Chrift the Mediator work coercively, with an irrefiftible power and force, to bring a man again to God? No, no more than the devil did to beguile man from God. Man might have ftood and continued in his ftate of innocency if he would; he might join with evil, and yield to the temptation of the devil, if he had a mind; he knew if he gave over his mind to evil, he fhould be ruined; and it proved fo. Man was refolved to try what it was to yield to the devil, and obey him. He told them that if they did eat of the forbidden fruit they fhould be as Gods, but they became more like the devil; this they got by being

ing obedient unto him, not that the devil laid an irrefiftible force upon them, you fhall eat of the fruit of this tree; but there was only a prefentation of it to them, and with that he prevailed, and fo came to the deftruction of mankind.

Chrift the Mediator, in order that he may prefent us to God, comes himfelf and prefents his commands to us, and his command is, that we muft break off from that fervitude and fubjection that the devil hath brought man into, and there muft be a fubjection unto Chrift; we muft believe in Chrift, and hearken to the word of God, and break off from fin; but where is the power? If God would have me holy, let him make me holy; if he would have me pure, let him make me fo, and give me ability to do that which of myfelf I cannot do; when it pleafeth God to give me grace and captivate my will, I fhall become a good Chriftian. Now here is a great miftake, that people fhould think they muft wait for an irrefiftible power to bring them back to God; there is a prefentation of love and mercy, and earneft invitations, and the long-fuffering and patience and goodnefs of God's long waiting upon finners. *God, who commanded light to fhine out of darknefs, hath fhined into our hearts, to give the light of the knowledge of the glory of God in the face of Jefus Chrift*, 2 Cor. iv. 6. What fhall I do with the light that fhines into my heart? I will fhut mine eyes againft it; I love darknefs rather than light, and evil more than good; this light will lead me to holinefs and righteoufnefs, I will quarrel with it, it comes to bereave me of my comforts in this world, of my merry companions, and of all my bravery, I will not hearken to it. Alas! for thefe; *this is the condemnation, that light is come into the world, and men love darknefs rather than light, becaufe their deeds are evil*, faith our Saviour. *If I had not come and fpoken to them, they had no fin, but now they have no cloak for their fin.*

Here is the gofpel preached by Chrift himfelf; here is the prefentation of an opportunity for every man and woman to return again; but I muft be in the way of returning, that is, by joining with that which prefents to me holinefs, righteoufnefs, chaftity and humility, that prefents and offers to the foul all the virtues and graces that are in Chrift, and fhews it the light and grace that comes from Chrift. Now this light and grace fhewing itfelf to my foul, I have a view of. Haft thou a view of it? Haft thou feen purity, humility, fobriety, meeknefs, and felf-denial, and an heavenly frame of fpirit in thyfelf or fomebody elfe? How doft thou like it? I like it not at all; I love to have honour and dignity, power and dominion, and my elbow-room in the world; I love not this meeknefs, humility and ftrictnefs of life, that a man muft have a care what he fpeaks, and fet a watch upon his lips, and upon his heart, tongue, and hands, I do not like this kind of life.

If thou doft not like a good life, fomebody will like it, and live in it; and notwithftanding all thy vapouring, thy hating, and defpifing it, when people come to live this kind of ife, they will outlive thee; thy proud life, they reigning life, and thy having elbow-room in the world, will at laft come to be limited; the hand of God is againft it, and it will bring down the pride of man. When thou comeft to lie upon thy dying pillow, expecting every moment to expire, and breathe thy laft, then thou wilt fay, O that I had been more ferious, and lived more like a Chriftian; lived a godly life, and given up my heart to God, and been more watchful over my thoughts, words and actions! There is fuch a friend of mine, that hath lived better than I; if I had lived fuch a life as he hath lived, I fhould have had more comfort; and they that are defpifers of the godly, tho' they do not like fuch a life now, they will like it then.

Friends, you that are lovers of your fouls, and meet together that you may become better, and have expectation and hope, that you fhall receive comfort and benefit by your meeting together, I tell you, as a fervant of God, and a lover of yours, it is but a little while, and you will wifh that you had chofen the moft holy, harmlefs, innocent life, that ever you faw yourfelves, or heard of from any body elfe; and you will wifh that you had been more watchful over your thoughts, words and actions. There is a day, a day approaching, when we muft give

an

The ACCEPTABLE SACRIFICE.

an account for every thing that we have done, *whether good or evil;* you muſt give an account for your curſed debauchery; for your ſwearing, lying, and inordinate paſſions; you muſt give an account for every vain thought, and every idle word.

If this will certainly come to paſs, how ſhall I prevent theſe idle words and evil actions? *Wherewith ſhall a young man cleanſe his way,* ſaith the Pſalmiſt? *By taking heed thereto, according to thy word.* I am not as thoſe that ſay lo here and lo there : I do not ſay, you muſt come and learn truth of me, but if you find it, you muſt find it in yourſelves : What if I live in the truth ? That will not ſerve *thee*; and if I be a holy man, that will not ſanctify *thee*; thou muſt hearken to truth's ſpeaking in thyſelf; thou mayeſt hear it ſpeaking in thine own heart; you may hear it call you to righteouſneſs and holineſs; and if you hear it, you may do it too, if you pleaſe; for there is a power that goes along with it.

I know enough, thou wilt ſay, but I cannot do what I know; I have not power. What ails thee that thou haſt not power ? If I had power, then would I abſtain from all ſin, and break off from my evil ways; but the devil throws this object and the other object in my way, and by his temptations he doth enſnare me, I have not power to reſiſt : Would you have me do more than I can do? and as long as I have not power I am to be excuſed.

Now here is a device of the devil to keep people in his net ſtill. If men would be true to themſelves, they would not be long without power: If thou art convinced of the evil of thy ways, and that it is thy duty to break off from ſin, there is a power offered to thee, that, if thou joineſt with, thou mayeſt overcome all temptations, and forſake thy ſin : I would have you all prove, and ſearch, and ſee whether I ſpeak truth or no; I am perſuaded there is not a man or woman here but they have ſometime abſtained from an evil work, which they were tempted to. How were you reſtrained; becauſe you knew it was an evil work, you durſt not do it; the devil had not a coercive power to force you to do it; I knew it was an evil thing, and I joined with that in my mind which diſſuaded me me from it; and I prayed to God to give me power to abstain from it. The devil tempted thee on still, who helped thee against the temptation? God restrained thee by his grace. Will not he be a present help unto thee? *he is the same yesterday, to-day, and forever;* depend upon him still, and he will be always ready to help thee, and support thee, and strengthen thee, and thou shalt be kept from sin in an hour of temptation: Consider that all power in Heaven and Earth is given to Christ, and if he be able to keep thee thou shalt not fall into it; *those that come unto me,* saith Christ, *none shall pluck them out of my hands, and my Father is greater than all.* If thou comest unto Christ, *he will in no wise cast thee out,* and if thou depend upon him, he will preserve thee, and *none shall be able to pluck thee out of his hand.* If thou join with the truth, and with that which is holy, thou shalt have strength and ability to withstand temptation and overcome it; and (I may speak with reverence) Christ hath bound himself to those that trust in him; *those that keep the word of my patience, I will keep them in the hour of temptation.* If I keep waiting upon his power, that is ready to help me, and have a mind to be purified and sanctified, and to have righteousness brought into my soul, and have mine eyes unto God, and my expectations from him, he *will work in me to will and to do of his good pleasure.*

Now here people have a fixed foundation for their faith; but there is no working at this rate without bearing a daily cross. There are a great many can receive the truth in words, and receive doctrines, and tenets, and that with delight; but there is no practising holiness and righteousness without a daily cross and self-denial. There are a great many who have come to truth, as far as it stands in words, but when it comes to something that they must do, to speak the truth, and live in the truth, they meet with so much of the temptation of the devil, so much lust and corruption, and ungodliness in themselves; they meet with such evil things that their souls join with and yield to, that they cannot go on in the ways of holiness, unless they look up to Jesus, and have an eye to their Saviour, and

and take up his crofs and follow him. Whatfoever reproaches, fufferings, and perfecutions they endure, they muft have a godly refolution to follow the Lord Chrift, and fay, I will obey his commands, he fhall have the rule and government of my life, and be the guide of my way; whatfoever ftands in my way, I will take up my crofs and deny myfelf; without this there is no good Chriftianity in the world.

There are a great many that feem to be religious and are profeffors of the truth: We all know there are many profeffors of the truth in notion, and with fome zeal will talk of it; but they do not know how to live and walk in the truth, they do not live uprightly and honeftly in it; they do not keep their words; they do not live juftly and honeftly with all men, nor do unto others as they would have others do to them: They can tell how to fpeak and act; then why do they not do it? They have got a notion that they are above the crofs of Chrift, and felf-denial is far below them. People will not live in the truth.

This is wanting in the whole world: If we look around we fhall find a great many are illuminated; there is abundance of knowledge and underftanding among profeffors, abundance of learning, and great numbers of learned men: What is the reafon that oaths, and curfes, and all manner of wickednefs run down the ftreets like a river; there is pride, and wrath, and envy, and revenge, and violence to be found among us, as if it would draw down vengeance upon us. They have heard preached in pulpits much of holinefs, humility, patience and meeknefs, *that a meek and quiet fpirit is an ornament of great price:* Men have heard much preaching againft pride, prophanenefs, and drunkennefs, and uncleannefs, but they have heard it *like a tale that is told*, not much concerned about it, and have given little credit or regard to what they have heard of thefe things. Why are people fo wicked? The reafon at laft refults in this, *men are lovers of pleafures more than lovers of God*, they are *not the fervants of Chrift, but ferve divers lufts, and pleafures, and are led captive by the devil, at his will;* and fo they go on in iniquity. No laws can reftrain restrain and curb them, when the law of Christ is not written in their hearts; but when men come to see a necessity of self-denial and taking up the cross, this will produce a reformation.

This is what I labour for, and all good men and women will do it: It is time to try for reformation. Vain fashions, and garbs, and pride have been cried up, why should not we cry for reformation before the wrath of a provoked God is kindled against us, and his vengeance poured down upon the nation? We must reform our lives. How shall men reform, you will say? By getting the *law of God within their hearts*, that is pure, and holy, and heavenly, that will be *as a light to mens feet, and a lanthorn to their paths*: Now till people come to this they will go on in sin and iniquity, till they be swept away with some overflowing and dreadful judgment.

So that, my friends, in the fear of God, and out of love to you, I seek that you may be brought to God, through Christ; that you may live in the love and fear of the Lord, and, when you come to die, you may have rest and peace for your souls. There is no rest for those that are evil-doers; *there is no peace, saith my God, to the wicked*. The ungodly cry, *peace, peace*, and talk of peace, but there is no peace for them, but they shall have for their portion *tribulation, and wrath, and anguish*; this shall certainly come upon every one that doth evil. It is no matter what religion you are of, if you do not obey the truth, but live in unrighteousness.

Now, friends, my exhortation to you all is, that you will return to the truth in your own hearts, and do it while you have time. I am not persuading people to love my opinion, but to love God's truth in their own hearts, to love it and obey it, and you cannot do this unless you resolve to take up a daily cross, and be followers of Christ, who is gone before to prepare a place for them that are his true disciples; and then he will present them to God, *as holy, harmless, and undefiled*, for these are heirs of that everlasting kingdom, *which God hath prepared for them that love him*.

SERMON

SERMON XXX.

CHRIST the WAY to ETERNAL LIFE.

Preached at GRACE-CHURCH-STREET, *May 6, 1688.*

THE defire of all nations is come; that which all people defire in their own way, is come in God's way; for all nations and all people on the earth defire eternal life; they would all be happy in the other world, and in order thereunto, they have fitted themfelves with divers ways and methods, in which they have propofed to themfelves the enjoyment of eternal life; but by reafon of the darknefs that is in them, they have erred in their ways, they have been fcattered, they have been driven and toffed hither and thither, and can never agree about the way that leads to eternal life.

This comes by reafon of the great darknefs that is over the fons and daughters of men in general, in which they have loft their way, and are endeavouring to find it again: But the fubtle adverfary led them out of the way, and as long as he leads and they follow, they will never find the right way: The great calamity that is come upon the world in this refpect, is very greatly to be lamented; for when the eye of the mind is opened, to behold the univerfal ftate of mankind, and to fee how they are fcattered hither and thither, and often left in confufion, by the craft and delufion of the wicked one, and that none of the ways that they have found, are like to bring them to the propofed end, becaufe they are defiled, becaufe they are unholy; this hath bowed down the fpirit of the Lord's fervants many times, and a great cry hath arifen in the hearts of thofe that have feen the fruition and enjoyment of life eternal; O, that the fons of men might hear! and O that they might confider their ways before they come to their latter end! for mark friends, this you may take for a certain doctrine, and a fure rule in judgment, concerning all the ways that the fons and daughters of men walk in; *if they be unholy, they will be unprofitable*; the

way

way of the Lord was, and is, and ever will be the way of holiness, and the people that walk therein, they were, and are, and they will always be a holy people; now the sons and daughters of men have not gone to meafure their way by this rule, but the greateſt endeavours that ever have been in the world, from the beginning (the greateſt endeavours that men did undertake) were to ſee how near they could approve their doctrine and practice with the ſcriptures of truth, and that hath been the bone of contention, that they have ſtumbled about from one generation to another, one crying my way is right; and here they have been contending, difputing, and jangling and debating one with another, and could never agree, and could never come to that underſtanding, which is given by the Holy Spirit, that moved holy men to write the Holy Scriptures of truth; if they had, it is manifeſt they would have agreed, for this one ſpirit muſt agree with itſelf, and will give judgment according to its own righteous judgment: Men being alienated from the life of God, by evil works, and by the ſuggeſtions of ſatan, they have not known the way of peace, and have not come to that which is the deſire of all nations, as now in the fulneſs of time, the Lord God eternal, who created the Heavens and the Earth, the ſea and the fountains of water, he hath looked down and beheld the miſerable calamitous ſtate of the ſons and daughters of men, and he hath ſeen how they have been ſcattered and driven to and fro by idle ſhepherds, and how every one hath indulged himſelf in his own way, though unholy and impure; and it is becauſe of the darkneſs of the night of ignorance that hath been over the people; and therefore in his infinite love and mercy, he is riſen, and hath brought forth his light and his truth, that the nations might be enlightened, that they might come and ſee with a divine eye that the truth is but one, and the way but one, and all that do really deſire to be inheritors of eternal life, muſt come to walk in that way. So that people are never brought back again out of that way wherein they have been ſcattered and driven about, till they come to ſee the way they practiſe to bring forth iniquity; they ſee there is no light to be had in them,

them, they see the anger of God kindled, and the indignation of God poured out by reason of sin and unholiness.

Now when they come to be convinced by the light of Christ Jesus of their disobedience, then they come to feel and find a principle, a seed and root that gives them a law which they should obey, and hear the right law-giver, and have respect unto him : Here is the revelation of Christ Jesus by his Spirit, and this extends itself in its operation and working to the sons of men, to them that are afar off, as well as to those that are nigh; therefore our continual exhortation, from time to time, according as the spirit hath given us utterance, is not so much to make profession of this and the other doctrine of Christianity, as to persuade all men every where, that they believe in the light, and hearken to the voice of the light in their own consciences, that they hearken to that which is purely of God in themselves, as we know, whosoever comes to love the light of Christ Jesus, wherewith they are enlightened, it would discover doctrine to them, and make known faith and practice too ; it will lead them in the way everlasting, it will open their understanding far above all preaching this and the other doctrine and tenet.

What signifies it to shew colours to the blind, or to speak words to the dead; till men come to have their senses opened, that they may discern things belonging to the spirit of truth, the carnal man cannot understand the things of the gospel of Christ, the carnal man is not subject to the law of God, neither indeed can be; there must be something done in the soul, to bring it out of its carnality, and bring it to something that is spiritual, before it is capable of understanding the things of the spirit : Therefore when our minds can witness what we came hither for, when we meet to serve and worship God, we shall have a hope to receive some illumination, some refreshment, some comfort, or some knowledge of things divine; it is in vain to attend religious doctrines with an irreligious mind. It is my judgment of charity, that every one that comes hither, hath some expectation of illumination in their understandings, some gift, or some instruction ; this they may receive from the God of Heaven, by the ministry of those
who

who muſt be the mouth of God, to ſpeak to them in his name: When people are thus prepared, and their minds fixed to hear the truth; if they do not find it in themſelves, if they come not to a ſenſe of the word of life in their own hearts, their hearing cannot give them life. We are commending ourſelves to every man's conſcience; let your minds be turned inward, ſearch and conſider, is there a light that enlightens every man that comes into the world? Is there a deſire of eternal life manifeſted in me? Is there that in me that puts me upon obedience to God, to mend my life and converſation, that I might be recommended to God? Is there ſomething in me that checks me when I ſpeak amiſs, and do amiſs? I do appeal to the witneſs of God in you; if that be ſo, then believe me for the word's ſake, the teſtimony of God in your hearts.

Let us next conſider, whether we had beſt agree on this concluſion, that God hath enlightened us, and whether we had not beſt obey that light; this is the beſt way, let us put the queſtion, and wait for an anſwer from ourſelves. There is much indeed to be ſaid on the other ſide: If I ſhould hear and obey that by which I am enlightened, if I ſhould hearken to the reproof of my own conſcience, I ſhould loſe a great deal of the pleaſure and of the comfort of the world, I ſhould loſe a great deal of the profit which I gain in my trade and calling, and of the delight and pleaſure I have with my neighbour.

This is not to be denied; I would have things put in the balance; I grant you will loſe ſome pleaſure, and ungodly gain, and the friendſhip of the world; but pray conſider, and let us go through the account: If thou obeyeſt this light of Chriſt Jeſus, this is God's way of drawing thee nearer to himſelf, to make thee an heir of his eternal kingdom; whereas by thy indulging thy carnal parts, thou wilt loſe thy immortal ſoul; if thou ſhouldeſt gain the whole world, and loſe thy own ſoul, what will it profit thee? Thou ſhouldeſt conſider, why I am enlightened; how comes it to paſs that my nature is evil, and I am fallen from my primitive ſtate, from the knowledge of God, and from the enjoyment of his preſence, and communion with him? How comes God to take notice

tice of me, and to enlighten me and kindle in me a desire of returing to him? why should he do this for me? Thou wilt never find a reason in thyself of this extraordinary kindness, of this singular mercy of God to thee; it is because his mercy moved him, and it was his compassion that stirred him up: He hath sent his Son Jesus Christ into the world, that men might have light in and through him, and have it abundantly. The mercy of God is a fountain from whence all this flows to us; if this prevail not upon thee, no argument will: What, was it meer mercy, meer grace, that God was not willing to see me perish, and run headlong to destruction? He was loath to execute his wrath upon me, therefore he found out a way by which I might return to him. This made a good man cry out, behold! what manner of love is this, wherewith the Father hath loved us? Here is the grace of God; here is the good will of God; here is the way; a way, what way? A way of coming to God; a way of being again reconciled unto God, whom we had provoked by our sins; a way of enjoying eternal life again, after we had lost all pretence to it.

The next question is, who will walk in the way that leads to eternal life? We would all have eternal life; it is the universal consent of all nations; all would have eternal life; but the question is, who will walk in the way that leads to it? Some of the nations round about, and many in this nation, they will walk in their own way, and yet they would have eternal life; but their way must be of the same nature and quality with the life they would have; if the way they walk in be not of the same nature and quality, it will not lead to it. Let every one examine their way; let every one examine their progress, and their lives and footsteps in this world; if they sow to the flesh, they shall of the flesh reap corruption; and if they sow to the spirit, they shall of the spirit reap life everlasting; a suitable fruit to that life they live, and the way they walk in. If we conclude with reason; with pure, found reason, we must conclude it is better for us all to walk in the way of holiness; and we shall have more reason to believe that we shall have life eternal, than in walking in an unholy way, therefore we should be resolved to walk in the way of holiness; and if people are brought to this, it is an easy thing to draw them to confession: You say true, it is better to walk in a holy way than an unholy way; but alas! we have not power so to do; we are feeble, weak, dark and ignorant; and we have many lusts, temptations and impediments, lying in our way, that it is not possible for any to walk in that way; we know the way, we understand the way well enough; you would have us walk by the light of Christ, and the dictates of our own consciencies, then we should never be condemned for any thing we do, but we should stand in an openness of access to God; when a man sinneth against God, sin lies at the door; but they that sin not, have an access to God. Alas, these things cannot be done! What can a poor creature do that wants power?

My friends, this excuse must go no further; let us try and consider in the presence of God this day, the powerful God that is the assister of his people; let us try how far this will go, I have no power of myself; all good men grant it to be true, you have not power to walk in the way of holiness: But let us ask another question; doth God require of thee and me to walk in the way of holiness, and doth he deny power to us to walk in it? We cannot walk in the way of holiness, but by the operation of his power working in us, unto the extinguishing of the life of sin and corruption, that hath hindered us all this while; God knows we cannot do it ourselves. Christ tells his disciples, without me ye can do nothing, nothing good, nothing that is right. This being concluded on, all power comes from God; the next question is, how, and which way must we receive power from God greater than our own power? Which is the way of people's receiving power from God? You have read how people came to have power; *to as many as believed, to them he gave power to become the sons of God.* What signifies this to them that do not believe? If believing be the way to obtain power, it is nothing to those that do not believe; there faith is necessary, in the first place, for obtaining of this power: This is a great mystery, such an odd saying, that the

world

world knows not what to make of it: Believers, we are all believers; I believe the truth of the principles of the Chriſtian religion, and I believe all the articles of the creed: To talk of believing at this time of the day, we have believed this twenty, or thirty, or forty years, but the firſt act of faith is yet to be done after your ſenſe: It is true, with the greateſt part of the nation; the firſt act of faith is not yet begun, for their faith is men's faith: We are for the faith that was delivered to the ſaints; it is the gift of God, it comes from the operation of God; ſo that I may conclude, whoſoever remains a ſtranger to the operation of God, he is a ſtranger to the true faith; and they who eſtrange themſelves from that which God worketh, are ſtrangers to the operation of God. Therefore, till people's minds are turned to Chriſt, whom God hath ſent, who is appointed to be for ſalvation to the ends of the earth; till men come to reduce the government both of the ſoul and body to him, as the captain of their ſalvation; till they come to be thus reſigned, they cannot come to the true faith.

Now when God worketh this reſignation in us, a man will reflect upon himſelf and ſay, alas I have been mine own keeper too long, I ſee I have gone off from God, now I will return to him, and reſign up myſelf to the Lord, that he may work in me what he pleaſeth to work: When men come to this reſignation of ſoul, they have faith given them, they muſt believe God will never leave them nor forſake them, but he will magnify his power in their weakneſs; I will reſt my ſoul upon him, and caſt my care upon him that careth for me; it is not faith barely in words, and in the articles of the creed, but it is a *faith in the Son of God, to whom all power in Heaven and Earth is given*; I may expect a ſhare of it, he will give me a little, if I come to him for it; and if I be faithful in a little, he will give me more; the reaſon why you want power, is, becauſe you want faith; and the reaſon of your want of faith, is, becauſe you want a reſignation to the will of God; you will be your own carvers, and your own keepers and guides. When you come to this reſignation to the will of God, God will give you power, and

and then you will find him the God of all grace; you are what you are by the grace of God, and by his power, and by that power you will obey his will: Here is faith that giveth glory to God, to that God that takes an unholy man and makes him holy; how doth he this? By his holy fpirit, which is as fire that burneth up that which is corruptible; then the man is well (I fpeak according to the dictates of the fpirit) when he is reconciled to God by Chrift Jefus, the Mediator between God and man, the Mediator of the new covenant, who maketh our peace. That you may come to the knowledge of the day of the Lord's vifitation, is what our fouls labour and travel for, that you may be in the unity of the fame fpirit after the defire of all nations is come; he is come to you, that you may all fay within yourfelves, *falvation this day is come to our houfes, and into our hearts.*

SERMON XXXI.

CHRIST ALL in ALL.

Preached at DEVONSHIRE-HOUSE, *June 10,* 1688.

THE Lord Jefus Chrift is the light, life and virtue that can only fatisfy. Chrift is all in all.

There is nothing can fatisfy the fouls of the upright, unlefs they feel life and *virtue* to flow from Chrift Jefus; and this, whether it flow inftrumentally or immediately, always comforteth; it always refrefheth the upright in heart.

Therefore all they that defire fatisfaction to their fouls, that meet together upon that account, they ought to have their eyes turned to the Lord, that they may be capable to underftand the miniftration of the fpirit, whether in themfelves, or through any other. For while they are exercifed outwardly, and the dependence of their fouls is upon that which is outward, there remains a *veil* upon the mind, that they many times hear excellent things fpoken of the kingdom of God, but they underftand them not,

not, becaufe they are alienated and eftranged in their minds from *that* of *God* in themfelves, that fhould give them an underftanding. We never pretend to give people an underftanding, we have always faid, that is the work of God. We have fpoken many things of the *kingdom of God*, excellent things have been revealed to us by his holy fpirit, and the fame fpirit hath given us utterance, to fpeak of the great things of the law of God; yet many, that have been conftant hearers of thefe things, remain ignorant, and are infenfible, becaufe they are not exercifed in their own meafure of the grace and light of the Lord Jefus Chrift, by which they fhould receive and underftand them.

This hath made me often lament the cafe of many of the people of this city and nation, who are daily hearers of the word of God preached, and retain it not in their hearts: The fowers are gone out to fow, but many receive it in the *high-way-ground*; the way that every thing can pafs in, there they receive the word fown, and the devil catcheth it away; and though they have heard excellent things, of the ftrength, ability and power of God, that he miniftreth to his people, they remain fo weak and fo feeble, that they are blown away with every blaft of the adverfary, with every temptation, and with every fnare and gin that is laid for them, they are catched, and enfnared, and taken; and fo thefe come to meetings again and again, one year after another: I might fay unto you, wherefore do you come? It may be you may fay, we defire to be fatisfied; we defire fatisfaction for our fouls. Do you fo? Then I tell you, you may come all the days of your life, and want it, and lay down your heads in forrow at laft for all that. For all the words in the world will never communicate that heavenly life and virtue which brings true fatisfaction to the foul, unto any, except to thofe that have an exercife in their own mind and fpirits, in that which they have of God; they muft firft be brought to know the way they fhould walk in, and to believe that is the way: When people believe this is my way, the light within is my way, the grace of God is my way; that fearches and tries my heart, that is my way I muft walk in, fpeak in, and think in, and do all

that

that I have to do in; when I believe this is that way, then this belief obligeth men to take heed to their ways, to their footsteps. And here they that are thus exercised, are in a tender care every step they take in their way; and so perhaps they may receive great benefits by hearing the reports they do daily hear from those that were in the way before them, and have travelled further in it, than they ever yet have done. The experiences of the servants of the Lord, are daily helpful to them, and they are daily comforted, strengthened, and confirmed, to hear how they have sped, that have travelled through their condition, and through their present state; the helps and advantages they have met with, will do thee good, and comfort thee: But what is this to those that are not in the way, that have not faith in the way? Tho' they have a clear belief of the doctrine and way itself, yet they are not exercising themselves to walk therein; for they do but as the rest of the world, saying, this good man, and the other good man, made a good sermon. Why was it good? Not for any good they found by it, but because he raised his doctrine well, and proved it from the scripture, therefore we are obliged to believe it.

But now this good doctrine, if it be ever so good, and ever so firmly proved, it brings forth no fruit to the amendment of life, saving in them that believe, saving in them where there is an exercise in the fear of God, where people are concerned for their soul's satisfaction. For they that look for true satisfaction by this, or that, or the other way of the world, they spend their days without satisfaction, and so at last they die in sorrow; and so it will be to the end of this, and all succeeding generations.

And therefore, my friends, though I confess it is not a grief to me, but a joy, to see people willing to hear the truth, and to come together in great assemblies; tho I say, this is not a grief, but a joy, for I am not about to discourage them that do so: Yet I must be plain with you; I know what I say, and you will know it too one day, that all this meeting together, and gathering in great assemblies, and hearing what is preached to you, with ever so great delight to your minds, it will do you no good,

unless

unless you believe in the grace of God, that hath been ministered to you through Jesus Christ.

And when people come to this foundation, and build on it, and grow every day more and more diligent in the exercise of their minds towards God, and examine their way, and examine their footsteps, how they have walked yesterday, how they have walked this day, and how their minds are exercised at this present time, whether they have answered the grace of God; when they come to be thus exercised, they will look upon themselves as bound in duty to give account to God every moment, for their thoughts, words and actions. When they are thus exercised, then let them come to meetings in the name of God, and hear the experiences of them that have gone before them, and treasured up sayings in their hearts for their encouragement, and they will find this will be a help to them: But if people go and build a religion upon the sayings of this and that man; nay, were it upon the sayings of Christ himself and his apostles, if they were here to preach to them, and build a religion upon their words, and sayings, and doctrines, without the operations of the Spirit of God upon their hearts, inclining them to holiness and righteousness, this religion will do them no good: By this, to make the best of it, they might make a shift to reach to a form of godliness; people conforming themselves outwardly, to the outward precept or command from without, it might amount to a form of godliness; yet it might be supposed and granted, that the power of God, the power of divine life and virtue, where it comes, it doth sanctify and season the mind, and bring men into an awful reverence of the living God, their Maker, that they might stand in awe, and not sin against him; for here is the life of religion.

This hath a great difference from the manner of building men in religion, that many have been acquainted withal. They tell us, our fathers before us were built up in these forms, and modes, and methods of religion; they received so many doctrines, ordinances, sacraments and articles; and when these are received, believed and professed, there's a saint for you, there's a child of God, and a member of the church. How came he to be so? He was instructed in all the principles of the Christian religion, and subject to all the ordinances of the church, saith one; and saith another, he could speak excellently concerning the doctrine of our religion; therefore he is certainly a child of God, and a member of Christ; but all this acceptation of the principles of the Christian religion, of doctrines, and ordinances, and sacraments; all this will not amount to the purifying of the heart, and cleansing and purging of the conscience; nay, it would not come to a far less matter, to the bridling of the tongue; but they would be in a passion upon the least provocation, and upon the least disgust and distaste given them, their tongues would run over into wrath, and into wantonness, and prophaneness; and upon any occasion and provocation given, their corrupted words would prevail, and lead them into deceit and covetous practices; and though the fruits and works of the old man remain, yet they will follow the principle of the regenerate, as far as they consist in words.

If our Lord Jesus Christ say, *except a man be born again he cannot enter into the kingdom of God*, then this old corrupt birth will preach a sermon upon this text, and profess it. How many have taken upon them to preach a sermon, upon some excellent sayings of Christ, that never knew what regeneration was; for the *new birth* always hath a *new life*; but they have lived the life of carnal corrupt fallen man, and yet preach a sermon upon regeneration: Thus the minister hath done, and the people have believed him, and have been gathered into such and such a church; for most put themselves into one church or other; they have been covenanted Christians, members of a church; but they have wanted that which makes a Christian, a religious man, *viz. the answer of a good conscience*.

A true Christian, he is bound to be an obedient child unto God, that begat him of his own will, by the word of truth; and such a one may be in expectation of an answer of peace from God, through Jesus Christ, in whom he hath believed, and by whom he is reconciled to God. If you take away this new birth, and this new nature, and an anſwer of peace, from God to the ſoul, then tell me what the Chriſtian religion is, more than the religion of *Heathens* and *Pagans*, that worſhip ſtocks and ſtones? All the reſt is but talk, and men are never a whit the better for it: One man may excel another in talk and diſcourſe: A debauched man many times hath been able to talk at a great rate, and to ſpeak notable things; and ſome have been ready to ſay, it is a pity a man of ſuch excellent parts ſhould lead a wicked life: But alas! if ſuch a one can talk of the power of God ſtill, and the devil hath power over him; or if he ſpeak highly of the wiſdom of God, yet he himſelf plays the fool abominably; ſo that by ſuch a kind of life, and ſuch a kind of religion, people never attain to ſatisfaction; after forty, or fifty, or ſixty years ſpent therein, they muſt after all, lay down their heads in ſorrow, when they have been conſtant keepers to the church, and ſayers of their prayers, and receivers of the ſacrament, and ſtedfaſtly believe the articles of the creed, and make profeſſion of all the parts of the Chriſtian religion; yet after all, they muſt lay down their heads in ſorrow: Why, what is the matter? what did they want? They wanted faith in the power of God, that ſhould enable them to overcome their ſin, and live in obedience to God; and they wanted to their outward profeſſion, the *anſwer of a good conſcience, and juſtification through Chriſt the Mediator.*

They talked of redemption through Jeſus Chriſt, but were never redeemed from their ſins: This is ſo evident and plain, that there is no ſpeaking to the contrary: If you ſee a drunkard, or a ſwearer, or an unclean perſon, and if he ſhall preach, and make an excellent ſermon of the redemption that there is in Chriſt, and therein tell you, what great benefits they receive by Chriſt, that are true believers; and that Chriſt is a Redeemer, and redeemeth them from the curſe of the law, and from the guilt of ſin, and reconcileth them to God; ſo that he that was under the curſe of the law, and an heir of wrath, is now a child of God: Now if you come to examine this man, and ask him, whether he is redeemed, and delivered from ſin, ſo that ſin hath no more dominion over him, he will tell

tell you, no: What not redeemed, when thou haft been a believer thus long? Art thou ſtill under the bondage and captivity of ſin? Then thou art under the government of ſome other maſter than Chriſt; ſome other maſter hath rule over thee, if thou art not redeemed from thy ſwearing, lying, drunkenneſs, and uncleanneſs; if thou art led to theſe things, thou art under the power and government of ſome other maſter than Chriſt. Now this hath ſtartled people, when they have been thinking, that they have been baptized perſons, and profeſſing Chriſtians, and they have flattered themſelves with a groundleſs confidence, let me die when I will, this night, or to morrow, I ſhall be ſaved by Chriſt; I am an heir of the kingdom of God: Let me tell thee, thou diſhonoureſt the name of God by thy preſumption.

When people come to examine matters, and read over the book of their conſciences, and ſee what ſervants they have been to the devil, how the devil hath led them up and down at his will, thoſe that were covenanted Chriſtians, followers of Chriſt; when the devil hath ſaid to them, follow me, then ſayeſt thou I will; when the devil ſaith, follow me to this and the other evil thing, I ſee I cannot reſiſt; I cannot withſtand the temptation; I was overtaken, and ſurpriſed, and led away by ſuch an allurement, and enſnared by it: I pray thee leave off profeſſing, for thou diſgraceſt the Lord Jeſus Chriſt; he and his diſciples did not ſo: He was tempted as thou art, and his diſciples were tempted as thou art; ſo were Chriſtians of old time; and Chriſtians that live in the preſent time do meet with many temptations, but they are not at the devil's beck and call, as thou art.

The apoſtle *Paul*, in one paſſage of his life, we find came to be awakened and ſtartled: There was a light from *Heaven* ſhone about him, he heard the voice of Chriſt ſpeaking to him, *Saul, Saul, why perſecuteſt thou me?* and he ſaid, *who art thou Lord?* and the Lord ſaid, *I am* JESUS *whom thou perſecuteſt; it is hard for thee to kick againſt the pricks*; and he trembling and aſtoniſhed ſaid, *Lord, what wilt thou have me to do?* Acts, ix. 4. He was brought to this paſs after his convincement, but before that he was overcome and led captive; and when he would do good,
evil

evil was prefent with him: *To will*, faith he, *is prefent, but how to perform I know not;* but he did not call this a happy ftate. He did not fay then, I am in a good condition, when I am led captive by the devil at his will: The good that I would do, I do not, and I am carnal, and fold under fin: He doth not fay, this is a good condition, I am fatisfied with it; fee what he calls that condition; he gives it a more right name than many do now-a-days, that fay, this is the ftate of God's children; that the beft of all God's children have not power to live without fin, and overcome all their corruptions, that they fin in their beft duties, and can do nothing but fin, and that fin mixeth itfelf in all their holy duties and performances: Many of their minifters tell them, that if they think they can perform any duty without fin, they deceive themfelves, and run the hazard of being accurfed. But they learned not this of Chrift, but of fome other mafter. Paul gave this ftate another name; I would you were as wife when you are in this ftate and condition. *O wretched man that I am, who fhall deliver me?* I fee a wretchednefs in this condition; I fee, if I be not delivered out of it, I muft perifh to all eternity. This is not a ftate to live in; who can live at eafe in fuch a condition as this? Who can but cry out, who fhall deliver me from this body of fin and death? Alas! we hear no fuch cry now among priefts or people, and feparate congregations: I fear this cry is almoft loft among us, unlefs it be fome few that hear the voice of God, and feel fuch a ftroke of the divine power as *Paul* did, and anfwer to the heavenly voice. I confefs that I myfelf have heard fuch a cry, and have been fenfible of my woful captivity and bondage, by reafon of fin. And though I had a mind to do good, I could not do it; it was my defire that I might fin no more, I would not fin againft the Lord, if I could avoid it; and when I would do good, I found that evil was prefent with me; but I was far from fitting down there, and faying, this is the ftate and condition of God's people; it is as well with me as it was with the apoftle Paul, therefore I will fit down in this ftate: The people of God cannot find fatisfaction in fuch a ftate as this; though I confefs, that God's peculiar people at firſt came to this ſtate, for their conviction; and the opening of their minds, and enlightening their underſtandings, to ſee the evil of their ways; but they do not come to this ſtate, as to their reſt, and then perſuade themſelves that they are in the condition of the children of God; but they give their ſtate a right name, and cry out, *O wretched man that I am!* what a miſerable condition am I fallen into! I did not ſee it before: Now my eyes are opened, now my underſtanding is illuminated, now I ſee that the corruption of my nature prevails againſt the grace of God; and when I would join with the grace of God, and the motions of his Holy Spirit, the enemy is preſent to lead me away; I am not now in a happy ſtate, but I am ſo far advanced that I am convinced of my miſerable and wretched ſtate and condition; if ſome way or other be not found for my deliverance, I ſhall never ſee the face of God with comfort. Then ariſes that cry, *who ſhall deliver me?* Thus the apoſtle *Paul* (*Rom.* vii.) ſets forth the ſtate of his convincement, and how miſerable a condition he was in: Then he goes further, and tells you how it was with him: *I thank God, through Jeſus Chriſt our Lord.* O! I have cauſe enough to thank God, I am not a wretched man now, I am not carnal, ſold under ſin; I am not led captive by the devil at his will now. Why how ſo? the apoſtle faith, *the law of the ſpirit of life in Chriſt Jeſus, hath ſet me free from the law of ſin and death.* Here is ſomething to glory, and to comfort the ſoul in: The law of the Spirit of life triumphed in his ſoul, and delivered him from the law of ſin and death, and redeemed him from the power of ſin, and made him ſerve God with freedom and liberty. *I thank God, through Jeſus Chriſt our Lord:* I would have all come to this, to thank God; not only in words, but in reality, in deed and truth. For one may teach a *parrot* to talk over theſe words; but it is the law of the ſpirit of life in Chriſt Jeſus, that will make you free from the law of ſin and death.

    This is a hard leſſon, therefore you muſt go home into your own conſciences, before you can make a right judgment of things, and give a right anſwer to yourſelves. The law of the ſpirit of life will ſet thee free from the law

CHRIST ALL in ALL.

law of thy paſſion, and of thy pride and covetouſneſs, and ſenſuality, and the law of thy carnal inclinations. Art thou ſet free from theſe?

Now when people come to examine themſelves, they have no way to flee to, but they muſt take up a daily croſs, and truſt to the Lord Jeſus for their deliverance; who hath enlightened them, to ſee their wretched and woful ſtate; and illuminated their underſtandings, that they might come to him, in order to their being delivered from the dominion of ſin.

The greateſt part of the world think this is a thing impoſſible, and therefore do not hope to be ſet free from the bondage of their ſins. Which of theſe ways is it that thou takeſt? I am afraid many of you have taken the wrong way: I judge no one in particular, but I ſpeak this in faithfulneſs and love to your ſouls.

If there be any here, that are ſenſible of their ſins, and in a captivated ſtate under ſin and ſatan, who have deſpaired of ever being ſet at liberty, and have ſaid, it is a vain thing to expect it; for ſome learned men have told them, that there is no deliverance from ſin in this world, therefore it is in vain for me to ſtrive, in vain for me to engage myſelf in a continual care and conflict, in a continual warring and watching againſt ſin; for this deliverance can never be obtained in this life: It is in vain to ſeek for a thing that can never be found, and to ſtrive for that which can never be obtained. If there be any ſuch here preſent, I have this to ſay to them, that the Lord, in his infinite mercy, hath done two great things for you, to help you out of this deſpair, of obtaining a full deliverance from the bondage of your ſins.

Firſt, God hath placed a witneſs for himſelf in your boſoms, in your conſciences. Let me ask you, have ye not got victory over many ſins and temptations, that you have been aſſaulted with, from your childhood to this day? I might challenge any perſon in this aſſembly, when a temptation hath been preſented before you, hath there not been ſomething within you, to tell you of the danger of complying with it? Hath not thy conſcience warned thee, and called upon thee, O take heed, do not this evil thing, do

not

not cheat thy neighbour, do not commit this fin; whether drunkennefs, or uncleannefs, or whatfoever fin thou waft tempted to: Now, didft thou join to that voice in thine own confcience? And did it not help thee over the temptation? And when thou didft efcape the fin, waft thou not glad of it? and didft thou not rejoice that thou obtainedft victory over it? Satan laid a fnare, and an opportunity before me, to commit fuch a fin; but I did not join with it, and now I am glad of it. It was not only the devil's fault, for he came to his own, but there was an evil inclination in my heart to it: How came it to pafs thou didft not do it? I knew it was a fin againft the Lord. How didft thou know that? I knew in my confcience, that if I did it, I muft fin againft light, and againft conviction, and againft grace received; and that was the reafon I did not do it. Thus thou acknowledgeft thine own confcience helped thee againft the temptation.

Now I appeal to all your confciences, that hear me this day, whether God hath not done this kindnefs for you; and there is none here but hath been fome time helped out of temptation? I do not believe that ill of any, that they comply with all the temptations they meet with, but the light in their confciences hath fhewn them the evil of fin, and they have been kept out of it, and they have been glad of it afterwards.

Now this is one great kindnefs, which God hath done for every one of you, in order to help you out of this defpair of being delivered from your fins.

Defpair in the common notion of it, is that which makes a man doubt of his eternal falvation: *I fhall go to hell when I die; there is no mercy for me.* This defpair hath fo wrought upon people, that many have loft their wits, and common fenfe, and at laft made away with themfelves; many have been diftracted and undone in this world, while they lived in it, and at laft have difpatched themfelves out of it. And there is another defpair; a defpair of getting victory over their corruptions, and obtaining a freedom from fin: This latter defpair, this nation is generally fallen into; though the effects of the other defpair is lamentable to behold, the effects of this will be as bad one day, if not
prevented

prevented by rectifying that miftake men lie under. Why fhouldeft thou defpair of the power of God to help thee, and of the grace of God, and of the good will of God for thy deliverance? if thou wilt not join with the grace of God, and the power of God that is ready to help thee, and give deliverance from thy fins, the confequence will be dreadful at the laft. Therefore believe in that grace of God, which hath helped thee againft fome temptations, and given thee victory over fome fins, that it will, if thou faithfully join with it, give thee victory over all.

Secondly, Confider God hath done another kindnefs for thee, he hath fent his *light and truth* into thy heart, to engage thee in a war againft fin : There are a great many faithful foldiers of Chrift, that have fought this battle before you, and have obtained the *victory*, and they will tell you, they never went out to war in their own names, but in the name of the Lord JEHOVAH: When they relied upon him, and in meeknefs and fear waited upon him, he gave them power to overcome; and they were made conquerors, and *more than conquerors;* for they have overcome thofe enemies, that fometimes overcame them; and Chrift hath fixed and fettled them in this conqueft, never to be overcome more. Here is both an outward and an inward evidence : The outward evidence will do you no good, till you come to lay hold of the inward evidence in your own hearts; then the outward evidence that God fends, will be ferviceable to you.

Therefore, my friends, I tell you (as I faid before) nothing will fatisfy the foul, but the virtue and life that flows into it from the fountain of life ; here is the way to it. If you fhould hear of a treafury, and ftore of bread laid up for all that are willing to come to it ; if you knew not the way to come to it, and were ready to perifh with hunger, what a cry would there be among you! If a man fhould come and tell you where there is fuch a *treafury of bread,* when you are ready to perifh with hunger, and tell you the way to it is intricate and narrow, but that he himfelf hath been there, and that he can tell you the ready way to it, and that he himfelf had relief and fupply, and great plenty beftowed upon him, and that he
would

would bring you thither, O how welcome would such a one be to you! O that you were as wife in spiritual things, and as much concerned for your souls, as you are for your bodies, and would take the advice of Gods ministers! They would turn you to the light within; the grace of God in your own hearts, which you are partakers of; and speaking to you in the name of God, desire you to follow the duties of your own consciences, and you will come quickly where there is bread enough. By that light within, you will see your state is not so good as you imagined it was. This *oracle* within, is that which you must live with, and dwell with; you must go home with it, and lie down with it, and you must rise with it, and follow the dictates of it; if you do so, before the week be out, you will have experience to tell me, if I should come and ask you, I have got more victory over my sins, by following the dictates of the light of the grace of God within my own bosom, than by all my reading, hearing and praying, and performing other duties.

Make a trial of this, and you will find the presence of God with you, and that he is a God at hand, and not afar off; and if you buckle on your spiritual armour, the captain of your salvation will not be far off, but be present before you.

Therefore keep your eye unto Jesus, the author and finisher of your faith, and you will be *able to do all things through Christ that strengthens you*; and you will be able to conquer those sins and temptations that have conquered you.

May the law of the spirit of life in Christ Jesus, break down the body of sin and death, and bring you into the glorious liberty which God hath prepared for his children.

SERMON

SERMON XXXII.

CHRISTIANS *should often think on the* NAME *of the* LORD.

Preached at DEVONSHIRE-HOUSE, *July* 17, 1692.

THE people of God in former ages, did *often think upon the name of the Lord*: I would it might be the daily practice of all that make profession to be the people of God in our days, to think *often* upon the name of the Lord. This you know is an inward exercise, invisible and known to none but God; he only knows when you are met together, whether you are thinking upon his name, whether the exercise of your minds is upon his power, or upon whatsoever else your minds are engaged. They whose exercise and desire is, to feel God's power, and to be acquainted with his name, the Lord is nigh to them, to reveal his mighty power, and his name to them, and they are a people that partake of his goodness and of his virtue, and have an experimental knowledge of the divers administrations of both his judgments and mercies to their own souls, and so they can proceed from thinking to speaking of the goodness of God from the experience that they have in themselves, that the Lord is good to them.

For all that some do in their manner of speaking of God and his goodness, and crying up the name of the Lord, it is all worth nothing, it is but noise: But every one that partakes in his own soul of something of the divine virtue and goodness that flows from God invisibly to him through Jesus Christ, he hath assurance in himself that he speaks the truth: It is not meer words, made ready to his hand, but it is his own knowledge and experience of that which God hath wrought in him by his own Spirit; there are none that think upon the name of the Lord, and his power, and the working of it, but they are able to speak of it effectually and truly.

I know it hath been, and is the practice among many, that they are able to speak of God's goodness from what they find in the writings and sayings of some that lived before them, that did bear an honourable testimony of God's goodness in their religion; and they learn to say it over again in their particular age: But what hath this tale that they have told, wrought? This report they have made, how God was with the Christians of old, the primitive Christians and martyrs; they have told a tale of these things, and what hath it effected? It hath either brought forth Christians, or it hath not.

The way for people to be grounded and settled in divine knowledge, is for every one to speak what they know: And if they know nothing of these things, to say nothing of them. And the way for them to come to receive divine knowledge, is, by thinking, by meditating, by considering of that converse that God hath with their own souls; for there is a way provided for all men to converse with God that made them: Every man and woman may ask questions of him, and may have answers from him, if they have patience enough to wait for them; every soul here present, that with seriousness of mind shall ask of God what their state and condition is, if they were to die presently, God will tell them, he will answer them; he will shine unto them by the *light of his Son Jesus Christ*, and let them know whether they are *in the gall of bitterness, and in the bonds of their iniquity* still, or whether they are redeemed out of it, and brought into covenant with himself: But will you believe his answer? I would have no man go about to ask such a question of God unless he hath a mind to believe the answer that God giveth him. To what purpose should men ask, if they *ask amiss*? If they ask without faith, they do not believe except the answer please them.

Many, in our days, have put up their petitions and prayers to God, that he would discover to them the state and condition of their souls: The Lord hath answered them, and notwithstanding all the profession that they have made of his name, and of their faith in his Son Jesus Christ, and of the work of redemption, yet he hath often declared
thou

on the NAME of the LORD.

thou art still unredeemed, thou art still in thy sin, and lusts, and concupifcence prevail over thee; thou art still in bondage. This is God's anfwer to many; but there is fomething arifeth in their minds, that they are not willing to believe this; I would think better of myfelf than this: What if thou doft think better of thyfelf? Thou art never the better, *for the word of the Lord stands sure.* There is no removing of it; there is no denial of the truth. If this truth condemn thee, all the world cannot juftify thee; and this truth by which God condemns the finner is in the finner's own heart: What will he do with it? It is in the finner's confcience; it doth not only condemn him by book, out of this chapter and that verfe, out of this author and the other author, but he is condemned by God's true and faithful witnefs, in his own confcience. Thou wilt not believe it; but if thou believeft not this, then thou remaineft in thy unbelief of the truth; and nothing elfe but believing it can fave thee; no counfel elfe can deliver or redeem thee.

So that the beft advice and counfel that I can give a people in this cafe, is this; that when they come to fuch a religious meeting as this is, they would come with a mind prepared and fitted to think upon the Lord; to think upon his name, and the way by which he brings people to himfelf; for no man can be called a child of God, that doth not partake of his nature. If a man be ever fo wife, and rich, and great in the world; if he be a prince or an emperor, without this he is a *child of wrath.* Now if thefe children of wrath meet with fomething that convinceth them; if they are touched and become a fenfible people, then crowns and diadems are nothing to them. Such a one will fay, if I be a *child of wrath,* a captive to fin and my own lufts and concupifcence, yet for all that I will go to a religious meeting, where I hope the word of God will be preached; I hope to meet with fomething there that will do me good; and I have a defire that I may be tranflated out of a natural ftate, from being *a child of wrath, to be brought into the kingdom of God.* If I have this defire in me, God that made me, wrought it in me; for by nature *we cannot fo much as think a good thought.* When men

men think of being better, and of amending their ways, and doing their souls good, these are very good thoughts in themselves. When such thoughts are begotten in any men's hearts, I would have them to ascribe them to the grace of God, and nothing else. Preachers may do much where these desires are begotten; but it is not in their power to beget these desires.

Many have come to a meeting with loose, prophane and wandering minds; and though many good things have been spoken to them, it hath not reached so far as to beget good desires, their hearts have been so alienated from the grace of God in themselves, which is the great superior worker, to which we are but servants and ministers; there is none can beget any thing, but he in whom all power is. They that are under the power of darkness, the devil begets in them wantonness and vanity, prophaneness and hardness of heart. Some go away from a meeting without being touched and persuaded, and they have no good hope of being better: But where people are really touched in their spirits, with a desire after something that will do them good, they must come to the fountain of good, the God that made them, and they must think upon him; if they cannot *see his glory, and hear his voice*, yet they can think upon him. This is the least duty of a Christian, to *think upon the name of the Lord*, when their minds are exercised about divine matters, about the state and condition of their poor souls. If I die this night, what will become of me? This and that sin I have committed; how shall I be able to answer to God for one of a thousand of all my loose thoughts, words and actions? They that come to a consideration of this, and a due sense of their state and condition, though it is such a state that they do not like; though it is not such as it ought to be, yet notwithstanding it may be better; they may be brought out of it into a better condition.

Now this is the duty of all, to wait upon God, the fountain of all good, that they may receive something from God, for *every good and perfect gift comes from above, from the Father of lights*, the Father of thy light and my light, that light comes to us from the Father of lights: If
we

we have any perfect gift bestowed upon us, it is bestowed by God; therefore you will grant that we are all obliged, from the greatest to the least, to wait upon him, if we have the least expectation from God, by meeting, otherwise we had better keep away.

But I am apt to judge that the most here are come with some desire, that if it please God they may receive benefit by their meeting: Where shall they have it? They say, if such a man preacheth, then I can edify much by him: This is a great mistake; for, let who will preach, there is nobody can receive any benefit, but it must be from the Lord, as the fountain of good; for the best preachers in the world are but instruments in the hands of God; if God doth not bless his labours, the preacher can do nothing to the souls of people; he can found the truth in their ears outwardly, but he can reach no further, God only speaks to the heart. If thou mind the preacher and not God that made thee, all his preaching will do thee no good; it may indeed help thee to a notion or speculation, but that comes not to the inside, that will be no better, the inside wants mending.

There are great deformities, scars, spots, stains, wounds and lameness upon the souls of men, by reason of their sins, lusts and corruptions; and there wants a remedy, and there is no physician of value but God that made us after his own image. The devil hath brought in deformity, he hath made one proud, another cruel, another wanton, another an oppressor, another malicious; this is all the devil's work: *And for this end Christ Jesus came into the world, that he might destroy the works of the devil.* He came to destroy pride, malice and lust; these are the devil's works, that Christ came to destroy: Why doth he not do it? He will destroy all the devil hath wrought in every man that will be subject to him: Can a chirurgeon set a bone, if the patient be not subject to his hand?

But this is far beyond all comparison; Christ hath *received all power in Heaven and Earth*, yet he always looks for a willing people; he sends the day of his power upon a people, and he worketh upon their hearts by an invincible power; he makes them willing to be helped, and

mended,

mended, and healed, and cured, and then he cures them. I dare say, there is not one here that is willing to be reformed, and to submit to Chrift to be faved and redeemed by him, but he will do it; *he that is willing and obedient, shall eat of the good of the land*, and shall know the good of redemption. See whether it be come to a state of redemption; here is univerfal grace offered; for the *light of Chrift Jefus enlighteneth every one of you*; it shews you your loft state and condition: When we fee our condition bad, that it is not as it ought to be, who would not have it better?

What means prayer, that Chriftian duty? What shall we pray for? Muft not people be fenfible in themfelves what they should pray for, before they come to pray? And what is it that will make them fenfible but the light and grace of God? They fee their own wants when God worketh faith in their hearts, and they believe that God can fupply thofe wants. Why should I go to a beggar, to pray him to give me an hundred pounds? I believe he cannot do it, therefore I will not pray to him for it: Now neceffity brings people to prayer, but there muft be faith in him to whom we pray, that he is able to fupply our wants, and relieve our neceffities. Upon this account the apoftle faith, *he that cometh to God muft believe that he is, and that he is a rewarder of them that diligently feek him*. He muft firft know that there is a God to come unto, and then that he is a rewarder.

Here is the foundation of all true religion and true worfhip; they that go to God and fay their prayers, and join with others in faying their prayers, if they have no fenfe of God, they had as good hold their tongues, for their praying is to no purpofe: They that pretend to believe in God, without an experimental power of God working upon their hearts, their belief is not worth a ftraw; without their refpect to the power of God, all their belief is nothing; but if they know that God hath fuch an operation upon them, that no man or woman in the world can difcover that to them, that God difcovereth, then they know that God is *the fearcher of hearts and the trier of the reins*, Jeremiah, xvii. 10.

Suppofe

on the NAME *of the* LORD.

Suppofe I know that there is a God, and at the fame time I believe that he will never hear me; that I am a reprobate creature, and that he hath caft me off forever, and that he hath fealed condemnation upon me, to all eternity. What reafon hath fuch a one to pray? This is a defperate condition. But while we believe there is a God, and that *he is a rewarder of them that diligently feek him,* it is not in vain to pray; yet there is fomething antecedent too to prayer; there is knowledge, and faith by reafon of that knowledge, that God is a rewarder: He that hath this, let him pray in God's name. But what muft he pray for? He muft *not offer the facrifice of fools;* he muft have regard to his lips; if it be mental prayer, he muft pray for that he ftands in need of; it is for fomething he prays, that God hath revealed by his Holy Spirit; this he ftands in need of; it is fomething that he needs; it is power to overcome corruption, and power to overcome temptation, that he ftands in need of; he ftands in need of a Mediator to procure for him the pardon of his fins: Thefe things he ftands in need of, then let him pray; *he that is afflicted, let him pray.*

So that if a man or woman go to prayer, they muft pray to God, in the belief of his goodnefs and mercy, that he will beftow fome blefling upon them, that may be for the better, that may be for their good. When they come to a meeting, to worfhip God, and hear the word fpoken outwardly, they muft pray for fomething that may be for their good; Lord give me fomething that may fupport my foul, and fomething that may enable me to withftand temptation. People fhould have their minds thus exercifed, and they fhould think upon the name of the Lord according to their particular neceffity; they fhould pour out their fupplication to the Lord: This is fuch worfhip as God looks for, and fuch as he is pleafed with; he will deliver thofe that thus pray to him out of temptations, fo that they fhall not prevail over them: One man's temptation is of one fort, and another's of another fort, but they are all delivered by the grace of God, and helped over them, upon their prayer to God; for they find by experience that *he is a God hearing prayers.*

Now

Now, when we have prayed, what is the next work? It is to wait for an anfwer of our prayer. I prayed the other day to God for power to withftand fuch a temptation; when that temptation comes again I do expect that God will anfwer my prayer. Doft thou fo? Then I pray thee have an eye to the fame grace of God that convinced thee, and fhewed thee the temptation; and have thy faith exercifed upon that grace of God, and thou wilt find it fufficient for thee, I will warrant thee: Let the devil come with a temptation ever fo fuitable and fubtil, keep thine eye upon the grace of God, and it will deliver thee. This was the cafe of *Paul*; *when a meffenger of fatan was fent to buffet him, he befought the Lord thrice*: The temptation did attend him, and God gave him an anfwer of his prayer; *my grace is fufficient for thee*. As if he had faid, let the devil come with ever fo much power he fhall never overcome thee.

I fpeak to thofe that are well skilled in this kind of work, and have met with fharp temptations, and fometimes perhaps they have been overcome by them, and at other times they have withftood them: What is the difference; why, one while they are loofe and carelefs, and did not pray for the affiftance of divine grace; another while they kept clofe to it, and were delivered.

Therefore when you come to meeting, with a defire to receive benefit from God, with your expectations Godward, to receive comfort from the hands of the Lord, let your eye be upon him, and the working of his grace in your own hearts, and hearken to that voice that is within you, and it will be more effectual than mine. If you find the work of grace in you to be the fame thing that I fpeak of, then believe me for the truth's-fake; believe me becaufe you find the fame work and teftimony within yourfelves. And I am perfuaded there is no one here, but fometime or other have withftood that temptation which they have met withal. Pray tell me how they did it? Why, the temptation came unto me, and it pleafed God to fhew me the evil of it, that it was a bad thing if I yielded to it. How didft thou refift it? had not the devil a coercive power over thee, to force thee to it, whether
thou

thou wouldeſt or not? That God that ſhewed me the evil of it, delivered me from the evil; I was not judged and condemned in myſelf, becauſe I found myſelf delivered from it; there are none of you, if you would not be lazy and idle, but you might be delivered every day, and have experience in your own ſouls, that when the devil comes and tempts, the Lord is at hand to deliver you by his grace and power.

So that the only way for people to be preſerved from ſin and iniquity, is to have a reverent reſpect to that grace of God which they have already received. I would have that vain conceit, that hath long reigned in the world, taken out of your head. When you ſee a wicked husband, wife, or child, you ſay, if they had grace they would be better; I ſay they have ſome degree of grace already; God hath ſent forth his grace and truth, to *teach men to deny ungodlineſs,* ſo that I would not pray that God would give my husband, wife, or child, or friend grace, but that he would break their hard hearts, that they may ſubmit to the grace of God that is already beſtowed upon them. I believe there is not a perſon here that is utterly void of all grace; but they walk not according to it, they trample upon it: For every one being endued with a meaſure of grace, through Chriſt, our duty therefore is to have a reverential regard to the grace of God, that we have received.

What grace have I received from God, may ſome ſay? I have received ſo much grace from God (thou mayeſt truly ſay) that I can tell when the devil brings a temptation to me; when he tempts me to uncleanneſs, theft, wrath, malice, or to deceive my neighbour, I have ſo much grace that I can tell I am tempted in ſuch a reſpect; the grace of God ſhews me this is a temptation of the devil: But the queſtion is, whether I am ſubject to the grace of God, and love his grace better than the profit or pleaſure of a temptation? It comes as a bait, but the devil cannot make me do that which he tempts me to; it is not in the power of all the devils in hell, or of his ſervants on earth, to make me do this evil thing: The light of my own conſcience ſhews it to be a temptation. Now I am free and at my choice, whether I will love the profit and pleaſure that comes with the temptation more than the grace of God: I believe there is no one that hath been tried by a temptation, but they can say so: I leave it to him *that searches and tries all your hearts, and knows your thoughts*, to judge whether you joined with the temptation, that you might have the profit and pleasure of it, or joined with his grace, that thereby you might have resisted the temptation: You that have done the one and the other, tell me which is the best bargain; when you have joined with the temptation, that you might have the profit and pleasure that came along with it; or when you joined with the grace of God, that shewed you the evil and danger of the temptation. The same God speaks to you that spake to *Cain, if thou doest well, shalt not thou be accepted? and if thou dost not well, sin lies at the door.* If thou hast yielded to a temptation, *sin lies at the door*, there is a breach made between God and thy soul.

The same man at another time, having smarted so deeply for it, being judged by his own conscience, when he meets the temptation again, he saith, let the profit or pleasure go where it will, if I yield to this temptation I cannot go to God but as a criminal to a judge; let the profit or pleasure be what it will, I will not join with this temptation. Can the devil force thee to comply with this temptation? No, if thou be true to the grace of God in thy own heart, it will make thee able to resist the strongest devil in hell. Christ hath purchased for the sons and daughters of men a power to withstand the devil's power, and all his devices and temptations, and you shall obtain victory, and have dominion over them. If you have a mind to grow in this dominion, when the devil comes to tempt you, resist him, and you shall, through the power of Christ, be enabled to overcome.

If satan tell thee of the profits and pleasures of this world, remember *that the world passeth away, and the lust of it*, but peace with God endures forever: By the grace of God you will be able to overcome the devil and all his angels. This power is given to all that believe and obey the gospel: If you would have benefit by it, you must be exercised in resisting of temptation, and have regard to the

grace

grace of God, and the workings of it in your own hearts; and then you will be able to say, when a temptation comes, promising profit and pleasure, *how can I do this great wickedness, and sin against God?* Turn your eye to God's *favour, which is better than life, and you will be more than conquerors;* you will say the fear of God seized upon my soul, and the grace of God came to my assistance, and was as a bulwark against temptation. Here praises will go up to God; here will be occasion for thee to speak good of his name. Remember what *David* said; *my soul, praise the Lord, that hath delivered me from the horrible pit.* Thus *David* and the saints of old praised God in their day, and why should not we? They breathed forth living praises and thanksgivings for the deliverances wrought for them; and shall not we do it?

Now this cannot be done without thinking upon his name, the name of that God that made us: Here I live in the world, I live and breathe still, I have health, and strength, and an estate, how came I by all this? Did I make myself? No, there is a God that gave me life, and breath, and being; he holds forth the hand of mercy to gather me to himself, and to *redeem me from all iniquity, that I might serve him without fear, in holiness and righteousness, all the days of my life:* If I believe this, I shall rejoice in him, and love and praise him, and daily wait upon him for the accomplishment of his work. *He desireth not the death of sinners:* If you believe the Almighty, *it is impossible for him to lie, all things are possible* to him except that; he saith, he *would not the death of him that dies:* What would he have then? He would have you *turn and live:* What means doth he use? What I would have done I would use means to accomplish it. You would say, what means hath he not used? What is it that God doth more wish for than that men would repent, *return and live,* and be happy forever? He hath created them, and given them life and breath, and continued his grace to them, that they might have time to prepare for eternity; and he hath given his good spirit to instruct them, *but they have rebelled against him.* He hath sent forth his word, the gospel of salvation, which hath been preached

ed to them; and *he hath waited to be gracious, and exercised much patience and long-suffering* towards them; so that I may say, what means hath he omitted? *He hath planted them as a vineyard, in a very fruitful hill; and he hath fenced it, and gathered out the stones thereof, and planted it with the choicest vine, and built a tower in the midst of it, and made a wine-press therein, and he looked that it should bring forth grapes, and it brought wild grapes. Judge, I pray you saith the Lord, between me and my vineyard: What could have been done more to my vineyard, that I have not done in it?*

But notwithstanding all your unfruitfulness, the day of your visitation is continued, the Lord is willing to shew mercy to your souls. This is all the Lord your God requires of you, that you would think upon his name, believe in him and trust in him, and wait upon him for the operations of his grace in the use of his ordinances, and your attendance upon them, and hearkening to his voice, and obeying it, and so *to hear that your souls may live.*

I will affirm, that there is none of you here present, whether you be Quakers or no, but you may meet with the divine operations of the power of God in your own hearts, if you will regard it, and when you meet with these operations and regard them not, I cannot help it; if you will resist the good things of the Spirit of God, I cannot help it; if you will be of that mind, *always to resist the Holy Ghost; if as your fathers did so do ye,* then you must all perish, both you and your fathers; there is no escaping but by being subject to Christ Jesus, and his quickening Spirit; if there be any divine operations that you meet with in your own hearts, let me persuade you to submit and have regard to them; for I know the devil is near at hand; and when people meet with divine operations in their souls, that humble them and bring down their pride, and convince them of the danger of their condition, he lies in the way and suggests some poisonous thing that takes off the edge of these operations, that they may dislike them: It is true, they meet with the convictions of sin; but they reckon they have that faith and belief in Christ, that doth in the sight of God obliterate all their sins that can be laid to

their

their charge, both paft and to come. If I would look, fay they, to the divine operation, or any thing wrought in me, it were enough to make me mad; I look wholly to the merits of Chrift; my mind is wholly fixed upon him who is *the author of eternal falvation* ; his meritorious fufferings and obedience can obliterate and blot out all my fins.

My friends, I tell you, many a poor foul hath fplit upon this rock by undervaluing the divine operations of the Spirit upon their hearts; they make a falfe and wrong application of the merits of Chrift, which indeed are fo great that nobody can overvalue them; but we muft not make a falfe application of them, *for this purpofe was the Son of God manifefted, that he might deftroy the works of the devil* ; he takes away the guilt of fin, not that you might live in it ftill : Whofoever believeth in Chrift, fhall have power over their fins and not be under the dominion and power of fin ; *fin fhall not have dominion over you ; for you are not under the law, but under grace. But God be thanked, you were the fervants of fin ; tho' you have obeyed from the heart, the form of doctrine which was delivered you : Being then made free from fin, ye became the fervants of righteoufnefs*, Rom. vi, 14, 18.

But thou wilt fay, I am guilty of a great deal of fin already, what fhall become of me for the guilt I have contracted?

If we confefs and forfake our fins, he is faithful and juft to forgive us our fins, and to cleanfe us from all unrighteoufnefs ; and the blood of Jefus Chrift his Son cleanfeth us from all fin ; 1 John, ix, 9. Here is a true application of Chrift, his merits and righteoufnefs ; when there is a confeffing of fin to God, and a forfaking of it, here is an offering and a facrifice made to God by our Lord Jefus Chrift for the expiation of fin ; he hath by his precious blood purchafed the pardon of all my fins, *that he might prefent me to God without fpot or blemifh* ; here is a true application of the righteoufnefs of Chrift ; but how can I apply it to myfelf while I live in fin?

Here God's witnefs in the confcience of a finner pleads againft the finner; when he endeavours to believe that his guilt is taken away, and all his fins, paft, prefent and to come, are pardoned, while he continues to live in fin, and fin hath yet dominion over him. Take

Take heed you split not upon this rock; if you be humble Chriftians, you will *think upon the name of the Lord;* and when ye find the operation of God's power begetting good defires in you to hate fin and love righteoufnefs, you will then believe; you will then pray to the God of all grace; for the *prayer of the faithful is acceptable to him: The effectual fervent prayer of a righteous man avails much*, James v, 16.

Let your fupplication therefore be poured forth unto God, to endow you with power and wifdom to fubdue all your fpiritual enemies, and to conquer your concupifcence, and the inordinate defires and affections of your own hearts, that you may take up the crofs of Chrift and follow him as your great pattern, and in his name, and by the help and affiftance of his Holy Spirit, you may know how to overcome all temptations.

His

His PRAYER after SERMON.

MOST glorious Lord God! wonderful is thy great power over all, which thou hast revealed and made manifest in this thy blessed day. Thy arm, O thou Almighty God! is stretched forth; thou hast touched a remnant with a sense of thy divine love, whom thou hast gathered unto thy name; thou hast revealed thy great salvation, and therewith thou hast made glad the souls of thy children; thou hast endeared thyself unto us by the discovery and manifestation of thy abounding love, who didst love us, when we were strangers, and didst preserve us when we were enemies, and brought a glorious day of visitation upon us, and opened our eyes to behold the light thereof, so that we were a people engaged to speak good of thy name. Thou hast declared and manifested to the sons and daughters of men thy good will, and thy universal grace that thou art daily extending to them, that all may be made partakers of the riches of thy house, and of thy great salvation which by the Lord Jesus Christ thou hast ordained.

And, O thou powerful God of Life! since the day that thou first gathered us, thou hast been with us, thou hast been our guide, and our eyes have been towards thee for instruction, thou hast taught us and led us in the way in which thou wouldest have us to walk; thou hast led us, O Lord, in the way everlasting with the poor, the humble and the meek of the earth; and thou hast placed our feet, O Lord, near the everlasting mountain, which thou hast exalted upon the high hills of the earth, and thou hast revealed the glory and the splendor of thy house, thy holy dwelling place, and hast raised breathings in the hearts of thy people, that they may dwell in thy courts forever: And now, Holy Father! thou hast gathered a remnant, and brought a peculiar people to trust in thy name; but still we do all that we do by thee; thou must be our keeper, thou must be our preserver, therefore we wait upon thee; we expect all from thy hand, therefore our applications are unto thee, that from day to day, and from time to time, we may find thy living presence in the midst of us.

And, O living God of Life! thou hast given thy children large experience that thou art a God nigh at hand to us, in all

His PRAYER after SERMON.

all our trials, in all our exercises; as our eyes have been turned to thee, thou hast preserved us, and revealed thy heavenly power, O Lord, in preserving and delivering thy church and people, that they may bear a testimony in their generation for thy great love, and the great salvation that thou hast wrought for them and made them partakers of.

Now blessed God of Life! the desires and supplications of thy people are unto thee, for the glorifying of thy power, and the exalting of thy glorious name.

O Lord! let the mighty operation of thy power bow down all stout and stubborn ones, that have rebelled against thee, and that have withstood the tenders of thy grace, and the motions and strivings of thy Holy Spirit: Thou art able to bow them, and to break their stony hearts; thou art able to speak effectually to their souls, and to make them submit themselves to thee.

Holy and living Father! let the progress of thy word and gospel be great in our day; let it have a free course and spread itself mightily to those that believe not, to beget a seed of faith in their souls, that they may believe in thy name, and trust in thy power, and wait to see the great work of redemption wrought for the salvation of their immortal souls, before the day of their visitation goes over.

Powerful God of Life! thy little remnant which thou hast redeemed, keep them by thy power, and preserve them in uprightness and cleanness of mind; preserve them in the places and stations wherein thou hast appointed them to dwell, that so in all the trials, and tribulations, and distresses, that may come upon them, they may be quiet and still, and in patience possess their souls; and let them have strong consolation in that everlasting covenant which in thy Son thou hast made with them, and revealed to them; and let them not be moved and tossed with the hurries of this world, with the tumults and disorders that evil men make in it, and the storms and the tempests that are raised; but let their hearts and minds be stayed upon thee, that they may know how to behave themselves towards thee and one another, and towards all that are without, and thereby glorify and magnify thy great name by the beauty of holiness shining in their conversations, which may reach the consciences of men,

His PRAYER after SERMON.

men that all that see them may say, these are the plants that the right hand of God hath planted, and see the fruits that are brought forth from that root of life revealed in Christ Jesus.

Powerful God of Life! carry on thine own work in this city and the whole nation, and in other places among the people which thou hast chosen and gathered to thyself out of the world.

Powerful God of Life! remember those that groan in of thy making their moan to thee, that they cannot lay hold, solation that ation for their souls: Prepare them for that con-
 d day wrestling with thee by earnest prayer, but what ..ll all their wrestling signify, except thy word and the power of thy grace assist them, and teach them to lay hold of thy strength, that they may fight the good fight of faith, that they may get the victory, and rejoice in thy salvation, and see the glory of it? Thou seest how the children of men are working and contriving divers ways for their own salvation; make them to know that all their own ways and inventions are in vain.

Blessed God of Life! confound the devices of the ungodly that seek to lay waste thy heritage; and all those that thou hast gathered by thy word, do thou preserve them, that they may serve thee with sincere and upright minds all the days of their lives; and offer up daily thanksgivings and living praises to thee, the true and living God, and Jesus Christ whom thou hast sent, through thy eternal Spirit, who alone art worthy, God over all, blessed forever and ever. Amen.

CONTENTS.

SERM.		Page.
I.	THE Great Mediator of the Everlasting Covenant,	3
II.	Heart Preparation for receiving the Gospel,	1-
III.	The First and Great Commandment,	22
IV.	The Standard of Truth,	45
V.	The Great Duty of remembering our Creator,	56
VI.	The Divine Monitor, or Light from Heaven,	70
VII.	The Inward Preacher, or the Office of Conscience,	84
VIII.	Saving Faith, the Gift of God alone,	96
IX.	Truth's Testimony against the Power of Sin and Satan,	104
X.	Bearing the Cross of Christ, the True Mark of a Christian,	111
XI.	The Spirit of Christ, the only True Guide,	126
XII.	Pure and Spiritual Worship,	138
XIII.	The Divine Life of Christ Jesus,	148
XIV.	The Kingdom of God within,	156
XV.	The undefiled Way to Eternal Rest,	165
XVI.	The Dawning of the Day of Grace and Salvation,	174
XVII.	The Excellency of Peace with God,	185
XVIII.	True Christianity,	196
XIX.	The Great Work of Man's Redemption,	208
XX.	The Word of God a Christian's Life,	222
XXI.	The Necessity of a Holy Life and Conversation,	234
XXII.	Baptism and the Lord's Supper,	250
XXIII.	Christ the Way, the Truth, and the Life,	264
XXIV.	Captive Sinners set free by Jesus Christ,	275
XXV.	The Sheep of Christ, hear his Voice,	291
XXVI.	No True Worship without the Right Knowledge of God,	301
XXVII.	The Wonderful Love of God to Mankind,	316
XXVIII.	Salvation from Sin by Jesus Christ,	327
XXIX.	The Acceptable Sacrifice,	335
XXX.	Christ the Way to Eternal Life,	
XXXI.	Christ All in All,	
XXXII.	Christian's should often think on the Name of the Lord. This last Sermon was preached at Devonshire-House, a short Time before his Decease.	

www.ingramcontent.com/pod-product-compliance
Lightning Source LLC
Chambersburg PA
CBHW032033220426
43664CB00006B/465